The Ellen Meiksins Wood Reader

Historical Materialism Book Series

The Historical Materialism Book Series is a major publishing initiative of the radical left. The capitalist crisis of the twenty-first century has been met by a resurgence of interest in critical Marxist theory. At the same time, the publishing institutions committed to Marxism have contracted markedly since the high point of the 1970s. The Historical Materialism Book Series is dedicated to addressing this situation by making available important works of Marxist theory. The aim of the series is to publish important theoretical contributions as the basis for vigorous intellectual debate and exchange on the left.

The peer-reviewed series publishes original monographs, translated texts, and reprints of classics across the bounds of academic disciplinary agendas and across the divisions of the left. The series is particularly concerned with encouraging the internationalization of Marxist debate and aims to translate significant studies from beyond the English-speaking world.

For a full list of titles in the Historical Materialism Book Series available in paperback from Haymarket Books, visit:
www.haymarketbooks.org/category/hm-series

The Ellen Meiksins Wood Reader

Edited by
Larry Patriquin

Haymarket Books
Chicago, IL

First published in 2012 by Brill Academic Publishers, The Netherlands
© 2012 Koninklijke Brill NV, Leiden, The Netherlands

Published in paperback in 2013 by
Haymarket Books
P.O. Box 180165
Chicago, IL 60618
773-583-7884
www.haymarketbooks.org

ISBN: 978-1-60846-279-7

Trade distribution:
In the US, Consortium Book Sales, www.cbsd.com
In Canada, Publishers Group Canada, www.pgcbooks.ca
In the UK, Turnaround Publisher Services, www.turnaround-psl.com
In Australia, Palgrave Macmillan, www.palgravemacmillan.com.au
In all other countries, Publishers Group Worldwide, www.pgw.com

Cover design by Ragina Johnson.

This book was published with the generous support of
Lannan Foundation and the Wallace Global Fund.

Printed in Canada by union labor.

10 9 8 7 6 5 4 3 2 1

Library of Congress Cataloging-in-Publication data is available.

Contents

Preface

Edited readers are becoming more important for both students and academics. Readers are ideal for those who are unable or unwilling to peruse thousands of pages of an author's output – and who would not know where to begin, even if they had the time. With the publication of eleven books (two co-authored) and dozens of articles, the writings of Ellen Meiksins Wood have reached a point where an edited collection is needed. This reader serves as an overview of her ideas; it will be helpful especially for those just beginning to encounter her works.

Like similar texts, the excerpts are presented in thematic, rather than chronological, order. Unlike many readers, however, I have refrained from the common practice of incorporating whole chapters or entire articles from the author. This approach seems to me to defeat the purpose of a reader. At the same time, I have avoided, for the most part, cutting the original texts into small fragments, which would have given the work a 'prison-notebooks' feel. I have tried to strike a middle-ground, in effect incorporating Wood's 'greatest hits', consisting of pieces both long and (relatively) short. The result, I believe, is a showcase for Wood's groundbreaking scholarship, with important insights on every page. Those making use of this collection are obviously free to skip through the text, though I recommend that it be read from start to finish, as the material in the opening chapters on capitalism, precapitalist societies, and the state informs, in important ways, the theoretical arguments developed in later chapters.

In the chapters, sections are taken from a variety of Wood's texts. Even when they are excerpted from the same book or article, however, the sections reprinted here often do not follow consecutively in the original works, so readers should assume the presence of an ellipsis before each sub-title. When excerpts do not begin at the start (or finish at the end) of a paragraph (as found in the original publication), these excerpts are preceded (or followed) by an ellipsis. Ellipses have also been used occasionally to remove sections of material, either large or small, though they have been employed typically to eliminate phrases such as 'in the previous chapter', 'as we have seen', and so on. Editorial interjections are made inside square-brackets. If information has been placed in square-brackets in the original works, ' – EMW' appears before the closing bracket.

Small changes were made to Wood's footnotes for consistency of style and to update information on cited works noted as forthcoming in the original publications. A few discursive notes were left out. One footnote was added in brackets, a brief explanation of the phrase 'New "True" Socialism'. I have also made slight changes to some sub-titles and added sub-titles when there were none in the original publications (for example, where Roman numerals were used in place of sub-titles).

Some of the excerpts are from books co-authored with Neal Wood. However, in the case of *Class Ideology and Ancient Political Theory*, the preface (p. x) indicates that while 'both of us have criticised and amended each other's works', Chapters Two and Four, from which material is included here, were written by Ellen Meiksins Wood. The other book is *A Trumpet of Sedition*, from which I have used a small excerpt on John Locke.

The 'Bibliography of Works by Ellen Meiksins Wood, 1970–2012', found at the end of the reader, does not include translations (which have appeared in more than a dozen languages), though it does include a few works (in German and French) which have not yet been published in English. A number of the entries in the bibliography are reprints of earlier works, some expanded and further developed, others reproduced 'as is'. Many of the articles have been incorporated, typically with revisions, into Wood's books (see the relevant acknowledgements-pages of these books for further details).

Acknowledgements

I would like to thank Sebastian Budgen and Peter Thomas for arranging the publication of the hardback-edition of this work in Brill's *Historical Materialism* Book-Series; Marti Huetink, Tessel Jonquiere, and Rosanna Woensdregt at Brill for guiding this work through the publication-process; David Broder for copy-editing the text; and Ellen Meiksins Wood for her assistance in arranging some of the reprint-permission agreements and double-checking the bibliography of her works.

At Nipissing University, I would like to thank Denise Gauthier, Donna Robinson, and Pauline Teal in the Faculty and Administrative Support Services office for their excellent work in scanning, formatting, and proofreading text. For funding to pay for reprint-permission agreements, I am grateful for the support received from Rick Vanderlee, Dean of the Faculty of Applied and Professional Studies, and the Special Request for Publication Support programme of the Office of Research Services and Graduate Studies. Without the financial contributions of the aforementioned parties, this project would not have seen the light of day.

I would like to thank a number of publishers for permission to reprint works: the American Journal of Ancient History, Blackwell Publishing, Brill, Cornell University Press, Giulio Einaudi editore s.p.a., History Today Ltd., Imprint Academic, Merlin Press, Monthly Review Press, *New Left Review*, Oxford University Press, Pluto Press, Princeton University Press, and Routledge/Taylor & Francis. I am also grateful to Cambridge University Press, in particular, for its permission to use the revised version of some of Wood's works as published in *Democracy against Capitalism*. A special thank you goes to Verso for its generosity in supporting this project by providing permission to use excerpts from a number of Wood's books.

The following is a complete list of the original copyright holders who have given their permission to reproduce their works in this Reader, all of which were written by Ellen Meiksins Wood (except where noted).

American Journal of Ancient History (gorgiaspress.com), 'Agricultural Slavery in Classical Athens', *American Journal of Ancient History*, 8 (1983): 8–10, 13, 17, 30–1.

Blackwell Publishing (wiley.com), 'The Question of Market Dependence', *Journal of Agrarian Change*, 2 (2002): 51, 53–9, 64–5, 67–8.

Brill (brill.nl), 'Infinite War', *Historical Materialism* 10, 1 (2002): 22–6.

—— 'Landlords and Peasants, Masters and Slaves: Class Relations in Greek and Roman Antiquity', *Historical Materialism*, 10, 3 (2002): 21–3, 26–7, 36–7, 44–5, 48–9, 58–62, 64–5.

—— 'Logics of Power: A Conversation with David Harvey', *Historical Materialism*, 14, 4 (2006): 12–13, 24–8.

Cambridge University Press (cambridge.org), *Democracy against Capitalism: Renewing Historical Materialism* (1995), pp. 289–92.

Cornell University Press (cornellpress.cornell.edu) 'Democracy: An Idea of Ambiguous Ancestry', in *Athenian Political Thought and the Reconstruction of American Democracy*, edited by J. Peter Euben, John R. Wallach, and Josiah Ober (1994), pp. 62–78.

Giulio Einaudi editore s.p.a., Torino (einaudi.it), 'Schiavitù e lavoro', in *I Greci: Storia, Cultura, Arte, Società*, Vol. 1, *Noi e i Greci*, edited by Salvatore Settis (1996), pp. 633–6.

History Today Ltd. (historytoday.com), 'A Tale of Two Democracies', *History Today*, 44, 5 (1994): 50–5.

Imprint Academic (imprint.co.uk), 'The State and Popular Sovereignty in French Political Thought: A Genealogy of Rousseau's "General Will"', *History of Political Thought*, 4 (1983): 284–8, 304–11, 314.

—— 'Capitalism or Enlightenment?', *History of Political Thought*, 21 (2000): 408–12, 421–3.

Merlin Press (merlinpress.co.uk), 'C.B. Macpherson, Liberalism, and the Task of Socialist Political Theory', in *The Socialist Register 1978*, edited by Ralph Miliband and John Saville (1978), pp. 227–38.

—— 'Liberal Democracy and Capitalist Hegemony: A Reply to Leo Panitch on the Task of Socialist Political Theory', in *The Socialist Register 1981*, edited by Ralph Miliband and John Saville (1981), pp. 180–1, 184–7.

—— 'Marxism without Class Struggle?', in *The Socialist Register 1983*, edited by Ralph Miliband and John Saville (1983), pp. 241–2.

—— 'The Uses and Abuses of "Civil Society"', in *The Socialist Register 1990*, edited by Ralph Miliband, Leo Panitch, and John Saville (1990), pp. 60–7, 72–4.

—— 'A Chronology of the New Left and Its Successors, or: Who's Old-Fashioned Now?', in *The Socialist Register 1995*, edited by Leo Panitch (with special coeditors Ellen Meiksins Wood and John Saville) (1995), pp. 39–42, 46–7.

Monthly Review Press (monthlyreview.org/press), What Is the "Postmodern" Agenda? An Introduction', *Monthly Review*, 47, 3 (1995): 4–10.

—— 'Class Compacts, the Welfare State, and Epochal Shifts: A Reply to Frances Fox Piven and Richard A. Cloward', *Monthly Review*, 49, 8 (1998): 32–6, 38–42.

—— 'Modernity, Postmodernity, or Capitalism?', in *Capitalism and the Information Age: The Political Economy of the Global Communication Revolution*, edited by Robert W. McChesney, Ellen Meiksins Wood, and John Bellamy Foster (1998), pp. 27–32.

'The Politics of Capitalism', *Monthly Review*, 51, 4 (1999): pp. 14–18, 23–6.

New Left Review (newleftreview.org), 'The Separation of the Economic and the Political in Capitalism', *New Left Review*, I, 127 (1981):   80–4, 86–9, 91–5.

Oxford University Press (oup.co.uk), *Class Ideology and Ancient Political Theory: Socrates, Plato, and Aristotle in Social Context*, with Neal Wood (1978), pp. 17–19, 26–7, 29–30, 36, 41, 45–6, 52–4, 61–2, 128–9, 133–4, 137–8, 147–8, 153–4, 183–4, 186–7.

—— 'Marxism and Ancient Greece', *History Workshop Journal*, 11 (1981): 10–11.

Pluto Press (plutobooks.com), *A Trumpet of Sedition: Political Theory and the Rise of Capitalism, 1509–1688*, with Neal Wood (1997), pp. 123–5, 130–4.

Princeton University Press (press.princeton.edu), 'Demos versus "We, the People": Freedom and Democracy Ancient and Modern', in *Dēmokratia: A Conversation on Democracies, Ancient and Modern*, edited by Josiah Ober and Charles Hedrick (1996), pp. 123, 127–8, 131–2.

Taylor & Francis (taylorandfrancis.com), 'Global Capital, National States', in *Historical Materialism and Globalization*, edited by Mark Rupert and Hazel Smith (2002), pp. 25–7.

Verso (versobooks.com), *The Retreat from Class: A New 'True' Socialism* (1986), pp. 14–15, 90–1, 97–9, 131–9, 145–51, 153–9, 164–6, 173–9, 188–90, 198–200.

—— *Peasant-Citizen and Slave: The Foundations of Athenian Democracy* (1988), pp. 55–6, 61, 65, 78–83, 104–6, 109–12, 114–15, 126–8, 132–6, 139.

—— *The Pristine Culture of Capitalism: A Historical Essay on Old Regimes and Modern States* (1991), pp. 1–8, 22–8, 75–9.

—— *The Origin of Capitalism: A Longer View* (2002), pp. 2–7, 11–14, 35–7, 74–8, 95–100, 147–52, 176–9, 182–6.

—— *Empire of Capital* (2003), pp. 26–37, 55–8, 126–30, 139–42, 156–7.

—— *Citizens to Lords: A Social History of Western Political Thought From Antiquity to the Middle Ages* (2008), pp. 11–16, 21–5, 114–19, 121–7, 166–77.

Addendum

In the hardback edition of this *Reader*, an error was made in the acknowledgement for the use of selections from *Class Ideology and Ancient Political Theory: Socrates, Plato, and Aristotle in Social Context*, by Ellen Meiksins Wood and Neal Wood. Permission should have been attributed to Wiley-Blackwell (wiley.com). We thank Wiley-Blackwell for its permission to reprint selections from the book in this edition.

Introduction: The 'Method' of Ellen Meiksins Wood

Larry Patriquin

Ellen Meiksins Wood is one of the most important political theorists writing in the English language.[1] She has written nine books, co-authored two others, and published dozens of major articles. She has focused extensively on social and political thought from antiquity to the late middle-ages, as well as on 'early-modern' and 'modern' thinkers such as John Locke, Jean-Jacques Rousseau, Karl Marx, and Max Weber. She has elaborated an innovative approach to the history of political thought that interprets the works of writers within their socio-economic contexts, ranging from ancient Athens to early-capitalist England, absolutist France, and late twentieth- and early twenty-first-century capitalism, reinterpreting concepts such as democracy, citizenship, liberalism, and civil society. She has also been a powerful critic of many of her fellow Marxists, especially on questions concerning historiography, class, liberal democracy, socialism, and the market. Her work since the mid-1990s or so has analysed the Enlightenment, postmodernism, globalisation, imperialism, and the relation between capitalism and democracy. Her latest books, *Citizens to Lords* and *Liberty and Property*,[2] mark a return to what can be seen as her original 'project', the social history of political thought.[3]

---

1. For Wood's personal background and intellectual trajectory, see Phelps 1999.
2. E.M. Wood 2008a and 2012.
3. Wood elucidates the strengths of the 'social history of political thought' approach, in contrast to rival approaches such as the 'Cambridge school' (whose 'members' include Quentin Skinner and J.G.A. Pocock), in E.M. Wood 2008a, pp. 1–27. See also

In recent years, Wood's publications have frequently been cited by scholars in a variety of disciplines in the social sciences and the humanities, and
have influenced a growing number of academics and students. She has been
described as the founder, together with the historian Robert Brenner, of
'political Marxism', an approach to historical materialism that has inspired
a research-programme spanning the fields of history, political theory, political economy, sociology, international relations, and international political
economy.[4] Her work has been praised not only for its breadth, but also for the
high quality of her scholarship, sustained over four decades of writing. To cite
just one example, Mark Rupert and Hazel Smith, in dedicating a collection of
essays to her, expressed 'special appreciation to Ellen Wood, whose work the
word "path-breaking" seemed designed for, and who has set standards for
scholarly and political inquiry which she would with characteristic modesty
be surprised to hear are standards which many would want to emulate but
few could surpass'.[5]

Given the wide-ranging subject matter of Wood's publications, it is difficult
to summarise her contributions to social and political thought in a relatively
brief introduction; but we can at least sketch out the basic principles of what
could be described as her 'method'.

In his book *Why Marx Was Right*, Terry Eagleton (who acknowledges his debt
to Wood) writes that: 'Two major doctrines lie at the heart of Marx's thought.
One of them is the primary role played by the economic in social life; the other
is the idea of a succession of modes of production throughout history.'[6] It is
precisely in her treatment of these ideas that Wood demonstrates the distinctiveness of her approach. While situating herself in the historical-materialist
tradition, she challenges some of its most common interpretations: not only
the idea of history as a succession of modes of production, but the idea that
this history has been driven by contradictions between the 'forces' and 'relations' of production, a general 'law' of technological progress according to
which one social form will be followed by another, more productive one.[7]

E.M. Wood 1994a, pp. 355–72; Wood and Wood 1978, pp. 1–12 and 1997, pp. 1–4; as well
as N. Wood 1978. It should be added that the strength of Wood's approach to political
theory rests on her understanding of the critical distinctions between capitalist and
precapitalist societies (the subject-matter of the first two chapters of this reader).

4. For more information on this approach to historical materialism, see the website
of the Political Marxism Research Group at: <http://politicalmarxism.wordpress.com>.
For critiques of 'political Marxism', see Callinicos 1990; and Blackledge 2002–3 and
2008.

5. Rupert and Smith 2002, p. 13.

6. Eagleton 2011, p. 31.

7. Wood's reinterpretation of historical materialism, and her engagement with
other writers, can be found in E.M. Wood 1995a, Part One, Chapters One to Five.
See also E.M. Wood 1986, pp. 76–89; 1981a, pp. 70–4 (a section featuring a critique of

Building on the work of Marxist historians such as E.P. Thompson and Robert Brenner, Wood has taken up what she regards as the greatest theoretical challenge for historical materialism.[8] The objective is not to construct abstract and static theoretical models of modes of production or their various structural 'levels', such as base and superstructure, but to capture and illuminate *process*, both the processes of historical change from one social form to another and also the specific dynamics of each social form. This emphasis on specific social processes does not imply an antithesis between history and theory, or between the empirical and the theoretical. Instead, it means taking seriously Marx's own principle that historical materialism is about 'practical activity', or agency, but that this agency takes place within specific historical conditions that impose their own constraints on human action.

The 'mode of production' is a useful concept when its principal focus remains on relations of exploitation, modes of surplus-appropriation, and social-property relations. Here, Wood takes her main inspiration from Marx's observation that the 'innermost secret' of any social structure is the specific form in which 'unpaid surplus-labour is pumped out of the direct producers'.[9] This means that the dynamics and the specific 'rules for reproduction' (to use a formula proposed by Brenner) that govern each specific social form are shaped above all by the way in which surplus-labour is extracted and appropriated. As Marx makes clear, this does not imply that the entire social structure, in all its empirical manifestations, is determined by the economic 'base'; but it allows us to investigate how modes of production – both capitalist and precapitalist – function and sustain themselves, and how they affect political relations and historical processes, while it encourages us to focus on human practices and struggles, within their specific historical contexts.

This principle also encourages us to see what is truly specific about capitalism, one of the over-riding themes in Wood's work. She emphasises two features of capitalism in particular. The first is the unique imperatives that follow from capitalism's specific form of social-property relations: the imperatives of competition, constant accumulation, and profit-maximisation, and the requirement to improve the productivity of labour. Wood's historical work starts from the premise that the distinctiveness of capitalism has tended to be lost in conceptions of history – Marxist as well as non-Marxist – that read

---

the work of G.A. Cohen, not reprinted in *Democracy against Capitalism*); 1984; 1989, pp. 59–75; 1990; and 2008b.

8. Wood's survey of the works of E.P. Thompson can be found primarily in E.M. Wood 1995a, pp. 49–107; but see also E.M. Wood 1992a; 1994b; 1994c; and 2002a, pp. 65–9. Wood's account of Robert Brenner's ideas can be found in E.M. Wood 1996 and 1999a as well as 1989, pp. 65–70; 1990, pp. 118–20; 1995a, pp. 115–21; and 2002a, pp. 50–64.

9. Marx 1981, p. 927.

the 'laws' of capitalism back into all history and treat the drive to improve the forces of production as a general law of history, instead of as a very specific imperative of capitalism and its specific mode of exploitation. To say that there has been, throughout history and over the long term, a tendency for the forces of production to improve, and that technological advances will occur somewhere, sometime, sooner or later, may be true in a very general sense; but this tells us very little about history, Wood argues. We do, however, learn a great deal about capitalism if we understand its very specific imperatives, its unavoidable compulsion, as a condition of its survival, to improve the productivity of labour and to lower its costs, in order to compete and to maximise profit. These imperatives never existed, even in the most commercialised societies, before the advent of capitalism, which occurred rather late in history, and specifically in English agriculture.

The second major principle of Wood's approach is her account of the complex relation between the 'economic' and the 'political' in capitalism. It is only in capitalism that it is possible to speak of the 'economy' as a distinct sphere, with its own principles of order and its own forms of power, domination, and hierarchy. This does not mean that capitalism is only an 'economic' mechanism. On the contrary, proceeding from Marx's important principle that capital is a social relation, Wood treats capitalism as a total system of social relations, a new configuration of social power, which has implications not only for our understanding of how the capitalist economy works, but also for our understanding of, among other things, imperialism and democracy, which she has explored in various articles and books. For example, Wood's analysis of democracy, ancient and modern, builds on her exploration of the changing relation between economic and political power; she argues that democracy must be redefined to include a wide range of human activities that now fall outside its reach, because they are subject to new forms of arbitrary power in the 'economic' sphere. Our freedoms in a capitalist-liberal democracy, she suggests, are limited more by the economic imperatives of the market than by the actions of the state; and markets, as well as relations of domination in the workplace, are subject to no democratic accountability. So we must devise a new conception of democracy capable of dealing not only with the arbitrary powers of the state but also those located in the 'economy'.

The bourgeois paradigm

In one of her most important earlier works, *The Pristine Culture of Capitalism*, Wood developed some of these themes in a historical essay on the distinctiveness of capitalism and its cultural manifestations, in everything from ideas of the state to the arts and landscape-gardening. Here, she introduced her idea of the 'bourgeois paradigm', the historical model that she was challenging and would continue to challenge in all her later work on capitalism, democracy, and the history of political thought. The 'bourgeois paradigm', implicit in most liberal and much Marxist historiography, identifies 'bourgeois' with capitalist, and represents capitalism as a natural product of commercialisation, the growth of cities, and the expansion of trade. The same model underlies some familiar dichotomies which are supposed to capture the passage from the medieval to the modern: rural vs. urban, agriculture vs. commerce and industry, status vs. contract, aristocracy vs. bourgeoisie, feudalism vs. capitalism, and superstition, magic, or religion vs. reason and 'enlightenment'. The burgher or bourgeois – by definition a town-dweller – in these accounts is the principal agent of progress, as a declining, backward-looking aristocracy is displaced by a rising, forward-looking bourgeoisie. These dualisms supposedly pinpoint the essence of the move from the old to the new, from the premodern to the modern. According to this paradigm, the transition to capitalism involved a process of removing barriers, such as the privileges of aristocracies, allowing a natural but latent system of profit-making to unfold. Commerce has existed since time immemorial, and capitalism is seen as 'simply more trade, more markets, more towns, and, above all, a rising "middle-class"', not a historically unique mode of production, a novel form of exploitation. The bourgeoisie – which, in this paradigm, is synonymous with the capitalist class – becomes 'the bearer of knowledge, innovation and progress – and, ultimately, the bearer of capitalism and liberal democracy'.[10]

It is typical of proponents of the bourgeois paradigm to suggest, implicitly or explicitly, that the rise of capitalism was a Western-European (or perhaps trans-European) phenomenon. In some cases, such as world-systems theory, the geographic origins are enlarged, with capitalism regarded as global from the moment of its inception. In opposition to this, Wood argues that the transition to capitalism occurred first in England. She highlights the uniqueness of the English case, contrasting it with France where the absolutist state in the early-modern era was at the apex of a society that was fundamentally precapitalist (or better yet, *non*-capitalist – 'precapitalist' implying that such societies were somewhere on the road to capitalism). In France, the monarchy typically used taxes to appropriate the surplus-labour of the peasantry, while aristocrats employed their lordly jurisdictions or state-offices to procure a surplus from peasants, who comprised the vast majority of the population. A

---

10. See Chapter One.

chief characteristic of this *ancien régime,* in other words, was what Marx called 'extra-economic' power, or what Brenner calls 'politically constituted property', in the form of various powers of jurisdiction or state-office as a means to appropriate the surplus-labour of direct producers in the form of rent or tax, while privileged classes were often exempted from various forms of taxation. The monarchical state competed with the 'parcelised sovereignty' and privileges of 'local' seigneurs who exploited peasants through rents, user-fees, and the like; but many aristocrats, and even prosperous members of the non-privileged classes, the bourgeoisie, were coopted into the central state by means of lucrative state-offices, which acted as a form of private property.[11]

In contrast, in England, the social bases for absolutism – in particular a nation of peasants with effective legal and social rights to land – had undergone major and irrevocable changes by the early seventeenth century, if not before. From the late-medieval era onwards, England's ruling class increasingly relied primarily on economic appropriation. England was the first society to have a specifically capitalist division between what we now describe as the 'economic' and the 'political'. In accounting for the development of capitalism, we need to explore how this unique formation came about, and this requires us to focus not on statistical measures of growth – such as the famous 'take-off' of industry – which tell us little about how this 'great transformation' occurred. Instead, we must examine 'the social relations that displaced politically constituted property, corporate privilege and fragmented jurisdiction'.[12] And we must ask not how trade expanded or how market-*opportunities* increased, but how market-*imperatives* and the compulsion to increase productivity came into being.

Historical materialism

With few exceptions, Wood argues, those who have sought to explain the origin of capitalism assume the very thing that needs to be explained. Capitalism's origins are simply taken for granted. Capitalism, at least in some embryonic form, is deemed to have always existed, in all forms of trade, awaiting the right circumstances to reach maturity. We cannot understand capitalism as it operates today, she insists, without acknowledging that its origin represented a profound historic rupture. Many analysts have applied some version of the bourgeois paradigm. Is there, then, any merit to the fol-

11. Wood's analysis of absolutist France, in comparison to capitalist England, can be found in E.M. Wood 1983a; 1991, pp. 24–31, 38–41, 45–9, and 60–2; 2000; 2002a, pp. 182–9; and 2010. See also her latest book, E.M. Wood 2012, pp. 147–209.
12. E.M. Wood 1991, p. 133.

lowing assessment of historical materialism by J.H. Hexter, one of Britain's most well-known historians? He concluded that with 'the advantage of hindsight now, at the dawn of the twenty-first century, the preoccupation of historians in the previous century with a view of the nature and destiny of man so palpably flawed at its foundations as that of the Marxists may seem either mysterious or utterly ludicrous'.[13] Are Hexter and others with similar views correct, especially now that we live in a 'post-Communist' era, or does historical materialism have anything left to offer historians and those who work in other disciplines, such as sociology and political science, where research-agendas often require a substantial reading of history?

Wood contends that the great British Marxist historian E.P. Thompson 'remains the closest thing we have to a theorist of historical materialism as I understand it'.[14] Thompson's classic works focused on life at the turn of the nineteenth century, at the end of England's (partly) non-capitalist society and the solidification of its (mostly) capitalist society, highlighting critical differences between the two.[15] He conducted a fine-grained analysis of *transformations*. In particular, he analysed the move away from 'custom', which regulated the relationship between landlords and peasants and provided the peasantry with substantial rights (including access to land), while also regulating the lives of many urban workers, in particular masters and apprentices. Thompson also considered the flipside to this process, the transition to the 'free market', which enshrined absolute private property in a way never before seen in human history, reducing individuals to mere commodities who would have to survive in a ruthless buy-and-sell marketplace, with a modicum of poor-relief available to them to tide over difficult times. Thompson put under a microscope the 'confrontation between market society and alternative practices and values', especially the change from independent craftsmanship to the externally-imposed work-discipline of the factory.[16] He proceeded on the assumption, akin to a European anthropologist in a 'foreign' country, that the practices of capitalism were unusual, and hence required explanation. Thompson gave an account of a 'historical dynamic of change within continuity', on how a working class was formed or made.[17] His method, and that of other British Marxist historians, has been described as 'class-struggle analysis'.[18]

---

13. Hexter 2003, p. 276.
14. E.M. Wood 1995a, p. 13.
15. See especially Thompson 1968 and 1993.
16. E.M. Wood 2002a, p. 65.
17. E.M. Wood 1995a, p. 68.
18. See Kaye 1984.

Wood follows Thompson's example in arguing that we need to explain *processes*. We can best accomplish this task by focusing on the 'dynamic of the relation between appropriators and producers'. In doing so, we have to discard the notion that all modes of production are hidden within their predecessors, like a butterfly waiting for the opportune moment to break out of its cocoon. Instead, we need to ask: How is productive activity, in particular surplus-appropriation, organised within an economic system? What is the architecture of exploitation? For instance, are 'central' state-officials the dominant exploiters, or do they compete with 'local' landlords for the same peasant-produced surpluses? What kind of class-struggles emerge from this system, and how do such struggles play themselves out (this requires integrating statuses such as gender and race into the analyses)? How are states (domestic and/or 'foreign') implicated in these conflicts? For example, in societies where most people are peasants, does the state defend the peasantry, or contribute to its eradication as a class? Where can we see examples of the formation of one social class and the destruction of another? How are institutions, both 'public' and 'private' (such as the police, social services, and the family), reconfigured to meet alterations in class-relations? How are 'public' and 'private' themselves redefined, their borders and their 'content' changed over time? How is the system of exploitation affected by external forces, such as colonialism and military invasions? These and similar kinds of questions provide 'a *general* guide to discovering the *specific* "logic of process" in any given social form'. In sum: 'Marxist theory can point us in the direction of class struggle as a principle of historical movement and provide the tools for exploring its effects, but it cannot tell us a priori how that struggle will work out'.[19]

Capitalist and precapitalist societies

Wood, then, challenges much of the scholarly literature on the history of capitalism, from postmodern theories of a supposed radical break in 'late' capitalism (sometime in the 1970s),[20] to the famous 'transition from feudalism to capitalism' debate between Marxists in the 1950s,[21] to Max Weber's notion of the city as a major conduit of capitalism.[22] Whereas most writers

---

19. E.M. Wood 1995a, pp. 77, 127, 141–2.
20. Wood's critique of postmodernism, especially its interpretation of recent economic history, can be found in E.M. Wood 1995b and 1997.
21. For Wood's critique, in particular of Maurice Dobb and Paul Sweezy, see E.M. Wood 1996, pp. 225–7; and 2002a, pp. 37–43 and 51–4.
22. For Wood's engagement with Max Weber, see E.M. Wood 1995a, pp. 153–78.

have emphasised the similarities between precapitalist and capitalist societies (trade, money, urbanisation, and so forth), Wood draws attention to the critically important distinctions between these social forms.

Precapitalist societies were dominated by peasants who, even though they owned (or at least possessed) means of production, were forced to hand over a significant portion of their surplus-labour because they were subjected to direct coercion by means of political, judicial, or military power in the hands of states or dominant classes. These societies were also marked by a type of state quite distinct from what exists under capitalism. In medieval Europe, for instance, feudalism developed in societies with established aristocracies for whom maintaining power depended on a privileged legal status. Even though peasants had some claims to the land, a few men were endowed 'with political authority as well as the power of surplus-appropriation'.[23] The lord became 'a fragment of the state invested with the very functions that gave him the power of surplus-extraction'.[24] This system, in which the 'political unit' and the 'unit of property' coincided, gradually evolved into feudalism. In the case of France, power-struggles resulted in new and different extra-economic powers moving 'upwards', from property to taxes and state-offices, on such a scale that the state served as a form of private property. In this instance, peasants were 'preserved by the monarchy from destruction by rent-hungry landlords in order to be squeezed by a tax-hungry state'.[25] As a consequence, agrarian property-relations in France were not significantly transformed, as one prominent historian has argued, until well into the twentieth century.[26] Meanwhile, social change was unfolding at a relatively rapid pace in early-modern England. Peasant-landlord struggles were occurring over the definition of property and its accompanying rights, in a society where, from the ruling-class perspective, 'traditional conceptions of property had to be replaced by new, capitalist conceptions of property – not only as "private" but as *exclusive*'.[27]

Wood maintains that capitalism's basic features are radically distinct from every society that preceded it, and hence the 'rise' of these features requires explanation. Some characteristics of capitalism are unique, but many analysts take these characteristics for granted, assuming that they have been present throughout most, if not all, human history. Capitalism is also understood as a generally urban phenomenon, because cities apparently supported the

---

23. See Chapter One.
24. Ibid.
25. See Chapter Three.
26. See Bloch 1970.
27. E.M. Wood 2002a, p. 108.

freedom of the individual and protected 'rational' economic action (profit and reinvestment). But Wood points out that commercial trading practices that represent mere opportunities stand in stark contrast to the imperatives of capitalist competition. Trade by itself does not 'generate the need to maximise profit and, even less, to produce competitively'.[28] Production is not necessarily transformed in 'commercial' systems. It is still, for the most part, controlled by peasants who possessed means of production. Profit was gained in the process of circulation – market-exchange – rather than surplus-value in the course of producing in a competitive environment. Arbitrage and long-distance merchant-activities, for example, are an indication of 'a fundamental separation between consumption and production'.[29] Precapitalist trade took the form of 'profit on alienation', 'buying cheap' in one market and 'selling dear' in another, rather than profit derived from competitive production in an integrated market.

In many models of the transition, capitalism is seen as merely the expansion of features that have always existed in latent form. In challenging these models, Wood points to capitalism's historically unique laws of motion and its unique social relations, including the fact that virtually all production is for exchange. Both direct producers (workers) and those who appropriate their surplus-labour are dependent on the market. The propertyless must sell their labour-power in order to gain access to the tools with which they will work. The ruling class has to respond to economic competition, hence their activities must be geared towards the accumulation of wealth, the maximisation of profit, and constant increases in productivity, which requires introducing the latest technologies. This is 'fundamentally different from rentier-aristocrats, who throughout history have depended for their wealth on squeezing surpluses out of peasants by means of simple coercion'.[30] In capitalism, the power of rulers 'to appropriate the surplus-labour of workers is not dependent on a privileged juridical or civic status, but on the workers' propertylessness'.[31] Another way of describing the transition from feudalism to capitalism, then, is to say that capitalism shifted 'the locus of power from *lordship* to *property*' and thus 'the benefits of political privilege gave way to purely "economic" advantage'.[32]

In developing her view, Wood elaborated on the work of the American historian Robert Brenner, who, alongside E.P. Thompson, can be seen as one of the

28. See Chapter One.
29. E.M. Wood 2002a, p. 84.
30. See Chapter One.
31. E.M. Wood 1995a, p. 201.
32. See Chapter Five.

two contemporary scholars who has had the greatest impact on her writings.[33] (It is interesting that, for someone who can best be described as a political theorist, Wood's approach to political theory has been most influenced by two *historians*.) In particular, Brenner maintained that market-dependence *preceded* proletarianisation. The lesson from his analysis is that economic 'units could be market-dependent – that is, separated from non-market access to the means of their self-reproduction – without being completely property-less and even without employing propertyless wage labourers'.[34] What made Brenner's work so important is that he did not assume that capitalism existed in the interstices of feudalism. Rather, he pointed to the unique nature of leases for land in England, which required leaseholders to produce competitively. This new economic 'reality' forced landlords and the farmers to whom they rented land to organise and control every detail of production, as part of a process that involved 'dispossession, extinction of customary property rights, the imposition of market-imperatives, and environmental destruction'.[35]

In sum, for Wood the essential questions are: 'in what specific conditions do competitive production and profit-maximisation themselves become survival-strategies, the basic condition of subsistence itself'?[36] And where were social relations first transformed in such a way as to require such survival strategies? If we should learn one thing from Marx, Wood maintains, it is that capital 'is a social relation and not just any kind of wealth or profit, and accumulation as such is not what brings about capitalism'.[37] This new class-relation is grounded in the market-dependence of both exploiter and exploited. Capitalism's uniqueness rests on this and the fact that market-'forces', as the terms implies, involve coercion. The 'distinctive and dominant characteristic of the capitalist market is not opportunity or choice, but, on the contrary, compulsion'.[38]

---

33. Brenner's major articles, 'Agrarian Class Structure and Economic Development in Pre-Industrial Europe' and 'The Agrarian Roots of European Capitalism', have been reprinted in Aston and Philpin (eds.) 1985, pp. 10–63 and 213–327. Brenner's other important historical works include 'The Origins of Capitalist Development: A Critique of Neo-Smithian Marxism' (Brenner 1977); 'The Social Basis of Economic Development' (Brenner 1986); 'Bourgeois Revolution and Transition to Capitalism' (Brenner 1989); and *Merchants and Revolution: Commercial Change, Political Conflict, and London's Overseas Traders, 1550–1653* (Brenner 1993), especially the postscript, pp. 638–716. For a brief review of Brenner's key ideas, see Patriquin 2007, pp. 35–44.
34. E.M. Wood 2002b p. 51.
35. E.M. Wood, 2002a, p. 194.
36. E.M. Wood 2002b, p. 55.
37. See Chapter One.
38. Ibid.

Rethinking social and political thought: liberalism, democracy, civil society

This brings us to capitalism's distinctive 'separation of the economic and political'. In the transition to capitalism, producers were separated from non-market access to the means of subsistence, in particular the land. Eventually, they were completely separated from the means of production, so that they were obliged to sell their labour-power for a wage in order to gain access to the means of labour itself. In tandem with this, the 'state divested the appropriating class of direct political powers and duties not immediately concerned with production and appropriation, leaving them with private exploitative powers purified of public, social functions'.[39] Politics in capitalism 'has a special character' because this mode of production maximises the 'differentiation of *class*-power as something distinct from *state*-power'.[40] Appropriators abandon direct coercive powers. Yet capitalists could not do what they do without 'their' state. The absolute/exclusive private property that is one of the essential features of capitalism, and the kind of social order necessary to permit the constant accumulation of capital, require the state to make use of coercive legal, policing, and military powers. But capitalism involves 'a new relation of authority, domination and subjection between appropriator and producer', as appropriation and coercion 'are allocated separately to a private appropriating class and a specialised public coercive institution, the state'.[41] More precisely, the separation of the economic (class) and the political (state) in capitalism 'is not merely a separation but a more perfect symbiosis, in effect a cooperative division of labour between class and state which allocates to them separately the essential functions of an exploiting class: surplus-extraction and the coercive power that sustains it'.[42]

The meaning of 'liberalism' is, to say the least, elusive; and what counts as the 'liberal' tradition remains a subject of dispute. Even if we say that all interpretations of liberalism make liberty the core-value, there are debates about what that means. At the very least, liberalism is understood to mean that individuals are entitled to protection from arbitrary power. In everyday discourse, 'liberalism' is often married to 'democracy', to the point where the terms are often regarded as interchangeable. However, as one prominent exponent of liberalism readily acknowledges, liberal government – or limited government – 'need not be democratic government'.[43]

39. Ibid.
40. Ibid.
41. Ibid.
42. See Chapter Five.
43. Gray 1995, p. 71.

Much of what we understand by 'liberalism' and its conceptions of individual rights against the state, Wood maintains, are rooted in medieval lordship and the attempt by lords to protect their privileges against a higher power. In early-modern Europe, the development of 'liberal' ideas was 'not a question of peasants liberating themselves from the political domination of their overlords but lords themselves asserting their independent powers against the claims of monarchy'. For Wood, this struggle by medieval lords may have contributed to the birth of liberalism, but it had nothing to do with democracy (which, of course, is much older than liberalism). Democracy in ancient Athens entailed the 'freedom of the *demos from* lordship' whereas the *Magna Carta* and other such milestones represented the 'freedom *of* lordship against both Crown and popular multitude'. Lords were 'a privileged stratum constituting an exclusive political nation situated in a public realm between the monarch and the multitude'.[44] This new philosophy – liberalism – helped to usher in a process in which the ancient-Athenian definition of democracy receded into the background, and was replaced, at the end of the eighteenth century, with a more 'modern' definition. A significant moment in the modern redefinition of democracy, Wood argues, occurred in the United States.

In its original meaning, democracy meant the power of the people, the *demos,* not simply as a political category but as something like a social class: the common people, or even the poor. In Athenian democracy, there were certainly slaves, as well as women, who enjoyed no civic rights; but, contrary to the view that society's labour was performed largely by slaves, the majority of Athenian citizens worked for their livelihood. Athenian peasants and craftsmen were members of the civic community; and membership, as it turned out, had its privileges.[45] Democratic citizenship did not do away with divisions between rich and poor. But, since the power to appropriate the labour of others derived in the main from 'extra-economic' power or 'politically-constituted property', granting political rights to producing classes gave them 'an unprecedented degree of freedom from the traditional modes of exploitation',[46] an instance where 'relations between classes were directly and profoundly affected by civic status'.[47]

The word 'democracy' would continue to be understood in the ancient-Greek sense, as rule by the common people or the poor, for centuries thereafter;

---

44. See Chapter Five.
45. Wood's analysis of ancient Athens can be found in Wood and Wood 1978 and 1986, and E.M. Wood 1981b; 1988; 1995a, pp. 181–225; 2002c; and 2008a, pp. 28–98.
46. E.M. Wood 1995a, p. 189.
47. See Chapter Five.

and dominant classes would fear it for precisely that reason. In the hands of the USA's 'Founding Fathers', Wood argues, a fundamental redefinition took place. Both terms that made up the ancient word, *demos* and *kratos*, people and power (or rule), changed their meaning. The *demos* lost its class-meaning and became a political category rather than a social one; and the power of the people would be wielded by their representatives. It is true that the idea of *representative* democracy was itself an innovation, a considerable departure from the Greek idea of direct and active citizenship. Representation meant the alienation or transfer of power away from the people, in a manner that was contrary to Greek conceptions of democracy. But what for Wood, is more important than the difference between direct and representative democracy is the particular conception of representation proposed by Federalist leaders like James Madison and Alexander Hamilton: not so much as an expression of popular power, but as a filter between the private citizen and public power. The revolutionary experience, and even the habits of local democracy in the colonial period, had made it impossible to contemplate a return to an exclusive citizen-body, but the Federalists sought ways to limit the damage of democracy. Their objective 'was to sustain a propertied oligarchy with the electoral support of a popular multitude', so they advocated a system of representation, and the elections that go with it, 'for the same reasons that Athenian democrats were suspicious of election: that it favoured the propertied classes'.[48] There would 'be no incompatibility between democracy and rule by the rich',[49] something ancient Athenians would have regarded as a contradiction in terms.

Although capitalism was at an early stage of development in the USA, there was already a growing division between the 'political' and the 'economic' which made it possible to relegate democracy exclusively to the 'political' level. For 'the first time, "democracy" could mean something entirely different from what it meant for the Greeks'.[50] With the development of capitalism, large 'segments of human experience and activity, and many varieties of oppression and indignity, were left untouched by political equality'.[51]

Wood's 'social-history' perspective of the rise of capitalism and the diminution of democracy has contributed to her reassessment of the 'private' sphere of capitalism. This sphere is typically referred to as 'civil society', a term that political scientists, politicians, and non-governmental organisations have had a virtual love-affair with for the past two or three decades. Each liberal-

---

48. Ibid.
49. Ibid.
50. Ibid.
51. Ibid.

democratic polity is characterised by an arena of life that is supposedly nei-ther state nor household, situated somewhere between 'public' governance and the atomised, 'private' family. Typical units of civil society include trade-unions, religious groups, and 'single-issue' organisations (women, ecology, Third-World development, and so forth). But often absent in this discussion, Wood notes, is that while civil society is composed of voluntary associations, it is also framed by the 'free market', an overarching umbrella of compul-sion and domination, both in the workplace and in the operation of market-imperatives. It is rarely acknowledged that the creation of a 'civil society' (in what has become the conventional sense) 'constituted a new form of social power, in which many coercive functions that once belonged to the state were relocated in the "private" sphere, in private property, class exploitation, and market-imperatives'. In Western conceptions of civil society, 'the totalising logic and the coercive power of capitalism become invisible', or if coercion and oppression are seen, they 'are treated not as constitutive of civil society but as dysfunctions in it'. For many advocates of civil society, private (economic) power is not even regarded as a power, a force. Rather, it is almost universally celebrated as a 'free' market, where choice reigns supreme. The culmination of centuries of liberal theorising is that we have reached a point where there is even a 'tendency to *identify* democracy with the "free market".'[52] It may be conceded that a capitalist market can exist without democracy, but the pro-tection of private property and the 'freedom' of the market are regarded as necessary conditions of democracy.

It is not enough to focus on the voluntary sector, as many civil-society advo-cates do, because the essential features of this sector, and the social tasks set out for it, are powerfully affected by capitalist social relations. The 'market' is not just another aspect of 'private' life, like a senior citizens' club or a Bible-study group. Civil society is 'a systemic totality within which all "other" institutions are situated and all social forces must find their way'.[53] One of the unique fea-tures of capitalism is the presence of an overwhelming private power.

This implies that democracy must be redefined to deal not only with state-power, but also with the power of capital, both in the workplace and in those spheres of life where it is now excluded by market-imperatives. Liberalism, first and foremost, addresses the question of how to hold political authority to account. At the same time, it 'has no interest in the *disalienation* of power'. As she notes, the *limitation* of power, the cornerstone of liberalism, 'is not the same thing as its disalienation', which is the focus of socialist theory. To

52. Ibid.
53. Ibid.

go beyond liberal democracy 'requires not simply the perfection of existing political institutions but a radical transformation of social arrangements in general, in ways that are as yet unknown'.[54]

Wood proposes that we should consider how democratic powers can be extended in the context of capitalism and its specific forms of power. If the political and civil rights of liberal democracy are aimed at limiting the power of the state and asserting the autonomy of individuals and communities against arbitrary power, we have to find ways of extending something like these principles to the distinct structures of power and coercion that capitalism has created outside the state, to defend our autonomy against that kind of power too – which means, among other things, taking certain basic social needs out of the market and giving them the same protection that liberal democracy accords to civil and political rights. This means that *decommodification* should be at the centre of the democratic project. But, while much can be accomplished by removing needs and services like health-care from the market, Wood warns us that we should have no illusions about how far it is possible to go in compelling markets to operate according to principles other than its basic imperatives of profit-maximisation.[55] As long as those imperatives continue to operate, there will be strict limits on freedom and democracy.

Conclusion

Ellen Meiksins Wood has spent decades engaged in a theoretical brush-clearing exercise in order to clarify the limits and possibilities of socialism. Her most explicit pronouncements on this matter appeared as part of *The Retreat from Class*, published in 1986 (it incorporated some writings from the late 1970s),[56] which dealt with then-fashionable currents such as 'post-Marxism'. While a few embraced her view, others ignored it; some even wrote it off as a regurgitation of 'well-worn theories and socialist dogmas',[57] committed to a 'defense of the "correct" Marxist line'.[58] Her critique of post-Marxism was based on assumptions that she has since drawn out in detail. Wood's arguments, especially her assertion that there is a chasm between 'democracy' in capitalism and the type of democracy required for socialism, are difficult

---

54. See Chapter Eight.
55. For Wood's analysis of the historical origins of market-imperatives, and how these imperatives impinge upon present-day mainstream economic policies, see E.M. Wood 1995a, pp. 284–93; 1999a; 1999b; 2001a, pp. 283–6; 2002a, pp. 193–8; 2002b; and 2009.
56. E.M. Wood 1986.
57. Bodemann and Spohn 1989, p. 120.
58. Bodemann and Spohn 1989, p. 111.

to grasp without first coming to grips with her redrawing of the social and political map. This redrawing is reflected in the excerpts that make up this reader (and it is why her views on socialism, though written relatively early in her career, have been placed in the final chapter).

With the rise of neoliberalism in the 1980s, and certainly after the fall of the Soviet Union in the early 1990s, many scholars on the political Left abandoned the critique of capitalism and gave up on the possibility of creating socialism. Instead, they encouraged activists to focus on small, 'realistic' social reforms, those deemed attainable within 'market-society'. Wood challenges this strategy. In her view, some of the bases of a humane and just community, such as gender- and racial equality, are in important ways achievable within capitalist societies, but other struggles, like the efforts to establish peace and initiate sustainable development, are likely to fail unless we challenge capitalism's basic *modus operandi*. While acknowledging the concerns raised by the 'new social movements', Wood is adamant that we cannot 'abandon the conception of the socialist project as a class struggle whose object is the abolition of class'.[59] This involves linking problems such as, for example, harmful environmental practices and gender- and race-inequalities, to the competitive imperative and the maximisation of profit that are requirements in a capitalist system. For Wood, this is just one of the reasons why socialist theory, rather than being abandoned, must be rethought and extended to confront contemporary problems and challenges.

---

59. See Chapter Eight.

Chapter One
Capitalism

The 'economic' and the 'political' in capitalism

What [...] does it mean to say that capitalism is marked by a unique differentiation of the 'economic' sphere? It means several things: that production and distribution assume a completely 'economic' form, no longer (as Karl Polanyi put it) 'embedded' in extra-economic social relations,[1] in a system where production is generally production for exchange; that the allocation of social labour and the distribution of resources are achieved through the 'economic' mechanism of commodity-exchange; that the 'economic' forces of the commodity and labour-markets acquire a life of their own; that, to quote Marx, property 'receives its purely economic form by discarding all its former political and social embellishments and associations'.[2]

Above all, it means that the appropriation of surplus-labour takes place in the 'economic' sphere by 'economic' means. In other words, surplus-appropriation is achieved in ways determined by the complete separation of the producer from the conditions of labour and by the appropriator's absolute private property in the means of production. Direct 'extra-economic' pressure or overt coercion are, in principle, unnecessary to compel the expropriated labourer to give up surplus-labour.

---

1. Polanyi 1957, pp. 57, 69–71.
2. Marx 1971, p. 618.

Although the coercive force of the 'political' sphere is ultimately necessary to sustain private property and the power of appropriation, economic need supplies the immediate compulsion forcing the worker to transfer surplus-labour to the capitalist in order to gain access to the means of production.

The labourer is 'free', not in a relationship of dependence or servitude; the transfer of surplus-labour and its appropriation by someone else are not conditioned by such an extra-economic relationship. The forfeiture of surplus-labour is an immediate condition of production itself. Capitalism in these respects differs from precapitalist forms, because the latter are characterised by extra-economic modes of surplus-extraction, political, legal, or military coercion, traditional bonds or duties, etc., which demand the transfer of surplus-labour to a private lord or to the state by means of labour-services, rent, tax, and so on.

The differentiation of the economic sphere in capitalism, then, can be summed up like this: the social functions of production and distribution, surplus-extraction and appropriation, and the allocation of social labour are, so to speak, privatised, and they are achieved by non-authoritative, non-political means. In other words, the social allocation of resources and labour does not, on the whole, take place by means of political direction, communal deliberation, hereditary duty, custom, or religious obligation, but rather through the mechanisms of commodity-exchange. The powers of surplus-appropriation and exploitation do not rest directly on relations of juridical or political dependence but are based on a contractual relation between 'free' producers – juridically free and free from the means of production – and an appropriator who has absolute private property in the means of production.

To speak of the differentiation of the economic sphere in these senses is not, of course, to suggest that the political dimension is somehow extraneous to capitalist relations of production. The political sphere in capitalism has a special character because the coercive power supporting capitalist exploitation is not wielded directly by the appropriator and is not based on the producer's political or juridical subordination to an appropriating master. But a coercive power and a structure of domination remain essential, even if the ostensible freedom and equality of the exchange between capital and labour mean that the 'moment' of coercion is separate from the 'moment' of appropriation. Absolute private property, the contractual relation that binds producer to appropriator, the process of commodity-exchange – all these require the legal forms, the coercive apparatus, the policing functions of the state. Historically, too, the state has been essential to the process of expropriation that is the basis of capitalism. In all these senses, despite their differentiation, the economic sphere rests firmly on the political.

Furthermore, the economic sphere itself has a juridical and political dimension. In one sense, the differentiation of the economic sphere means

simply that the economy has its own juridical and political forms whose purpose is purely 'economic'. Absolute property, contractual relations and the
legal apparatus that sustains them are the juridical conditions of capitalist
production-relations; and they constitute the basis of a new relation of authority, domination and subjection between appropriator and producer.

The correlative of these private, economic juridical-political forms is a separate, specialised public-political sphere. The 'autonomy' of the capitalist state
is inextricably bound up with the juridical freedom and equality of the free,
purely economic exchange between free expropriated producers and the private appropriators, who have absolute property in the means of production
and therefore a new form of authority over the producers. This is the significance of the division of labour in which the two moments of capitalist
exploitation – appropriation and coercion – are allocated separately to a private appropriating class and a specialised public-coercive institution, the state:
on the one hand, the 'relatively autonomous' state has a monopoly of coercive
force; on the other hand, that force sustains a private 'economic' power which
invests capitalist property with an authority to organise production itself – an
authority probably unprecedented in its degree of control over productive
activity and the human-beings who engage in it.

The direct political powers that capitalist proprietors have lost to the state,
they have gained in the direct control of production. While the 'economic'
power of appropriation possessed by the capitalist is separated from the coercive political instruments that ultimately enforce it, that appropriative power
is integrated more closely and directly than ever before with the authority to
organise production. Not only is the forfeit of surplus-labour an immediate
condition of production, but capitalist property unites to a degree probably not
enjoyed by any previous appropriating class the power of surplus-extraction
and the capacity to organise and intensify production directly for the purposes of the appropriator. However exploitative earlier modes of production have been, however effective the means of surplus-extraction available
to exploiting classes, in no other system has social production answered so
immediately and universally to the demands of the exploiter.

At the same time, the powers of the appropriator no longer carry with
them the obligation to perform social, public functions. In capitalism, there
is a complete separation of private appropriation from public duties; and
this means the development of a new sphere of power devoted completely
to private rather than social purposes. In this respect, capitalism differs
from precapitalist forms, in which the fusion of economic and political powers meant not only that surplus-extraction was an 'extra-economic' transaction separate from the production-process itself, but also that the power
to appropriate surplus-labour – whether it belonged to the state or to a

private lord – was bound up with the performance of military, juridical and administrative functions.

In a sense, then, the differentiation of the economic and the political in capitalism is, more precisely, a differentiation of political functions themselves and their separate allocation to the private economic sphere and the public sphere of the state. This allocation separates political functions immediately concerned with the extraction and appropriation of surplus-labour from those with a more general, communal purpose. This formulation, suggesting that the differentiation of the economic is in fact a differentiation within the political sphere, is, in certain respects, better suited to explain the unique process of Western development and the special character of capitalism. It may, then, be useful to sketch this historical process of differentiation before looking more closely at capitalism.

Class-power and state-power

If the evolution of capitalism is viewed as a process in which an 'economic' sphere is differentiated from the 'political', an explanation of that evolution entails a theory of the *state* and its development. For the purposes of this discussion, the state will be defined in very broad terms, as 'the complex of institutions by means of which the power of the society is organized on a basis superior to kinship'[3] – an organisation of power which means a claim 'to paramountcy in the application of naked force to social problems' and consists of 'formal, specialized instruments of coercion'.[4] These instruments of coercion may or may not be intended from the outset as a means for one section of the population to oppress and exploit the rest. In either case, the state requires the performance of certain common social functions which other less comprehensive institutions – households, clans, kinship-groups, etc. – cannot carry out.

Whether or not the essential object of the state is to maintain exploitation, its performance of social functions implies a social division of labour and the appropriation by some social groups of surplus produced by others. It seems reasonable to suppose, then, that however this 'complex of institutions' came into being, the state emerged as a means of appropriating surplus-product – perhaps even as a means of intensifying production in order to increase surplus – and as a mode of distributing that surplus in one way or another. In fact, it may be that the state – at least some form of communal or public power –

---

3. Fried 1967, p. 229.
4. Fried 1967, p. 230.

was the first systematic means of surplus-appropriation, and perhaps even the first systematic organiser of surplus-production.[5]

While this conception of the state implies that the evolution of a specialised, coercive-public authority necessarily entails a division between producers and appropriators, it does not mean that private appropriation is a necessary precondition to the emergence of such an authority. The two may develop together, and a long historical process may intervene before private appropriation clearly dissociates itself from public power. Propositions about the relation between *class* and state must, therefore, be cautiously formulated. It may be misleading to suggest, as Marxist arguments often seem to do, that there is a universal sequence of development in which class precedes state.

What *can* perhaps be said is that, whichever came first, the existence of a state has always implied the existence of classes – although this proposition requires a definition of class capable of encompassing all divisions between direct producers and the appropriators of their surplus-labour, even cases in which economic power is scarcely distinguishable from political power, where private property remains undeveloped, and where class and state are in effect one.[6] The essential point is the recognition that some of the major divergences among various historical patterns have to do with the nature and sequence of relations between public power and private appropriation.

This point is especially important in identifying the distinctive characteristics of the historical path leading to capitalism, with its unprecedented degree of differentiation between the economic and the political. The long historical process that ultimately issued in capitalism could be seen as an increasing – and uniquely well-developed – differentiation of *class*-power as something distinct from *state*-power, a power of surplus-extraction not directly grounded in the coercive apparatus of the state. This would also be a process in which private appropriation is increasingly divorced from the performance of communal functions. If we are to understand the unique development of capitalism, then, we must understand how property- and class-relations, as well as the functions of surplus-appropriation and distribution, so to speak liberate themselves from – and yet are served by – the coercive institutions that constitute the state, and develop autonomously.

_____

5. See Sahlins 1974, Chapters Two and Three, for some illuminating suggestions about how a public authority might emerge as a means of intensifying production.

6. Problems may emerge out of such an inclusive definition of class, not the least of which are their implications for the analysis of Soviet-type states, which have been analysed, alternatively, as autonomous from class or as a particular form of class-organisation.

Feudalism and private property

The capitalist organisation of production can be viewed as the outcome of a long process in which certain *political* powers were gradually transformed into *economic* powers and transferred to a separate sphere.[7] The organisation of production under the authority of capital presupposes the organisation of production and the assembling of a labour-force under the authority of earlier forms of private property. The process by which this authority of private property asserted itself, uniting the power of appropriation with the authority to organise production in the hands of a private proprietor for his own benefit, can be viewed as the privatisation of political power. The supremacy of absolute private property appears to have established itself in large part by means of political *devolution*, the assumption by private proprietors of functions originally invested in a public or communal authority. [...]

[T]he opposition of the 'Asiatic' mode of production at one extreme and the capitalist mode at the other helps to place this devolutionary process in perspective. From this point of view, the crucial issue is not the presence or absence of private property in land as such. China, for example, had well-established private landed property from a very early stage; and, in any case, some form of property in land was often a perquisite of office in the 'Asiatic' state. The important point is the relation between private property and political power, and its consequences for the organisation of production and the relation between appropriator and producer. The unique characteristic of Western development in this respect is that it is marked by the earliest and most complete transfer of political power to private property, and therefore also the most thorough, generalised, and direct subservience of production to the demands of an appropriating *class*.

The peculiarities of Western feudalism shed light on the whole process. Feudalism is often described as a fragmentation or 'parcelisation' of state-power; but while this description certainly identifies an essential characteristic, it is not specific enough. Forms of state-power vary, and different forms of state-power are likely to be differently fragmented. Western feudalism

---

7. I would now emphasise the specificity of capitalist development much more than I did when I first wrote this essay (in 1981). Although I would still say that the particular characteristics of Western feudalism I am outlining here were a necessary condition of capitalism, I would now also stress their *insufficiency*. Capitalism seems to me only one of several paths out of Western feudalism (quite apart from the variations within feudalism), which occurred in the first instance in England, in contrast, for example, to the Italian city-republics or French absolutism. For a discussion of the contrast between English capitalism and French absolutism, see E.M. Wood 1991.

resulted from the fragmentation of a very particular form of political power. It is not here simply a matter of fragmentation or parcelisation, but also of *privatisation*. The state-power whose fragmentation produced Western feudalism had already been substantially privatised, located in private property. The form of imperial administration that preceded feudalism in the West, built upon the foundations of a state already grounded in private property and class-rule, was unique in that imperial power was exercised not so much through a hierarchy of bureaucratic officials in the manner of the 'Asiatic' state, but through what has been described as a confederation of local aristocracies, a municipal system dominated by local private proprietors whose property endowed them with political authority as well as the power of surplus-appropriation.

This mode of administration was associated with a particular kind of relationship between appropriators and producers, especially in the Western Empire where there were no remnants of an older redistributive-bureaucratic state-organisation. The relationship between appropriators and producers was in principle a relationship between individuals, the owners of private property and the individuals whose labour they appropriated, the latter directly subject to the former. Even taxation by the central state was mediated by the municipal system; and the imperial aristocracy was notable for the degree to which it relied more on private property than on office for the accumulation of great wealth. If, in practice, the landlord's control over production was indirect and tenuous, this still represents a significant contrast to early bureaucratic forms, in which producers were typically more directly subject to an appropriating state acting through the medium of its officials.

With the dissolution of the Roman Empire (and the repeated failures of successor-states), the imperial state was in effect broken into fragments in which political and economic powers were united in the hands of private lords whose political, juridical and military functions were at the same time instruments of private appropriation and the organisation of production. The decentralisation of the imperial state was accompanied by the decline of chattel-slavery and its replacement by new forms of dependent labour. Slaves and formerly-independent peasants began to converge towards conditions of dependence, in which the economic relationship between individual private appropriator and individual producer was, at the same time, a political relationship between a 'fragment' of the state and its subject. In other words, each basic 'fragment' of the state was, at the same time, a productive unit in which production was organised under the authority and for the benefit of a private proprietor. Although in comparison to the later developments of capitalism the power of the feudal lord to direct production remained far from complete, a considerable step had been taken towards the integration of surplus-extraction and the organisation of production.[8]

The fact that the property of the feudal lord was not 'absolute', but 'conditional', does not alter the fact that feudalism represents a great advance in the authority of private property. In fact, the conditional nature of feudal property was, in a sense, a hallmark of its strength, not a sign of weakness, since the condition on which the lord held his land was that he must become a fragment of the state invested with the very functions that gave him the power of surplus-extraction. The coincidence of the political unit with the unit of property also meant a greater coincidence between the unit of appropriation and the unit of production, so that production could be organised more directly in the interests of the private appropriator.

The fragmentation of the state, the fact that feudal relations were at once a method of governing and a mode of exploitation, also meant that many *free* farmers now became subject, with their properties, to private masters, forfeiting surplus-labour in exchange for personal protection, in a relationship of dependence that was both political and economic. As many more independent producers were brought into dependence, more production fell within the scope of direct, personal exploitation and class-relations. The particular nature of the exploitative relation in feudalism and the fragmentation of the state also, of course, affected the configuration of class-power, eventually making it both more desirable – in some respects, even necessary – and more possible for private appropriators to expropriate direct producers.

The essential characteristic of feudalism, then, was a privatisation of political power which meant a growing integration of private appropriation with the authoritative organisation of production. The eventual development of capitalism out of the feudal system perfected this privatisation and integration – by the complete expropriation of the direct producer and the establishment of absolute private property. At the same time, these developments had as their necessary condition a new and stronger form of centralised public power. The state divested the appropriating class of direct political powers and duties not immediately concerned with production and appropriation, leaving them with private exploitative powers purified of public, social functions.

---

8. See Rodney Hilton's discussion of the limited control exercised in practice by feudal lords over the productive process: Hilton 1978, pp. 9–10. It should be noted, however, that, in stressing the limited nature of feudal lordship, Hilton is not comparing feudalism to other precapitalist formations, but, at least implicitly, to capitalism, where the appropriator's direct control of production is more complete because of the expropriation of the direct producer, and the collective, concentrated nature of capitalist production.

Capitalism as the privatisation of political power

It may seem perverse to suggest that capitalism represents the ultimate pri-vatisation of political power. This proposition, on the face of it, runs directly counter to the description of capitalism as uniquely characterised by a differ-entiation of the economic and the political. The intention of this description is, among other things, precisely to contrast capitalism to the 'parcelisation' of state-power which unites private political and economic power in the hands of the feudal lord. It is, after all, capitalism that is marked not only by a specialised economic sphere and economic modes of surplus-extraction, but also by a central state with an unprecedented *public* character.

Capitalism is uniquely capable of maintaining private property and the power of surplus-extraction without the proprietor wielding direct politi-cal power in the conventional sense. The state – which stands apart from the economy, even though it *intervenes* in it – can ostensibly (notably, by means of universal suffrage) belong to everyone, producer and appropriator, without usurping the exploitative power of the appropriator. The expropriation of the direct producer simply makes certain direct political powers less immediately necessary to surplus-extraction. This is exactly what it means to say that the capitalist has economic rather than extra-economic powers of exploitation. [...]

There are, then, two critical points about the capitalist organisation of pro-duction which help to account for the peculiar character of the 'political' in capitalist society, and to situate the *economy* in the political arena: first, the unprecedented degree to which the organisation of production is integrated with the organisation of appropriation; and second, the scope and general-ity of that integration, the virtually universal extent to which production in society as a whole comes under the control of the capitalist appropriator.[9]

---

9. Chattel-slavery is the precapitalist form of class-exploitation about which it might most convincingly be argued that the exploiter exercises a continuous and direct con-trol over production; but, leaving aside the many questions surrounding the nature and degree of the slave-owner's control of the labour-process, one thing is clear: that, even among the very few societies in which slavery has been widespread in produc-tion, it has never come close to the generality of wage-labour in advanced-capitalist societies, but has always been accompanied, and possibly exceeded, by other forms of production. For example, in the Roman Empire, where ancient slavery reached its culmination in the slave-*latifundia*, peasant-producers still outnumbered slaves. Even if independent producers were subject to various forms of surplus-*extraction*, large sec-tions of *production* remained outside the scope of direct control by an exploiting class. It can be argued, too, that this was not accidental; that the nature of slave-production made its generalisation impossible; that not the least obstacle to its further expansion was its dependence on direct coercion and military power; and that, conversely, the uniquely universal character of capitalist production and its capacity to subordinate virtually all production to the demands of exploitation is inextricably bound up with the differentiation of the economic and the political.

The corollary of these developments in production is that the appropriator relinquishes direct political power in the conventional, public sense, and loses many of the traditional forms of personal control over the lives of labourers outside the immediate production-process that were available to precapitalist appropriators. New forms of indirect class-control pass into the 'impersonal' hands of the state.

At the same time, if capitalism – with its juridically-free working class and its impersonal economic powers – removes many spheres of personal and social activity from direct class-control, human life generally is drawn more firmly than ever into the orbit of the production-process. Directly or indirectly, the demands and discipline of capitalist production, imposed by the exigencies of capitalist appropriation, competition and accumulation, bring within their sphere of influence – and thus under the sway of capital – an enormous range of activity, and exercise an unprecedented control over the organisation of *time*, within and without the production-process.

These developments betoken the existence of a differentiated economic sphere and economic laws, but their full significance may be obscured by viewing them only in this light. It is at least as important to regard them as a transformation of the *political* sphere. In one sense, the integration of production and appropriation represents the ultimate 'privatisation' of politics, since functions formerly associated with a coercive political power – centralised or 'parcelised' – are now firmly lodged in the private sphere, as functions of a private appropriating class relieved of obligations to fulfil larger social purposes. In another sense, it represents the *expulsion* of politics from spheres in which it has always been directly involved.

Direct political coercion is excluded from the process of surplus-extraction and removed to a state that generally intervenes only indirectly in the relations of production, and surplus-extraction ceases to be an immediately political issue. This means that the focus of class-struggle necessarily changes. As always, the disposition of surplus-labour remains the central issue of class-conflict; but, now, that issue is no longer distinguishable from the organisation of production. The struggle over appropriation appears not as a political struggle, but as a battle over the terms and conditions of work.

The localisation of class-struggle

Throughout most of history, the central issues in class-struggle have been surplus-extraction and appropriation, not production. Capitalism is unique in its concentration of class-struggle 'at the point of production', because it is only in capitalism that the organisation of production and of appropriation so completely coincide. It is also unique in its transformation of struggles over appropriation into apparently non-political contests. For example, while the wage-struggle in capitalism may be perceived as merely 'economic' ('economism'), the same is not true of the rent-struggle waged by medieval peasants, even though the issue in both cases is the disposition of surplus-labour and its relative distribution between direct producers and exploiting appropriators. However fierce the struggle over wages may be, the wage-relationship itself, as Marx points out, remains intact: the basis of the appropriator's extractive powers – the status of his property and the propertylessness of the labourer – are not immediately at stake. Struggles over rent, wherever appropriation rests on 'extra-economic' powers, tend more immediately to implicate property-rights, political powers and jurisdictions.

Class-conflict in capitalism tends to be encapsulated within the individual unit of production, and this gives class-struggle a special character. Each individual plant, a highly organised and integrated unity with its own hierarchy and structure of authority, contains within it the main sources of class-conflict. At the same time, class-struggle enters directly into the organisation of production: that is, the management of antagonistic relations of production is inseparable from the management of the production-process itself. While class-conflict remains an integral part of the production-process, which it must not disrupt, class-struggle must be *domesticated*.

Class-conflict generally breaks into open war only when it goes outdoors, particularly since the coercive arm of capital is outside the wall of the productive unit. This means that when there are violent confrontations, they are usually not directly between capital and labour. It is not capital itself, but the state, that conducts class-conflict when it intermittently breaks outside the walls and takes a more violent form. The armed power of capital usually remains in the background; and, when class-domination makes itself felt as a direct and personal coercive force, it appears in the guise of an 'autonomous' and 'neutral' state.

The transformation of political into economic conflicts and the location of struggles at the point of production also tend to make class-struggle in capitalism *local* and *particularistic*. In this respect, the organisation of capitalist production itself resists the working-class unity which capitalism is supposed to encourage. On the one hand, the nature of the capitalist economy – its national, even supra-national, character, the interdependence of its constituent parts, the homogenisation of work produced by the capitalist labour-process – make both necessary and possible a working-class consciousness and class-organisation on a mass-scale. This is the aspect of capitalism's effects on class-consciousness that Marxist theory has so-often emphasised. On the other hand, the development of this consciousness and this organisation must take place against the centrifugal force of capitalist production and its privatisation of political issues.

The consequences of this centrifugal effect, if not adequately accounted for by theories of class-consciousness, have often been remarked upon by observers of industrial relations, who have noted the growing, rather than declining, importance of 'domestic' struggles in contemporary capitalism. While the concentration of working-class battles on the domestic front may detract from the political and universal character of these struggles, it does not necessarily imply a declining militancy. The paradoxical effect of capitalism's differentiation of the economic and the political is that militancy and political consciousness have become separate issues.

It is worth considering, by contrast, that modern revolutions have tended to occur where the capitalist mode of production has been less developed; where it has coexisted with older forms of production, notably peasant-production; where 'extra-economic' compulsion has played a greater role in the organisation of production and the extraction of surplus-labour; and where the state has acted not only as a support for appropriating classes, but as something like a precapitalist appropriator in its own right – in short, where economic struggle has been inseparable from political conflict, and where the state, as a more visibly centralised and universal class-enemy, has served as a focus for mass-struggle. Even in more-developed capitalist societies, mass-militancy tends to emerge in response to 'extra-economic' compulsion, particularly in the form of oppressive action by the state, and also varies in proportion to the state's involvement in conflicts over the terms and conditions of work.

These considerations again raise questions about the sense in which it is appropriate to regard working-class 'economism' in advanced capitalist societies as reflecting an undeveloped state of class-consciousness, as many socialists do. Seen from the perspective of historical process, it can be said to represent a more, rather than a less, advanced stage of development. If this stage is to be surpassed in turn, it is important to recognise that the so-called 'economism' of working-class attitudes does not so much reflect a lack of political consciousness, as an objective shift in the location of politics, a change in the arena and the objects of political struggle inherent in the very structure of capitalist production.

These are some of the ways in which capitalist production tends to transform 'political' into 'economic' struggles. There are, it is true, certain trends in contemporary capitalism that may work to counteract these tendencies. The national and international integration of the advanced-capitalist economy increasingly shifts the problems of capitalist accumulation from the individual enterprise to the 'macro-economic' sphere. It is possible that capital's powers of appropriation, which the state has so far left intact, indeed reproduced and reinforced, will be subverted by capital's own growing need for the state – not only to facilitate capitalist planning, to assume liabilities or to conduct and contain class-conflict, but also to perform the social functions abandoned by the appropriating class, indeed to counteract its anti-social effects. At the same time, if capital in its mounting crises demands, and obtains, the state's complicity in its anti-social purposes, that state may increasingly become a prime target of resistance in advanced capitalist countries, as it has been in every successful modern revolution. The effect of this may be to overcome the particularism and the 'economism' imposed on the class-struggle by the capitalist system of production, with its differentiation of the economic and the political.

In any case, the strategic lesson to be learned from the transfer of 'political' issues to the 'economy' is not that class-struggles ought to be primarily concentrated in the economic sphere or 'at the point of production'. Nor does the division of 'political' functions between class and state mean that power in capitalism is so diffused throughout civil society that the state ceases to have any specific and privileged role as a locus of power and a target of political action, nor, alternatively, that everything *is* the 'state'. Indeed, the opposite is true. The division of labour between class and state means not so much that power is diffuse, but, on the contrary, that the state, which represents the coercive 'moment' of capitalist class-domination, embodied in the most highly specialised, exclusive, and centralised monopoly of social force, is ultimately the decisive point of concentration for all power in society.

Struggles at the point of production, then, even in their economic aspects as struggles over the terms of sale of labour-power or over the conditions of work, remain incomplete as long as they do not extend to the locus of power on which capitalist property, with its control of production and appropriation, ultimately rests. At the same time, purely 'political' battles, over the power to govern and rule, remain unfinished until they implicate not only the institutions of the state, but the political powers that have been privatised and transferred to the economic sphere. In this sense, the very differentiation of the economic and the political in capitalism – the symbiotic division of labour between class and state – is precisely what makes the unity of economic and political struggles essential, and what ought to make socialism and democracy synonymous.

England vs. the dominant model of capitalism

The capitalist system was born in England. Only in England did capitalism emerge, in the early-modern period, as an indigenous national economy, with mutually-reinforcing agricultural and industrial sectors, in the context of a well-developed and integrated domestic market.[10] Other capitalist economies thereafter evolved in relation to that already-existing one, and under the compulsions of its new systemic logic. Unprecedented pressures of economic competition generated a constant drive to improve the forces of production, in an increasingly international market and a nation-state system where advances in productivity conferred not only economic, but geo-political and military advantage.

Yet though England was the world's first capitalist system, Western culture has produced a dominant image of capitalism to which the English experience fails to conform: a *true* capitalism is essentially an urban phenomenon, and the *true* capitalist is by origin a merchant, a *bourgeois*. Because the capitalist economy in England originated in the countryside, dominated by a landed aristocracy, it is, at least according to some versions of this dominant model, imperfect, immature, inadequately modern and, above all, peculiar – a kind of 'bastard-capitalism', with a pre-modern state and antiquated ruling ideologies. England may have been the first and even the first *industrial* capitalism, but it reached its destination by a detour, almost by mistake, constitutionally weak and in unsound health. Other European capitalisms, after a late start, headed in the right direction, under the guidance of a bourgeoisie with an appropriately 'rational' state at its disposal, and arrived in a healthier condition, more mature, more perfectly formed, more thoroughly modern.

This model implies that there is a *natural* course of capitalist development which has little to do with the real *historical* process that produced the world's first capitalist system, and probably also that the evolution of capitalism was inevitable, though when it actually emerged it did so at the wrong time and in the wrong place. It is not hard to see how such an approach might encourage a certain amount of circular reasoning. Since, for instance, the British economy did not develop in accordance with the bourgeois model, its weaknesses and failures must be due to its deviant development.

But, suppose we break out of this question-begging circle by just beginning with the simple fact that a capitalist economy *nowhere* and *never* developed in a more 'modern' or more 'bourgeois' society before English capitalism had imposed its own economic and geo-political pressures on its principal rivals.

---

10. See Brenner 1985b, pp. 323–7. Brenner emphasises that even the Dutch Republic, which in the early-modern period possessed a progressive commercial agriculture, did not go on to constitute an integrated capitalist economy, but, like other European economies, succumbed to the stagnation and crisis of the seventeenth century. England alone broke through to a self-sustaining economic growth and industrial development, as well as demographic increases which ended the age-old Malthusian cycles.

Might the very features that have been ahistorically defined as the marks of modern capitalism turn out, on the contrary, to be the tokens of its absence? Might the absence of those features signal the presence of capitalism? And what would this tell us about the nature of capitalism? Might it mean, among other things, that the weaknesses of the British economy are not so much the symptoms of arrested or deviant development as the contradictions of the capitalist system itself?

The bourgeois paradigm

There is a historical paradigm so general and firmly fixed in Western culture that it determines the framework of nearly all historical debates, often – probably even more often than not – without conscious acknowledgement by the participants, whatever side they are on. The deviant- or incomplete-development theory of English history, for instance, clearly assumes a particular standard of historical development against which the case of England can be measured. But even those 'revisionist' historians who deny that 'social change' models apply at all to English history[...]or those who reject the 'social interpretation' of the French Revolution, tend to define what qualifies as 'social change' in the terms of this dominant paradigm.

There is a particular conception of progress and the passage to modernity so deeply-ingrained that when historical evidence fails to sustain it – and, more particularly, when there are strong ideological reasons for discarding it (such as those associated with the rise of neo-conservatism or the current fashions in capitalist triumphalism) – there seems to be little alternative but to deny historical process altogether. This, for example, is the preferred escape-route of the 'revisionist' currents which have come to dominate both English and French history, especially the history of seventeenth-century England and the French Revolution. If the evidence of history fails to conform to the conventional paradigm of progress (and especially if that paradigm is associated with Whiggery or Marxism, at a time when rejection of both is a fashionable ideological trend), then history must be reducible to unstructured contingency, a series of episodes rather than a historical process.

What, then, is the dominant paradigm of progress and historical change? It can be expressed by a few simple oppositions: rural vs. urban, agriculture vs. commerce and industry, communal vs. individual, unreason (magic, superstition, even religion) vs. reason, status vs. contract, coercion vs. freedom and, above all, aristocracy vs. bourgeoisie. The principle of movement between these polarities of ancient and modern is, in one form or another, the progressive development of human knowledge, reason or, more specifically, technology; but these developments tend to take the shape, within a general framework of rising and falling classes, of a triumphant bourgeoisie, the bearer of knowledge, innovation and progress – and, ultimately, the bearer of capitalism and liberal democracy.

The curious thing about this paradigm is that, while it contains significant elements of truth, it does not correspond to any actually-existing pattern of historical development. In England, there was capitalism, but it was not called into being by the bourgeoisie. In France, there was a (more-or-less) triumphant bourgeoisie, but its revolutionary project had little to do with capitalism. Nowhere was capitalism the simple outcome of a contest between a (falling) aristocracy and a (rising) bourgeoisie, and nowhere was it the natural product of a fatal encounter between urban dynamism and rural idiocy. The model is, rather, a composite-picture formed largely by a retrospective superimposition of the French-revolutionary experience upon the example of English capitalism, and, conversely, an interpretation of the French political experience in the light of English economic development. It is only the French Revolution, seen through the eyes of post-revolutionary French historians (and German philosophers), that conferred upon the bourgeoisie its historic status as agent of progress. Through the prism of this self-congratulatory bourgeois ideology, relations not only between classes, but between town and country, agriculture and commerce, and all related dichotomies, took on a new colour.

Before this retrospective ideological intrusion, the evolution of capitalism in England did not present itself to contemporary observers in the terms demanded by the bourgeois paradigm. The dynamism of English agrarian capitalism; the active involvement of the landlord-class in commerce; the absence of a clear opposition between bourgeoisie and aristocracy: all this would have suggested a rather different model of historical change. John Locke, for example, for many the archetypal bourgeois philosopher, saw matters in another light. The relevant opposition, the criterion of difference, between old and new certainly had to do with the progress of knowledge, but it was not embodied in a class-distinction between aristocracy and bourgeoisie, nor in the confrontation between town and country, agriculture and commerce. In Locke's treatment of property, the relevant distinction is between the productive and the unproductive, between passive rentier-property and agricultural 'improvement'.[11] These criteria could be applied equally to landlord and town-dweller, aristocrat and bourgeois, with passive appropriators, urban or rural, on the side of antiquity, and productive 'improving' proprietors in the vanguard of progress.

---

11. See N. Wood 1984.

By the late eighteenth century, there had evolved a conception of prog-ress according to which 'commercial society' represented the highest stage of human development, and a tendency to distinguish between traditional landed wealth and commerce as representing different (though perhaps equally necessary) moral qualities. The association of 'commercial soci-ety' with progress is certainly an assumption that runs through, say, David Hume's *History* or classical political economy. But, even here, the issue is not the stagnation of agriculture as against the dynamism of commerce, nor is it a matter of class-conflict between an agrarian aristocracy and an urban bourgeoisie. Certainly, there are rising and falling classes; but it was Hume who gave us the rising gentry, a dynamic agrarian class which, in contrast to the 'ancient barons' who dissipated their fortunes, instead 'endeavoured to turn their lands to the best account with regard to profit', and thereby increased the cities and enhanced the wealth and power of 'the middle rank of men'.[12]

Adam Smith, too, takes as given the productivity of English agriculture, and sets out to explain economic growth on that assumption.[13] He attributes development to the division of labour between manufacture and agricul-ture, separately allocated to town and country, which encourages trade and increases productivity through specialisation. But, if trade is the motor of development, and if the nexus between town and country is critical to it, the force of this development is not to be found in some dynamic principle exclu-sive to the town itself or to the quintessentially urban class, the bourgeoisie, as against a parasitic class of landlords. Like Hume, Smith takes for granted the model of English agrarian capitalism – a formation which should, according to the bourgeois paradigm, represent a contradiction in terms.

In France, too, there emerged a school of economic thought, the physio-crats, which identified agriculture as the source of all wealth and develop-ment and looked to England for its model of productive agriculture.[14] But all this was to be overlaid, if not obliterated, by the French Revolution. The French setting was substantially different from the English, with no agrar-ian capitalism; indeed, agrarian stagnation, and more antagonistic relations between bourgeoisie and aristocracy. Yet even here, the model that was to be constructed in the wake of the Revolution did not quite fit the facts. The association of the bourgeoisie with capitalism – indeed, the absolute identifi-cation of 'bourgeois' with 'capitalist', which was eventually to emerge out of

---

12. Hume 1773, pp. 488–9.
13. See McNally 1988.
14. Ibid.

the composite-paradigm – had less to do with the realities of bourgeois life in France, than with the aspirations of French liberals to English-style progress.[15] The revolutionary bourgeoisie had been composed in large part of professionals and office-holders, not capitalists or even merchants and traders of a more classic variety; and the career of the rentier remained a bourgeois ideal. But, in retrospect, and in the light of English economic development, together with England's earlier advances in parliamentary government, the dramatic and exemplary struggle of the French bourgeoisie against aristocratic privilege was made to stand for every struggle against economic stagnation and political exclusion.

Through the powerful lens of this post-revolutionary ideology, even the history of England began to take on the colour of a rising bourgeoisie – with, of course, some adjustments so that Hume's rising gentry, or perhaps the enterprising yeomanry, could be assimilated to the bourgeoisie. It may even have been French historians – like [Augustin] Thierry and [François] Guizot – who first conferred upon the English Civil War its status as a 'bourgeois revolution', a class-struggle by a modern, progressive bourgeoisie against a backward, feudal aristocracy. The French-revolutionary model of social change is responsible even for the characterisation of English industrial development in the terms of 'revolution' – though this revolution now typically appears in the dominant paradigm as if it took place outside the history of social relations, belonging, instead, to some kind of natural process, the impersonal evolution of technology, an autonomous technical development called 'industrialisation'. Finally, the composite paradigm became a pan-European model, projecting a single, if uneven, pattern of development for Europe – and, ultimately, the world.

One paradoxical consequence of this ideological development was that the particularity of *capitalism* as a historically-specific social form, with its own distinctive laws of motion, was concealed from view. The specificity of capitalism was less clearly visible in the identification of 'capitalist' with 'bourgeois' than it had been in, say, the writings of Locke, still firmly focused on the model of English agriculture. To the extent that Locke's conceptual framework – like that of the agricultural 'improvers' – fixed his attention on the difference between productive and unproductive uses of property, to the extent that he was preoccupied not so much with commerce or commercial profit-taking, the ancient practices of buying cheap and selling dear, as with *productivity* and the wealth to be derived from 'improvement', he came

---

15. See Hobsbawm 1990, pp. 11–20.

much closer to the distinctive systemic logic of capitalism than did those who identified capitalism with classic 'bourgeois' activities or the simple growth of towns and trade. The system of property-relations described by Locke, drawn from the dynamic agricultural regions of southern England which he knew best, was not simply an extension of age-old commercial activities, with a long historical pedigree reaching back to antiquity; it set in motion a wholly-new social dynamic of self-sustaining growth and accumulation based on the improvement of labour-productivity generated by the imperatives of competition.

There was very little in these new arrangements that could have been deduced simply by extrapolating from the traditional commercial practices of the merchant in classical antiquity or the medieval burgher. Yet the identification of 'capitalism' with 'bourgeoisie' has brought with it a tendency to regard the capitalist system, its characteristic activities, motivations and imperatives, as little more than an extension of these apparently ageless social forms. Capitalism is simply more trade, more markets, more towns, and, above all, a rising 'middle-class'.

This tendency has had another significant effect, the treatment of capitalism as historically always present – at least latently, and at least as far back in history as it is interesting to go – requiring only the removal of obstacles standing in the way of its natural development. Capitalism is a long-deferred *opportunity*, rather than a new and historically-specific *imperative*. The bearers of that opportunity – trader, merchant, burgher, bourgeois – have existed as long as there have been cities and markets, and obstacles have stood in their way as long as there have been privileged aristocrats and communal restrictions. These obstructions have been tenacious, and they may have required violent struggle to remove them; but, if there is anything here that demands explanation, it is the removal of obstacles, not the coming-into-being of a new social force.

The same tendency may help to explain why such developments as the rise of individualism, the rise of freedom and the rise of the middle-classes seem enough to account for the evolution of capitalism. And, of course, such accounts have been very congenial to those who would like to see capitalism as the natural order of things. Nothing could be better than a view of history that acknowledges the incontrovertible fact that capitalism, or 'commercial society', has not always existed, and that identifies it as the final destination of progress, while at the same time claiming for it a universal and trans-historical status, a conception of progress that acknowledges the historicity of capitalism as an evolutionary stage, and yet denies its specificity and transience.

Begging the question

Capitalism is a system in which goods and services, down to the most basic necessities of life, are produced for profitable exchange, where even human labour-power is a commodity for sale in the market, and where all economic actors are dependent on the market. This is true not only of workers, who must sell their labour-power for a wage, but also of capitalists, who depend on the market to buy their inputs, including labour-power, and to sell their output for profit. Capitalism differs from other social forms because producers depend on the market for access to the means of production (unlike, for instance, peasants, who remain in direct, non-market possession of land); while appropriators cannot rely on 'extra-economic' powers of appropriation by means of direct coercion – such as the military, political, and judicial powers that enable feudal lords to extract surplus-labour from peasants – but must depend on the purely 'economic' mechanisms of the market. This distinct system of market-dependence means that the requirements of competition and profit-maximisation are the fundamental rules of life. Because of those rules, capitalism is a system uniquely driven to improve the productivity of labour by technical means. Above all, it is a system in which the bulk of society's work is done by propertyless labourers, who are obliged to sell their labour-power in exchange for a wage in order to gain access to the means of life and of labour itself. In the process of supplying the needs and wants of society, workers are at the same time, and inseparably, creating profits for those who buy their labour-power. In fact, the production of goods and services is subordinate to the production of capital and capitalist profit. The basic objective of the capitalist system, in other words, is the production and self-expansion of capital.

This distinctive way of supplying the material needs of human-beings, so very different from all preceding ways of organising material life and social reproduction, has existed for a very short time, barely a fraction of humanity's existence on earth. Even those who most emphatically insist on the system's roots in human nature and its natural continuity with age-old human practices would not claim that it *really* existed before the early-modern period, and then only in Western Europe. They may see bits of it in earlier periods, or detect its beginnings in the middle-ages as a looming threat to a declining feudalism but still-constrained by feudal restrictions; or they may say that it began with the expansion of trade or with voyages of discovery – with, say, Columbus's explorations at the end of the fifteenth century. Some might call these early forms 'proto-capitalism', but few would say that the capitalist system existed in earnest before the sixteenth or seventeenth century, and some would place it as late as the eighteenth, or perhaps even the nineteenth, when it matured into its industrial form.

Yet, paradoxically, historical accounts of how this system came into being have typically treated it as the natural realisation of ever-present tendencies. Since historians first began explaining the emergence of capitalism, there has scarcely existed an explanation that did not begin by assuming the very thing that needed to be explained. Almost without exception, accounts of the origin of capitalism have been fundamentally circular: they have assumed the prior existence of capitalism in order to explain its coming-into-being. In order to explain capitalism's distinctive drive to maximise profit, they have presupposed the existence of a universal profit-maximising rationality. In order to explain capitalism's drive to improve labour-productivity by technical means, they have also presupposed a continuous, almost natural, progress of technological improvement in the productivity of labour.

These question-begging explanations have their origins in classical-political economy and Enlightenment-conceptions of progress. Together, they give an account of historical development in which the emergence and growth-to-maturity of capitalism are already prefigured in the earliest manifestations of human rationality, in the technological advances that began when *Homo sapiens* first wielded a tool, and in the acts of exchange human-beings have practised since time immemorial. History's journey to that final destination, to 'commercial society' or capitalism, has, to be sure, been long and arduous, and many obstacles have stood in its way. But its progress has, nonetheless, been natural and inevitable. Nothing more is required , then, to explain the 'rise of capitalism' than an account of how the many obstacles to its forward movement have been lifted – sometimes gradually, sometimes suddenly, with revolutionary violence.

In most accounts of capitalism and its origin, there really *is* no origin. Capitalism seems always to *be* there, somewhere; and it only needs to be released from its chains – for instance, from the fetters of feudalism – to be allowed to grow and mature. Typically, these fetters are political: the parasitic powers of lordship, or the restrictions of an autocratic state. Sometimes, they are cultural or ideological: perhaps the wrong religion. These constraints confine the free movement of 'economic' actors, the free expression of economic rationality. The 'economic' in these formulations is identified with exchange or markets; and it is here that we can detect the assumption that the seeds of capitalism are contained in the most primitive acts of exchange, in any form of trade or market-activity. That assumption is typically connected with the other presupposition: that history has been an almost natural process of technological development. One way or another, capitalism more-or-less naturally appears when and where expanding markets and technological development reach the right level, allowing sufficient wealth to be accumulated so that it can be profitably reinvested. Many Marxist explanations are fundamentally the same – with the addition of bourgeois revolutions to help break the fetters.

The effect of these explanations is to stress the *continuity* between non-capitalist and capitalist societies, and to deny or disguise the *specificity* of capitalism. Exchange has existed more-or-less forever, and it seems that the capitalist market is just more of the same. In this kind of argument, because capitalism's specific and unique need constantly to revolutionise the forces of production is just an extension and an acceleration of universal and transhistorical, almost *natural*, tendencies, industrialisation is the inevitable outcome of humanity's most basic inclinations. So, the lineage of capitalism passes naturally from the earliest Babylonian merchant through the medieval burgher to the early-modern bourgeois and, finally, to the industrial capitalist.[16]

There is a similar logic in certain Marxist versions of this story, even though the narrative in more recent versions often shifts from the town to the countryside, and merchants are replaced by rural commodity-producers, small or 'middling' farmers waiting for the opportunity to blossom into full-blown capitalists. In this kind of narrative, petty commodity-production, released from the bonds of feudalism, grows more-or-less naturally into capitalism, and petty commodity-producers, just given the chance, will take the capitalist road.

Central to these conventional accounts of history are certain assumptions, explicit or implicit, about human nature and about how human-beings will behave, if only given the chance. They will, so the story goes, always avail themselves of the opportunity to maximise profit through acts of exchange; and in order to realise that natural inclination, they will always find ways of improving the organisation and instruments of work in order to enhance the productivity of labour.

Opportunity or imperative?

In the classic model, then, capitalism is an opportunity to be taken, wherever and whenever possible. This notion of *opportunity* is absolutely critical to the conventional understanding of the capitalist system, present even in our everyday-language. Consider common usage of the word that lies at the very heart of capitalism: the 'market'. Almost every definition of *market* in

---

16. In E.M. Wood 1991, I called this model of history the 'bourgeois paradigm'.

the dictionary connotes an *opportunity*: as a concrete locale or institution, a market is a place where opportunities exist to buy and sell; as an abstraction, a market is the possibility of sale. Goods 'find a market', and we say there is a market for a service or commodity when there is a demand for it, which means it can and will be sold. Markets are 'opened' to those who want to sell. The market represents 'conditions as regards, opportunity for, buying and selling' (*The Concise Oxford Dictionary*). The market implies *offering* and *choice*.

What, then, are market-*forces*? Does not force imply coercion? In capitalist ideology, the market implies not compulsion, but freedom. At the same time, this freedom is guaranteed by certain mechanisms that ensure a 'rational economy', where supply meets demand, putting on offer commodities and services that people will freely choose. These mechanisms are the impersonal 'forces' of the market, and if they are in any way coercive, it is simply in the sense that they compel economic actors to act 'rationally', so as to maximise choice and opportunity. This implies that capitalism, the ultimate 'market-society', is the optimal condition of opportunity and choice. More goods and services are on offer, more people are more free to sell and profit from them, and more people are more free to choose among and buy them.

So what is wrong with this conception? A socialist is likely to say that the major missing ingredient is the commodification of labour-power and class-exploitation. So far, so good. But what may not always be so clear, even in socialist accounts of the market, is that the distinctive and dominant characteristic of the capitalist market is not opportunity or choice but, on the contrary, compulsion. Material life and social reproduction in capitalism are universally mediated by the market, so that all individuals must, in one way or another, enter into market-relations in order to gain access to the means of life. This unique system of market-dependence means that the dictates of the capitalist market – its imperatives of competition, accumulation, profit-maximisation, and increasing labour-productivity – regulate not only all economic transactions but social relations in general. [...]

The commercialisation-model

The traditional account – which appears in classical-political economy, Enlightenment-conceptions of progress, and many more modern histories – is as follows. With or without a natural inclination to 'truck, barter, and exchange' (in Adam Smith's famous formulation), rationally self-interested individuals have been engaging in acts of exchange since the dawn of history. These acts became increasingly specialised with an evolving division of labour, which was also accompanied by technical improvements in the instruments of production. Improvements in productivity, in many of these explanations, may in fact have been the primary purpose of the increasingly specialised division of labour, so that there tends to be a close connection between these accounts of commercial development and a kind of techno-logical determinism. Capitalism, then, or 'commercial society', the highest stage of progress, represents a maturation of age-old commercial practices (together with technical advances) and their liberation from political and cultural constraints.

Far from recognising that the market became capitalist when it became compulsory, these accounts suggest that capitalism emerged when the market was liberated from age-old constraints, and when, for one reason or another, opportunities for trade expanded. In these accounts, capitalism represents not so much a qualitative break from earlier forms, as a massive quantitative increase: an expansion of markets and the growing commercialisation of eco-nomic life. [...]

[One] of the most common assumptions associated with the commercial-isation-model [...] [is] the association of capitalism with cities – indeed, the assumption that cities are, from the beginning, capitalism-in-embryo. In the early-modern period, Henri Pirenne argued,[17] cities emerged with distinctive and unprecedented autonomy, cities devoted to trade and dominated by an autonomous burgher- (or bourgeois) class, which was to free itself once and for all from the fetters of the old cultural constraints and political parasitism. This liberation of the urban economy, of commercial activity and mercantile rationality, accompanied by the inevitable improvements in techniques of production that evidently follow from the emancipation of trade, was appar-ently enough to account for the rise of modern capitalism.

All these explanations have in common certain assumptions about the con-tinuity of trade and markets, from their earliest manifestations in exchange to their maturity in modern industrial capitalism. The age-old practice of com-mercial profit-taking in the form of 'buying cheap and selling dear' is not, in these accounts, fundamentally different from capitalist exchange and accu-mulation through the appropriation of surplus-value.

The origin of capitalism, or 'commercial society', then, does not in this model represent a major social transformation, so much as a quantitative increment. Commerce becomes more widespread and encompasses ever more commodi-

---

17. Henri Pirenne's most famous work was *Mohammed and Charlemagne* (Pirenne 1956), but a general summary of his whole thesis is presented in a series of his lectures, *Medieval Cities: The Origins and the Revival of Trade* (Pirenne 1969).

ties. It also brings with it ever more wealth – and here, in classical political economy, we encounter the notion that commerce and the economic rationality that it engenders – the prudence and frugality of rational economic actors engaged in commercial transactions – encourages the accumulation of sufficient wealth to permit investment. This 'previous' or 'primitive' accumulation, when it reaches a critical mass, brings commercialisation to fruition in a mature 'commercial society'. This notion, 'the so-called primitive accumulation', would [...] become the focal point of a major shift in explaining the origin of capitalism, when Marx subjected it to critical scrutiny in Volume I of *Capital*.

There also tends to be another common theme in these histories of capitalism: the bourgeois as agent of progress. We have become so used to the identification of *bourgeois* with *capitalist* that the presuppositions secreted in this conflation have become invisible to us. The burgher or bourgeois is, by definition, a town-dweller. Beyond that, specifically in its French form, the word was once conventionally used to mean nothing more than someone of non-noble status who, while he worked for a living, did not generally dirty his hands and used his mind more than his body in his work. That old usage tells us nothing about capitalism, and is likely to refer to a professional, an office-holder, or an intellectual, no less than to a merchant. The convergence of 'capitalist' and 'bourgeois' was implanted in Western culture by means of conceptions of progress that joined British economic development with the French Revolution, in a composite-picture of historical change. In the slippage from town-dweller to capitalist via the merchant that occurs in the later uses of 'bourgeois', we can follow the logic of the commercialisation-model: the ancient town-dweller gives way to the medieval burgher, who in turn develops seamlessly into the modern capitalist. As a famous historian has sardonically described this process, history is the perennial rise of the middle-classes.

Marx on the transition

[...][The] classic commercialisation-model, first laid out systematically by Adam Smith, suggests that the prelude to 'commercial society' was a process of prior accumulation in which wealth was amassed by means of commercial acumen and frugality, eventually reaching a point at which it was sufficient to permit substantial investment. This process represents the 'primitive' accumulation of 'capital' – which simply means the collection of material wealth. Variations on this theme have continued to appear even in contemporary explanations of capitalist development, for instance in those accounts that explain the origin of capitalism as a result of 'capital' accumulation by means of colonial exploitation and unequal exchange. In these arguments, again, capitalism, or 'commercial society', is a quantitative expansion of commerce and wealth, and there is little conception of a *transition*, a qualitative shift, from one social system with its own 'laws of motion', to a very different one with a very different dynamic and very different conditions of existence.

Marx, in his critique of 'so-called primitive accumulation', diverged sharply from classical political economy and its commercialisation-model. The general principles spelt out in his critique of political economy – in particular, his insistence that wealth by itself is not 'capital', and that capital was a specific social relation – are here applied to the transition from feudalism to capitalism. It follows from these principles that the mere accumulation of wealth was not the decisive factor in the origin of capitalism. The 'primitive accumulation' of classical-political economy is 'so-called', because capital, as Marx defines it, is a social relation, and not just any kind of wealth or profit, and accumulation *as such* is not what brings about capitalism. While the accumulation of wealth was obviously a necessary condition of capitalism, it was far from being sufficient or decisive. What transformed wealth into *capital* was a transformation of social property-relations.

The essence of Marx's critique of 'so-called primitive accumulation' (and people too-often miss the significance of the phrase 'so-called') is that no amount of accumulation, whether from outright theft, from imperialism, from commercial profit, or even from the exploitation of labour for commercial profit, by itself constitutes capital, nor will it produce capitalism. The specific precondition of capitalism is a transformation of social-property relations that generates capitalist 'laws of motion': the *imperatives* of competition and profit-maximisation, a *compulsion* to reinvest surpluses, and a systematic and relentless *need* to improve labour-productivity and develop the forces of production.

The critical transformation of social-property relations, in Marx's account, took place in the English countryside, with the expropriation of direct producers. In the new agrarian relations, landlords increasingly derived rents from the commercial profits of capitalist tenants, while many small producers were dispossessed and became wage-labourers. Marx regards this rural transformation as the *real* 'primitive accumulation' not because it created a critical mass of wealth, but because these social-property relations generated new economic imperatives, especially the compulsions of competition, a systematic need to develop the productive forces, leading to new laws of motion such as the world had never seen before.

Towns and trade

The association of capitalism with cities is one of the most well-established conventions of Western culture. Capitalism is supposed to have been born and bred in the city. But, more than that, the implication is that *any* city, with its characteristic practices of trade and commerce, is, by its very nature, potentially capitalist from the start, and only extraneous obstacles have stood in the way of *any* urban civilisation giving rise to capitalism. Only the wrong religion, the wrong kind of state, or other ideological, political, or cultural fetters tying the hands of urban classes have prevented capitalism from springing up anywhere and everywhere, since time immemorial, or at least since technology has permitted the production of adequate surpluses.

What accounts for the development of capitalism in the West, according to this view, is the unique autonomy of its cities and of their quintessential class, the burghers or bourgeois. In other words, capitalism emerged in the West less because of what was present, than because of what was absent: constraints on urban economic practices. In those conditions, it took only a more-or-less natural expansion of trade to trigger the development of capitalism to its full maturity. All that was needed was a quantitative growth, and the accumulation of wealth that came with it, which occurred almost inevitably with the passage of time (in some versions, of course, helped along, but not originally caused, by the 'Protestant ethic').

There is much that is questionable in these assumptions about the natural connection between cities and capitalism, but, above all, the tendency to naturalise capitalism, to disguise its distinctiveness as a historically-specific social form with a beginning and, potentially, an end. The tendency to identify capitalism with cities and urban commerce has, as we have seen, generally been accompanied by an inclination to make capitalism appear a more-or-less automatic consequence of practices as old as human history, or even the consequence of a 'natural' inclination, in Adam Smith's words, to 'truck, barter, and exchange'.

Yet there have, throughout history, been a great many towns and a great deal of trade that never gave rise to capitalism. For that matter, there have been elaborate urban settlements – such as the temple-cities of ancient empires – that have not been commercial centres. More particularly, there have been societies with advanced urban cultures, highly-developed trading systems, and far-flung commercial networks, that have made ample use of market-*opportunities*, but have not systematically experienced what we have been calling market-*imperatives*.

These commercial powers have often produced a rich material and cultural infrastructure, far in advance of developments in the European backwater that first gave rise to capitalism. No reasonable person would deny that, in Asia, Africa, and the Americas, there were 'high' civilisations, which in some cases developed commercial practices, as well as technological advances of various kinds, that far surpassed those of medieval England. But the emergence of capitalism is difficult to explain precisely because it bears no relation to prior superiority or more advanced development in commercial sophistication, science and technology, or 'primitive accumulation' in the classical sense of material wealth.

Nor was the autonomy of cities the decisive factor. Free urban communes in Europe may have provided fertile ground for trade, prosperous burghers, and urban patriciates, but there is no obvious correlation between the success of such autonomous commercial centres and the rise of capitalism. Vastly successful commercial city-states like Florence did not give rise to capitalism, while capitalism did emerge in England, whose cities, in the context of a precociously centralised monarchical state, were arguably among the least autonomous in Europe.

The critical factor in the divergence of capitalism from all other forms of 'commercial society' was the development of certain social-property relations that generated market-imperatives and capitalist 'laws of motion', which imposed themselves on production. The great non-capitalist commercial powers had producing classes, and especially peasants, who remained in possession of their means of subsistence, and land in particular. They were ruled and exploited by dominant classes and states that relied on 'extra-economic' appropriation or 'politically-constituted property' of various kinds. These great civilisations were not systematically subjected to the pressures of competitive production and profit-maximisation, the compulsion to reinvest surpluses, and the relentless need to improve labour-productivity associated with capitalism. […]

The simple logic of trade is 'the exchange of reciprocal requirements'. This can take place within a single community or among adjacent communities, and this simple logic can still operate where the direct exchange of products is replaced by circulation of commodities mediated by money. It does not by itself generate the need to maximise profit and, even less, to produce competitively. Beyond such simple acts of exchange, there are more complex transactions between separate markets, involving commercial profit-taking (buying cheap in one market and selling dear in another) in the process of conveyance from one market to another or arbitrage between them. This kind of trade may have a logic different from the simple exchange of reciprocal requirements, at least to the extent that requirements of commercial profit intervene. But here, too, there is no inherent and systematic compulsion to transform production.

Even in precapitalist societies, there are, of course, people who live by profit-taking, people who make a living by profitable trade. But the logic of non-capitalist production does not change simply because profit-seeking middlemen, even highly developed merchant-classes, intervene. Their strategies need have nothing to do with transforming production in the sense required by capitalist competition. Profit by means of carrying trade or arbitrage between markets has strategies of its own. These do not depend on transforming production, nor do they promote the development of the kind of integrated market that imposes competitive imperatives. On the contrary, they thrive on fragmented markets and movement between them, rather than competition within a single market; and the links between production and exchange may be very tenuous.

The trading networks of medieval and early-modern Europe, for instance, depended on a degree of local or regional specialisation that allowed merchants to profit by carrying goods from one locale, where they were produced, to others, where they were not, or not in adequate quantities – to say nothing of their ventures much further afield, in a growing network of long-distance trade. But here as elsewhere in the non-capitalist world, though profit-seeking was a common and highly developed activity, it was separate from, if not actually opposed to, 'efficient' production.

Fierce commercial rivalries certainly existed, both between major economic powers and even within them, among their cities and local merchants. There were even major wars over trade. But these rivalries generally had less to do with competitive production of the capitalist kind, than with 'extra-economic' factors such as superior shipping, domination of the seas and other transport-routes, monopoly privileges, or highly-developed financial institutions and instruments of arbitrage, typically supported by military force. Some of these extra-economic advantages, such as those in shipping or, indeed, military superiority, certainly depended on technological innovations, but this was not a matter of a systematic need to lower the costs of production in order to prevail in price competition.

Even later than the seventeenth century, most of the world, including Europe, was free of market-imperatives. A vast system of trade certainly existed, extending across the globe. But nowhere, neither in the great trading centres of Europe, nor in the vast commercial networks of the non-European world, was economic activity – and production in particular   driven by the imperatives of competition and accumulation. The dominant principle of trade everywhere was not surplus-value derived from production, but 'profit on alienation', 'buying cheap and selling dear'.

Agrarian capitalism

For millennia, human-beings have provided for their material needs by working the land. And probably for nearly as long as they have engaged in agriculture, they have been divided into classes, between those who worked the land and those who appropriated the labour of others. That division between appropriators and producers has taken many forms, but one common characteristic is that the direct producers have typically been peasants. These peasant-producers have generally had direct access to the means of their own reproduction and to the land itself. This has meant that when their surplus-labour has been appropriated by exploiters, it has been done by what Marx called 'extra-economic' means – that is, by means of direct coercion, exercised by landlords or states employing their superior force, their privileged access to military, judicial, and political power.

In early-modern France, for example […] where production was dominated by peasant-owner/occupiers, appropriation took the classic precapitalist form of politically-constituted property, eventually giving rise not to capitalism, but to the 'tax/office' structure of absolutism. Here, centralised forms of extra-economic exploitation competed with, and increasingly supplanted, older forms of seigneurial extraction. Office became a major means of extracting surplus-labour from direct producers, in the form of tax; and the state, which became a source of great private wealth, co-opted and incorporated growing numbers of appropriators from among the old nobility as well as newer 'bourgeois' office-holders.

Here, then, is the basic difference between all precapitalist societies and capitalism. It has nothing to do with whether production is urban or rural, and everything to do with the particular property-relations between producers and appropriators, whether in industry or agriculture. Only in capitalism is the dominant mode of appropriation based on the complete dispossession of direct producers, who (unlike chattel-slaves) are legally free, and whose surplus-labour is appropriated by purely 'economic' means. Because direct producers in a fully developed capitalism are propertyless, and because their only access to the means of production, to the requirements of their own reproduction, even to the means of their own labour, is the sale of their labour-power in exchange for a wage, capitalists can appropriate the workers' surplus-labour without direct coercion.

This unique relation between producers and appropriators is, of course, mediated by the 'market'. Markets of various kinds have existed throughout recorded history and no doubt before, as people have exchanged and sold their surpluses in many different ways and for many different purposes. But the market in capitalism has a distinctive, unprecedented function. Virtually everything in capitalist society is a commodity produced for the market. And even more fundamentally, both capital and labour are utterly dependent on the market for the most basic conditions of their own reproduction. Just as workers depend on the market to sell their labour-power as a commodity, capitalists depend on it to buy labour-power, as well as the means of production, and to realise their profits by selling the goods or services produced by the workers. This market-dependence gives the market an unprecedented role in capitalist societies, as not only a simple mechanism of exchange or distribution, but the principal determinant and regulator of social reproduction. The emergence of the market as a determinant of social reproduction presupposed its penetration into the production of life's most basic necessity: food.

This unique system of market-dependence has specific systemic requirements and compulsions shared by no other mode of production: the imperatives of competition, accumulation, and profit-maximisation, and hence a constant systemic need to develop the productive forces. These imperatives, in turn, mean that capitalism can and must constantly expand in ways and degrees unlike any other social form. It can and must constantly accumulate, constantly search out new markets, constantly impose its imperatives on new territories and new spheres of life, on all human-beings and the natural environment.

Once we recognise just how distinctive these social relations and processes are, how different they are from the social forms that have dominated most of human history, it becomes clear that more is required to explain the emergence of this distinctive social form than the question-begging assumption that it has always existed in embryo, just needing to be liberated from unnatural constraints.

The question of its origins can be formulated this way: given that producers were exploited by appropriators in non-capitalist ways for millennia before the advent of capitalism, and given that markets have also existed 'time out of mind' and almost everywhere, how did it happen that producers and appropriators, and the relations between them, came to be so market-dependent?

Now, obviously, the long and complex historical processes that ultimately led to this condition of market-dependence could be traced back indefinitely. But we can make the question more manageable by identifying the first time and place that a new social dynamic of market-dependence is clearly discernible. [...] [We previously] considered the nature of precapitalist trade and the development of great commercial powers that flourished by availing themselves of market-opportunities without being systematically subjected to market-imperatives. Within the precapitalist European economy, there was one major exception to the general rule. England, by the sixteenth century, was developing in wholly new directions.

We can begin to see the differences by starting with the nature of the English state and what that reveals about the relation between political and economic power. Although there were other relatively strong monarchical states in Europe, more-or-less unified under monarchy, such as Spain and France, none was as effectively unified as England (and the emphasis here is on England, not other parts of the British Isles). In the eleventh century (if not before), when the Norman ruling class established itself on the island as a fairly cohesive military and political entity, England already became more unified than most countries. In the sixteenth century, England went a long way towards eliminating the fragmentation of the state, the 'parcelised sovereignty', inherited from feudalism. The autonomous powers held by lords, municipal bodies, and other corporate entities in other European states were, in England, increasingly concentrated in the central state. This was in contrast to other European states, where powerful monarchies continued for a long time to live uneasily alongside other post-feudal military powers, fragmented legal systems, and corporate privileges whose possessors insisted on their autonomy against the centralising power of the state – and which continued to serve not only 'extra-economic' purposes, but also as primary means of extracting surpluses from direct producers.

The distinctive political centralisation of the English state had material foundations and corollaries. Already in the sixteenth century, England had an impressive network of roads and water-transport that unified the nation to a degree unusual for the period. London, becoming disproportionately large in relation to other English towns and to the total population of England (and eventually the largest city in Europe), was also becoming the hub of a developing national market.

The material foundation on which this emerging national economy rested was English agriculture, which was unique in several ways. First, the English ruling class was distinctive in two related respects.[18] On the one hand, demilitarised before any other aristocracy in Europe, it was part of the increasingly centralised state, in alliance with a centralising monarchy, without the parcelisation of sovereignty characteristic of feudalism and its successor-states. While the state served the ruling class as an instrument of order and protector of property, the aristocracy did not possess autonomous 'extra-economic' powers or 'politically constituted property' to the same degree as their Continental counterparts.

On the other hand, there was what might be called a trade-off between the centralisation of state-power and the aristocracy's control of land. Land in England had for a long time been unusually concentrated, with big landlords

---

18. This discussion of the particularities of English property-relations is deeply indebted to Brenner 1985a and 1985b.

holding an unusually large proportion, in conditions that enabled them to use their property in new ways. What they lacked in 'extra-economic' powers of surplus-extraction, they more than made up for with increasing 'economic' powers.

This distinctive combination had significant consequences. On the one hand, the concentration of English landholding meant that an unusually large proportion of land was worked not by peasant-proprietors, but by tenants (the word 'farmer', incidentally, literally means 'tenant' – a usage suggested by phrases familiar today, such as 'farming out'). This was true even before the waves of dispossession, especially in the sixteenth and eighteenth centuries, conventionally associated with 'enclosure', and was, in contrast, for example, to France, where a larger proportion of land remained, and would long continue to remain, in the hands of peasants.

On the other hand, the relatively weak extra-economic powers of landlords meant that they depended less on their ability to squeeze more rents out of their tenants by direct, coercive means, than on their tenants' success in competitive production. Agrarian landlords, in this arrangement, had a strong incentive to encourage – and, wherever possible, to compel – their tenants to find ways of reducing costs by increasing labour-productivity.

In this respect, they were fundamentally different from rentier-aristocrats, who, throughout history, have depended for their wealth on squeezing surpluses out of peasants by means of simple coercion, enhancing their powers of surplus-extraction not by increasing the productivity of the direct producers, but rather by improving their own coercive powers – military, judicial, and political.

As for the tenants, they were increasingly subject not only to direct pressures from landlords, but also to market-imperatives that compelled them to enhance their productivity. English tenancies took various forms, and there were many regional variations, but a growing number were subject to economic rents – rents fixed not by some legal or customary standard, but by market-conditions. There was, in effect, a market in leases. Tenants were obliged to compete not only in a market for consumers, but also in a market for access to land.

The effect of this system of property-relations was that many agricultural producers (including prosperous 'yeomen') became market-dependent in their access to land itself, to the means of production. [...]

Market-dependent producers

In his historical work, [Robert] Brenner has shown how the systemic pressures deriving from market-dependence, the imperatives that have driven the development of capitalism, operated before, and as a precondition for, the proletarianisation of the workforce. Economic units could be market-dependent – that is, separated from non-market access to the means of their self-reproduction – without being completely propertyless, and even without employing propertyless wage-labourers. This early form of market-dependence, which subjected producers to the imperatives of competition and profit-maximisation, set in train the development of capitalism, and with it mass-dispossession and the mature relation between capital and labour. In his earlier work, Brenner explained the nature of market-dependence in English agrarian capitalism, and he has now offered an account of a different path to market-dependence in the Low Countries.[19]

One implication of Brenner's argument on the nature of market-dependence as in a sense independent of, and prior to, the class-relation between capital and labour, has been his emphasis, especially in his recent account of the contemporary global economy,[20] on imperatives and contradictions rooted in the 'horizontal' relations among capitals, the relations of competition. This emphasis has aroused much hostility among other Marxists. More particularly, Brenner's critics have reacted strongly against a conception of capitalism that, in their view, displaces the class-relation between capital and labour as the defining feature of the system, giving pride of place to 'horizontal' relations. [...]

In his analysis of the Low Countries, Brenner's first premise is that market-dependence, of a kind that sets in train the process of capitalist development, can be created simply by the producers' need to obtain basic 'inputs' from the market (not necessarily, it seems, the factors of production, but the basic condition of survival, namely food), and to produce other commodities for the market in order to obtain those basic inputs. The corollary is that the production of these commodities must be adapted to meet the requirements of competition and its price-cost pressures. So, let us explore whether, or in what specific conditions, the need to exchange the outputs of production for basic inputs, and notably food, will generate the kinds of imperatives that Brenner is talking about.

There is no mystery [...] about the fact that throughout history there have existed many kinds of markets and that agricultural producers have entered them in diverse ways, with various different purposes and consequences. There is presumably no need here to spell out, for instance, the differences between, on the one hand, a 'market-system', in which virtually all commodities are produced for the market and where all factors of production,

19. Brenner 2001.
20. Brenner 2006a.

including land and labour, are treated as commodities; and, on the other hand, peasant-markets in which producers who own, or securely possess, the means of production – in particular, land – sell their surpluses as an adjunct or supplement to their own production for subsistence.

But even this relatively clear distinction raises questions about the point at which reliance on the market becomes vital to subsistence or, in Brenner's terms, the point at which, short of complete separation from the means of production, a loss of non-market access to the means of subsistence becomes decisive in establishing market-dependence, setting in train a process of economic development. This question is particularly difficult to answer in the case of the Northern Netherlands, even more than in the English case.

In the latter, the critical factor, convincingly explained by Brenner in his earlier work, was the loss of non-market access to the land itself. In what has long seemed to me his most important historical insight, he demonstrated how this kind of market-dependence could exist well short of complete dispossession. Non-market access to the means of production was lost well before the complete commodification of labour, in the form of tenancies that operated on 'economic' principles. The pivotal point of his argument was the relation between tenant-producers who held their land (*de jure* or *de facto*) on 'economic' leases and paid 'economic' rents, and landlords who, lacking extra-economic powers of surplus-extraction – the powers of direct coercion to squeeze more surplus from producers – instead depended for their wealth on the productivity, competitiveness and profitability of their tenants. In other words, both producers and appropriators depended on the market for access to the conditions of their self-reproduction, and the relation between them was mediated by the market. Brenner's argument may not have been uncontroversial, but in his explanatory framework the dividing line between market-dependence and its absence was relatively clear, determined by the logic of the property-relations he described, rather than by some elusive quantitative measure.

By contrast, in the Netherlands, the decisive factor is not some kind of market-mediated property-relations or market-access to the land itself. Instead, Brenner invokes the ecologically-determined inadequacy of the land which made its possessors – outright owners, no less than tenants – unable to supply their own subsistence needs, specifically their need for food-grain, without entering the market. Producers, here, were market-dependent simply in the sense that they were obliged to sell commodities they produced in order to obtain basic necessities they were unable to produce.

In such a case, it seems much harder to avoid confronting the quantitative question: to what extent must people rely on the market to purchase the means of survival before they become market-dependent? At what point does the loss of non-market access to subsistence-goods become market-dependence? Does it require dependence on the market for the *full* costs of self-reproduction, or would something short of the full costs still constitute market-dependence in the relevant sense? Why, for instance, is the case of Dutch farmers – who presumably consume some of their own dairy-products and meat, vegetables from their own kitchen-gardens and eggs from their own chickens – differ fundamentally from peasants elsewhere, who produce much or most of their own food but still require exchange to obtain certain basic necessities? At what point does a quantitative difference become a qualitative one? For that matter, precisely how does the economic logic of the Dutch farmer differ from that of craft-producers, even more dependent on the market for their basic food-needs, in a commercial centre like Renaissance Florence?

But let us accept that there is a critical difference between, on the one hand, producers who generally produce their own food but enter the market to supplement their 'subsistence/safety-first strategies', even if these ventures into the market are for the purpose of acquiring necessary goods, and, on the other hand, producers who must produce for the market even to gain access to their most basic food-requirements, particularly grain. The question still remains whether, or in what conditions, the need to produce and sell commodities (of whatever kind) in order, in turn, to buy food on the market creates a pressure to produce competitively and maximise profit in the capitalist manner. Or, to put it another way, the essential question is this: in what specific conditions do competitive production and profit-maximisation themselves become survival-strategies, the basic condition of subsistence itself?

Strategies for survival are identical with strategies for maximising profit, at least for producers, only in capitalism. The conditions of capitalist competition require 'maximising' strategies because capitalists have no guarantee of 'realisation' in advance. They cannot know whether their commodities will sell, or even what conditions and production-costs would ensure sale at all, let alone profit. Lacking the capacity to control prices in a competitive market, they must adopt strategies that will optimise the price/cost-ratio, and their only available strategy is to reduce costs by enhancing labour-productivity, to achieve the maximisation of surplus-value.

But such competitive conditions cannot simply be assumed, even in the presence of well-developed markets and trading networks, so we need to know more about market-dependence and how it engenders imperatives of competition. Brenner seems to suggest that the decisive factor is the degree of specialisation, which, if not a cause, is at least an index, for him, of market-dependence and capitalist development. Needless to say, the more special-ised producers become, the more they must look elsewhere, particularly to the market, to obtain the necessary goods they do not themselves produce. But there have been many cases of specialisation that have not been directed at 'efficient' – i.e. 'competitive' – production. So specialisation for purposes of 'efficiency', in the interests of profit in a competitive market, requires further explanation.

It is important to recognise that specialisation, which, for Brenner, is a critical index of capitalist development, may have no connection whatever with 'efficiency'. Specialisation has existed in non-capitalist economies not driven by the imperatives of competition. In such cases, the object, far from generating maximum-profit, or indeed profit at all, has been to supply the community's needs by means of division of labour and exchange, and methods of production as well as opportunities for profit have been limited by all kinds of mutual expectations, obligations and customs.

Take the example of so-called 'sectional' markets in which specialisation is the dominant principle of economic organisation.[21] Here, traditional, even hereditary, communities of geographically-separated monopolistic specialised producers regularly meet each other in the marketplace to supply their various needs. Yet, despite variation not only in the quality, but in the price, of goods on offer from various producers of the same commodity, unless these markets are integrated into an already-capitalist economy, there is no intrinsic reason why these markets should be competitive in the capitalist sense; and their effects on the methods and costs of production – which may still be deeply rooted in the traditions of the peasant-community and the communal solidarities that are their basic conditions of survival – may be minimal, or even non-existent.

The opportunities of export-trade in precapitalist societies could also encourage specialisation, without transforming social-property relations or methods of production. This was the case, for instance, in France. Even in the middle-ages, at a time when French agriculture in general was striving for self-sufficiency in grain-production, some rural communities were, where possible, already completely given over to viticulture, because wine was a distinctively valuable and uniquely exportable commodity. Later, with the resumption and growth of trade, that specialisation increased, yet this labour-intensive agricultural craft, far from signalling a movement towards capitalist property-relations, has even been credited with preserving the traditional French peasantry.[22]

---

21. On sectional markets, see Wolf 1966, pp. 40–1.
22. See for example, Braudel 1986, p. 316, where he even suggests that 'it was chiefly through the spread of the vine' that France acquired its distinctive character as a nation of small landowners and independent peasants.

We cannot even assume the producers' desire for profit-maximisation in exchange on the grounds that it would give them the best return for their labour and other inputs. We cannot presume the kind of calculation of returns to factors specific to capitalism, which may be quite alien to non-capitalist peasant-economies, where all kinds of other considerations enter into the calculation of the 'value' of labour and land. But, even when peasants do respond to the market with some kind of 'economic rationality', it may be in ways very different from capitalist responses to market-imperatives.

For instance, farmers may respond to rising prices for their particular commodities – typically in cases of growing demand – by increasing their output of those commodities as much as possible, perhaps by bringing more land under cultivation, or even by employing more (cheap) labour, in order to take advantage of the opportunities for increased profits. The typical response to *falling* prices would, in such cases, be to reduce or withdraw from production. In that sense, these producers are indeed price-sensitive. But this kind of motivation is very different from the *cost*-sensitivity of a capitalist producer who strives for increasing labour-productivity at lower cost, especially by transforming the methods of production, in a competitive market with many producers.

The latter kind of market-response presupposes conditions that have not prevailed in most societies, throughout most of human history. There must, of course, be the material possibility of systematic innovation in the methods of production, which is seldom present in peasant-communities with limited resources. But we cannot simply assume that peasants would so respond if only they *could* systematically improve the forces of production and that nothing but their poverty prevents them from doing so. There are also social constraints, the requirements and regulations of the peasant-community, which may themselves be essential to survival.

Yet even these communal constraints, with or without the material limits of peasant-property, are not enough to account for the absence of systematic development of productive forces of the kind we associate with capitalism. In fact, it is, on the whole, a mistake to think in terms of *blockages*. The self-sustaining development unique to capitalism requires not just the removal of obstacles to development, but a positive *compulsion* to transform the forces of production, and this comes only in competitive conditions, where economic actors are both free to move in response to those conditions and obliged to do so. No one has taught us more than Brenner about the specificity of such conditions.

Nor has anyone demonstrated more effectively that even the need to produce surpluses for exploiting classes or states has not, throughout most of history, by itself transformed the methods of production in that way, even production for exchange. Where exploiters – whether rent-taking landlords or tax-hungry states – have had at their disposal the extra-economic means of surplus-extraction, the direct military, political and judicial powers of coercion to squeeze more surpluses from peasants, there has been no systematic compulsion to enhance labour-productivity. Indeed, the effect of exploitation has typically been to impede such transformations of productive forces. Coercive 'extra-economic' modes of surplus-extraction have both lacked the incentive to promote the development of productive forces, and positively hindered it by draining the resources of direct producers. What capitalist development requires is a mode of appropriation that must extract maximum-surplus from direct producers, but can do so only by encouraging or compelling producers to increase their labour-productivity and by enhancing, rather than impeding, the development of productive forces. That kind of appropriation is a rare and contradictory formation, with very specific and stringent conditions of existence.

We shall return to the question of appropriation. But, for now, the question remains why, and in what highly unusual conditions, people would abandon their old survival-strategies, which were not based on profit-maximisation by means of 'efficient' production, and begin pursuing a strategy that did take this form. We need to know more to explain how survival-strategies came to be united with profit-maximising strategies, and even how profit-maximisation and 'efficiency' were joined, or, for that matter, specialisation and efficiency.

When farmers in the maritime northern Netherlands switched to dairy-production, for instance, in response to a huge and growing demand, especially in the cities of neighbouring Brabant and Flanders, they may have had more freedom to alter production in response to market-conditions than has been typical of peasants throughout history constrained by communal requirements. But they seem, at first glance, to have been responding according to a logic not fundamentally different from the strategies of peasants in many other times and places, reacting to a seller's market in conditions of rising demand (and probably, rising prices). There seems to be nothing in their behaviour to suggest that they were doing anything but increasing output to meet increasing demand. Of course, switching from one commodity to another to meet an unfilled need, or even specialising in order to take advantage of growing demand for a particular commodity, is different from merely increasing already-existing production to meet a growing need. But these strategies surely have more in common with each other, than either has in common with adjustment of production to meet the *constraints* of a competitive market where supply always threatens to exceed demand, with a downward pressure on prices.

It may be possible to argue that these farmers – dependent as they were on buying in their basic food-requirements – would have had no, or little, option to limit production in a tight market, and even less option to withdraw altogether. They would, therefore, have had no choice but to reduce their costs of production in order to stay in contention. But there is nothing in Brenner's account to suggest that they were operating in a market of that kind. On the contrary, every indication is that they enjoyed the dual advantage of a growing market and a dominant commercial apparatus.

The 'competition' that certainly took place in European trading networks was principally among merchants and commercial centres, the mercantile interests of the Netherlands, say, against the Hanse, and later, even within the Dutch Republic, between Amsterdam and rival commercial cities. Here, it was, in general, less a question of price-competition among producers of particular commodities, than a contest among merchants or whole commercial cities for control of markets. Even when this kind of competition (rivalry might be a better and less question-begging word) was intended to corner a larger share of the market for domestic producers, it was an essentially 'extra-economic' contest. It had less to do with the methods and costs of production, than with either politically-enforced restrictions and privileges, or with superiority in the instruments, methods and range of commercial activity, to say nothing of superiority in shipping and navigation and military might.

The question, then, is whether the markets so skillfully-negotiated by the Dutch were already operating according to different principles. The Dutch situation described by Brenner's principal source, De Vries and Van der Woude,[23] seems to be one in which the growth of commercial agriculture involved increasing production for growing demand, but not necessarily the kinds of competitive pressures that would systematically drive uncompetitive producers off the land. In a sense [...] the Dutch Golden Age was a period of growing market-*opportunities* for more total output with more or less guaranteed sale, rather than a period of market-*imperatives* requiring the systematic improvement of labour-productivity to meet the demands of competition.

Not even the technical advances pioneered by Dutch farmers, nor the massive reclamation projects which extended cultivable land, by themselves argue for the need to 'compete or go under', as distinct from expanding production to meet expanding demand. This is not to deny that the Dutch did pioneer certain advances in productivity, not least in agriculture. But it is not at all clear [...] that the success of the Dutch economy, or the survival of individual

---

23. De Vries and Van der Woude 1997.

producers, depended on these advances in productivity, more than on 'extra-economic' advantages in commercial rivalries. Dutch investment in production could signal not so much the emergence of a capitalist dynamic, as a precapitalist logic taken to its absolute limits.

A different kind of market-dependence?

[...][We] must surely distinguish between the need to sell even in order to survive, and the need to attain an average rate of profit in order to survive, irrespective of one's own consumption-needs. The English tenant may not have been compelled to attain an average rate of profit in the manner of a modern-capitalist producer, but his particular relation to the landlord already made production for profit beyond his own subsistence-needs a *presupposition* of production for his own subsistence. In that sense, he was subject to price/cost-pressures in a wholly new way.

When a farmer in the northern Netherlands switched from grain to dairy-production, and supplemented his income by producing summer-grains for beer, he was doing so to meet his own consumption-needs and those of his household, even if he did so by means of exchange, consumption-needs that were, within reason, under their own control. When English land-use was switched from arable to sheep-pasture, driving many producers off the land, and when later, in conditions where rents for arable were rising again, landlords derived their rents from productive agriculture, the driving force was something very different from the consumption-needs of the producer. The requirements of the surplus-appropriating landlord were imposed on production from the start, and the requirements of that landlord were different from the pressures exerted by landlords or states that could rely on extra-economic coercion.

We begin to see, in the English case, something more like a capitalist dynamic, in which the immediate object of production is not consumption, or even exchange, but profit; and perhaps for the first time in history, production was directly subjected to the requirements of profit-maximisation, which became a condition of self-reproduction. It is certainly true that Dutch farmers, even independent owner-occupiers, were subject to the requirements of appropriators, notably the state, in the form of taxation. But, again, on its own, this kind of surplus-extraction, in the absence of capitalist property-relations, does not compel competitive production. Perhaps the point can be made simply by considering the conditions in which agricultural producers were in danger of losing their access to land. To be sure, even owner-occupiers in non-capitalist societies may not only suffer poverty, but, in extreme cases, may even be forced to give up their land, if the exigencies of inadequate land, together with burdens of rent or taxation, make survival impossible. But it takes something other than the pressures of inadequacy to make possession dependent on competitive production. The pressures of a capitalist economy are such that even a prosperous farmer, like the English yeoman-tenant, is subject to them, making his continuing possession of good land dependent on his cost-effective production.

At any rate, if Dutch commercial farmers in the earlier phases of development were simply responding to a new market or an absolute rise in demand, it is not even clear whether, or to what extent, they were confronted by rival producers aiming for the same consumers, let alone competitors in a specifically capitalist sense – that is, producers always driven to lower their costs of production, and not only in times of economic decline, in order to maintain their positions in an integrated market where there is always a threat of over-capacity. At the very least, we need to know a great deal more to determine whether, or how, they were subjected to pressures that obliged them to produce competitively – or whether, even if there existed the productive potential for more supply than demand, they were simply availing themselves of the 'extra-economic' advantages enjoyed by their compatriot-merchants, such as the command of trade-routes and trading networks or outright monopolies, superior shipping, and so on.

Competitive markets

We cannot fully understand the difference between these divergent forms of market-dependence without exploring more closely the market-dependence of *appropriating* classes, no less than that of the direct producers. First, however, let us consider the relevant markets themselves.

Let us look first, in very general outline, at the logic of precapitalist trade. The simple logic of trade is 'the exchange of reciprocal requirements'. This can take place within a single community or among adjacent communities, and this simple logic can still operate where the direct exchange of products is replaced by circulation of commodities mediated by money. It does not by itself generate the need to maximise profit and, even less, to produce competitively.

Beyond such simple acts of exchange, there are more complex transactions between separate markets, involving commercial profit-taking (buying cheap in one market and selling dear in another) in the process of conveyance from one market to another or arbitrage between them. This kind of trade may have a logic different from the simple exchange of reciprocal requirements, at least to the extent that requirements of commercial profit intervene. But here, too, there is no inherent compulsion to transform production.

Even in precapitalist societies, there are, of course, always people for whom profit-making (profit-taking might be a better term) is indeed a survival-strategy, people who make a living by trade. But the logic of non-capitalist production, even specialised production, does not change simply because profit-seeking middlemen, even highly developed merchant classes, intervene. Their strategies need have nothing to do with transforming production in the sense required by capitalist competition. Profit by means of carrying trade or arbitrage between markets has strategies of its own. These do not depend on transforming production, nor do they promote the development of the kind of integrated market that imposes competitive imperatives. On the contrary, they thrive on fragmented markets and movement between them, rather than competition within a single market, and the links between production and exchange may be very tenuous. The trading networks of medieval and early-modern Europe, for instance, depended on a degree of local or regional specialisation that allowed merchants to profit by carrying goods from one locale where they were produced to others where they were not. But here as elsewhere in the non-capitalist world, though profit-seeking strategies may indeed have been survival-strategies, profit-seeking was separate from, if not actually opposed to, 'efficient' production.

What, then, constitutes a competitive market? I want to emphasise again that the ultimate issue here is the conditions in which the market constitutes a system of social-property relations. But let me leave aside for now my suggestion that there is a fundamental difference between the situation Brenner describes, in which producers must exchange in order to obtain basic goods, and a system of social-property relations that makes profit, and not just exchange, the immediate object of production. Are there any irreducible conditions without which there can be no competitive market?

Certain simple conditions must surely prevail. The simplest requirement is that buyers must have ready access to alternative suppliers. This means not only that productive capacities must be sufficient to meet and, at least potentially, to exceed demand, but also that supply and demand are reasonably accessible to one another, even if by means of middlemen. But that is only a necessary and far from sufficient condition. The relation among various producers must be such that they can affect each other's costs of production. Price-competition presupposes various suppliers responding to the same or similar conditions, some common standard of measure – not only some common standard of monetary exchange but, more particularly, some compelling social average of labour-costs and the 'socially-necessary labour-time' that underlies it.

It can, of course, happen that producers in social conditions that yield low labour-costs, even without productivity-enhancing technologies or methods of production, can drive down the price of a commodity in ways that affect producers of the same commodity in other, higher-cost social environments, compelling them to lower their costs by increasing labour-productivity. This is, needless to say, a familiar situation in the modern global economy, though throughout most of human history it has probably been uncommon to find the same commodities, produced in very different social environments, regularly competing for the same market. At any rate, even when the same commodity is available from different sources with substantially different costs of production, very specific conditions, both technological and social, must be present to permit the costs and methods of production in one locale systematically to affect those in another, distant one, not to mention modern means of transport and communication – conditions very rare until quite late in history.

The link between production and consumption must also be such that, while production and consumption are separate and mediated by the market, there is a relation between them that creates price/cost-pressures and generates the need for cost-effective production. We need not get embroiled in fruitless calculations of the relation between 'value' and 'price' in order to recognise that competition – the kind of competition that entails price/cost-pressures and compels cost-effective production – presupposes a relation between costs at the point of production and price at the point of consumption. Various factors may weaken that relation: for instance, there may be a great distance between production and consumption, with one relatively inaccessible to the other; social conditions at the poles of production and consumption may be so different that a commodity bought by merchants in a 'cheap' environment can easily be sold relatively 'dear' in another more affluent one without straining the buyers' resources; there may be complex and multiple interventions by merchants whose relative advantages are determined by extra-economic factors; and so on. The more mediated the relation between production and consumption, the less direct will be the effect of commerce on the process of production.

Chapter Two

Precapitalist Societies

Class and state in China and Rome

The Roman case is significant not only because Western images of empire are self-consciously rooted in it, or even because it was, by the standards of its time, very large and widespread, but also because Rome created and administered its vast empire in a distinctive way, which would thereafter represent the criterion, whether positive or negative, of European imperialism. In a sense, it was the first colonial 'empire', as we have come to understand the word.

Early-imperial China, by contrast, had established, already by the third century BC, a very different pattern of rule. This pattern – which, with some variation, formed the framework of Chinese imperial rule for many centuries thereafter – was based on a centralised bureaucratic state, unifying a hitherto-fragmented collection of warring states under the rule of the emperor and administered by a vast apparatus of office-holders. Underlying the coercive powers of the state, needless to say, was military force; but its mission was not colonisation of a kind that marked later European empires.

The Chinese imperial state reproduced, on a large scale, a pattern of state-formation that was probably more the rule than the exception in 'high' civilisations of the non-capitalist world: a bureaucratic hierarchy descending from a monarch to administrative districts governed by royal functionaries and fiscal officials, who extracted surplus-labour from subject-villages of peasant-producers for redistribution up the hierarchical chain. Something like this pattern is visible in many of the most highly organised civilisations, from the relatively small and modest states of Bronze-Age Greece, to the more elaborate and powerful New Kingdom of Egypt, and even, much further afield, the vast empire of the Incas.

The material base of imperial China was the peasantry, which was directly taxed by the state, both to sustain its administrative functions and to line the pockets of its office-holders. The imperial state often took measures to block the development of powerful landed classes, even prohibiting the ownership of land by mandarins in the provinces they governed; but office was itself a route to wealth. This meant that, while peasants lived under oppressive conditions, the imperial state had good reason to preserve the peasantry and its possession of land. It also meant that, while the position of the landed aristocracy fluctuated with the rise and fall of China's successive empires, at the height of China's imperial powers, especially in later centuries, truly great wealth was associated with office. This was less an empire than a single large and over-arching territorial state; and its mode of 'extra-economic' exploitation was less like what we think of as colonial exploitation, than like the direct exploitation of peasants by a tax-office state, which, in another form, existed even in, say, absolutist France.

Like other empires ruled by central bureaucracies, the Chinese imperial state always confronted a dilemma: the direct reach of the central state was necessarily limited, while the means by which that reach could be extended – a proliferation of officers with local administrative and fiscal powers – always threatened to create local power-centres and dynasties that might challenge the central imperial power. This tension, no doubt, limited the state's imperial ambitions.

The Romans were not similarly inhibited. In keeping with its own specific social-property relations at home, the Roman Republic, dominated by a self-governing aristocracy of landowners, made a virtue of necessity in its project of imperial expansion by mobilising, and even creating, landed aristocracies elsewhere as an instrument of empire from the start. They embarked on a ruthless programme of territorial expansion, a massive land-grabbing operation. The transition from republic to empire certainly required the development of a complex imperial state. But, even after the republic was replaced by imperial rule and bureaucracy, the Romans administered their empire with a relatively small central state, through what amounted to a wide-ranging coalition of local landed aristocracies, with the help of Roman colonists and colonial administrators.

If the 'redistributive' kingdom of the ancient world was the foundation of other great non-capitalist empires, the basis of the Roman Empire was a very different social and political form. The ancient-Greek and Roman states were 'city-states' governed not by monarchies or bureaucracies, but by self-governing communities of citizens, with varying degrees of inclusiveness. The state-apparatus was minimal, and the governing bodies were assemblies of one kind or another, with relatively few standing offices. Although peasants as well as landlords were citizens in, for instance, both Athens and Rome, the balance of relations between rich and poor, large landowners and peasants, varied, and was reflected in different political dispensations, such as the democracy in Athens or the aristocratic republic in Rome. But, in all cases, land, not state-office, was the principal source of wealth; and taxation was never the problem for Greek and Roman peasant-citizens that it has been for other peasants throughout history. At the same time, the peasants' relative freedom from dependence, protected even in aristocratic Rome by their civic status as citizens of the city-state, encouraged the development of slavery as an alternative source of surplus-labour for larger landowners.

The city-state, or *polis*, became the basis of the Hellenistic empire, which created a new kind of imperial hierarchy. Here, although there was a monarchical centre, the hierarchy descended from the monarch to the *city*, dominated by a local aristocracy of private landholders, who often had land-grants from the monarch. The Romans essentially took over this form of imperial rule, adopting its 'municipal' structure. Although, in the East, the Empire tended to be superimposed on already well-developed political and economic institutions, the Western parts of the Empire were reshaped by this 'municipal' form of organisation. But, while the *polis* in ancient Athens had been remarkable for its democracy, the Romans, in keeping with their aristocratic base at home, used the municipal form (even in rural areas with no real urban centre) to organise and strengthen local aristocracies. In fact, where no sufficiently dominant propertied class existed, the Romans were likely to create one; and everywhere they encouraged the development of Romanised local propertied elites.

The material base of the Empire was correspondingly distinctive. The growth of slavery certainly marked out the Roman Empire from other great empires. But, although slavery became very important in the imperial homeland, it never dominated the Empire as a whole; and throughout Rome's imperial history, peasants probably still remained the majority of the population outside Rome itself. There is certainly a sense in which the peasantry was no less the basis of the Roman Empire than it was of the Chinese imperial state, but peasants played a very different role in Rome than they did in China.

In many parts of the empire, local peasantries continued to play their traditional role as producers of surplus-labour for the landlord and the state, by means of rent and tax, especially in those regions in the Eastern empire and

North Africa where the Romans largely took over already well-developed political and economic structures. But the Roman peasant himself was a different story. He was the military backbone of Rome's imperial expansion. Many peasants experienced exploitation more as soldiers than as rent-producers or taxpayers, and their creation of the empire was the principal means by which they enriched their aristocratic compatriots. Their military role, and their long absences on military campaigns, also made them vulnerable to expropriation at home, which certainly encouraged the concentration of land and the replacement of peasants by slaves to work the large estates. The proposition that the Empire rested on the peasantry must, then, be amended to take account of the fact that, in the process of imperial expansion, the army was increasingly professionalised, as soldier was increasingly detached from peasant.

The revenues of empire, no doubt, helped to keep Roman peasants relatively free from the burden of taxation, at least for a time. Imperial expansion also provided an alternative income, and even allowed them, up to a point, to replace their ancestral lands with new colonial possessions. As for their replacement by slaves, 'one of the main functions of slavery', as a distinguished historian of Rome has put it, 'was that it allowed the elite to increase the discrepancy between rich and poor without alienating the free citizen-peasantry from their willingness to fight in wars for the further expansion of the empire'. Nevertheless, the fact remains that 'Roman peasant soldiers were fighting for their own displacement'.[1]

The Roman propertied classes were vastly enriched by this whole process, from expropriation of peasants at home, appropriation of great wealth from imperial revenues and, above all, from land. It may seem strange to say so, but the Roman 'élite' was arguably more dependent on the acquisition of land than any other ruling class had ever been before. In other 'high' civilisations, the possession of extra-economic power through the medium of the state had been a primary means of appropriation, even where private property existed and commerce was very well-developed.

In China, even during the last imperial dynasty, when private property was well advanced and trade conducted on a very large scale, the Manchu conquerors (who ruled China until 1912) derived their wealth less from appropriating land, than from seizing hold of the bureaucracy and its apparatus of office and tax. Truly great wealth in the empire derived from office rather than property, and the imperial state had an interest in obstructing the growth of the landed aristocracy, while preserving peasant-possession as a source of taxation. By contrast, the Roman aristocracy, at home and abroad, was, above

---

1. Hopkins 1978, pp. 14, 30.

all, a class of landowners. There have been societies in which wealth derived from land has been an avenue to lucrative public office – such as absolutist France or even the highly commercialised Dutch Republic. For the Romans, conversely, office was an avenue to land. Even as imperial administrators, they were primarily interested in looting local populations (officially or unofficially), largely for the purpose of investing the profits of office in land. While this preoccupation with land did not prevent the Roman aristocracy from engaging in large-scale commercial enterprises, land was nevertheless its only secure and steady source of wealth. That fact alone goes a long way towards explaining their ruthless imperialism and militarism.

Rome and the empire of private property

Unlike other imperial states, whose overbearing power tended to impede the development of private property, the Roman Empire consolidated the rule of property as an alternative locus of power apart from the state. This combination of the imperial state and strong private property was reflected in the Roman law, which produced both a distinctive conception of absolute individual property [*dominium*] – very different from the loose conceptions of possession characteristic, for example, of the ancient Greeks – and also something approaching a notion of sovereignty [*imperium*] – a public right of command attached to civil magistrates and then the emperor – which distinguished Roman ideas of the state from the Greek idea of the *polis* as simply the community of citizens. While the conceptions of *dominium* and *imperium* had roots in the Republic, they developed in tandem and came to fruition in the administration of the Empire, by means of the alliance between property and state.

This mode of imperial administration did not, of course, preclude the need for military force. On the contrary, the Empire was, above all else, a military construction, and the word *imperator* applied to great military commanders before it designated emperors. If anything, the Empire's dependence on private property made it even more reliant on military power, in the form of a huge standing army. The presence of Roman legions throughout the Empire was a necessary bulwark of local administration, a substitute, in a sense, for a top-heavy centralised state at home in Rome.

The Roman Empire, then, rested on a dual foundation: a strong system of private property and a powerful military force. This proposition may seem self-evident, even banal. But, just as it cannot be taken for granted, even in societies with well-developed private property, that the greatest wealth necessarily derives from it, we cannot assume that imperial expansion is always an extension of appropriation by that means. More commonly, before the advent of European imperialism, extending the reach of imperial rule meant, above all, extending direct appropriation by the state. Just as states and dominant classes at home derived great wealth from taxation, so, too, did imperial domination extend that mode of appropriation, through the medium of tribute and tax.

The Roman case represents a significant departure from this pattern, but not because it ceased to depend on imperial taxation – which it certainly did not. It is even possible to say that the Romans, like others, exploited their empire largely by means of taxation (especially since taxes at home were more limited). But taxation, here, was a medium for other modes of appropriation, more than a means of direct exploitation itself. Private land, and the wealth derived from it, were the essence of the imperial exercise; and even the Roman mode of administration, while forging bonds of empire by granting various privileges, and even offices, to imperial subjects, depended, above all, on strengthening the rule of private property in the hands of local elites, as well as colonial settlers and administrators.

Maintaining the army was the primary cost of the Empire, and this, in turn, affected the use of land, as a direct source of supplies or as the basis of taxation. Yet the logic of this empire derived not from tax-hungry office-holders, but from a land-hungry aristocracy of private property. The reliance on colonists and local propertied classes certainly allowed the Empire to reach far beyond the grasp of its central state-administration (in a way that, for instance, the Chinese imperial state did not), but it also created its own problems of enforcement. The Empire relied on such a huge standing army precisely because its defining purpose was the private acquisition of land, and because, in the absence of a vast state-apparatus, the Empire depended on a fragmented coalition of local aristocracies, whose own powers were grounded in their private property, in a dangerously disjointed polity policed by widely-dispersed Roman legions.

The fragmentation and particularism of the Empire also placed a premium on cultural ties and on universalistic ideologies that could help bind the fragments together. The network of communication and the remarkable system of roads which enabled military and commercial movements also served as conduits of Roman culture. The Roman citizenship, which was extended beyond Rome to the empire, was geographically and ethnically inclusive in its conception, quite unlike, for example, the exclusive Athenian idea. Athenian citizenship, at least in principle, designated active political agency in a direct democracy, and was, therefore, resistant to very wide extension. The Roman citizenship – perhaps because it had always been, even in the republican period, associated with aristocratic dominance over a majority of lesser citizens – was more adaptable to spatial expansion and extension to local elites, who were allies, as much as subjects, of their Roman rulers. Active republican citizenship increasingly gave way to a more passive legal identity, which had more honorary or symbolic value than political force.

The Roman law, as it developed to encompass the Empire, was also conceived in universalistic terms, first in the form of the *ius gentium*, which was meant to apply to all peoples, as distinct from the *ius civile*, specific to Roman citizens, until the citizenship spread and rendered the distinction irrelevant. The Roman law countered (up to a point) the particularisms of local laws and customs; and its principles were essential to the Roman definition of property, which spread throughout the empire. But its dominance depended upon its willing acceptance and implementation by Romanised local élites. Both Roman law and Roman citizenship played a major part in unifying the empire, but they did so by creating an ideological – at least as much as a political or administrative – unity.

It would also be hard to explain the spread of Christianity if Roman imperial functionaries – including, finally, the Emperor Constantine, who 'Christianised' the Empire – had not recognised the utility of the 'universal' religion, the first of its kind, as an instrument of imperial order. The very idea of a 'universal' church, as distinct from the traditional local or tribal cults, which included Jewish monotheism, would probably not have emerged if the Roman Empire itself had not been conceived as 'universal', claiming to represent a universal human community.

In order to play that imperial role, the Christian religion had to undergo a significant transformation. It had to be transformed from a radical-Jewish sect, which opposed the temporal authority of the Empire, into a doctrine amenable to, and even encouraging, imperial obedience. That transformation can be traced from St. Paul to St. Augustine, both of them Romanised imperial subjects – one a citizen of Rome in its imperial ascendancy, the other as Bishop of Hippo who witnessed the imperial decline – and two of the most ingenious ideologues any empire has ever produced. In their hands, Christianity became not a politically rebellious sect of a tribal religion, but a 'universal' spiritual doctrine that sought salvation in another world and 'rendered unto Caesar' his unchallenged temporal authority.

The pattern of imperial decline very clearly reveals the logic of the Empire. The mode of administration, and the system of private property on which it was based, meant that the Empire tended towards fragmentation from the start; and in the end, that tendency prevailed. The imperial bureaucracy grew, above all for the purpose of extracting more taxes – as always, largely to maintain the Empire's military power. But the growth of the bureaucracy was a sign of weakness, not of strength. With no significant new conquests after the first century AD, the Roman army was over-stretched in keeping control of the existing empire, while the burdensome bureaucracy and the tax-hungry state grew in order to sustain the army. The burden this imposed on Rome's imperial subjects simply hastened the decline. The so-called 'barbarian' invasions were less a cause than an effect of Rome's disintegration. By the time these incursions became a fatal threat, and not just an annoyance, a crumbling state had long-since become an intolerable burden to peasants and a dispensable nuisance to landlords.

It is a striking fact that the so-called 'fall' of the Empire took place in the West, and not in the imperial East, where the pattern of rule was more like that of other ancient empires: a bureaucratic state in which land remained largely subordinate to office. It was in the Western Empire, where state-rule was diluted and fragmented by aristocracies based on huge landed estates, that the weaknesses of the Empire proved fatal.

As the imperial state imploded, it left behind a network of personal dependence binding peasants to landlord and land – a development encouraged by the state itself when, in a time of crisis, it tied many peasants to the land, no doubt for fiscal purposes. A new form of dependent peasantry, the colonate – in which tied peasants and freed slaves merged – came to replace the old forms of chattel-slavery. In the centuries following the 'decline and fall', there would be various attempts to recentralise this fragmented system under one or another dynastic monarchy, with successive cycles of centralisation and repeated fragmentation, as one or the other element in the uneasy Roman fusion of political sovereignty and landed property prevailed. But the fragmentation of the Roman Empire is still recognisable in European feudalism, a system of parcelised power based on property, with political and economic power united in a feudal lordship dominating and exploiting a dependent peasantry without the support of a strong central state.

The city-states of Florence and Venice

The distinctive position of Italian city-states in the European economy may be rooted in certain more-or-less unbroken continuities with the Roman Empire. Older Roman landholding patterns persisted, with a larger proportion of free peasants, as distinct from serfs. The relatively strong position of the towns perhaps also owed something to the Roman municipal system, in which towns were the social and political domain of Romanised local élites, who effectively governed the surrounding countryside. But, while the imperial elites had been overwhelmingly landed classes, a new kind of urban ruling class emerged in medieval Italy.

Cities like Florence and Venice became what have been called collective lordships, dominating the *contado*, the surrounding countryside, and extracting wealth from it in one way or another, not least to sustain the public offices that, directly or indirectly, enriched many members of the urban élite – in a pattern reminiscent of other tax/office-states we have encountered. In this respect, they were unambiguously non-capitalist in their mode of exploitation, depending on the coercive power of the city to appropriate surplus-labour directly, not only for the purpose of maintaining civic revenues, but also for the benefit of urban élites who owed their power and wealth to their civic status. But, while rural production was needed to provide the city with supplies and revenues, the real wealth of these city-states and their dominant classes was generated by commerce and financial services. Exploitation of the countryside was more a means than an end, a service to the urban economy. The question is whether the logic of that economy was capitalist, or whether the commercial system itself still followed a non-capitalist logic.

Florence and Venice certainly traded in commodities produced in their own cities, such as Florentine textiles or Venetian silk and glass; and the ruling urban classes certainly encouraged and exploited not only commerce, but production, with merchants organising and investing in production as long as market-opportunities were attractive enough. But, while production in these city-states was substantial, the circulation of goods and the provision of financial services were the sources of great commercial wealth. Trade was conducted on non-capitalist principles, depending not on cost-effective production and enhanced labour-productivity in a market driven by price-competition, but rather on extra-economic advantages, such as monopoly-privileges, with the aid of especially sophisticated commercial and financial practices (double-entry book-keeping for instance, is supposed to have originated in Florence). In some cases, where these city-states imposed their military force on colonies, they could exploit forced labour in the production of marketable commodities – as the Venetians did, for instance, by funding the use of slaves for sugar-production in Crete and Cyprus. But Venetian gains from slavery derived not only from the republic's own exploitation of slaves, but from its central role in the early slave-trade, supplying slaves to the Arab Caliphate already in the eighth century. In any case, while Italian merchants could and did benefit from the extra-economic exploitation of producers, at home and elsewhere, the most militant commercial interests were engaged in speculation, not production.[2]

---

2. Hale 1993, p. 150.

This is not to say that production could not, or did not, adapt to changing conditions and market-opportunities. But the ultimate secret of success in these commercial city-states was their command of trading networks. This, in turn, depended not only on the quality of the products they produced, but also on the extra-economic advantages that gave them superiority in controlling and negotiating markets or conveying goods between them, both their own domestic goods and particularly those produced elsewhere. Political power in the city was, at the same time, economic power; and, in external trade, which was by far the most lucrative commercial activity, military force remained the basic condition of commercial success.

The urban élite was likely to respond to inadequate commercial opportunities not by enhancing labour-productivity and improving cost-effectiveness, but by squeezing producers harder by means of extra-economic coercion. They might, in fact, find it more profitable to withdraw from production altogether, and even from trade. In Florence, for instance, the greatest commercial families, notably the Medici, moved into more lucrative non-productive enterprises, such as financial services for monarchs and popes, and, indeed, public office, up to and including dynastic rule of the city-state. Even for those who remained in trade, appropriation of great wealth still depended on civic powers and privileges, on their status in the city and on the extra-economic power of the city-state itself.

At bottom, then, the commercial success of these city-states was based on military force. Economic competition in these non-capitalist economies was less a matter of price-competition than rivalry among merchants, commercial cities or states over direct control of markets. The city-states of northern Italy were constantly at war with their neighbouring rivals, to maintain control of the *contado* as well as dominance in trade; and local wars among Italian cities occurred with the normality and regularity of football-fixtures. In the process, both Florence and Venice, for a time, established control not only over their own *contado*, but over neighbouring cities and their surrounding countryside.

A major feature of these commercial societies was the commercialisation of war (the Italian *condottiere* was, after all, the model mercenary-soldier). But nowhere was the connection between commerce and war more symbiotically close than in the construction of Venice's commercial empire. The city's location gave it privileged access to trade between East and West, but to preserve its commanding position required control of eastern Mediterranean sea-routes. This, naturally, brought Venice into regular military conflict with rivals, to say nothing of pirates. Maintaining its commercial expansion also required control over rivers and mountain-passes on the Italian mainland, which was a strong motivation to establish a territorial empire on Italian soil and beyond.

The Venetians turned military force not only into a means of directly policing their commercial dominance, but into an exchangeable commodity in its own right. From the beginning, the city-state's commercial success depended on expanding its reach beyond Italy, and that demanded not only military force and a vastly superior navy, but commercial ingenuity, particularly the exploitation of war as a commercial resource. In the early days, for instance, Venetian commercial expansion relied on trade-concessions from the Byzantine Empire, which granted Venice commercial privileges and rights to trading posts in exchange for military aid.

Master and slave vs. landlord and peasant

It is not[…]only[…]free producers themselves who were affected by their unique civic status. The whole system of production and surplus-extraction, including the emergence and development of slavery, must be understood against the background of the peasant-citizen. It has often been said that slavery made Athenian democracy possible. This proposition has often been associated with the profoundly mistaken view that Athenian citizens were generally free from the necessity to labour, and that production rested essentially on slave-labour. Since it is now a generally accepted fact that the majority of citizens worked for a livelihood – in agriculture, crafts, or trade – and since the contribution of slaves to production, especially in agriculture, is, to say the least, open to question, the association of democracy with slavery must be formulated somewhat differently.

One possibility is to say (as Michael Jameson does, for example)[3] that slaves *supplemented* the labour of the ordinary farmer in a way that made possible his performance of civic and military functions. Even this formulation, while it assumes that agricultural slavery was essential and widespread, implies that the growth of slavery *presupposed* the emergence of the farmer-citizen. The argument is not simply that because slaves somehow became available in large numbers, Attic farmers found themselves able to become citizens. On the contrary, the object of an argument like Jameson's is precisely to explain what was unique about ancient Athens that compelled farmers to seek an unusual means of responding to increasing demands on their productive capacities. In other words, according to this view, it is because the Athenian farmer had

---

3. This is, in fact, the essence of his article; see M. Jameson 1977–8, pp. 122–45.

attained the apparently unprecedented status of full citizenship, that he was obliged to seek the assistance of slaves.

This formulation, though it places slavery and the farmer-citizen in the correct order, will not quite do. Since [...] the civic status of the farmer actually restricted the need for surplus-production by limiting the pressures of surplus-extraction in the form of rent and taxes, the citizenship of the peasant could just as easily be regarded as a limitation on his need for slave-assistance.[4] What can, however, be said with some assurance is that the status of the peasant-citizen and his freedom from dependence created an incentive for wealthier landlords to seek alternative sources of labour; and it is almost certainly true that slavery grew as Athenian smallholders themselves became unavailable as dependent labourers.

Even here, caution is needed. Not only must we keep in mind that smallholders remained available to their wealthy compatriots as tenants, share-croppers, and casual wage-labourers, and also that there were propertyless citizens who required employment; but we must also consider the extent to which the relations between landlords and peasants restricted the form and extent of slave-utilisation itself. In particular, the configuration of class-power within the citizen-body, to the extent that it curtailed concentration of property, also limited the possibilities of slave-exploitation. As long as properties remained small and peasant-tenures relatively secure – and even wealthier landlords tended to own several scattered smaller holdings – the scope for the utilisation of labour in production beyond the peasant-family was limited. In the forms of exploitation more appropriate to smallholdings and a free peasantry – tenancy, sharecropping, casual wage-labour – family-labour would still have been the predominant productive force. The growth of the urban economy, craft-production, and trade expanded the scope of slave-exploitation (though the extent of these developments should not be exaggerated, since production for the market remained undeveloped); and it is worth noting that the very few known large slave-enterprises in Athens, in addition to the mines, were 'industrial' rather than agricultural. In sharp contrast to Rome, the intensive exploitation characteristic of *latifundia* worked by slave-gangs, made possible by enormous accumulations of property, never existed in classical Greece. These significant differences between Greek and Roman slavery reflect different configurations of power and property that characterised the relations between peasants and landlords in the two cases. [...]

---

4. In E.M. Wood 1983b, I elaborate this argument in reply to Jameson's contention that the utilisation of slave-labour was probably the norm on ordinary small farms, because it was the best way to intensify labour without sacrificing the farmer's civic status. This article forms the basis of Chapter Two of E.M. Wood 1988.

The question of slavery, then, is first and above all the question of the peasantry. How, why, and under what circumstances were relations between landlords and peasants transformed in such a way as to displace peasants on a significant scale as agricultural producers, and to permit or necessitate a massive intrusion of slaves into the Roman economy? The question becomes even more pressing if (as Hopkins convincingly argues) slavery was a difficult and costly mode of exploitation and 'by no means an obvious solution to the élite's needs for agricultural labour'[5]...

How and why did slavery on such a scale become an option in the first place? If slavery was the result of conquest and empire, how and why did Roman imperial expansion become possible and necessary, and why did the Romans transform captives into slaves, when this disposition of conquered peoples was far from an obvious or universal practice? It can hardly be maintained that the influx of slaves provided the original impetus for expropriation, since the very motivation for large-scale slavery presupposes a significant degree of land-concentration; therefore, where did this impetus come from, and how did it become possible to expropriate peasants on such a scale that vast numbers of slaves could be employed? One might even ask why it became *necessary* for landlords to adopt a form of exploitation that required concentration of property to make it economically feasible. At any rate, what made the advantages of this burdensome form of exploitation outweigh its disadvantages?

Whatever the answers to these questions, the important thing is that they are there to be asked. In other words, slavery cannot be taken for granted. [...]

Free producers and slaves

If the mode of surplus-extraction and exploitation is the essential characteristic of any society, then the *fact* of exploitative surplus-extraction is more fundamental still. In other words, the first essential characteristic of any society is *whether* surplus is 'pumped out of the direct producers' by someone other than themselves. One cannot simply set aside free producers on the grounds that they neither exploit others nor suffer exploitation themselves. Especially if they exist in substantial or even preponderant numbers, and perhaps even account for a greater proportion of basic production than do other forms of labour, it must in itself be a highly significant fact that they are *not* exploited and that much or most of production takes place outside the system of exploitation and without surplus being pumped out of the direct

---

5. Hopkins 1978, pp. 9, 108ff.

producers. The existence or non-existence of exploitation, the organisation of production in exploitative rather than non-exploitative ways, is, after all, the difference between a class-system and a classless society. The freedom of so many direct producers from exploitation *must* be treated as an essential factor in describing and explaining the nature of social arrangements, class-conflict, ideology, and the form of the state. One must ask how such a strikingly unusual arrangement came about, and precisely what in the system of social organisation, class-relations, and political power made it possible. And, at the very least, in explaining the nature and function of slavery itself, one must ask whether the unusual development of slave-production was cause or effect of the equally unusual system of class-relations in which so many direct producers managed to free themselves, or to remain free, from exploitation.

At the same time, it must be said that the form in which *production* is carried out cannot be treated as peripheral, even if we place surplus-extraction at the centre of our analysis. If it turned out that the bulk of production was performed by free men, rather than by slaves (as seems to be the case in Athenian agriculture), this alone might raise questions about slavery as the primary form of surplus-*extraction*. At the very least, it would be necessary to ascertain whether the proportion of social production carried out by slaves was sufficient to account for the amount of surplus appropriated by the propertied classes. After all, surplus must first be *produced*, in order to be extracted. […]

[To] conflate the various forms of unfree labour is to obscure a truly fundamental question: why slavery and *not* other forms, and why in Greece and Rome, and nowhere else in the ancient world; or, for that matter, in very few places at any time? Perhaps the answer is that the civic status of Greek and Roman peasants and artisans made them unavailable as dependent labourers and made necessary other forms of surplus-extraction. This, by itself, cannot prove that slavery predominated in production, if we do not accept without question [G.E.M. de] Ste. Croix's first premise about the intrinsic superiority of unfree labour over free, or his assumption that abstract superiority means historical predominance. What such an argument *would* suggest, however, is precisely that the importance of slavery depended upon the condition of free producers; that the growth of slavery cannot be taken for granted as predetermined by its inherently greater effectiveness as a mode of exploitation; and cannot be explained without first accounting for the special character of Greek and Roman peasants and their relations to landlords.

There are, in fact, hints of doubt in Ste. Croix's own argument. In at least one place, for example, he suggests that, in the late-Roman Empire, when there was 'a considerable increase in the exploitation of small free producers, the use of slave-labour in the strict sense was in principle less necessary'.[6] This statement would seem to run counter to the assumption that slave-labour as a mode of surplus-extraction is *in principle* and fundamentally preferable to the exploitation of small free producers (rent-paying peasants and craftsmen, not hired labourers). The suggestion now seems to be that slavery is preferable only when free producers are not available for exploitation.

Here is, at least, a hint of how the crucial question might be posed: why, and under what conditions, did free producers cease to be readily available for exploitation; how, and under what conditions, was their availability restored and increased; and why did their exploitation take the particular forms that it did? [...]

Slavery and the 'decline' of the Roman Empire

[...] The question of the decline of Rome and the rise of feudalism could, then, be reformulated, again more inclusively, as follows: what factors led to changes in the form and extent of peasant-exploitation, including – temporarily – its *relative* decline and *partial* replacement by slave-exploitation, and its re-establishment in the new forms of medieval serfdom? Related to and co-extensive with this question – and again more inclusive than the issue of slavery – are other questions concerning changes in the nature of appropriating classes and the state. This mode of analysis, among other things, has the advantage of focusing on continuities, rather than upon a radical break between the Roman Empire and what came afterwards. The myth of Rome's decline and fall, whether viewed as a sudden cataclysmic collapse or a gradual dissolution, has tended to make feudalism appear out of nowhere (or, at best, out of the alien barbaric North). First, Rome declines and falls in accordance with its inner logic and inadequacies, then feudalism fills the void. What is needed, instead, is a vantage-point from which the continuities are clearly visible and which permits us to discern the emergence of specifically 'feudal' relations and institutions within the social and institutional framework of imperial Rome.

European feudalism was characterised by three essential features: the 'parcelisation' of the state and its replacement by a patchwork of jurisdictions in which state-functions were both vertically and horizontally fragmented; a 'parcelisation' of the economy, contraction towards a 'natural' economy; and,

---

6. See de Ste. Croix 1981, p. 113. He makes a similar suggestion about the relationship between the unavailability of free producers for exploitation and the rise of slavery in Athens on p. 141.

above all, a significant growth of personal dependence, a condition of serf-dom which, to an unprecedented degree, bound formerly-free producers both to the land and to individual appropriators in a relationship of dependence that was – at once and inextricably – economic and political. These three fea-tures can be viewed as three aspects of a single phenomenon: a new mode of surplus-extraction constituted by a decentralised fusion of political and economic power.[7] This new form of exploitation took the shape of a juridical-political relationship between producer and appropriator, so that each unit of production and appropriation was at one and the same time a fragment of the state, and the lord was both private exploiter and ruler at once. The ques-tion of the transition from imperial Rome to Western feudalism should, there-fore, focus on whatever there was in the logic of Roman social relations that tended towards fragmentation of the state, the growth of a parcelised unity of political and economic power, and the increasing personal dependence of for-merly free producers. The specific institutional forms assumed by these new relationships – the forms of infeudation and subinfeudation, vassalage, etc. – may owe a great deal to alien-intrusions; but, even these, together with the manorial system, have Roman antecedents, and could not, in any case, have been implanted if an appropriate matrix of social relations had not already developed to receive them in Rome.[8]

The 'logic' of slavery vs. the logic of capitalism

The whole analogy between slavery and capitalism is especially problematic, not least because slavery did not and could not have an ability – or a need – to squeeze out other modes of production comparable to capitalism's unprece-dented tendency to do so. If capitalist relations of exploitation have promoted the development of a particular system of *production* – factory-production, with a concentrated, integrated, and centrally controlled labour-force – it is not at all clear that slavery carried with it a similar impulse towards latifun-dial production. Capitalism encourages certain forms of production because it creates unprecedented pressures for accumulation and competition, and because the capitalist owns only the labour-power of the worker, and only for a fixed period of time. Capitalism, therefore, typically responds to the pres-sures of competition and accumulation by increasing labour-productivity, and this requires transformations in the organisation of the labour-process.

7. See P. Anderson 1974, pp. 147–8; and E.M. Wood 1981a, pp. 86–9. A modified version of this article is included as Chapter One of E.M. Wood 1995a.
8. For a brief summary of the ambiguities in the evidence concerning the provenance of specific feudal institutions, see P. Anderson 1974, pp. 130–1.

The resulting high productivity, within the competitive system, tends to drive out less productive forms of labour. The same pressures of accumulation and competition and the need to increase labour-productivity are not present in slavery – especially since the master owns the worker's *person* and not simply his labour-time.

Slavery may create pressures to concentrate property; but this is, arguably, less because of its inherent superiority as a mode of production and exploitation, than because of its *dis*advantages, the need to compensate for its costs and its shortcomings in competing with other forms of exploitation. So, for example, a need may arise to consolidate holdings in order to employ slaves full-time, by mixing crops, etc., because the investment in their *persons* might otherwise exceed the returns, a problem that does not arise with wage-labourers or tenants. In this case, the question is not how a 'primordial' system of exploitation, by its own inherent natural logic and superior strength, squeezes out other forms of production, but rather, how, and under what specific historical restrictions, such a difficult mode of exploitation becomes the most eligible one. It is also worth stressing that the 'logic' of slavery depended very much on surrounding circumstances. For example, it might, in certain conditions, adapt itself to prevailing forms of production, rather than establish forms of its own which tended to drive out others. Especially in classical Athens, under the constraints of the democracy, traditional forms of individual craft-production were never superseded by gang-production, and slaves commonly produced as individual craftsmen. Even the few known large enterprises that employed many slaves under one roof never achieved anything like the integrated labour-force and division of labour characteristic of the modern factory, but essentially brought together in juxtaposition a number of individual craft-producers.

The question raised by [Pierre] Dockès's analysis of slavery and its internal dynamic may point to another, more fundamental question: if there *was* a tendency towards concentration of property and a consequent – and contradictory – need for a strong centralised state, should that tendency be traced to the logic of slavery at all, or to some other, prior source?[9] In other words, is the developmental logic for which we are looking the distinctive logic of a slave-society at all?

It is true that the possibility of large-scale slave-utilisation, especially with 'centrally managed large-scale production-units', presupposes land-ownership on a scale sufficient to require and make possible a large labour-force. This is almost tautological, but it does not necessarily mean that the tendency towards concentration is produced by slavery. Apart from the fact that lati-

9. Dockès 1982.

fundial slavery was only one form of slave-utilisation, temporally and geo-graphically limited, it could just as easily be argued that the very motivation to acquire a large force of slaves was preceded, and in some sense caused, by a tendency towards concentration of property. Dockès does little but assert – usually by analogy with capitalism – that the logic of slavery was to drive out small producers and concentrate property, except to say that the mas-sive influx of slaves helped to ruin the independent small peasant in Italy by making him unable to compete in the market not only with imported goods, but with produce from large Italian estates. Questions must, however, be raised about the degree to which peasants depended on the market for survival, especially markets in which they would be forced to compete with large estates. Peasant-production was largely subsistence-farming, and the markets in which they operated were essentially local 'peasant'-markets in which petty producers exchanged necessities with one another.[10] Dockès may, here again, be imposing the logic of capitalism and capitalist competition on Roman society. But, even granting that the logic of slavery encouraged con-centration of property, this logic presupposes the existence of large estates and a prior process of concentration which slavery only aggravated.

At the same time, and paradoxically, the growth of slavery seems also to presuppose a failure on the part of large landowners to reduce the peasantry to dependence – that is, a failure to deny peasants access to the means of subsis-tence and reproduction without being compelled to perform involuntary labour for others. Again, slavery rose and declined in inverse ratio to the availability of free producers for exploitation. This would seem to suggest that slavery might be most necessary precisely where peasants remained in possession of the means of production. Is this true, and does it contradict our earlier assumption that slave-utilisation and peasant-expropriation go hand in hand?

The 'slave-mode of production'

The relation between citizens and slaves, then, is difficult to characterise as a simple class-relation based on a social division of labour. The citizen-body itself was, from the beginning, internally divided in ways which cannot be dismissed as *merely* a division between rich and poor. It can be argued that the Athenian state, the *polis*, developed in response to an internal class-opposition between two agrarian classes – an aristocracy of noble landholders and a producing class of peasant-proprietors; and while the internal class-struggle was transformed by both the development of slavery and the growth of free *urban* producing classes, it never ceased to play a central role in the social

---

10. Finley 1973, p. 107.

life of the Athenian *polis*. Indeed, the class-conflict among citizens is, in many respects, the essential fact of Athenian political history. Even though it was the surplus-labour of slaves, more than that of poor but free producers, that was appropriated by wealthy citizens, the opposition between rich and poor took a particularly definite form in Athenian eyes, as the opposition between citizens who were compelled to labour for a livelihood and citizens who, by virtue of their property, were able to live on the labour of others. This opposition figured prominently in philosophical speculations, playing an essential role in the theories of Plato and Aristotle. Above all, the division between two kinds of citizens expressed itself in political conflicts. These political struggles cannot be dismissed as *merely* political, as oppositions peripheral to the basic relations of production within a fundamentally united ruling class. In precapitalist societies which still rely on 'extra-economic' modes of surplus-extraction – by means of direct legal, political, or military coercion – the political struggles of the poor, even poor proprietors, may represent resistance to *economic* exploitation. In this sense, the conflicts between democrats and oligarchs in Athens cannot be fully understood without reference to class-oppositions within the citizen-body.

In all these respects, the concept of the 'slave-mode of production', and the transparent social relations it implies, is put in question by the facts of Athenian social history. If one further considers the differences between Greece and Rome, the notion of *the* slave-mode of production becomes even more problematic. It should be noted, in the first place, that this 'mode of production' is usually so conceived that it covers a time-span of more than a millennium. This is a considerable slice of historical time, whose magnitude may be judged by comparing it to a period which in modern Europe encompassed all the historical transformations from early feudalism to industrial capitalism. The rate of epochal change in classical antiquity may not have been quite so dramatic, but this period does cover the rather significant transformations which separate the early Greek *polis* from the later Roman Empire, and the peasant-economy of Attica from the 'senatorial' economy of the late-Roman Republic or the latifundial production of the Western Empire.

If one essential form of production binds together these very different 'social formations', it is arguably *peasant*-production rather than slavery. While it can be said more-or-less categorically that, in both Athens and Rome, large-scale enterprises, urban and rural, were dominated by slave-labour, it must also be said that, especially in Athens, there were few such enterprises.[11]

---

11. M.I. Finley emphasises the role of slaves in large enterprises in Finley 1980, p. 82. His designation of Greece and Rome as *slave-societies*, incidentally, has certain advantages over the 'slave-mode of production' since it acknowledges the importance

In particular, the 'fully-developed' slave-mode of production, based on large estates worked by slave-gangs, was never characteristic of Greece at any time, and existed – let alone predominated – in Rome for only part of the period concerned, and even then, in only part of the Empire: in the West, and particularly in Italy and Sicily. Even then, at the height of latifundial slave-production, the majority of the population were peasants, who were arguably still the productive backbone of the Empire. Indeed, it is only by keeping this fact in mind that the continuities in the transition from antiquity to feudalism can be understood.[12]

The concept of 'slave-mode of production' is questionable, even if its essential characteristics are reduced to the existence of a 'juridically pure' condition of chattel-slavery (in contrast to the 'mixed types of servitude[...]in an amorphous continuum of dependence and unfreedom' which characterised slavery elsewhere in the ancient world)[13] and the systematic use of this juridical category as the dominant type of surplus-extraction. The seeming precision of this criterion dissolves when one considers the widely divergent forms of slave-utilisation, the profoundly different labour-processes (that is, literally, modes of production) into which this juridical category was inserted, and the different locations of slaves in the economies of Greece and Rome. It is also questionable whether one can speak of slavery as a single type of 'surplus-extraction', or, for that matter, as a 'pure', 'absolute' condition, if one considers the 'continuum of unfreedom' which separates slaves in the Attic silver-mines or the plantations of imperial Rome from the slave-craftsmen of Athens, living and working independently and paying a kind of rent to their owners, or slaves in managerial or civil-service functions, including the police-force of Athens.

Above all, the role of free labour, its relation to slavery and its position in the class-structure, cannot simply be excluded from an analysis of the dominant mode of production and relegated to the periphery as a secondary characteristic of an 'impure' 'social formation'.[14] It is not so easy to determine whether it is

---

of slavery without suggesting that the systematic use of chattel-slaves necessarily implies a particular system of production, or even appropriation.

12. See, for example, Hopkins 1978; and Hilton 1973, p. 10.

13. See P. Anderson 1974, p. 21. Finley also stresses the uniqueness of chattel-slavery as a form of dependence. See, for example, Finley 1980, pp. 71–7, where he discusses the unique characteristics of slavery: 'the slave's property status, the totality of power over him, his kinlessness' (p. 77); and their consequences. It is clear from Finley's account, however, that while the distinct juridical status of slaves had profound consequences for their social condition and for their usefulness to their owners, it did not imply a particular form of labour, a particular location in the division of labour, or even a particular form of surplus-extraction.

14. See, for example, P. Anderson 1974 p. 22.

the position of slavery, or that of free labour, which acts as the 'general illumi-
nation which bathes all the other colours' of the social formation.

The presumption in favour of slavery as the 'dominant mode of production' probably has less to do with the actual preponderance of slaves over
free labourers, either in numbers or in their relative importance to the economy, than with the fact that, especially from the vantage-point of the modern world and the predominance of juridically free labour, it is slavery alone
which seems *extraordinary*. It is true that Greco-Roman civilisation employed,
systematically and on a large scale, slaves who were clearly defined in law as
chattels; and it would be absurd to deny the significance of this fact. On the
other hand, it can be argued that at least as remarkable and extraordinary
as slavery in the ancient world was the position of *free* labour, peasants and
craftsmen, especially in Athens. Their juridical, civic and political status was
unique; and in social formations where 'extra-economic' forms of surplus-
extraction predominated, this was a matter of no small consequence.

Agricultural slavery and the peasant-citizen

Peasants have been defined – in contrast to 'primitive agriculturalists' – as
cultivators who depend for their subsistence on certain rights in land and
family-labour, but who are involved in a 'wider economic system' which
includes non-peasants. Essential to this definition is the fact that the peasant-
family operates as a productive unit (rather than as an 'entrepreneurial unit',
as in the modern family-farm).[15] In this sense, the small farmers of Attica
can be called peasants. More specifically, peasants have been characterised
as 'rural cultivators whose surpluses are transferred to a dominant group of
rulers that uses the surpluses both to underwrite its own standard of living
and to distribute the remainder to groups in society that do not farm but
must be fed for their specific goods and services in turn'. The production of
a 'fund of rent' – the payment in labour, produce, or money to someone who
'exercises an effective superior power, or *domain*, over a cultivator' – is, by
this definition, regarded as the characteristic 'which critically distinguishes
the peasant from the primitive cultivator',[16] whether that 'rent' takes the

---

15. See, for example, Finley 1973, p. 105.
16. Wolf 1966, pp. 3–4, 9–10. The term 'surplus' is used here in a particular sense
which perhaps requires some explanation. In purely technical terms, one could speak
of 'surplus-labour' to describe any labour above what is needed to provide 'the minimum required to sustain life [...], the daily intake of food calories required to balance
the expenditures of energy a man incurs in his daily output of labor' (Wolf 1966, p. 4),
plus what is required to maintain and replace the supplies and equipment necessary

form of payments to private landlords, or a tax or corvée-labour for some state or religious authority. It has been a general characteristic of peasants that a large proportion of their surplus-production has been accounted for by rent and/or taxes. What distinguishes the Attic peasant from others in this respect, as we shall see, is the limited degree to which he was subject to such obligations.

Clearly, the need to intensify production has varied in large part according to the extent of such obligations. Patterns of surplus-*production*, therefore, have varied in response to the demands of surplus-*appropriation*. These patterns have been determined not only by 'objective' factors of population, ecology and technology, cultural factors and the standard of expectations, but in particular by social and political relations and the balance of power between producing and appropriating classes. In fact, demographic pressures themselves cannot be considered in abstraction from these relations.[17] The level at which population-growth begins to strain available resources and productive capacities varies *inter alia* according to how much production is syphoned off by leisured appropriators. This is especially true in non-capitalist societies, where appropriating classes tend to extract surplus 'unproductively', increasing their surplus by coercively squeezing the direct producer, rather

---

for the production of that caloric minimum – to repair or replace instruments, feed livestock, maintain buildings, fences, fields, etc. Such 'purely technical' terms are, of course, affected by cultural factors, changing technologies and expectations. For the purposes of the present argument, however, the critical issue does not concern the precise measure of biological needs, cultural necessities, or the cost of the 'replacement-fund'; nor are we primarily concerned with how much of the producer's 'surplus' is produced voluntarily in order to enhance his or her own comfort or affluence. The essential issue, here, is the disposition and distribution of goods and services between primary producers and others not engaged in the production process. When society 'is no longer based on the equivalent and direct exchanges of goods and services between one group and another' (Wolf 1966, p. 3), when in particular the goods and services of some groups are appropriated by others whose claims rest on a position of dominance, a distinction emerges between what the primary producers produce for their own and their families' use and maintenance (whether directly or through the medium of exchange), and what they produce for others without equivalent exchange. The question of 'surplus-production', then, has to do with the form and extent of the labour performed by primary producers for non-labouring appropriators. More particularly, the issue is the *compulsory* labour performed by the primary producer in order to meet the demands of a dominant appropriator. The point at issue, then, is the nature and extent of any external social compulsions which may determine the nature and extent of the producer's labour beyond what is required for self-maintenance and the continuance of the family unit. See Wolf 1966, pp. 2–10, for a more detailed discussion of some of these points.

17. See Brenner 1985b, pp. 223–4, for a particularly lucid statement of this principle.

than by enhancing the *productivity* of labour through technical improvements. The more surplus appropriated by non-producers, the lower the population-'ceiling', the level at which 'overpopulation' occurs, and the level at which population-growth requires intensified production. That Jameson has failed to take account of such considerations is illustrated by the fact that his central concern is to identify the source of the poorer citizen's free time, without asking about the source or degree of the rich citizen's wealth.

Athens can be contrasted in these respects with other ancient civilisations which were also subject to demographic pressures and technological limitations, and where production was also sufficiently intensive to support elaborate material cultures as well as state-forms far more complex than the Athenian *polis*. In the ancient Near East, for example, wealthy ruling strata, monarchs, and religious institutions were supported not by chattel-slavery, but by the heavy dues and labour-services of subject peasant-populations. The difference does indeed seem to lie in Athenian *citizenship* and the social limitations that it placed upon surplus-production. But the critical point, here, is that the demands of citizenship determined not only the form of surplus-production, but also its extent. The civic status of the small producer limited the pressures for intensified production by limiting the two principal forms of surplus-extraction, rent and tax. The wealth and power of landlords, and hence the demands they could make on the society's productive capacities, were restricted by the configuration of social and political power represented by the democracy, which limited opportunities for concentrating property and afforded legal protections to small producers against certain forms of dependence. As for the tax-burden so often borne by peasants, not only was the Athenian state-apparatus relatively simple, but exemption from regular taxation, as M.I. Finley has suggested, was a hallmark of 'that novel and rarely repeated phenomenon of classical antiquity, the incorporation of the peasant as a full member of the political community'. For the Greeks, a 'tithe or other form of direct tax on the land [...] was the mark of a tyranny'.[18] In this

---

18. Finley 1973, pp. 95–6. The Athenians, again, generally avoided direct and regular taxation on the property or persons of citizens. Metics paid a head-tax, the *metoikion*, while propertied citizens were occasionally obliged to pay a war tax, the *eisphora*, from which 'roughly everyone below the hoplite status' was exempt (Finley 1981, p. 90). There was also a substantial number of indirect levies, such as harbour-taxes, taxes on property-transactions or for operating mines; but these too would have fallen more heavily on the rich, as would taxes on property owned outside one's own deme. A substantial portion of public revenues came from the liturgies, by which individual wealthy citizens took responsibility for certain public functions, including entertainments and the maintenance of ships. Thus, the burden on poorer citizens was exceptionally light. It is worth noting that, as Finley has pointed out, there is no evidence that taxation, so often the object of grievance for the poor in other times and places,

respect, classical Athens (and Rome before the growth of her empire) differed dramatically from other societies in which kingdoms and empires have rested on the backs of a tax-burdened peasantry. [...]

In fact, in a very important sense, the essence of citizenship for the Athenian peasant was protection from certain kinds of surplus-extraction, both in the form of taxation (as Finley pointed out in the passage quoted above), and in the form of dependence on the rich. In Rome, the transition from republic to empire at first permitted the rich to avoid the burden of state-revenue without transferring the full fiscal weight of empire to the peasants, by exploiting the provinces; but, eventually, in contrast to Athens, the tax-burden was increasingly shifted to the poor, while the public financial burden of the rich diminished even further.[19] In Athens, no such decline of the peasant-as-citizen took place while she remained an independent *polis*.

It is true that the relative unavailability of Athenian free producers for exploitation was itself a critical factor leading to the growth of slavery. In a sense, the free time of the poor was won at the expense of slave-labour for the rich. This, however, tells us little about the use of slaves by the small proprietors themselves, which is Jameson's principal concern. Furthermore, while the relative freedom of the Athenian small producer encouraged slave-utilisation by the rich, that freedom itself placed *limits* on what the rich could do, even with slaves. The relations between appropriating classes and free producers restricted not only the total amount of surplus-production in general, but also the extent and form of slave-exploitation itself. In particular, the configuration of class-power between producing and appropriating citizens in Athens obstructed the concentration of property which could have made possible more intensive forms of slave-production like the latifundial slavery of Rome. [...]

Hired labour has, after all, never been the predominant form of surplus-appropriation, until the very recent and localised predominance of capitalist appropriation. Where wage-labour has existed in precapitalist or non-capitalist economies, it has generally been an adjunct to other forms of labour and surplus-appropriation, often as a means of supplementing the incomes of smallholders whose land – whether owned or held conditionally – has been insufficient for subsistence. In such cases, wage-labour has tended to be casual or seasonal, employed particularly at the harvest. Wage-labour as a predominant form presupposes a labour-force composed of people who are juridically free, but devoid of land or any other property essential to

---

ever figured among the complaints of the Athenian *demos*. By contrast, the burden borne by the rich seems to have been a major theme in anti-democratic grievances.

19. Finley 1973, p. 96.

production – whether held in ownership or some kind of conditional possession such as tenancy – and therefore dependent for their livelihood upon the
sale of their labour-power for a wage on a regular, continuous basis. The predominance of such a labour-force has been unique to the capitalist economy,
which emerged in early-modern Europe. In non-capitalist economies, where
peasants have tended to dominate production, propertied classes have derived
their wealth primarily from rents, labour-services, dues, fines, taxes, tithes, or
tributes, imposed upon producers who have been in various ways dependent
upon them, either in legal bondage, for example as serfs or debt-bondsmen, or
in otherwise subordinate positions, as sharecroppers or tenants. [...]

A mixture of various rent-forms – fixed or variable, ranged along a continuous scale, extracted in various ways by landlords from tenants and sharecroppers, with varying degrees of security of tenure according to prevailing needs
and possibilities – has been typical of many agrarian economies. At the very
least, we must entertain the possibility that such forms of tenancy, leasing,
or 'management' – and not just slavery or wage-labour – were available as
significant options to Athenian landowners looking for ways to exploit labour
'profitably'. Indeed, since wealthy Athenians so often owned several smaller
properties, rather than large concentrations of land, 'farming' out these smallholdings in one form or another may have been the easiest way.

What, then, might the Attic countryside in classical times have looked like?
Most properties would be worked by peasants and their families. Often these
smallholders would, as in other peasant-communities, assist their neighbours, especially at harvest-time.[20] Some smallholders would be able to afford
a slave or two, whose principal functions would probably be in the house,
but who might lend a hand in the fields. Land owned by wealthy citizens
would, in the typical case of small scattered properties, be let out to tenants or
sharecroppers, who would work the land in much the same way as any other
peasant, using principally family-labour. Larger estates – of which there were
relatively few – could be supervised directly by the landowner or by bailiffs.
In such cases, the basic permanent stock of farm-labourers would consist of
slaves, but this stock would not be very large. It is possible, too, that the size
of a farm would not be the sole consideration, since even a small home-farm,
owned by a wealthy leisured proprietor as one of several fragmented holdings, might be worked by slaves, even if his other properties were farmed
by peasant-labour. Casual labour would probably be available for hire at all
times in the form of propertyless citizens and the many small farmers whose

20. See Osborne 1985, pp. 144–6, for a discussion of evidence suggesting non-
monetary cooperation between neighbours, as well as kin, in agricultural labour.

properties (whether owned or leased) were insufficient to support their families. These labourers would be especially busy at the harvest, but would be available for various kinds of work throughout the year. It would be to the advantage of the landowner to employ them whenever possible – buying their labour-power at very low wages, and only when needed – instead of investing in slaves and incurring the risks and responsibilities of owning their *persons*, keeping them alive and (relatively) well through both productive and unproductive periods. As long as the concentration of property remained limited and peasant-tenures reasonably secure, and while even large landowners often held their properties in separate scattered parcels, the scope for labour on the land beyond that of the peasant-family unit would continue to be restricted.[21] This picture cannot, of course, be confirmed by positive proof, but it is historically plausible and fits the available evidence. Unless and until new evidence emerges different from what now exists, 'widespread' agricultural slavery must seem very much more fanciful.

The bulk of Athenian slaves, then, would be found in domestic service and in the silver-mines, the two areas of labour that they more-or-less monopolised. The rest – relatively few, if we assume something less than the maximum-estimates of slave-numbers – would be scattered throughout the division of labour: apart from small numbers in agriculture, they would work in public service (what Finley has called the lower civil service), including the Scythian archers, who represented the nearest thing to an Athenian police-force – functions in which slaves predominated over citizens; various crafts, entertainment, and so on. The large numbers in the mines and in domestic service were, certainly, 'essential' to the Athenian economy, and their absence, if such a thing can be imagined, would have transformed Athenian society. Silver was vital to the Athenian economy; and an Athens without domestic servants – that is, an Athens without wealthy households, or one in which poor citizens served in the households of their wealthy compatriots – would have been something very different from the Athenian democracy. And the productive functions of the household-crafts – which supplied many of the citizens' daily needs, in the absence of large-scale production for the market –

---

21. See Andreyev 1974 and Audring 1974, for some indications of the persistence of these conditions. Andreyev discusses the distribution of land in Attica, arguing that there was a 'rather numerous' class of peasant-proprietors owning from about 3.6 to 5.3 hectares of land, which he estimates was approximately the amount needed to maintain a family. He stresses the stability of this peasant-property and questions the extent of upheavals and dispossessions at the end of the fifth century BC and in the fourth. Audring also notes the stability (and stagnation) of the peasant-economy, the limits it imposed on land-concentration, and the consequent restrictions on slave-utilisation.

should not be underestimated. But if slaves undoubtedly belonged to the essence of Athenian life, it was in a very different sense from that suggested by the 'slave-mode of production' which displaces the labouring citizen from the heart of the productive 'base'.

The nexus of freedom and slavery in democratic Athens

There is a sense in which [Jacob] Burckhardt and the others were right when they singled out as an essential characteristic of Athenian democracy the fact that the poor were free, or relatively so, from the compulsion to 'do work which the rich needed done'.[22] This claim [...] must be distinguished from the simple myth of the idle mob, according to which the poor were excessively free from work as such, leaving slaves to carry on the labour of day-to-day life while citizens disported themselves in the assembly, the theatre, and especially in the courts, where the poor were constantly occupied in persecuting and expropriating the rich. If the idle mob bears little resemblance to historical reality, there is an important grain of truth in the more subtle proposition with which the myth is often associated, namely that, while the multitude did work for a livelihood, the bonds between rich and poor in Athens were weak, to the extent that the two classes were not firmly bound to one another by the ties of dependence that link master and servant.

The independence of the labouring poor, which, for [William] Mitford[23] and Burckhardt, was the major source of Athens's ills, may indeed supply the key to Athenian democracy. To put it this way is already to recognise that, even if an intimate connection undoubtedly existed between the freedom of the citizen and the bondage of the slave, that connection did not take the simple form suggested by the myth of the idle mob or by its Marxist inversion, the slave-mode of production. The connection between democracy and slavery is not simply that the labour of slaves made possible the leisure which citizens could devote to political activity. The connection is to be found in the *independence* of the citizens, not in their leisure, nor in the relegation of productive labour to slaves.

To put it another way – and this may be taken as the central thesis of the present study – the distinctive characteristic of Athenian democracy was not the degree to which it was based on dependent labour, the labour of slaves, but on the contrary, the extent to which it *excluded* dependence from the sphere of production, that is, the extent to which production rested on free,

22. Burckhardt 1929, pp. 254–5.
23. Mitford 1814.

independent labour, to the exclusion of labour in varying forms and degrees of juridical dependence or political subjection. Athenian slavery, then, must be explained in relation to other forms of labour which were *ruled out* by the democracy. It should be treated not as the productive base of the democracy, but rather as a form of dependence permitted and encouraged by a system of production dominated by free and independent producers, and growing, as it were, in the interstices of that system. The central question about Athenian slavery would, then, be what social needs remained to be filled by some kind of dependent labour which the dominant forms of free labour were unable to accommodate.

There are two common ways of formulating the historical connection between the rise of democracy and the growth of slavery. The first suggests that an increase in the supply of slaves, by whatever means, made the democracy possible, by liberating the citizen-body for civic participation. This 'explanation' begs every important question and is, in any case, chronologically flawed. Nowhere in Greece does slavery seem to have been economically important until the sixth century BC, and in Athens it reached its peak rather later than in other prosperous cities.[24] Even if we hesitate to accept the convention which identifies the Solonian reforms (594/3 BC?) as the founding moment of Athenian democracy, they certainly represent a critical turning-point in the liberation of the peasantry; and in that sense, it can be said with reasonable confidence that Athenian democracy had implanted its roots before slavery became a significant factor in the Attic economy. The alternative explanation of the connection between democracy and slavery is that the growth of the democracy and the status it accorded to the poorer citizens of Athens, peasants and artisans, made them unavailable as dependent labour, thereby creating an incentive for their wealthier compatriots to seek alternative modes of exploitation. M.I. Finley, for example, has argued that 'the peasantry had won their personal freedom and their tenure on the land through struggle, in which they also won citizenship, membership in the community, the polis. This in itself was something radically new in the world, and it led in turn to the second remarkable innovation, a slave society'.[25]

This seems the most fruitful line to follow, though it requires considerable elaboration and specification. We need to know, first, precisely what social functions the peasant-citizen was no longer available to perform, and what limits his existence placed on the possible forms in which labour could be organized in the *polis*. If it was not labour as such which was precluded by the

---

24. For a brief discussion of this point, see Murray 1980, pp. 226–8.
25. Finley 1980, pp. 89–90.

status of citizenship, and certainly not the agricultural labour that constituted the material base of this agrarian society, then what possibilities *did* citizenship foreclose, and where were the spaces which slavery could grow to fill? It must also be said, however, that slaves did not simply step directly into places left vacant by peasant-citizens. The very existence of that unique social formation, the distinctive relations between landlords and peasants embodied in the *polis*, and the democracy in particular, not only created new economic opportunities, but also restricted the possibilities of production and appropriation – for example, by limiting the concentration of property and thereby, as we have seen, limiting the scope of slave-utilisation itself. So we need to know a great deal more about the needs, possibilities, and limits created by this 'radically new' phenomenon, the peasant-citizen, if we are to understand the functions of both democracy and slavery. [...]

[The] independence of the peasantry meant that certain kinds of labour-services, apart from agricultural production, which in other peasant-societies have been drawn from the peasant-family – notably various kinds of domestic service for the rich, as well as corvée-labour, both public and private – insofar as they continued to exist at all, had to be performed by some other kind of dependent labour-force not associated with the peasant-family. As a general rule, it might be expected that slavery would grow most dramatically in those areas left vacant by the transformation of the peasant's relation to landlord and state: the detachment of his household from dependence on that of the lord, and his conversion from subject to citizen. The one limited the forms in which the peasant could be made to work for the lord, excluding those that entail personal bondage to landlord or land; the other limited the forms in which he could be made to work for the state, curtailing the scope of taxation and corvée-labour. [...]

It can be stated, as a general rule, that 'power over men', in the sense here-intended – that is, the power to command the service of dependent labourers who are obliged to serve by virtue of their juridical or political status – is typically the most highly prized possession of the propertied classes in pre-capitalist societies. And although in such societies, and especially when the money-economy is undeveloped, the attachment of non-kin to the household by various juridical means has been a common method of procuring regular personal service beyond the work of the family or the obligations of kinship, chattel-slavery has not been the predominant or even the preferred form in which such power has been exercised. Indeed, one of the disadvantages of chattel-slavery may be that the slave, unlike the dependent peasant, is less likely to be accompanied by a subject-*household*, available as a source of labour and a 'nursery' of workers. A broad spectrum of peasant-dependence, ranging from serfdom to clientship, has been a far more widespread way of commanding a variety of labour-services.

It is this spectrum of dependence that was precluded by the democracy in Athens; and it can be argued that the kind of economic power still exerted by Athenian landlords over their poorer compatriots did not extend much beyond the forms described by [Georges] Duby as belonging to those prosperous peasants in the twelfth century 'who owned more land than they could cultivate themselves' and leased out the excess to tenants.[26] This kind of economic power, or that of the landlord over the casual wage-labourers who supplemented his work-force in times of special need, was certainly not inconsiderable or unprofitable; but it was more limited in its scope than various forms of peasant-dependence, and it left open whole areas of personal service which dependent peasants, serfs, and clients have performed throughout history.

To be a citizen, to belong to the *polis*, was precisely not to belong to an *oikos* other than one's own. We should not be surprised to find these empty spaces filled by the one remaining form of attachment to the master's household – chattel-slavery. In his relations with free peasants, the dominance of the Athenian landlord over his fellow citizens rested not on exclusive possession of the state and its tributary system, nor on a privileged juridical status, but on possession of more and better property. And the juridical status of the slave was itself determined by the replacement of traditional tributary relations with the relations of private property, as personal servitude became synonymous with the reduction of human-beings to chattel-property.

In a society where agricultural production was dominated by smallholders whose availability for personal service to the rich and public service to the state, except as citizens and soldiers, was limited; where a degree of freedom from personal dependence unequalled in any other advanced civilisation of the time had produced a culture in which independence and self-sufficiency were among the most prized and deep-seated values, where might one except to find room for the labour of slaves? Is it too much to say that we might expect to find the largest space for slavery precisely where the evidence suggests it was: in domestic service; in long-term employment, public and private, whether in the most degraded and servile occupations such as mining, or in managerial positions; and in those areas of production outside the traditional domain of the peasant-citizen; in other words, in the interstices of the peasant-régime, and not in the society's agrarian material base?

---

26. Duby 1968, p. 220.

Chapter Three
The State in Historical Perspective

Class and state in ancient society

Greece and Rome are distinguishable from other ancient civilisations not only by their utilisation of slaves in unprecedented ways and degrees, but also by their distinctive relations between landlords and peasants and between both these classes and the state. The typical ancient state was the 'bureaucratic' kingdom in which the state exercised substantial control over the economy; property in land tended to be closely bound up with state-service; and peasant-producers were subject to surplus-extraction, less in the form of personal subjection to individual private proprietors, than in the form of collective subjugation to the appropriating, redistributive state and its ruling aristocracy, especially through taxation and compulsory services.[1] Classes confronted each other not simply as individual appropriators and producers, or large and small proprietors, but collectively as appropriating states and subject peasant-villages. Although states of this kind, at least on a small scale, seem to have existed in Bronze-Age Greece (as the archaeological remains of Mycenaean civilisation and the decipherment of Linear B reveal), they completely disappeared and were replaced by new forms of social and political organisation. Unfortunately, the process by which this replacement occurred remains obscure.

---

1. For a more detailed discussion of the contrast between these different forms of state, see E.M. Wood 1981a, pp. 82–6. A modified version of this article is included as Chapter One of E.M. Wood 1995a.

What is important, from our point of view, is that in Greece and Rome, in the absence of this form of state and its characteristic relations between ruling and subject-groups, appropriators and producers confronted one another more directly *as individuals* and as *classes*, as landlords and peasants, not primarily as rulers and subjects. Private property developed more autonomously and completely, separating itself more thoroughly from the state. In other words, a new and distinctive dynamic of *property-* and *class*-relations was differentiated out from the traditional relations of (appropriating) state and (producing) subjects. We have seen this specific dynamic at work in the struggles over land, which were so central to Graeco-Roman history. Indeed, one might say that Greece and Rome were distinctive precisely in the degree to which a differentiated dynamic of *class*-conflict was at work, with a logic of its own.

New forms of *state* emerged out of these relations. The ancient 'bureaucratic' state had constituted a ruling body superimposed upon, and appropriating from, subject-communities of direct producers. Although such a form had existed in Greece, both there and in Rome, a new form of political organisation emerged that combined landlords and peasants in one civic and military community.[2] The very notions of a *civic community* and *citizenship*, as distinct from a superimposed state-apparatus and rulership, were distinctively Greek and Roman. The unity of appropriators and producers, rich and poor, embodied in this new form of state, was, as it were, a 'harmony of opposites' (to adopt a concept beloved by the Greeks), imbued throughout with the tensions and contradictions, the internal dynamic, of the conflicts between and within these two classes. [...]

Private property and class-exploitation require coercive power to sustain them; and the appropriating powers of the individual lord *always* depend in various ways and degrees on a collective class-power. Direct producers, even when exploited individually, never confront their exploiters *solely* as individuals. Even peasant-proprietors who are relatively isolated in production tend to be organised in communal groups, especially in village-communities.[3] Appropriators must find ways of counteracting the divisions *within* their own class, the *intraclass*-conflict which results from private property and competition over land and limited sources of surplus-labour. It can also be argued that the balance of power between appropriators and producers may be less one-sided in favour of the former when petty producers are confronted by

---

2. This description does not, of course, apply equally to all parts of Greece. Sparta and Crete are the most notable examples of Greek states in which the citizen-community ruled over a subject-population of producers.

3. See Brenner 1985a, pp. 40–6, for an example of how village-organisation can function as a kind of peasant-class organisation and affect the relationship between landlords and peasants.

private appropriators, divided and competing among themselves, rather than by a centralised 'public' appropriator. There is, therefore, always a tendency towards centralisation which will permit individual exploiters to withstand resistance by producers and to maintain their hold on property.

That tendency, however, is accompanied by countervailing forces. The resistance of producers may itself act as a force against centralisation, as may the intraclass conflict within the ruling class. More particularly, to the extent that the dominant class is not directly organised as an appropriating state – in other words, to the extent that *class* and *state* are not co-extensive – they will represent two separate and often competing powers. Until the advent of capitalism, in which appropriators can rely on 'economic' modes of surplus-extraction which depend not on the coercive extraction of surplus, but on increasing the *productivity* of labour, the dominant *class* and the *state* must confront each other, in varying degrees, as competing 'extra-economic' powers of appropriation. Both landlords and state must rely on the application of direct force to extract surplus from the same limited source, the same peasant-producers, one in the form of rent, the other in the form of tax (in this context, a kind of centralised rent).

The emergence of the *polis* in ancient Athens

[...] The palace-controlled, 'redistributive' economy indicated by the archeological evidence, and especially the testimony of Linear B-inscriptions, suggests that the Mycenaean kings, either actually or effectively, owned most, if not all, arable land; that their subjects were, in effect, their serfs, bound to transfer surplus-product to the king for unequal redistribution among his subjects; and that the apparently wealthy aristocrats who joined the king in ruling his subjects were probably not large landowners in their own right, but rather, men who occupied positions in the state-hierarchy, which entitled them to a greater share of the goods distributed by the king, and sometimes to land-allotments associated with their offices. If the beginnings of private property existed, if the aristocrats or the peasant-subjects had any independent claims to land, the dominance of king and palace over land and men remained the essential characteristic of the society. The new 'Homeric' aristocracy, on the other hand, is one whose power clearly rests on property, on ownership of the best land. It is not at all an aristocracy of royal officials or palace-dominated warrior-nobles; rather, the Homeric lords have something in common with tribal chieftains, but chieftains who have gradually become divorced from their community by the acquisition of property, and whose unchallenged claim to political, military, religious, and judicial functions and to the labour of others, is already a matter of hereditary property-rights. It is possible that the developments that produced this new aristocracy had already begun under the Mycenaean kings; but the full evolution of this new phenomenon had to await the disappearance of palace and king (the Homeric 'kings' hardly deserve the name); and the reversion of land to the community, giving way to the dynamic that transformed communal property into private or class-property, the tribal community into a class-divided society, and chieftains into an aristocratic ruling class.

Homeric society, then, lies somewhere between the tribal society based on kinship and the community of citizens embodied in the *polis*. Its principal social and economic unit is the *oikos*, the household, and more particularly the aristocratic *oikos*, dominated by its lord, with his kin and retainers, and supported by the labour of various kinds of dependents. The *oikos*-system is, in one sense, more particularistic than the tribal community, reflecting a gradual privatisation and individuation of property; but this also means that the foundation for a wider community based on new, civic principles is being laid. Although there is a community of sorts among households, and a limited recognition of *public* matters, which are taken up occasionally by a communal assembly, the community beyond the household is of secondary importance. Most matters of concern to the members of the community are private matters, to be dealt with among kinsmen and friends. Duties are primarily to the members of one's household, kinsmen, and friends; rights are 'strictly private rights privately protected'.[4] At the same time, however, households are bound together not only by bonds of kinship among household lords, but by ties of class-interest among them, reinforced by the traditional ceremonies and obligations of 'guest-friendship'. The society is tribal in the sense that kinship is still crucial. Tribal law still prevails in the sense that essential social functions – the disposal of property, the punishment of crime – are dictated by customary rules of kinship. Property is largely inalienable, transmitted strictly according to traditional rules of inheritance, and to that extent is still tied to the tribal community, rather than to an individual propertyholder. Crime is essentially a family-matter, to be avenged by kinsmen according to the ancient customs of blood-vengeance. On the other hand, the community is anti-tribal in the sense that it is already bound together by a territorial principle that transcends kinship-ties, with an urban centre as the focal point of the territorial community. There are also other principles independent of kinship dictating relations among members of the community: the potentially antagonistic relations between master and servant, and the bonds

---

4. Finley 1965, p. 117.

among masters – in short, relations of class, particularly the ties among members of the ruling class, the household-lords, whose common class-interests gradually override tribal and household-bonds. In this sense, class is the foremost anti-tribal force; and even 'tribal' law is administered in an anti-tribal way, once jurisdiction becomes the exclusive prerogative of the ruling class, instead of a communal function belonging to the tribe as a whole.

The growth of class out of tribal relations and its consolidation in the *oikos*-system is a turning-point in the establishment of the political principle, its triumph over traditional principles, and the birth of a community of citizens. At first, as the aristocracy increased its power through a growing monopoly of land, the effect of this consolidation of class was simply to fragment the community. The aristocracy became more and more an isolated ruling society, its members increasingly bound together by class-interests and cut off from their non-aristocratic associates. Eventually, however, the very conditions of this fragmentation became the basis of a new kind of community, more focused on the *city*, the urban centre, the *polis*. Initially, the urban centre in most Greek communities had been largely the focal point for activities of the ruling society, its meeting-place, the centre of jurisdiction and government; but, as the city grew in economic importance, it also became the focal point of a new community, which encompassed the isolated nobility and, ironically, undermined its power, acting as an arena for the struggles of the lower classes. The significant economic changes that took place during the period following the Homeric age can be generally characterised as a decline of the self-sufficient household-economy and the growing economic importance of market-place and city, together with an increase in the number of people whose livelihood was not derived from possession of land, tenancy, or service in a noble *oikos* – an increase to which the consolidation of aristocratic power itself contributed. […]

As *polis* replaced *oikos* as the primary economic unit, the city, born as a centre for the governing activities of the ruling class, became the natural home of the growing classes that depended on it for their livelihood; and gradually it became the source of their power, economic and political, as the *oikos* had been for the landlords. It was in the *polis*, which brought them together and in so doing created in them a heightened consciousness of their position, that the aspirations of the economically and politically dispossessed classes – the peasants, then the growing classes of craftsmen, traders, and landless workers – found their expression. And, while the nobles continued, for a long time, to dominate the political life of the *polis*, in it their monopoly of power was increasingly undermined. The rise of the *polis* meant that the civic community replaced the exclusive ruling class as the source of law and justice and the arbiter of social order, and the rule of law replaced the arbitrary expression of aristocratic will. [...]

The 'essence' of the *polis*

[...] [We] can go on to look for the 'essence' of the *polis*, that which constitutes its most significant and revolutionary contribution to the development of social organisation. Unfortunately, the greatest admirers of Athens have not always been the most helpful in identifying its most remarkable characteristics. Indeed, there has been a tendency among classical scholars to obscure the most significant qualities, even to regard Athens as corrupt precisely to the extent that these qualities were developed. We can, however, begin by accepting certain aspects of the prevailing interpretation.

It is generally agreed, first of all, that the *polis* represents a new concept of social organisation, different from that of any other contemporary civilisation in the known world. More particularly, it is not the kind of social structure characteristic of the other advanced and stratified civilisations of the Mediterranean world and the East. The typical pattern for all these civilisations, as it apparently was for the Minoan and Mycenaean civilisations of ancient Greece, was some form of monarchy, in which king and palace dominated men and land and the essential 'political' relationship was that of master and subject. The advent of the *polis* marks a radical break with this mode of social organisation. Palace and king are replaced by a community of free men or *citizens*; it is not the king, but the citizen-body – whatever portion of the population it constitutes – which represents and embodies the *state*. It is this principle of citizenship – which submerges the qualitative differences among men in a common civic identity – and the identity of state and citizen-body that are the most obviously unique characteristics of the *polis*. That is why, for example, Ehrenberg suggests that democracy, as the most perfect identity of citizen-body and state (both in the sense that a greater portion of the population has citizenship, and in the sense that there is an identity of citizenship and sovereignty insofar as the citizen-body consists entirely of citizens with full, not unequal, rights), is, so to speak, the *telos* of the *polis*; why it can be argued that the *polis*, having established the principle of citizenship and the identity of citizen-body and state, has a tendency towards equality and democracy.[5]

Greek writers often appear to distinguish between *politics* – as the life of a community of citizens – and other kinds of social relations that we have come

---

5. See Ehrenberg 1969 and 1973.

to call 'political'. If *politics* represents a truly distinctive form of association, then it is with the *polis* that politics was born – not simply in the etymological sense, but as a new form of communal relationship which is neither tribe (though it bears certain similarities to early tribal democracy) nor, like the Eastern state, a patriarchal and hierarchical household writ large. The social relations and modes of governing in states other than the *polis* are not, in this sense, 'political'. Political relations exist where kinship and tribal custom, as well as the relation of master and subject and the arbitrary will of the master, have been overtaken by civic bonds, a territorial organisation, and the rule of law as the fundamental principles of social order; where the command- and obedience-relations and the arbitrariness of the master-subject nexus have, at least in principle, been superseded by deliberation by a free citizen-body within a framework of law; where reason and *persuasion*, rather than the force of a master or the violence of the tribal vendetta, are regarded as the essence of social order. In all these respects, too, democracy can be said to be the most perfectly *political* form of state, the form in which these departures from traditional associations are most developed.

There can be no doubt that these developments in political institutions and ideas represent a significant innovation in human social organisation; but there is more to the Greek invention of 'politics' than this conventional account suggests. Perhaps the most important aspect of 'politics' as it evolved in Greece – particularly in the democratic *polis*, which is the most 'political' – is that it constitutes a crucial development in class-relations, a milestone in the relations between appropriators and producers.

The Greek *polis*, at least in its democratic form, was a radical departure from all other existing states, not only in its form or its modes of organisation, but in its essential purpose. Before the emergence of the *polis*, in every known civilisation of the ancient world where the state had replaced tribal organisation as the dominant social system, the state was essentially a means of organising and extracting labour from largely-dependent labouring populations, a means of maintaining a fundamental division between producers and appropriators, an instrument for the exploitation of the former by the latter. The democratic *polis* may have been the first form of state to be based on a different, even antithetical, principle. [...]

Let us look more closely at the ways in which the Greek *polis* differed from other states of the ancient world. The advanced civilisations outside the Greek world – Egypt, Persia, Babylonia, even China – appear to have been founded on an economic base similar to that of the Mycenaeans, though on a larger scale. They were, in varying degrees, centralised states dominated by palace or temple, which exercised control of the economy through a vast bureaucratic and military apparatus. Land seems to have belonged in large part to the central authority, which to a great extent also controlled manufacture and trade. The crucial fact from our standpoint is that, in general, surplus-labour belonged to the central power, which used its elaborate military and bureaucratic establishment to organise and enforce the appropriation of surplus-product and to redistribute it very unequally to the population, largely to the non-productive elements – officials, soldiers, priests, and other privileged groups. The rigidly hierarchical social division of labour, as well as the often highly luxurious condition of the court and the upper strata, was based on this very effective system of extracting surplus-labour. So, too, of course, were often-impressive feats of civil engineering and public works, like the Egyptian irrigation-system; but if this mode of economic organisation served to provide useful, even necessary, public services which enabled the subject-populations to exist, it also ensured that they did little more than exist, often in conditions of extreme hardship, while creating and maintaining a luxurious culture and a ruling establishment whose condition of life was in sharp contrast to this minimal existence. There were, of course, differences among the various states in the degree to which they departed from this simple model. Private property and independent labour in the form of urban crafts and trade had, no doubt, developed to some extent in all of them, more in some than in others. Money and a system of commodity-production and exchange developed to some extent, alongside the palace-controlled system of production for use and redistribution in kind. Nevertheless, the dominant fact of economic, social, and political life in all these states was the centralised, appropriating despotism. Egypt and Persia, two states which were to figure most prominently in Greek political consciousness, were perhaps the most true-to-type.[6]

There are, then, two overwhelmingly central facts about this economic formation, as it concerns the nature of the state. First, the *state* was the direct appropriator of surplus-labour; this was, indeed, its essential function. In other words, the state was not simply a 'third power' designed to bring order to the class-struggle between appropriating and producing classes; nor was it even, as in a fully developed class-state, an instrument acting on behalf of an appropriating class but entering only indirectly into the process of class-exploitation. It *was*, in effect, the appropriating 'class', the direct master of a huge dependent labour-force, with the apparatus of the public power directly engaged in the process of surplus-extraction. This meant, secondly, that to

---

6. This social type can, with certain qualifications, be equated with Marx's 'Asiatic mode of production', in its 'despotic' form. For Marx's most systematic discussion of this mode of production, see Marx 1973, pp. 472–4.

be a *subject* of the state, for the great majority of subjects bound to render labour-services or transfer surplus-product on demand and virtually without condition to the public master, was immediately – and by definition – to be a dependent labourer, a servant, a serf. Slaves were owned by the palace, the temples, and the privileged groups, sometimes on a large scale; the primary form of dependent labour, however, was not chattel-slavery, but a kind of 'general slavery', as Marx calls it, in which whole populations, continuing to live in village-communities and occupying – if not owning – land, laboured as virtual serfs of the central power to whom their surplus-labour belonged. In a sense, the state was a household writ large, in which the fundamental 'political' relationship was that between producing servant and appropriating master. [...]

Perhaps it can be said that, paradoxically, the incomplete 'liberation' of Athenian producers – incomplete because, unlike Spartan citizens, they remained producers in the absence of an alternative labour-force – is what gave the Athenian situation its revolutionary implications. Instead of creating a class of non-labouring appropriators whose freedom rested on the labour of others, the Athenian revolution created a radically new kind of class – a producing class that was free in a very different sense. One is even tempted to ask why, once an alternative to citizen-labour became available in the form of a sizeable slave-population, Athens did not become the city of Plato and Aristotle's dreams, ruled like Sparta by a free citizenry completely relieved of the necessity of labour by its command of a subjected producing class. If the Athenian *polis* was, in its essence, an 'association against a subjected producing class',[7] it was a singularly ill-defined and imperfect one; on the other hand, it was more successful as an association for the liberation of a subjected producing class, having created what in the historical context was a radically new phenomenon – a sizeable class of free producers, whose independence lay not simply in their freedom from personal bondage, but in their role in self-government. It is perhaps not excessive to say that the labouring citizenry of Athens came as close to being *free* and independent labourers as is possible where a *class* of labourers exists at all – more independent, of course, than the free proletariat of the modern age, and, because of their political role, more free even than later 'petty-bourgeois' classes of independent producers. [...]

The democratic *polis*, in its elaboration of the 'political' principle, its extension of active citizenship to the lower classes, established a realm in which the social division of labour and the fundamental division between labourer and non-labourer was non-essential. It is all very well to dismiss citizenship

---

7. Marx and Engels 1947, p. 12.

as a fictional, ideal substitute for real social equality; but the fact is that in Athens it was more than that. It gave the labouring class a freedom and power that it had never possessed before and, in many respects, has never regained since. We cannot judge the importance of this civic revolution for the condition of labour simply in terms of citizenship in a capitalist society, which plays a more peripheral role in determining the status of the working class. In modern capitalist society, the appropriation of surplus-labour by a propertied class is inseparable from, essential to, the process of production itself. In precapitalist societies, 'non-economic' means of control, more-or-less extraneous to the productive process – tribal, religious, legal and political authority and military coercion – play a more central role in extracting surplus-product, in the form of forced labour, rents, or taxes. This form of exploitation can be applied not only to the serf, but to the 'free' peasant, who is not *in principle* – like the modern proletarian – deprived of the means of production and, therefore, not so clearly dependent on an appropriating class for access to the very conditions of his labour. Therefore, access to 'non-economic' power may have far greater significance. The *polis* at least so far modified the traditional social division of labour that it began to undermine its *hierarchical* nature by attacking the perfect coincidence of economic position and political power, thereby attacking one of the traditional instruments of economic domination and the command of labour. Furthermore, the political role assumed by the labouring class of the *polis* meant that, despite the contempt for labour which is often said to characterise the ancient world, the radical idea of a labourer capable of self-government had entered Western culture.

Class in the democratic *polis*

It cannot be emphasised enough that, contrary to a very popular myth, slaves and metics did not constitute, for all practical purposes, the labour-force of Athens. To begin with, most Athenian citizens worked for a living, many if not most of them in 'banausic' occupations, some as wage-labourers;[8] and while only citizens were permitted to own property, ownership of property was *not* a condition for citizenship. The importance of slaves to the Athenian economy, and probably their number, have been exaggerated until recently, and the role of citizens in the productive process underplayed. It must be remembered not only that the majority of citizens were compelled to earn their livelihood and were engaged in productive activities, but also that,

---

8. See Finley 1973, p. 68; Ehrenberg 1962, especially Chapters Five to Seven; Jones 1969, pp. 10–18.

on the other hand, there was virtually no occupation in which slaves did not engage.[9] Not only were citizens labourers, many slaves were not. Slaves occupied every possible position from mineworker to banker or business-man, even labour-contractor, to civil servant. Finley, in fact, reports that Pasion, 'the manager of the largest banking enterprise in fourth-century BC Athens', was a slave, later freed and granted citizenship.[10] 'Free and slave-labour stood on the same economic level,' writes Ehrenberg.[11] Some slaves were actually wage-earners, and in any case, slaves and free men worked side-by-side at the same tasks. Citizens avoided long-term service to a single employer in the form of regular wage-labour or salaried employment, pre-ferring, if possible, to leave such dependent roles to slaves; but the effect of this was not a division between labouring slaves and non-labouring citizens. On the contrary, the consequence was often that citizens remained common labourers – even casual wage-labourers – while slaves undertook manage-rial functions. Competition between slave and free labour does not seem to have been a significant factor. If anything, the availability of slaves may, by encouraging the ambitious public construction-projects undertaken by the democracy, actually have created work for otherwise unemployed citizens, many of whom worked beside slaves on the famous monuments of Athens. In any case, slave-labour did not constitute a different form of production in competition with free labour. In particular, there was no opposition between independent small-scale craft-production, on the one hand, and on the other, some kind of large-scale 'factory'-production with a specialised division of labour within an organised, integrated labour-force consisting of slave-gangs. The latter type of production simply did not exist. Instead, slaves, like citi-zens, even in the relatively few cases where many slaves worked for one master under one roof, generally worked as independent small producers or craftsmen, labouring, in a sense, on their own accounts, and paying a 'body-rent' to their master. [...]

The division between labouring and non-labouring classes was the *class*-distinction that figured most prominently in the literature and philosophy of the democratic age, as well as in the civil strife of the democracy: the political conflicts between the aristocratic-oligarchic faction and the democrats. The old, essentially agrarian class-opposition principally between aristocratic and peasant-landholders, which had been the motivating force of early political development, had now been transformed into a new conflict focused on the

9. See Finley 1973, p. 72; Ehrenberg 1962, p. 183.
10. Finley 1973, p. 62.
11. Ehrenberg 1962, p. 183.

polis: a conflict which expressed itself particularly in a political opposition between, on the one hand, rich citizens, who felt victimised by the democratic *polis*, the role it gave banausics, its redistributive function extracting funds from the rich and conferring public payments on the poor; and, on the other hand, poorer citizens who stood to gain from the institutions of the democracy, its checks on the rich and its diversion of surplus-product to subsidise the political and judicial activities of the poor. This class-division, however, though it played a significant role in the relations among citizens, did not determine the distinction between citizen and non-citizen, or even free man and slave.

It is precisely the fact that political standing is *not* determined by a fundamental class-division between labourers and non-labourers, or even producers and appropriators, that makes the democratic *polis* so important in the history of class-relations, and particularly in the history of the working classes. That a distinction between citizen and non-citizen – especially citizen and slave – exists at all, as distasteful as it is, should not obscure the significance of the fact that the distinction is not based on the division of labour and that the status of labourer, no matter how 'base and mechanical' – even dependent labourer (since wage-earners may be citizens) – does not determine exclusion from the political realm. Paradoxically, the very sharpness of the conceptual and legal difference between free man and slave inherent in Athenian citizenship may suggest a significant change in the status of labour, if one recalls the vagueness of the distinction between free labourer and slave to the Homeric aristocrat, for whom all labourers are natural inferiors and servants. In an important sense, a similar vagueness is implicit in any rigidly hierarchical society where all labourers, free men or slaves, are merely *subjects*, at the complete mercy of an economically dominant and hereditary ruling class, a class of masters. The fact that Athens has *citizens* – that is, full and active members of the body-politic – not merely 'free' subjects, and that the distinction between citizen and non-citizen does not correspond to the social division of labour, must, in light of previous historical experience in Greece and other advanced civilisations, be regarded as a revolutionary development, even if the fact that the distinction between citizen and slave survives at all indicates a tragically incomplete revolution.

What is important about the Athenian case is not only the immediate fact that the 'banausic' classes achieved unprecedented power in their struggle against domination and that, as we have said, the principle of a hierarchical social division of labour was thereby weakened, but also that a new attitude towards labour and the labourer was introduced into European consciousness. The attitude of Plato – and other aristocrats, Xenophon and even Aristotle –

towards the *banausos* and his incapacity for a fully rational, moral life should illustrate, by contrast, the significance of the Athenian reality. This attitude will be discussed at some length in the subsequent chapters. For the moment, suffice it to say that the whole of Plato's political philosophy is grounded in the conviction that to earn a livelihood, and especially by means of manual labour, corrupts the soul and disqualifies a man for politics, making it not only justifiable but necessary for him to subject himself to the command of others. Moreover, the incapacity of the *banausos* for politics and self-rule is not simply a consequence of his lack of leisure-time, but inheres in the corruptive nature of labour itself, so that even granted sufficient time for political participation – which many 'banausic' Athenians had – he would be disqualified. Plato's attitude is typical of his class, and in general seems to have characterised – if not always so extremely – all non-democratic cultures; but while commentators sometimes like to regard Plato's view as typical of Athens in general and often make reference to the Athenian contempt for labour, the reality of Athens suggests that a very contrary attitude is also at work. No culture in which the working class has the kind of political role the 'banausics' played in Athens – a role in many ways unequalled in most, if not all, modern democracies – could have retained such contempt for the labourer. The attitude expressed by Protagoras (or even Pericles), who, if Plato's testimony is to be believed, affirmed the fundamental capacity of shoemakers and smiths for politics, is clearly more typical – if the realities of Athenian political life were not enough to prove that Plato's view is a *class*-prejudice and not a cultural ideal.[12]

It is one thing to say that everyone, landowner and labourer alike, regarded a life of leisure as preferable to a life of toil; it is quite another to suggest that the kind of contempt for the *banausos* expressed by Plato and his fellow-aristocrats was a universal cultural prejudice. Whatever the average Athenian may have thought about a life of poverty and labour, the political role of the *banausos* – even the wage-labourer or the landless *thes*, who was often a casual labourer – indicates a very different attitude from one which relegates the working classes to a sub-human status virtually devoid of reason and moral worth. One need not glorify a life of labour, which the Athenians certainly did not, to recognise the labourer as a fully rational and moral being, qualified

---

12. Of course, in the oligarchic cities, which in varying degrees restricted the political rights of craftsmen, labourers, and traders, sometimes prohibiting citizens from engaging in any occupation, the contempt for labour did more nearly approach a cultural norm – or, to put it another way, in these cities, the class-prejudice exemplified by Plato was that of the *ruling* class.

for access to the political realm and self-rule. It is important to distinguish in Greek attitudes between a recognition of the woes of labour or the pleasures of leisure – an attitude that was no doubt widespread – and an aristocratic contempt for the labourer and his moral capacities. The conventional attitude towards labour among the common people of Athens is probably reflected in the ethic of craftsmanship, the concept of *technē*, the emphasis on the technical arts and skills, as the mainsprings of civilisation, which figure so prominently in the writings of the democratic age. It is also worth noting that the Greeks appear to have been the first to rescue craftsmen from anonymity, in sharp contrast to the great civilisations of the Near East and Asia.[13] [...]

On the face of it, if the most explicit divisions of the population, those with the most obvious consequences – the distinctions between citizen and non-citizen, free man and slave – do not correspond to class or to the social division of labour, it would appear that the class-division is of secondary importance. Yet it is precisely here that the crucial importance of class becomes most evident. Again, it is a question of looking at the situation historically. It is useless simply to isolate the relationship – or apparent lack of it – between citizenship and class that prevails in the democratic age from the *process* of dissociation that led to it. Viewed in isolation, the independence of citizenship from class in democratic Athens appears to indicate the relative unimportance of class. Seen as a process – the product of a development, even a struggle, that led from the perfect coincidence of class-division and political hierarchy in Homeric Greece, to the dissociation of class and citizenship in democratic Athens – that dissociation proves the vital importance of class in the social life of Athens. The dissociation of citizenship from class – indeed, the principle of citizenship itself – was clearly the consequence of a challenge by subordinate classes to the exclusive power of the ruling class, associated with the changes involved in the transition from an *oikos*- to a *polis*-economy. The gradual dissociation of political rights from class and the social division of labour hardly proves the insignificance of the latter. On the contrary, the elaboration of the political principle itself, and the principle of citizenship transcending class-boundaries, was a response to the social division of labour and the conflicts arising from class-divisions. The *polis,* with its principles of citizenship and law, was a way of dealing with class-divisions and the social cleavages brought about by the hierarchical social division of labour – and a radically new and unique way of dealing with what was, and still is, a universal social problem. Again, what is most significant, from our point of view, about this new method of dealing with class-relations is that, by beginning to dissociate political power from

---

13. See Burford 1972, pp. 20, 212ff.

the social division of labour, it was beginning to attack the very principle of a hierarchical social division of labour. In all other advanced civilisations, state-power was a means of coercing and controlling dependent labour and main-taining the social division between leisured masters and labouring servants.[14] The *polis*, therefore – particularly in its democratic form, in which the disso-ciation of political power from class had progressed the farthest – represents something very new in class-relations and a significant victory for subordi-nate classes, undermining a traditional instrument of class-domination. It is an achievement that cannot be imagined without a considerable degree of class-consciousness, a fairly developed perception of common interests and a common class-enemy, on the part of the subordinate classes as well as on the part of their rulers. In that sense, the lack of coincidence between class and citizenship in democratic Athens represents a triumph of class-consciousness, not a proof of its absence.

Village and state, town and country, in democratic Athens

[...] The critical difference between the Attic village and the 'typical' peasant-community lies in the relation between the village and the larger political organisation in which it was embedded. Shanin describes the peasant-commune as both socially self-sufficient and politically dependent; it is self-contained, both in the sense that it constitutes virtually the whole of the peasant's world, and in the sense that the world of its rulers is *alien*.[15] In other words, the peasant-commune is by definition dominated and exploited by 'alien, political hierarchies', political entities to which the peasant in no way belongs except as *subject*. The relation between state and village is the dichotomous relation between ruler and subject, as well as between producer and appropriator, whether in the nexus of feudal lord and serf, manor and vil-lage, or redistributive state and tribute-paying peasantry. This dichotomous relationship was, to a certain extent, compromised throughout the Greco-Roman world wherever the peasant was granted the status of citizenship, even when, as in Rome, the peasant's civic status was limited. But nowhere has the typical pattern been broken as completely as it was in the democratic *polis* in Athens. The breakdown of the opposition between village and state

---

14. In such states, even apparently free and independent labour – the labour of an independent 'petty-bourgeois' craftsman or artisan – often assumes the character of dependent labour, to the extent that surplus-labour is extracted by the ruling class through rents, taxes, and so on, with the aid of its complete monopoly of state-power.

15. Shanin 1971, p. 244.

was the very foundation of Athenian democracy, as the village-community became the basic constituent unit of the *polis*.

The reforms of Cleisthenes are commonly regarded as having established the organisational basis of Athenian democracy. Although the intention and significance of his reforms remain in dispute, there can be little doubt that his system of *demes* – the smallest constituent units of the new political order – had the effect of reposing political power in the ordinary people of Athens, the *demos*, to a degree unprecedented in the known ancient world. These demes, which seem to have varied greatly in size, from hamlets to the equivalent of medieval English market-towns, were largely based on existing villages [*demoi*], most corresponding to single villages, though new and artificial units may have been created in some cases.[16] By this means, Cleisthenes, in Osborne's words, 'politicised the Attic countryside and rooted political identity there'.[17]

It was through his deme that a man became a citizen, retaining his deme-identity – the mark of his citizenship – throughout changes of residence. The association of citizenship with the local identity of the deme among other things freed the right of citizenship from aristocratic control. It was also in the local democracy of the deme that peasants probably played their most active political role. If it remained true that the central assembly in Athens was generally dominated by wealthier citizens, especially those who maintained a residence in the city as well as owning properties in the countryside and especially in the demes where they were inscribed as citizens, there was

---

16. On the relationship between demes and pre-existing villages, the size of demes, etc., see Osborne 1985, pp. 42–5. Both Osborne and Whitehead 1986, pp. 23–30, emphasise the 'natural' character of the deme-system, its 'organic' growth out of traditional village-life, questioning the extent to which even *city*-demes were artificially created and stressing that the *asty* itself grew out of a collection of villages (Whitehead 1986, pp. 25–7). Whitehead suggests, too (following Wesley Thompson), that the establishment of the deme-network by Cleisthenes may not have been the outcome of an elaborate cartographic survey to fix territorial boundaries, but may have been simply the 'natural' result of an ordinance that every man must register in his home-village, leaving it to the people concerned to determine which centre was the appropriate one (pp. 29–30). See also Andrewes 1977. One cannot help but note here the contrast between the Attic system of registration in a village for the purpose of claiming the rights of citizenship, and village-registration in other societies where the reward of registration was the obligation to pay tax to a central authority. Whitehead also concludes that, although the evidence is sparse, the likelihood is that people generally tended to remain in their ancestral demes (Whitehead 1986, pp. 353–7). Osborne, too, stresses that citizens generally retained strong links with their ancestral demes (Osborne 1985, Chapter Three, and p. 225, n. 90).

17. Osborne 1985, p. 189.

no discontinuity between the *polis* and the deme.[18] The deme was the basic constituent unit of the *polis*, and not simply its subject. All demesmen had the same civic rights, and were entitled to attend the central assembly and serve on the juries through which so much of what we would consider *political* business was done; there was no distinction between villager and townsman in this respect, nor between peasant and landlord. Every citizen could become the *demarch*, the chief official of the deme through whom the local administration of the *polis* was mediated – and, in fact, the evidence is that demarchs were generally men of moderate means and relatively humble status.[19] Every citizen could also serve on the *boulē*, the council which set the central assembly's agenda – in fact, it is likely that most citizens must have sat on the *boulē* at least once.[20]

If the exigencies of labour, distance from Athens, and certain exclusive offices continued to give the advantage to wealthier citizens in the assembly at Athens, and if the most active politicians at the centre always tended to come from prosperous families, the fact remains that the democracy was unique in both principle and practice. In principle, it granted full civic status to ordinary peasants and artisans, and in practice such people actually did participate not only in local self-government through the deme assemblies, but also – if not as regularly as their wealthier compatriots – in the administration of the *polis* as a whole. The democracy no doubt worked imperfectly; but by giving (in Osborne's words)[21] political status to the villages, breaking down the discontinuity between village and state, between the peasant-community and the political order, it radically transformed the character of both. [...]

[How] was it possible for people whose livelihood and wealth were so overwhelmingly derived from the land to be so active in the city, especially in the case of the most active citizens, whose prominent role in the political life at the centre was facilitated by more-or-less permanent residence in the city? There is a temptation here to revert to the traditional view that the life of citizenship was dependent upon slavery, in the straightforward sense that the leisure of one was dependent upon the labour of the other. The flaws in this equation have already been examined in our discussion of slavery in Athenian agriculture.

----

18. Osborne suggests that the rich, who might own property in the *asty* as well as in the countryside, 'saw the whole polis as their field of activity, while those less well-off were also less mobile' (Osborne 1985, p. 87).

19. Osborne 1985, pp. 84–5.

20. Osborne 1985, pp. 91.

21. Osborne 1985, p. 184.

In the case of the working farmer, the peasant – keeping in mind that, in practice, he tended to be more active in the local politics of his deme than in the city-centre, that agricultural labour was marked by sharp seasonal fluctuations which left the farmer 'underemployed' at various times in the year, and that some peasants lived in or near the city while farming lands in its immediate surroundings – we need to remember the ways in which the democracy limited the demands on surplus-production, whether by peasants or even by slaves. In a sense, even to ask the question about the city's material base, in the way we have done, is to make unwarranted assumptions about the level of surplus-production required to sustain the democracy. If the political role of the peasant made unique demands on his time, we must also remember the demands that were *not* made on his labour. There was no large state-apparatus to sustain, no royal bureaucracy, no massive and wealthy ecclesiastical establishment, no huge disparities of wealth marked by conspicuous luxury, aristocratic magnificence and a flourishing market for manufactured luxury goods;[22] and military obligations were circumscribed by the capacities, objectives and rhythms of the smallholder. In short, the social, political and economic demands upon the tax- and rent-fund – in the form of rents, fees, dues, tithes, tributes, taxes and labour-services – typically produced by peasants elsewhere were relatively limited. Even if, as seems likely, Athenian peasants produced more of their richer compatriots' wealth, through rents of one kind or another, than is supposed by those who insist on the importance of slavery in agriculture, the demands on peasant-produced surplus – and indeed, on surplus-production in general – were restricted in Athens. [...]

The rise and fall of Rome

Rome, like Athens, developed as a small city-state; and like the Athenian *polis*, the Roman Republic was governed by a small and simple state-apparatus. By 265 BC, the Republic was already governing most of Italy south of the Po, and its subjects outside Rome were 'citizens' only in very loose terms. Yet even then, the ruling aristocracy, more powerful than its Athenian counterpart, was keen to maintain the state in its rudimentary form and long resisted the

---

22. See Osborne 1987, pp. 22 and 108–10. Osborne remarks on the 'limited place' of luxury goods even in the properties of wealthy landowners, despite their role as prestige-items for the urban rich. It would probably be safe to assume, too, that items such as clothing (which does seem to figure prominently in the wealth of rich Athenians like Alcibiades) were typically produced by domestic servants. Fine pottery, one luxury-item produced for the market of which there is ample evidence, turns out, according to Osborne, to have been of 'trivial economic importance' (p. 109).

emergence of a professional state-apparatus, preferring to govern themselves as amateurs. The aristocracy governed collectively, with individuals holding office for limited periods and every senator subject to principles of collegiality. But if this arrangement suited their purposes, it created problems of its own, requiring, again as in Athens, careful management of often tense relations between aristocracy and people and among rival aristocrats themselves.

In Rome, with its dominant aristocracy, the political form of the accommodation was not a democracy in the Athenian manner, but a republic dominated by the aristocratic senate. Yet, while aristocratic dominance is a constant theme of Roman politics throughout both Republic and Empire, there was from the beginning a tension at the heart of the Republic. It was a state built on private wealth, an instrument of individual ambition and acquisition for a ruling class of private proprietors who competed with one another for wealth and power, but whose class-position, in the absence of a superior state-power, was sustained only by their own fragile collegiality. This form of state also implied an ambiguous relationship between the aristocracy and subordinate classes. Like Athens, Rome departed from the pattern of other ancient 'high' civilisations where a clear division existed between rulers and producers, monarchical states and subject peasant-communities. In Rome, as in Athens, peasants and urban plebeians belonged to the community of citizens. While the balance of class-forces between landlords and peasants in Rome, unlike Athens, had produced an aristocratic state, its dominant class was obliged to enlist the political and military support of its subordinate fellow-citizens, so that here, as in Athens, some of the characteristic legal and political arrangements of the Republic are traceable to aristocratic conflicts and accommodations with popular forces – such as the office of tribune, in which a member of the élite was elected by the people to represent their interests (though tribunes were never regarded as 'magistrates', which meant that their office did not entitle them to sit in the senate).

In the early years of the Republic, the Roman peasantry was relatively strong, but the history of the Republic is a story of peasant-decline and an increasing concentration of land and power in aristocratic hands. While the expansion of Rome into a huge territorial empire depended on the peasantry, which manned what was to become the largest military force the world had ever known, their mobilisation and deployment away from Rome made them more vulnerable to expropriation at home. As the army was effectively professionalised, peasants were turned into soldiers and the aristocracy benefited on the home-front too, while the agricultural labour-force in the imperial homeland was increasingly given over to slaves, available in unprecedented numbers through conquest and trade.

As new lands were captured in Rome's imperial expansion, the issue of their distribution loomed very large on the political agenda, particularly the issue of land set aside as *ager publicus*, state-lands available for colonisation by citizens or for leaseholds at nominal rents. Some members of the aristocracy who served as tribunes of the people did seek to utilise the *ager publicus* to redress the balance between the rising aristocracy and increasingly impoverished peasants; but they were bitterly opposed by the ruling class in general, and the reforming agrarian laws seem to have had no lasting effect. The most famous attempt to effect a more equitable land redistribution, the reforms of the Gracchi, ended with the murder of the tribune Tiberius Gracchus at the hands of the aristocratic opposition, and later the violent death of Tiberius's brother Gaius, who had sought to continue and extend his brother's reforms and seems, unlike Tiberius, to have had a radical anti-senatorial political agenda.

With slaves and peasants (whether as tenants or as soldiers) creating wealth for the landlords, and urban masses in the huge metropolis of Rome living in appalling slums, overcrowded, unsanitary and dangerous, the differences of income between rich and poor at their peak have been estimated at twenty-thousand to one, in contrast to the ratio of a few hundred to one in Athens after the Peloponnesian War. 'No administration in history', as one distinguished historian of Rome has remarked, 'has ever devoted itself so wholeheartedly to fleecing its subjects for the private benefit of its ruling class as Rome of the last age of the republic.'[23]

By the time the republican era drew to a close, replaced by an imperial state (conventionally dated from the foundation of the principate under Augustus Caesar in 27 BC), the Roman ruling class had amassed private fortunes of staggering proportions, by means of exploitation and corruption at home – from their landed estates, urban slum-tenements, usury, trading in property, government-contracts, and so on – and even more spectacularly by systematic plunder of their expanding empire. The administration of the empire provided the Roman aristocracy with unprecedented opportunities for looting and extortion. Proconsular office in imperial domains was a sure means of lining the pocket and for the most prominent Roman oligarchs to consolidate their personal power by acquiring what increasingly amounted to private armies. The Empire also had the advantage of shifting the burden of taxation – at least for a time – away from citizens, including peasants, and onto imperial subjects. This undoubtedly lowered the risk of popular unrest

---

23. Badian 1968, p. 87.

in Rome, but the price paid by peasants was the increasing concentration of land in the hands of the aristocracy.

Yet the very success of the Republic as an instrument of aristocratic gain proved its undoing. The irony is that it was the triumph of the aristocracy which eventually led to the fall of the Republic, as the weakness of the threat from below deprived the ruling class of any unity it might have had in the face of a common enemy. The growth of the Empire aggravated the inherent weaknesses of the republican state by enlarging the scope of oligarchic competition and raising the stakes. With an increasingly unruly oligarchy, the vast military apparatus of imperial expansion was bound to be deployed in the service of personal ambition and intra-oligarchic rivalry. The Empire also placed intolerable strains on the administrative capacities of the Republic and its principle of government by amateurs. With no strong state to keep the warring aristocracy in check, the Republic descended into chaos. It is not surprising that the fabric of republican government gave way under the strain.[24]

The most famous period of Roman history, the moment of Julius Caesar and Marcus Tullius Cicero, was the end of the Republic: a time of unceasing intra-oligarchic conflict and violence, corruption, and breakdown of order, which spilled over into the vast expanses of the Empire as ambitious aristocrats brought their proconsular armies into play. The time of troubles was brought to an end, and the cohesion and class-power of the oligarchy preserved, only by the establishment of an imperial state in place of the city-state form of the Republic. If the class-interests of the oligarchy had created and sustained the Republic, the acquisitive and expansionary logic of that same oligarchy had now driven it beyond the narrow bounds of the republican form.

What is most striking about the history of Rome, and what is most important for our understanding of its political and cultural life, is the Roman preoccupation with private property. The monumental scale of its land-grabbing project, both in the concentration of oligarchic property at home and in imperial expansion, was unprecedented and unequalled in the ancient world. It reflected a distinctive system of social relations and class-reproduction, quite different from other ancient civilisations where centralised states ruled subject peasant-communities and access to the surplus-labour of others was typically achieved by direct possession of the state. State-appropriation in these other civilisations did not, as we have seen, necessarily preclude private possession of land, either for those who acquired it as a perquisite of office or for peasant-smallholders; but access to substantial wealth – that is, to the surplus-labour of others on a large scale – tended not to be a function of property as such,

---

24. The classic discussion of this period is Syme 1960.

but rather of state-power. In Rome, by contrast, landed property was the only secure and steady source of wealth.

As in other precapitalist societies, juridical status and political power remained critical factors in the relations of exploitation. But, in the absence of a centralised-appropriating state superimposed on subject-communities of producers, and without a clear monopoly of juridical privilege and political power for the ruling class, private property became an end-in-itself in unprecedented ways. Land-ownership became the major condition of surplus-extraction, and there developed a compelling pressure to acquire land, even to dispossess smallholders. Since the citizenship of peasants precluded their juridical dependence, their exploitation – as tenants or casual labourers – depended on their economic vulnerability. If expropriated, they could be replaced by slaves as a labour-force on large estates; and in the last century of the Republic, in Roman Italy (agricultural slavery was less important in other parts of the empire such as North Africa or the East) one-third of the population consisted of slaves. As the Empire grew, the juridical and political status of the peasantry declined, while the burden of taxation increased.

The collective power of the aristocracy was sufficient (unlike that of ancient Athens) to achieve an unprecedented concentration of land in the hands of the oligarchy; and the principal career for the Roman ruling class was the acquisition and management of property. Even imperial service in the provinces was a way of looting subject-populations to obtain the means of investing in property. Public office was, in general, just a moment in that career; and, while imperial office was certainly a road to fame and fortune, aristocrats were not always keen to take it. The characteristic aspiration of the Roman aristocracy was *cum dignitate otium* [leisure with dignity], and their principal motivation for seeking release from public duties was quite simple: 'Their primary function and activity after all was the supervision and maintenance of their wealth.'[25]

When the distinctive social-property relations of Rome outgrew the republican state, they produced a new imperial system, an 'undergoverned' Empire. Although some parts of the Empire were under more direct Roman rule than others, its administration of such far-flung territories could not have been achieved without a network of more-or-less self-governing cities (often newly founded and in largely rural areas), which amounted to a massive class-federation of local aristocracies. This municipal system made possible what has been described as 'government without bureaucracy'. While the imperial state did, of course, have its share of centrally-appointed officials, the

---

25. Starr 1982, p. 63.

Empire 'remained undergoverned, certainly by comparison with the Chinese empire, which employed, proportionately, perhaps twenty times the number of functionaries'.[26]

This imperial system, with its diffuse administration, enhanced and extended the power of private property. The Roman Republic had established the rule of property as never before, and the Empire pushed forwards the frontiers of that régime. It constituted a historically unprecedented partnership between the state and property, in contrast to all other known civilisations, in which a powerful state meant a relatively weak régime of private property. Even many centuries later, in late-imperial China, for instance, with its long history of well-developed property in land, the imperial state consolidated its power by expanding the smallholder-economy while discouraging large land-ownership, and centralised administrative power by co-opting large proprietors into the state. The result was a huge imperial bureaucracy, living off taxation of the peasants, while great wealth and power resided not in the land, but in the imperial state, in an élite at the top of which stood the court and imperial officialdom. The Roman Empire was very different, with its distinctive mode of coexistence between state and private property.

The culture of property: Roman law

We can begin to appreciate the specificity of Roman political culture by considering more closely how the Roman resolution of its early social conflicts differed from the Athenian. The Athenians, as we saw, managed the conflicts between peasants and landlords, 'mass' and 'élite', largely on the political plane. The effect of their democratic reforms was gradually to dilute legal or status distinctions among free Athenians in the common identity of citizenship. The Romans to some extent also pursued the political course, and the citizen-body also included both rich and poor; but, while property increasingly trumped heritage, even status-distinctions among citizens, notably between patricians and plebeians, continued to play a role, with patricians enjoying privileged status and disproportionate representation in assemblies. The Romans did, to be sure, devise political institutions and procedures to regulate relations between different types of citizen – such as the particularly distinctive office of the tribune. But, while influenced at first by Greek law, the Romans constructed a much more elaborate legal apparatus, relying more than the Greeks on the law to manage transactions between mass and élite, between propertied classes and less prosperous citizens. Social relations

---

26. Garnsey and Saller 1987, p. 26.

between these groups were in large part played out not in the public domain of political life, but in the sphere of private law – a distinctively Roman category; and the regulation of property would constitute by far the largest part of Rome's civil law.

The founding moment of the Roman law, the enactment of the Twelve Tables in the middle of the fifth century BC, was understood by Romans looking back at their legal history as a response to plebeian grievances about the old system of customary law, which had been interpreted and applied by patrician judges. But the Twelve Tables probably did not fundamentally transform the substance of traditional law or its aristocratic bias, and certainly did not dilute the distinction between patricians and plebeians. Instead, plebeians had to make do with the commitment of the law to a written code, which explicitly outlined their rights. While many adjustments and additions would later be required, especially as the Republic grew into a massive empire, the system of private law which emerged from this early written code would remain the basis of the Roman law.

Both in its origins and in its substance, the Roman law was rooted in the old relations between patrician landlords and plebeian farmers, many of whom may, in the early years, have been in a dependent condition, occupying and working surplus-land allowed them by landlords in exchange for political and military support. This traditional relation of *patronus* and *cliens* would soon change its form, and the division between patricians and plebeians would no longer entail the same relation between landlords and dependent peasants; but patronage would continue to denote a relationship between men of unequal status, in which a member of the Roman élite would offer help and protection to social inferiors (or sometimes, in a public capacity, to groups and even cities) who became his clients, in exchange for their loyalty, deference, political support and various kinds of service. The distinctively Roman conception of patronage and the relation between patron and client, which had no Athenian analogue, would continue to shape Roman conceptions of social and political dependence.

Even in the absence of the personal relation between patron and client, social relations between classes continued to play themselves out in the private sphere, where the law regulated property and all the various rights and obligations associated with it. This bespeaks a concept of the public realm very different from the Greek. The Greeks made various distinctions between state- and non-state spheres [...] for instance, in Sophocles's play, *Antigone*. But a reminder of what was at issue in that play may also help to clarify the ways in which these Greek distinctions differed from the Roman antithesis of public and private. Although *Antigone* is often read as a clash between the individual conscience and the state, it has more to do[...]with the opposition between two conceptions of *nomos*, Antigone representing eternal unwritten laws, in the form of traditional, customary and religious obligations of kinship, and Creon the laws of a new political order. The play also deals with two conflicting loyalties or forms of *philia*: on the one hand, the ties of blood and personal friendship and, on the other, the public demands of the civic community, the *polis*, whose laws are supposed to be directed to the common good. In neither of these cases is the non-state realm adequately described as *private*, since both *polis* and non-*polis* principles concern communal obligations.

The Greeks come closest to a public-private dichotomy in the distinction between *oikos* and *polis*. As Thucydides makes clear in his account of Pericles's 'Funeral Oration', Athenians certainly distinguished between a citizen's domestic concerns, or an individual's own business, and the common affairs of the *polis*. But, in Greek political theory, the distinction between *oikos* and *polis*, as elaborated most clearly by Aristotle, has to do with two forms of association and the different principles that govern them – in particular, the inequality of household-relations and the civic equality of the *polis*, or the *oikos* as the realm of necessity and the *polis* as the sphere of freedom. A man denied access to the political sphere because of his bondage to necessary labour was, for Aristotle, not so much a private individual, as against a citizen, but rather a 'condition' of the *polis*, as against a 'part' of it. Democrats would have disagreed with Aristotle about the political consequences of social inequality, or whether a life of necessary labour disqualified people from politics; but they would have shared his view that the distinctive characteristic of the political sphere was civic equality – which is, of course, why democrats and anti-democrats disagreed so fiercely about access to that privileged sphere for the poor and labouring classes.

The Romans, by contrast, elaborated some fairly clear distinctions between public and private, yet these had little to do with the criteria which, for the Greeks, distinguished *oikos* from *polis*. For the Romans, for instance, inequality was formally present in the political sphere and was not, therefore, the criterion that marked off public from private. It was certainly not a question of distinguishing between a domestic sphere in which superior ruled inferior and a civic sphere in which social unequals met as political equals. In Rome, relations between social unequals in the private sphere of property were reflected in the public sphere of hierarchical citizenship. The Romans created a new, probably unprecedented, kind of private sphere; and their distinction between public and private represented a new form of dichotomy, which is clearly visible in the distinction between public and private law that lay at the heart of the Roman legal system.

The only extant elaboration of the distinction defines it like this: 'Public law is concerned with the Roman state [*status rei Romanae*], while private law is concerned with the interests of individuals, for some matters are of public and others of private interest. Public law comprises religion, priesthoods, and magistracies.'[27] Private law was by far the greater concern of the Roman legal system, and the apparatus of law to deal with matters of public administration was fairly rudimentary by comparison. The primacy of private law is in itself significant, as is the mere fact that the Romans felt the need to draw such a clear line between public and private. The determining factor cannot have been simply the growth of the state. The Republic had a minimal, virtually amateur state, while even the Empire was 'undergoverned'; and other ancient civilisations had far more elaborate states. What set the Romans apart from all other high civilisations was their property-régime, with its distinctive legal conception of property; and with it came a more sharply delineated private sphere in which the individual enjoyed his own exclusive dominion.

The contrast with Greece, here, is particularly striking. It has often been remarked that the Greeks had no clear conception of ownership, indeed no abstract word for it at all. An Athenian might claim a better right than someone else to some piece of property, but certainly nothing like the exclusive claim entailed by the Roman concept of *dominium*. In disputes over property, the difference in practice may not have been as great as it seems in theory, but its significance should not be underestimated. It tells us a great deal about how the Romans conceptualised the social world. The word *dominium* 'and the actual law relating to ownership', writes one commentator on Greek law, emphasising the contrast with Rome, 'serve to underline the strongly individualistic character of Roman ownership, which comes out forcibly in the plaintiff's words in a *vindicatio* [the ancient legal action in which a Roman citizen asserted a more-or-less exclusive right of ownership over something – EMW]':[28] 'I claim that this thing is mine by the *ius Quiritum*', that is, by the legal right of private exclusive individual ownership which only Roman citizens could enjoy. In this way, the 'Roman citizen asserts a claim against all

---

27. This formulation is by the Roman jurist, Ulpian (d. 228 AD). The compilation of the Roman law under the emperor Justinian I (c. 482–565) – the *Digest* of Justinian – is said to owe something like one third of its content to Ulpian and begins with this distinction between public and private law.

28. Harrison 1968, p. 201. It may be misleading to call Roman property 'absolute', but perhaps no more misleading than is the concept of 'absolute' property itself. If 'absolute' means completely inviolable, without restrictions on its use, or without any obligations (such as taxation) attached to it, there has never been a truly absolute form of property. But it would be a mistake not to acknowledge the distinctively *exclusive* quality of Roman property, the degree to which it belonged to the individual to the exclusion of others, even if certain obligations might be associated with it.

the world, based on an act of his own will'.[29] The concept of *dominium*, then, marks out the private sphere with an unprecedented clarity, and the private is inseparable from property.

The idea of an exclusive private and individual sphere of mastery contained in the concept of *dominium* would develop in tandem with the concept of a distinctly public form of rule. The *imperium*, which designated military command and also the right of command attached to certain civil magistrates, would evolve to encompass the rule of the emperor, eventually approaching something like a notion of sovereignty, which distinguished the Roman idea of the state from the Greek conception of the *polis* as simply a community of citizens. The partnership of *dominium* and *imperium*, then, sums up both the distinction between public and private and the alliance of property and state that was so distinctively Roman.

To say that the Romans devised a conception of property more individualistic and exclusive than ever before, or that they differentiated private and public in historically unprecedented ways, is not to say that they anticipated modern liberal individualism. Their concern was not, for example, the protection of individual rights from incursions by the state. Indeed, they scarcely had a conception of the state, or of individual rights, of the kind that would be required to think in these terms; nor were their social relations and institutions of a kind to generate such ideas.

Rome was not a capitalist society, nor a 'liberal democracy'. It is certainly true that, unlike any other ancient civilisation, the Romans created a régime with two distinct poles of power, in which a well-developed central state coexisted with strong private property; and it is no doubt also true that, as the imperial state grew, there were tensions between propertied classes and an increasingly burdensome state. But there never existed in Rome a system of appropriation, like capitalism, which depended on intensive growth, rooted in profitably competitive production, rather than on the extensive growth of property in a massive grab for land. Territorial expansion in the Empire was an extension of land-concentration at home; and the public power of the state, its coercive force, played a more immediate role in the acquisition of private wealth.

Roman ideas of property and its relation to the public sphere expressed this distinctive partnership of property and state. The emblem of the Roman state, SPQR, *Senatus Populusque Romanus* ('the Senate and the Roman People'), does not convey a formal, abstract concept of the state, so much as a snapshot of the relations between dominant and subordinate classes, as well as alliances

---

29. Ibid.

and rivalries within the ruling class itself. It is significant that *Senatus* is distinguished from, and placed ahead of, *Populus*, in a formula that denotes the dominance of the propertied classes in the senate and their limited accommodation with the people, a 'mixed constitution' containing popular elements but governed by an aristocracy. The absence of any abstract notion of the state is particularly clear in the Republic, with its amateur government by members of the propertied elite taking time out from the management of their private wealth. In that context, the distinction between private and public represented not an antithesis between two poles of power, but rather the dominant class in its two different aspects.

The clear delineation of public and private spheres, then, was not, in the main, intended to protect the private from public intrusion. It was more a matter of managing the private sphere itself. In the first instance, especially in the form of private law, it contributed to the regulation of relations between classes by recognising the sanctity of property while spelling out the rights and obligations associated with it. Later, the ruling class's descent into self-destructive conflict would add a new dimension to the management of the private sphere [...] and, as Republic gave way to Empire, the relation between public and private would inevitably change. Yet, even when the polarities increased with the growth of the imperial bureaucracy, the state remained a distinctive collaboration between property and state, as private appropriation continued to depend on imperial power, while the imperial system relied on a network of alliances among landed élites.

The Roman law also mapped the social world in other significant ways. The distinction between the *ius civile*, the law specific to Roman citizens, and the *ius gentium*, which applied to other peoples, contains a wealth of information about the Roman world. This distinction between the Roman civil law and the law of nations in the first instance set Roman citizens apart from others, while at the same time acknowledging the need to provide some means of regulating the transactions between Romans and non-Romans, in a growing system of international trade and an expanding empire. The idea of the *ius gentium* both acknowledged that other peoples operated according to their own laws and customs, and also sought to find principles common to all which could form the basis of transactions among them and be applied in Roman courts. This applied not only to principles having to do with relations among nations, such as the inviolability of treaties, but also to a wide range of private-law matters concerning the performance of contracts, conditions of buying and selling, and so on.

The exclusiveness of the civil law became increasingly irrelevant as the Roman citizenship expanded, but the *ius gentium* continued to serve other

purposes. The identification of certain universal principles accepted by all
peoples had opened the way to a concept of *natural* law, a *ius naturale*, deriving from natural reason. At the same time, the idea of the *ius gentium* as simply
the observable commonalities among social practices in various nations also
allowed for the kind of Roman pragmatism that could, for example, regard
slavery as an essentially unnatural institution while treating it as legitimate,
just on the grounds that it was (allegedly) a universal practice accepted by
many particular systems of custom and law.

The 'undergoverned' Roman Empire, composed of diverse and loosely connected fragments and relying on an alliance of propertied elites spread over
a huge territory, depended for its cohesion not only on a vast military force,
but on cultural ties and universalistic ideologies that could help to bind the
imperial fragments together. The part played by the Roman law in maintaining the cohesion of the empire had at least as much to do with its cultural and
ideological effects as with its role in governance. Even at the height of imperial dominion, Roman law never completely overshadowed the particularities
of local law and custom; but the spread of the empire was accompanied by an
increasing assertion of universalism against legal, political and cultural particularisms of various kinds, a universalism expressed in the natural law or
the *ius gentium* no less than in Stoic cosmopolitanism and, finally, in Christian
doctrine and the 'universal Church'.

From imperial Rome to 'feudalism'

Between the sixth and tenth centuries, the period commonly identified as the
era of feudalisation, the Roman Empire was replaced by what has been called
the 'parcelisation of sovereignty'.[30] Persuasive arguments have recently been
made that the process was much more sudden than medieval historians have
conventionally suggested, and that there was a 'feudal revolution' only at the
end of this period;[31] but whether the process was gradual or revolutionary,
the imperial state gave way to a patchwork of jurisdictions in which state-
functions were vertically and horizontally fragmented. Domination by an

---

30. P. Anderson 1974, p. 148ff.
31. There have long been fluctuations between histories of feudalism that insist on
continuities and those that emphasise more revolutionary transformations. A case
for a 'feudal revolution' was made by T.N. Bisson, 'The "Feudal Revolution"', *Past
and Present*, no. 142 (1994): 6–42, which generated a debate among several historians
in subsequent issues (no. 152, 1996; and no. 155, 1997). Among the participants was
Chris Wickham, who, with some reservations about Bisson's argument, judiciously
and persuasively defended the idea of a 'feudal revolution'.

overarching imperial state was replaced by geographic fragmentation and organisation by means of local or regional administration, perhaps in the form of contractual arrangements within the ruling class, between kings and lords or lords and vassals – though these arrangements could take many different forms, and the very existence of vassalage has been put in question.[32] This administrative, legal and military patchwork was generally accompanied by a system of conditional property, in which property-rights entailed jurisdictional and military service.

This is not the place to consider whether, or to what extent, feudalism was a product of Germanic influences – even if it were possible to identify any single 'Germanic' entity or culture. It is, however, misleading to imagine invasions of the Roman Empire by more-or-less pristinely 'Germanic' tribes, emerging more-or-less untouched from the forests of the north. The interactions between the Romans and the 'Germans' go much further back than the late mass-migrations commonly regarded as 'barbarian invasions'. These included long-standing relations of exchange, which served to aggravate social differentiation within the German tribes and to destabilise relations among Germanic communities themselves, provoking constant warfare and increasing militarisation. By the time their incursions into Roman territory became a decisive factor in determining the fate of the Empire, the Germans were already deeply marked by their long interactions with Rome.

There has been considerable debate about whether relations between landlords and peasants should be included in the definition of feudalism. At one extreme is the argument that relations between seigneurs or manorial lords and their dependent labourers cannot be called feudal, because feudalism has to do not with domination and dependence, but with contractual relations among juridical equals – at least among people of lordly status, even if some owed service to others. At the other extreme is a definition of feudalism entirely based on relations among landlords and peasants, which is sometimes applied not only to the specifically Western medieval forms of

---

32. Susan Reynolds, in particular, has argued that the concept of vassalage is virtually meaningless, while even the concept of 'fiefs' is too vague and variable to be very useful; see Reynolds 1994. The argument here, as will be explained in what follows, in no way depends on the existence of vassalage or, indeed, on the notion of fiefs. Reynolds has also taken issue with arguments that, in her view, attribute too much importance to intellectual constructs, including the revival of ancient-Greek philosophy, in constituting social and political relations in the middle-ages. She emphasises 'traditional bonds of community' and communal practices established long before, and independently of, such ideas. It should already be clear that this criticism cannot apply to the concept of feudalism employed in this chapter.

peasant-dependence, but to any type of agrarian exploitation by means of rent-extraction. Both these extremes seem unhelpful.

On the one hand, it should go without saying that feudal lords, however we define them, depended for their very existence on their relations with peasants. Wherever there were lords, there were peasants whose dependent labour sustained them. On the other hand, a diluted definition of 'feudalism', which embraces any kind of relationship between landlord and peasant, obscures the specificities of agrarian relations in the medieval West. What is distinctive about the Western case is the exploitation of peasants by lords in the context of parcelised sovereignty – with or without the relations of vassalage. The concept of 'feudalism' is useful because, and to the extent that, it draws attention to this distinctive formation.

In the very particular unity of economic and extra-economic power that emerged in medieval 'Europe', economic relations of appropriation were inextricably bound up with political relations, as they had been in ancient bureaucratic states. But, in sharp contrast to those ancient civilisations where subject-peasants were ruled by monarchical states, the feudal state was fragmented by parcelised sovereignty; taxation by the state gave way to levies collected by lords and appropriation in the form of rent; and lordship combined the power of individual appropriation with possession of a fragment of state-power. Lordship, which constituted a personal relation to property and command of the peasants who worked it, took over many of the functions performed in other times and places by the state. The effect was to combine the private exploitation of labour with the public role of administration, jurisdiction and enforcement. This was, in other words, a form of 'politically constituted property', a unity of economic and extra-economic power, which presupposed the uniquely autonomous development of private property in ancient Rome.

In the preceding chapters, there was some discussion of property-relations in ancient Greece and Rome, emphasising their distinctiveness when compared to other 'high' civilisations. Property in land was more thoroughly separated from the state than in the 'bureaucratic' kingdoms, where it tended to be closely bound up with state-service. In such kingdoms, peasant-producers were subject to surplus-extraction, less in the form of exploitation by individual private proprietors, than in the form of collective subjugation to an appropriating, redistributive state and its ruling aristocracy, typically in the form of taxation and compulsory services. In Rome, private property developed as a distinct locus of power in unprecedented ways; and peasant-producers were more directly subject to individual private appropriators, who extracted surplus-labour in the form of rent. These developments, as we have seen, were reflected in the Roman law, which formally recognised the exclusiveness of private property and elaborated a distinction between two forms of domination, the ownership of property and the power of state-rule, the powers of *dominium* and *imperium*. The conceptual elaboration of these two distinct foci of power would have enormous implications for the development of political theory.

When a massive imperial state did emerge, with its own bureaucracy and system of taxation, it was already fundamentally different from the other imperial or monarchical states of antiquity. Even at the height of the Empire, the primary form of appropriation by dominant classes was not through state-office by means of taxation, but the acquisition of land and direct exploitation of the labour that worked it, whether peasants or slaves. Landlords and peasants confronted each other more directly as individuals and classes, as distinct from rulers and subjects, while imperial governance itself depended on a network of local landed aristocracies, especially in the Western Empire. This mode of imperial rule had the effect of strengthening property, in contrast to other ancient states which impeded the full and autonomous development of private property or propertied classes independent of the imperial bureaucracy. When the Empire adopted the expedient of paying for military services by grants of land, this property in land preserved the attributes of Roman ownership.[33]

---

33. An interesting but, in my view, flawed argument has been proposed by an eminent historian of late Rome and the middle-ages, Chris Wickham, who has more recently modified his view but without completely replacing what seem to me its most problematic aspects. In his original formulation, he invoked the notion of the 'tributary system', in which surplus-extraction takes place by means of taxation, and contrasted it to feudalism, in which surplus-extraction takes the form of rent instead of tax ('The Other Transition: From the Ancient World to Feudalism' and 'The Uniqueness of the East', originally published in 1984–5 and both republished in Wickham 1994). The tributary system includes the bureaucratic-redistributive kingdom as I have described it here; but in Wickham's view, it also includes the 'ancient' form exemplified by Greece and Rome, in which the city, rather than a central monarchical state, is the tax-extracting entity. The Greco-Roman case was distinctive, he argues, also because the tributary form coexisted with 'feudalism'. The transition occurred, he suggests, when the tensions between these two coexisting modes of production led to the decline of the tributary element (in particular, the imperial state) and the growing predominance of the feudal form.

I find this account problematic for several reasons: each category, the 'tributary' and the 'feudal', is far too undifferentiated and explains very little – especially because any relations of rent-extraction between landlords and peasants are called 'feudal', which tends to obscure the particularities of Western landlord/peasant-relations, while any form of taxation appears to partake of the 'tributary' form. The approach is more taxonomic than historical, positing two modes of production with no historical beginning and no internal dynamic that might help to explain the transition – the 'feudal' form is simply there and, in its tension with the 'tributary form', there is no apparent reason for its eventual predominance; and above all, this approach fails to capture the specificity of the 'ancient' form. It is not enough to say that the tributary

The existence of two poles of power, the state and private property, meant that there was a tendency to fragmentation at the very heart of the imperial state. When the Empire disintegrated – precisely in the West, where state-rule existed in tension with aristocracies based on huge landed estates – aristocratic autonomy would continue to grow, even when some form of public power continued to exist. The devolution of public functions to local lords occurred even where monarchical powers succeeded, at least for a time, in their attempts to recentralise the state. Monarchies typically depended, to varying degrees but always unavoidably, on territorial aristocracies which exercised functions – judicial, administrative and military – formerly belonging to the state.

Even when, in the eighth century and thereafter, the Franks, especially under Charlemagne, restored some kind of unity and order to the chaotic remnants of the Western Empire, creating their own large imperial dominion, the Frankish realm was administered by regional counts, while newly conquered territories were controlled by local military strongmen. This fragmented administration continued even after Charlemagne's coronation in

---

form here was different because the city was the tax-extracting entity, or even to say that it coexisted with 'feudalism'. The point, at the very least, is that the city and even the empire, with their systems of taxation, were themselves already shaped by the uniquely autonomous development of private property. The city-state of the Roman Republic was constituted by specifically Roman relations between landlords and peasants, and the empire that grew out of it presupposed the development of a historically unique landed class.

More recently, Wickham has replaced his distinction between tributary and feudal *modes of production* with a distinction between two types of *polity* or state: one based on taxation and the other on land. This distinction has certain advantages over the other, but it is still far from characterising the specificities of the Roman tax-based state and the differences between it and, say, a tax-based state like imperial China, where the relation between state and landed property was significantly different. For that matter, it is difficult to do justice to the divergences between the Western and Eastern Roman Empires without acknowledging such differences in their state/property-relations. In the East, the imperial state was typically superimposed on already existing and highly developed state structures. In the West, where no such structures had existed, the development of aristocratic landed property – and its centrifugal effects – went much further, and it was here that the Empire disintegrated. In any case, except in some ahistorical taxonomy, there probably has never existed a simple land-based state, in opposition to a tax-based state. Wickham's model for the land-based form seems to be the fragmentation of the state or 'parcelisation of sovereignty' based on a hierarchy of landed property which emerged in feudal Europe (he cites the great historian of feudalism, Marc Bloch, as the scholar who has best analysed it); but that feudal form surely presupposes the distinctive development of Roman property and Rome's landed aristocracy, as well as the Roman imperial state, with its system of taxation. Wickham's own magisterial and persuasive analysis of the early middle-ages confirms this, yet his conceptual framework tends to obscure it. See Wickham 2005.

800 as *Imperator* in the Roman manner, which appeared to revive the universal empire. The so-called Holy-Roman Empire which ensued would, in the centuries that followed, even aggravate the conflicts of fragmented jurisdiction, adding yet another claim to temporal authority, in an already combustible mix of lordly, royal and papal authority.

Kingship in the medieval West was always characterised, in varying degrees, by a tension between monarchical power and lordship, between centralised and local authority. This tension would produce uniquely Western conceptions of rule, in which a resolution between competing claims to authority was sought not by asserting the simple and unambiguous predominance of central over local power, but rather by invoking some kind of mutuality, an agreement between two legitimate forces conceived in contractual or, eventually, constitutional terms.[34] It is hard to imagine how such a dispensation could have emerged without the distinctively Western development of property as an autonomous force in tension – yet in tandem – with the state.

After the end of the ninth century, there was, in effect, no sovereign state, if the hallmark of state-sovereignty is legislative power (as distinct from the application of existing law). Some public institutions, particularly certain kinds of courts, continued to exist; but there was effectively no legislation at all for two centuries, except for changes in customary law. The disintegration of Western Frankish rule in the tenth century left local castle-lords in command, while the East, particularly Germany, was controlled by powerful duchies. By the early eleventh century, even the functions of public courts fell into the hands of local lords, with regional counts appropriating jurisdictions not as public offices but as private property. If any legal and political order existed in these regions, it has been said, the only sector of the population that remained subject to any social discipline was the peasantry, under the control of individual lords.[35] Aristocratic autonomy now truly became the parcelisation of sovereignty.

To put it another way, the public or civic sphere completely disappeared. This was so not only in the sense that the state-apparatus effectively disintegrated, but also in the sense that public assemblies in which free men could participate, of a kind that survived throughout the Carolingian realm, no

---

34. See Coleman 2000, p. 18, for a discussion of the peculiarly Western resolution of tensions between local and central authorities.

35. It is argued by R. van Caenegem that the coincidence of lordship and ownership, which made peasants both tenants and subjects at once, applied throughout the West, including England (See Van Caenegem 1988, p. 195). As we shall see, however, the English case was exceptional, because the coincidence of lordship and ownership did not take the form of parcelised sovereignty in the way that it did on the Continent.

longer existed.[36] Clear distinctions between free men and slaves gave way to a complex continuum of dependent conditions. The category of 'free' man effectively disappeared in the former Frankish Empire, where even owners of free land might be subject to seigneurial jurisdiction and feudal obligations, while the concept of slavery was overtaken by a spectrum of dependence, in relations between lords and 'their' men.

By the thirteenth century, more firmly established feudal monarchies restored effective systems of administration. This was also a period when the Holy-Roman Empire, now led by German kings, achieved its greatest power as a central European state, while the papacy was asserting its own authority in the temporal domain. Yet even then, although the feudal subjection of peasants to lords was eased to some extent, the autonomous powers of lords, with their administrative and jurisdictional challenges to royal authority, would remain defining features of the medieval order. When a public realm and spheres of civic participation re-emerged, it typically took the form of corporate entities, internally self-governing yet bound by charters defining their corporate relation to superior authorities. Far from resolving the old jurisdictional conflicts, the new configuration of power in the later middle-ages created even more virulent contests, with seigneurial and corporate claims to autonomous jurisdiction vying with, and intensified by, the powers of emperors and popes.

There were, to be sure, patterns of social order in Europe other than the characteristically 'feudal' relations between landlords, peasants and kings, even at the height of feudalism. Where urban concentrations had survived the collapse of the Roman Empire, and where landholding-patterns produced a larger proportion of free peasants as distinct from serfs, the seigneurial system was comparatively weak. This was true in northern Italy, where towns had remained relatively strong, and the legacy of the Roman municipal system was more persistent. Just as towns had been the social and political domain of Romanised local élites, who effectively governed the surrounding countryside, the city continued to be the administrative centre of the secular and ecclesiastical authorities that carried on the legacy of Rome. A typical pattern was administration by bishops who preserved something of the Roman Empire and its municipal government, though this relatively unified civic administration increasingly gave way to a more fractured system of governance by various corporate entities and guilds. While the imperial élites had been overwhelmingly landed classes, in medieval Italy – especially from the beginning of the eleventh century – there emerged a powerful urban patriciate. Some of

---

36. I owe this point to George Comninel.

the urban communes became prosperous commercial centres, with dominant classes enriched by commerce and financial services for kings, emperors and popes. Collectively, they dominated the surrounding countryside, the *contado*, extracting wealth from it in one way or another, not least to sustain the public offices that, directly or indirectly, enriched many members of the urban élite.

Much confusion has been generated by historical accounts of feudalism that identify commerce with capitalism, treating money and trade as inimical to feudal relations. Yet money-rents were a prominent feature of relations between landlords and peasants, while commercial transactions – typically, in luxury goods – were very much a part of the feudal order.[37] The thriving commercial centres of northern Italy may have stood somewhat apart from the seigneurial system, but they served a vital function in the larger European feudal network, acting as trading links among the segments of that fragmented order and as a means of access to the world outside Europe.

Nor did these cities escape the parcelisation of sovereignty. While other parts of Europe were experiencing feudalisation, municipal administration was undergoing its own fragmentation. The communes became and remained, in varying degrees, loose associations of patrician families, parties, communities and corporate entities with their own semi-autonomous powers, organisational structures and jurisdictions, both secular and ecclesiastical, often in fierce contention with each other and in battle among warring civic factions. A lethal ingredient in this mix was the intrusion of papal and imperial powers. Even while civic communes were to a greater or lesser extent autonomous from larger temporal authorities, they were often fierce battlegrounds in those wider power-struggles, which played themselves out as vicious factional rivalries within the civic community – what would come to be known as the conflict between Guelf (papal) and Ghibelline (imperial) factions; typically, but not necessarily, corresponding to divisions between merchant classes and landed *signori*.

Interpretations of medieval 'republicanism', especially conceived as a foretaste of political modernity, can be misleading not only because cities with effective civic self-government were essentially oligarchies, but also because they never constituted a truly united civic order with a clearly defined public sphere detached from private powers of various kinds. In moments of more effective republican government, greater efforts were made to unite the civic

---

37. The view that capitalism emerged when and because the expansion of trade destroyed feudalism was decisively challenged in the so-called 'transition-debate', sparked in the early 1950s by a debate between Maurice Dobb and Paul Sweezy, followed by a discussion among several other Marxist historians. See Sweezy et al. 1976.

community; but no medieval Italian commune ever succeeded in transcending its inherent fragmentation or the fusion of public power with private appropriation. The triumph of more despotic oligarchies did not represent a major rupture with republican forms but belonged to the same dynamic of what we might call urban feudalism. Nor did their attempts to extend and consolidate their own rule truly overcome the feudal fragmentation of governance. Even the most centralised of 'Renaissance'-states in post-medieval Italy would continue to be divided by party, privilege and confused jurisdictions.

The most notable exception to the feudal breakdown of state-order in the West was England, with significant implications for later European development and for the history of political theory. Although the collapse of the Roman Empire in Britain seems to have produced a breakdown of material and political structures more catastrophic than anywhere else in the West, and a more drastic discontinuity with Roman forms, in Anglo-Saxon times a process of state-formation was already well-advanced, with kings, landlords and church-hierarchy working in tandem to produce an unusually centralised authority. While France was disintegrating, the English forged a unified kingdom, with a national system of justice and the most effective administration in the Western world. There also began to emerge a new kind of national identity – 'the Anglo-Saxons', and later 'the English'.

Anglo-Saxon kingdoms were, certainly, administered with the help of local aristocracies who had considerable powers; yet local lords governed – in principle and even in practice – not as autonomous regional counts, but as partners in the royal state from which their administrative authority derived. In England there would emerge a distinctive relation between central government and the lesser nobility. Local élites, with considerable local authority, would govern not as feudal lords, but, in effect, as delegates of the royal state, and not in tension with the central state, but in tandem with the rise of a national parliament as an assembly of the propertied classes ruling in partnership with the Crown.

In the eleventh century the Normans would bring with them elements of Continental feudalism, but the feudal parcelisation of sovereignty never took hold in England as it did elsewhere. The Norman ruling class arrived and imposed itself on English society as an already well-organised and unified military force, and consolidated the power of its newly established monarchical state by adapting Norman traditions of aristocratic freedom to Anglo-Saxon traditions of rule.

It is certainly true that lords of the manor in England had substantial rights and jurisdictional powers over their tenants; but the centralised power of the monarchy remained strong, and a national system of law and jurisdiction emerged very early, in the shape of the common law, the king's law. The development of the English monarchy was, and continued to be, at bottom, a cooperative project between monarchs and landlords.[38] Even when open conflict and, indeed, civil war, erupted between king and aristocracy, the stakes had less to do with a contest between centralised government and parcelised sovereignty, than attempts to correct imbalances in the partnership between monarchs and lords. The baronial challenge to monarchy in the documents that make up *Magna Carta*, for example, can certainly be construed as an appeal to reinstate some kind of feudal right; but, while barons may have been demanding that they should have the right to be tried by their peers in their own courts, they were not asserting their own jurisdiction over other free men. Unlike their counterparts in France, where seigneurial and royal jurisdiction would long continue to be regarded as in conflict with each other, English barons were claiming their rights at common law, that is, as rights deriving from the central state. The barons took that state for granted hardly less than did the king himself; and this would continue to be true in every episode of conflict between the monarchy and propertied classes, up to and including the Civil War and the Glorious Revolution of the seventeenth century.

The relative strength of the centralised state in England , however, did not mean the weakness of the landed aristocracy. In significant ways, the contrary is true. There emerged a cooperative division of labour between the central monarchical state and the landed class, whose power rested not on fragmented sovereignty, but on its command of property. It is true that the Roman system of property, like the Roman state, suffered a more complete disruption in England than elsewhere in the former empire; but, just as effective central administration was re-established in England more quickly than elsewhere, a strong and exclusive form of property would emerge in England as it did nowhere else.

English property-law would, on the face of it, become the most 'feudal' in Europe. This was so in the sense that here, as nowhere else in feudal Europe, there were no exceptions to the principle of 'no land without its lord', and there was no allodial land. Yet the paradox of English 'feudalism' is that the condition for the complete feudalisation of property was the centralised monarchy, together with its law and courts – not parcelised sovereignty but, on the contrary, its absence. If all land had its lord, it was only in the formal

---

38. For a discussion of relations between aristocracy and monarchy in the process of feudal centralisation in England, in contrast especially to France, see Brenner 1985b, especially pp. 253–64.

sense that the monarch was conceived as the supreme landlord. Yet, in practice, tenements held directly, in common law, under the jurisdiction of the king – including certain types of humble property held by tillers and freeholders who owed no military service and were free of lordly jurisdiction – constituted private property more exclusive, and less subject to obligations to an overlord, than anything that existed on the Continent, despite (or in some ways because of) the growing dominance of common law in preference to Roman law.[39] Monarchical rule and exclusive private property, in other words, were developing together.

For all the feudal trappings of English property, and the departures of the common law from the legal traditions of Rome, private and exclusive property would develop more completely in England than in any of the Continental states where Roman law survived and where the parcelisation of sovereignty prevailed. In England, the total breakdown of the Roman imperial order may have had the paradoxical effect that when the Roman legacy was reintroduced from the Continent – not only by the Norman Conquest, but even before, by Anglo-Saxon kings availing themselves of Continental legal expertise – the régime of exclusive private property was more forcibly implanted and rigorously imposed.

Nonetheless, despite this significant exception, parcelised sovereignty continued to be a dominant theme in medieval European history. It is true that, by the end of the twelfth century, more-or-less stable political administrations began to re-establish themselves in various parts of Europe, either in the

---

39. It should be emphasised here that the development of the common law in England and its relation to the establishment of exclusive rights of property was not, as is often suggested, the simple transition from feudal relations of mutuality under feudal law to individual and exclusive property rights in common law, defensible in a common, national court. See, for instance, Coleman 1988, p. 616. The common law had its roots in Anglo-Saxon England and thus preceded 'feudalism', so that, when the Normans brought feudal law from the Continent, it was implanted in the context of an already-established common law. It is also important to recognise that the possibility of defending property-rights before a national court, as existed elsewhere in Europe too, did not in itself represent a negation of feudal property. In France, for example, when peasants had the right to defend their property in royal courts, property was still held on feudal principles, with attendant obligations, and each seigneurie continued to have its own system of law and its own autonomous jurisdiction. Nor did the fact that the land might be alienable change the feudal obligations associated with it or the right of the seigneur to interpose himself in the transaction. It is misleading to suggest that, by the late middle-ages, property both in England and on the Continent was well on the way from feudal to capitalist, simply because property-rights were increasingly defensible at law, before a national court. Quite apart from the misleading conflation of absolute property with capitalism, the fact remains that property in England developed in ways quite distinct from other European cases, and even with its feudal trappings was more 'absolute' and exclusive than anywhere else.

form of monarchical states or as autonomous urban communes. The classics of medieval-political philosophy belong largely to this later period, and are preoccupied not so much with tensions between feudal lords and monarchical states, as with conflicts among kings, popes and Holy-Roman emperors. Nevertheless, even as kings contended with ecclesiastical and imperial hierarchies, monarchs would continue to rely on, and compete with, the lordly jurisdictions of landed aristocracies; and corporate entities of one kind or another continued to assert their autonomy against various claims, secular and ecclesiastical, to a higher unified sovereignty.

In all these cases, the question of legal and political sovereignty was always inseparable from tensions between the authority to govern and the power of property; and political conflicts were often conducted through the medium of controversies on property-rights. In the feudal unity of property and jurisdiction, institutions claiming legal or administrative powers of any kind were inevitably obliged to confront competing rights of property; and questions about the relation between *imperium* and *dominium* were bound to pose themselves with special urgency.

Absolutism and the modern state

The absolutist state had followed an economic logic of its own, which owed more to its precapitalist antecedents than to an emerging capitalist economy. Here, the state itself was a primary instrument of appropriation, a private resource for public officeholders. Just as feudal lords had appropriated the surplus-labour of peasants by means of their political, military and jurisdictional powers and by virtue of their juridical privileges, so their successors continued to rely not only on the vestiges of these old powers and privileges but on new forms of proprietary political power, new forms of politically constituted property. Office in the absolutist state represented a 'centralisation upwards' of feudal exploitation, in which peasant-produced surpluses were appropriated in the form of tax, instead of rent.

It is this 'economic' function, as much as any 'political' purpose, that accounts for the elaborate administrative apparatus which distinguished the French monarchy from its English counterpart. In England, the ruling class had long enjoyed a uniquely extensive and concentrated control of land and was increasingly drawing its wealth from the productive use of property, in particular, land cultivated by tenants responding to the imperatives of competition. Private, purely 'economic' (capitalist) modes of appropriation were far more developed, and the state as an instrument for appropriating surplus-labour from direct producers was far less important, as were other forms of politically-constituted property, corporate privilege and the fruits of jurisdiction. It is in this sense that absolutism, specifically the tax/office-structure of the French state, was in England 'interdicted'.

This is not to say that the English ruling class lost all interest in sinecures and offices; in fact, exploitation of the state by the great aristocracy acquired a new lease of life for a time at the peak of agrarian capitalism in the eighteenth century, when 'Old Corruption' was so avidly plundering the national wealth. But, by that time, the state was not itself the direct instrument of surplus-extraction, appropriating 'centralised rents' in the form of taxation from peasant-producers; nor did the state compete with other forms of politically constituted property for a share of peasant-surpluses. On the contrary, while the propertied class *taxed itself* by Parliamentary consent, a section of that class used the state as a medium for creaming off a part of the gains accumulated in the 'private' sphere by means of purely economic appropriation.

All this may help to account for what Perry Anderson has called 'the historic achievement of the English governing class in all its metamorphoses', an achievement that has proved the undoing of British capitalism: 'its long maintenance of the supremacy of civil society over the state'.[40] This 'achievement' is expressed in 'three main idiosyncrasies of the structure of power in Britain: the relative insignificance of bureaucratic or military forms, the exceptionally immediate strike-capacity of economic forms, and the ultimate, crucial importance of ideological and cultural forms'.[41]

But if these are, indeed, the most distinctive features of the British state, they have more to do with the relative maturity of capitalist social-property relations than with their incomplete development. British capitalism may have suffered for its uniquely well-established subordination of the state to civil society; but the supremacy of 'civil society', of 'economic' forms over political or military – indeed the very separation of civil society from the state – is a defining characteristic of capitalism itself, which distinguishes it from other social forms. Anderson's account of 'the structure of power in Britain' [...] does not require us to ascribe all British failures to the persistence of anachronisms, or all Continental successes to a more perfect modernity and more thorough bourgeois revolutions.

The idea of the state

England and France produced centralised states long before any other European country. But it was the French experience that was to give the

<hr>

40. P. Anderson 1964, p. 51.
41. P. Anderson 1964, p. 47.

world its dominant paradigms of political modernity. The French Revolution is the most obvious instance, but the idea of the modern state is no less indebted to the pre-revolutionary history of France. Indeed, the concept of the state itself attained more-or-less its modern meaning in the sixteenth century, principally in France, and it was absolutism that first gave the idea a solid purchase in European culture.

In France, the process of state-centralisation, which was to prove very protracted, began early, as the feudal 'parcelisation of sovereignty' was challenged by a single, monarchical power forged in a process of 'patrimonial expansion' which set one feudal power above its competitors.[42] But, for all its successes of centralisation, French absolutism never completely conquered the fragmentation of its feudal past. Indeed, the defining characteristic of royal absolutism was a continuing tension between monarchical centralisation and feudal parcelisation, based on a division between competing forms of politically constituted property: on the one hand, rent, together with the fruits of jurisdiction or juridical privilege; and on the other, the 'centralisation upwards' of those feudal powers in the form of office and taxation by an appropriating state. The benefits accruing to the ruling class from the process of feudal centralisation did not resolve the tensions and conflicts between the state and the independent powers of the aristocracy as competing forms of politically-constituted property or fragments of sovereignty, both appropriating peasant-labour. These conflicts were only partially resolved by co-opting large numbers of aristocrats into the state, with its lucrative offices.

The assertion of royal absolutism against competing jurisdictions, the tension between monarchical centralisation and feudal fragmentation, put the concepts of sovereignty and the state on the ideological agenda as never before. The quintessential political theorist, here, is Jean Bodin, who, in the second half of the sixteenth century, elaborated the first systematic theory of absolute and indivisible sovereignty, and a concept of the state as an embodiment of sovereignty, as a means of joining in 'harmony' a disorderly welter of baronial powers and corporate jurisdictions.

But if the centralising mission of the absolutist monarchy was accomplished in the realm of theory, it never completely succeeded in practice. It remained for the Revolution, and more particularly Napoleon, to carry through the project of centralisation. Napoleon set out to create a modern state by sweeping away any neo-feudal remnants left by the Revolution, the 'intermediate bodies' and corporate powers, the internal barriers to political and economic unity, the fragmented jurisdictions. There remained, however, another stage

---

42. For a comparison of French and English patterns of feudal centralisation, see Brenner 1985b, pp. 253–64.

in the evolution – and the conceptual definition – of the state, its clear differentiation from 'civil society', a separation of the economic and political powers which had been fused, in their respective ways, by both feudalism and
absolutism. That job was not completed in France until the state had been
transformed from a parasitic growth, fed in large part by peasant-produced
taxes, into a catalyst of capitalist development.

If the Napoleonic project was fuelled by the competitive pressures of an
already-capitalist England, the military threat of the 'modern' Napoleonic
state, in turn, served as an impetus to nation-building elsewhere on the Continent and to the economic development which alone could make it possible.
From then on, the processes of state-integration and economic – that is to say,
capitalist – development went hand-in-hand.

In the post-revolutionary era, it was Hegel who in this respect captured the
spirit of the age. His theoretical project of creating a truly 'modern' state was
motivated by the inadequacies of the small and fragmented German principalities in relation to the political unity and military power of the Napoleonic state. The first major thinker systematically to elaborate the conceptual
distinction between 'state' and 'civil society', he looked to Napoleon as his
inspiration for a truly modern state, and to the British political economists
such as [Sir James] Steuart and [Adam] Smith for his model of civil society.
The result of this thought-experiment in grafting foreign social forms on to a
'backward' German reality was a curious amalgam of the 'modern' state with
archaic feudal principles. In particular, Hegel proposed to adapt feudal corporate institutions and to retain 'intermediate powers' whose destruction by
Napoleon he regarded as damaging to the organic unity of the state, depriving it of the necessary mediations between the 'particularity' of the individual
and the 'universality' of the state.

When, later in the nineteenth century, German unity was finally effected,
the process was still imbued with a precapitalist logic, driven by the external
pressures of geo-political competition and war. Just as state-centralisation was
achieved by imposition-from-above and in response to external impulses, so
too German capitalism was driven beyond its own organic level of development by motivating forces from without and above. German and French
state-centralisation thus had this in common: both were accomplished by a
coercive process of integration-from-above (though in France, the process
began much earlier and was more protracted), just as in both cases, though in
varying degrees, the state gave an external impetus to the progress of capitalism. The very externality of the relation between the post-absolutist state and
the development of capitalism in these cases brought out in sharp relief the
conceptual differentiation of state and civil society.

The peculiarities of the English state

The case of England was very different. The early unity of the ruling class in England had provided a much earlier and more organic basis for state-unification. Here, the early process of state-formation was not a matter of one baronial power gaining ascendancy over its competitors. Instead, feudal centralisation in England was the collective project of the dominant propertied class.[43] Indeed, it can be said that the English ruling class was born united, as the Norman Conquest brought to England a class of rulers already organised as a cohesive political-military unit. Despite episodes of baronial and dynastic conflict, England never lapsed into a feudal parcelisation. The early emergence of a unitary national parliament, and the traditional formula of 'the Crown in Parliament', testify to the process of state-formation which so sharply distinguished the English monarchical state from the French, with its fragmented jurisdictions and representative institutions vertically and horizontally divided by class and region.

The English pattern of state-formation was associated with the evolution of a ruling class which did not depend either on feudal 'extra-economic' powers or on the centralisation of these powers in the tax/office-nexus of absolutism. In the early-modern period, when the absolutist state was being consolidated in France, English lords were following a different path. With a large proportion of landed property in their direct control, but without the parcelised jurisdiction of French 'banal' lords or their seigneurial descendants, and demilitarised before any other aristocracy in Europe, they relied increasingly on purely 'economic' modes of appropriation, the productive and competitive utilisation of land, rather than on directly coercive surplus-extraction. Even exploitation of the state as a resource – in the form of offices, sinecures, patronage and outright corruption – was to a great extent dependent on recycling the wealth accumulated by these economic means. The political corollary of these distinctive economic relations was a formally autonomous state which represented the private, 'economic' class of appropriators in its public, 'political' aspect. This meant that the 'economic' functions of appropriation were differentiated from the 'political' and military functions of rule – or, to put it another way, 'civil society' was differentiated from the state – while at the same time the state was responsive, even subordinate, to civil society.

Yet the historical differentiation of state and civil society was reflected in their conceptual conflation. It is a striking fact that, no sooner had the 'state' entered the English political vocabulary in more or less its modern sense – in the sixteenth century, as in France – when it almost immediately receded

---

43. Brenner 1985b, pp. 254–8.

into the background of English political thought, as the already obstructed progress of royal absolutism was decisively derailed in the revolutionary decades of the seventeenth century. In the political language of that era, 'commonwealth', 'political society' or even 'civil society' in England occupied the conceptual place increasingly held elsewhere in Europe by the 'state'. The character of the ruling class and its relation to the state, the subordination of the state to civil society, were more aptly expressed by concepts in which the state was dissolved into the 'political nation' of private proprietors. It is not surprising that Hegel, the principal Continental exponent of the state/civil-society antithesis, would later criticise English political thinkers for theorising about politics in terms derived from the private sphere.

Contrasting states: France vs. England

The historical configuration of 'political dilemmas' that confronted [Jean-Jacques] Rousseau in eighteenth-century France and the conceptual instruments, the particular 'traditions of discourse', that had evolved to deal with them, can be traced back at least as far as the centralisation of the feudal monarchy and its gradual consolidation into an 'absolutist state'. The divergences between French and English patterns of feudal centralisation, the different structures of class-forces that underlay these divergent paths of state-formation, can be discerned not only in the future development of class and state in the two countries, but also, correspondingly, in their 'traditions of discourse' about class and state.[44] In France, the monarchy grew out of competing feudal powers and the ascendancy of one such power over and against others, while in England, the crown developed in close conjunction with the self-centralisation of the feudal class as a whole.[45] The French mode of feudal centralisation produced a monarchy that never quite overcame the particularisms and 'parcelised' power of its feudal origins, always contending with – and yet, in many ways dependent upon – the survival of seigneurial powers, privileges, and exemptions, as well as a variety of corporate institutions, local liberties, and competing jurisdictions. This mode of centralisation was reflected in the character of French representative institutions – for

44. For a ground-breaking discussion of the differences between English and French traditions in medieval-political thought and their relation to the differences in historical experiences, see Nederman 1983.

45. See Brenner 1985b, especially pp. 253–64, for a discussion of these divergent developments in state-formation. The following discussion of feudal centralisation in England and France is much indebted to this article and to its predecessor, 'Agrarian Class Structure' (Brenner 1985a).

example, in the corporate and regional fragmentation of the Estates, in sharp contrast to the unitary and national organisation of the English Parliament. At the same time, the monarchy established a strong apparatus of centralised state-power. The power of this state derived not only from the need of the feudal ruling class for improved instruments of political administration and military coercion to support its private powers of surplus-extraction and maintain order, but also from the new system of *centralised* surplus-extraction which the monarchy made available in the form of state-*office*, as well as the opportunities it offered for plunder, internal and external, through war.

This development of the French state as a centralised instrument of private appropriation, an extension of feudal 'extra-economic' surplus-extraction, defines many of its essential characteristics: the monarchy's reliance on the proliferation and distribution of offices, not only to maintain fiscal solvency by the sale of offices, but to constitute its power-base; the dependence of the propertied classes on the state, not only as a means of enforcing their private powers of appropriation, but as a private resource in its own right; the particular salience this gave to the problem of taxation – and exemptions from it – both for those who benefited from them, and for those who bore the burden.

This tax/office-structure implied complex and ambiguous relations between the state and various classes. The state served as a source – direct or indirect – of private income for members of the landed classes, while at the same time competing with them for the same peasant-produced surplus. The bourgeoisie stood to gain from the proliferation and venalisation of offices, which might give them access to power and a lucrative resource, and yet also suffered from the resulting increases in the burden of taxation. The peasantry, which was the major source of tax-revenue and the social base on which the whole tax/office-structure rested, had to be preserved by the monarchy from destruction by rent-hungry landlords, in order to be squeezed by a tax-hungry state. The role of the state as a private resource, and the consequent structure of social relations based on the tax/office-nexus, remained a central theme of French political life in theory and practice, up to and beyond the Revolution, and long continued to determine the issues and shape the contours of political discourse.

The English state generated a different set of problems. While feudal centralisation, here too, had the function of enhancing the powers of 'extra-economic' surplus-extraction, English landed proprietors were able more successfully to develop private and increasingly 'economic' means of extraction – with the coercive support of the state – and never came to rely so much on the state as a direct resource. The state also remained largely free of fragmentation inherited from feudal corporate institutions, regional privileges, and politically autonomous urban communes. A strong centralised state thus coexisted with – indeed rested upon – a strong propertied class much less fragmented than the French. Royal taxation never played the same role for the English propertied classes that it did for the French; the state never had the same reasons for either squeezing or protecting the peasantry as did the French absolutist state, and the English peasantry duly succumbed to larger landed proprietors. Thus, the relations among classes, and between class and state, differed considerably from the French, as did – necessarily – the issues contested among them.

Each form of state- and class-rule naturally generated its own characteristic grievances, provoked its own resistances, and erected its own defences. The relative importance of different modes of surplus-extraction and accumulation, and the varying functions of the state in furthering or hindering them, played a central role in establishing the terms of struggle. English property-owners, when seeking to protect and augment their increasingly 'economic' means of appropriation, might struggle to defend their private rights of property against incursions by the Crown, to establish the supremacy of Parliament as an association of property-holders, to thwart the consolidation of an absolutist monarchy by establishing 'limited government', while at the same time staving off threats from below. The propertied classes of France, who confronted the state both as a competitor for surplus-labour and as a means of access to it, contended over taxation, the proliferation of offices and the means of distributing them, often struggling less to limit the state than to acquire property in it or prevent others from doing so. The English commoner, in defence against the landlord's efforts to augment his economic powers of extraction, struggled against the enclosure of common and waste-land. The French peasant, more oppressed by 'political' forms of extraction, rebelled against royal taxation and seigneurial privilege. Englishmen asserted their individual rights; Frenchmen defended their corporate and regional privileges.

Many of the essential qualities of the French political 'problematic' can be summed up by contrasting the English concern with the relation between the state and private property and the French concern with the state *as* private property. French anti-absolutism was not simply a matter of resistance to political tyranny but also an attack on the state as, so to speak, a private racket, a 'semi-institutionalized system of extortion and embezzlement'.[46] Popular resistance, too, often focused on exploitation by the state. Thus, for example, exploitation by means of direct seigneurial exactions might take second place to taxation (or the tax-exemptions of others) as an object of grievance, just as

---

46. Franklin 1969, p. 16.

the landlord might be less concerned about losing economic powers such as the right of enclosure than about relinquishing tax-exemptions and political privileges.[47]

French political thought, then, was preoccupied with a complex of problems at the centre of which stood a fragmented polity consisting of many particularisms whose unifying principle was yet another particularistic power, yet another proprietary interest: the monarchical state and its growing administrative and fiscal apparatus conceived, if not as a means of production, certainly as a means of appropriation.

In absolutist thought itself, the justification of monarchy – especially its right to distribute offices and impose taxes – often took the form of claims for its generality against the partiality and particularity of other elements in society. The king embodied the *public* aspect of the state as against the private character of his subjects. Such arguments suggested that a single superior *will* was required to bind together the particular interests in the polity and produce a common good.[48]

Arguments against absolutism voiced concern not only with the particularisms that divided the polity, but also with the particularity of the state-apparatus itself and the consequences of its use as private property – the proliferation and venalisation of offices, the corruption of administration, the tax-burden. Even here, however, the public interest or common good might be presented as an emanation of a unifying will or mind; though now, the unifying, generalising will of the monarch, who was 'particular and single', was replaced by the collective will of the public council, 'one mind compounded out of many'.[49]

The contrast with England is striking. It is, of course, often argued that England never experienced absolutism at all, or at least that English absolutism was short-circuited. If the tax/office-structure so characteristic of French absolutism and associated with the evolution of the state as a mode of appropriation is regarded as an essential characteristic, for example, then English absolutism hardly existed – and in this respect, the problem of the state as private property hardly arose. It is no doubt significant that only two thinkers have entered the canon of English political thought as spokesmen for royal

---

47. For an example of such a case, see Le Roy Ladurie 1980, p. 72.

48. See Keohane 1980 for indications of how the concept of 'will' and the 'general will' were used in French traditions of discourse and their association with the idea of monarchical power acting as a unifying force among particularistic powers and interests. Other writers have also traced the lineage of the 'general will', but from a somewhat less historical and more abstractly philosophical point of view; for example, Hendel 1934; Derathé 1970; and Riley 1978.

49. Hotman 1969, p. 68.

absolutism, [Thomas] Hobbes and [Robert] Filmer; and of these only Hobbes is acknowledged as one of the 'greats'. But what is more significant is the mode of argumentation surrounding the question of state-power. Hobbes stands out not simply because absolutist thinkers are relatively rare in England and great ones even more so, but because he alone among significant English theorists regards an indivisible sovereign power as the essential condition of the polity's very existence, without which civil society itself would dissolve. This is an assumption no other important English thinker feels obliged to make, not even that unregenerate absolutist, Filmer. It is an idea that is much more at home in 'parcelised' France. Indeed, the concept of *sovereignty* itself is a matter of little concern to early-modern English thinkers. Given the long years spent by Hobbes in France and his close association with French thinkers, it is tempting to say that he is precisely the exception that proves the rule.

Chapter Four
Social and Political Thought

The social history of political theory

The 'social history of political theory' [...] starts from the premise that the great political thinkers of the past were passionately engaged in the issues of their time and place.[1] This was so even when they addressed these issues from an elevated philosophical vantage-point, in conversation with other philosophers in other times and places, and even, or especially, when they sought to translate their reflections into universal and timeless principles. Often, their engagements took the form of partisan adherence to a specific and identifiable political cause, or even fairly transparent expressions of particular interests, the interests of a particular party or class. But their ideological commitments could also be expressed in a larger vision of the good society and human ideals.

At the same time, the great political thinkers are not party-hacks or propagandists. Political theory is, certainly, an exercise in persuasion, but its tools are reasoned discourse and argumentation, in a genuine search for some kind of truth. Yet if the 'greats' are different from lesser political thinkers and actors, they are no less human and no less steeped in history. When Plato explored the concept of justice in

---

1. For a discussion of the term 'social history of political theory', see N. Wood 1978.

the *Republic*, or when he outlined the different levels of knowledge, he was certainly opening large philosophical questions and he was certainly in search of universal and transcendent truths. But his questions, no less than his answers, were[...]driven by his critical engagement with Athenian democracy.

To acknowledge the humanity and historic engagement of political thinkers is surely not to demean them or deny them their greatness. In any case, without subjecting ideas to critical historical scrutiny, it is impossible to assess their claims to universality or transcendent truth. The intention, here, is certainly to explore the ideas of the most important political thinkers; but these thinkers will always be treated as living and engaged human-beings, immersed not only in the rich intellectual heritage of received ideas bequeathed by their philosophical predecessors, nor simply against the background of the available vocabularies specific to their time and place, but also in the context of the social and political processes that shaped their immediate world.

This social history of political theory, in its conception of historical contexts, proceeds from certain fundamental premises, which belong to the tradition of 'historical materialism': human-beings enter into relations with each other and with nature to guarantee their own survival and social reproduction. To understand the social practices and cultural products of any time and place, we need to know something about those conditions of survival and social reproduction: something about the specific ways in which people gain access to the material conditions of life; about how some people gain access to the labour of others; about the relations between people who produce and those who appropriate what others produce; about the forms of property that emerge from these social relations; and about how these relations are expressed in political domination, as well as resistance and struggle.

This is certainly not to say that a theorist's ideas can be predicted or 'read off' from his or her social position or class. The point is simply that the questions confronting any political thinker, however eternal and universal those questions may seem, are posed to them in specific historical forms. The Cambridge school agrees that, in order to understand the answers offered by political theorists, we must know something about the questions they are trying to answer, and that different historical settings pose different sets of questions.[2] But, for the social history of political theory, these questions are posed not only by explicit political controversies, and not only at the level of philosophy or

2. For the major founders of what has come to be called the Cambridge school, see Skinner 1978 and Pocock 1985.

high politics, but also by the social pressures and tensions that shape human interactions outside the political arena and beyond the world of texts.

This approach differs from that of the Cambridge school both in the scope of what is regarded as a 'context' and in the effort to apprehend historical *processes*. Ideological episodes like the 'Engagement Controversy' or the 'Exclusion Crisis' may tell us something about a thinker like Hobbes or Locke; but unless we explore how these thinkers situated themselves in the larger historical processes that were shaping their world, it is hard to see how we are to distinguish the great theorists from ephemeral publicists.

Long-term developments in social relations, property-forms and state-formation do episodically erupt into specific political-ideological controversies; and it is undoubtedly true that political theory tends to flourish at moments like this, when history intrudes most dramatically into the dialogue among texts or traditions of discourse. But a major thinker like John Locke, while he was certainly responding to specific and momentary political controversies, was raising larger fundamental questions about social relations, property and the state generated by larger social transformations and structural tensions – in particular, developments that we associate with the 'rise of capitalism'. Locke did not, needless to say, know that he was observing the development of what we call capitalism; but he was dealing with problems posed by its characteristic transformations of property, class-relations and the state. To divorce him from this larger social context is to impoverish his work and its capacity to illuminate its own historical moment, let alone the 'human condition' in general.

If different historical experiences give rise to different sets of problems, it follows that these divergences will also be observable in various 'traditions of discourse'. It is not, for instance, enough to talk about a Western or European historical experience, defined by a common cultural and philosophical inheritance. We must also look for differences among the various patterns of property-relations and the various processes of state-formation that distinguished one European society from another and produced different patterns of theoretical interrogation, different sets of questions for political thinkers to address.

The diversity of 'discourses' does not simply express personal, or even national, idiosyncrasies of intellectual style among political philosophers engaged in dialogue with one another across geographical and chronological boundaries. To the extent that political philosophers are, indeed, reflecting not only upon philosophical traditions, but upon the problems set by political life, their 'discourses' are diverse in large part because the political problems they confront are diverse. The problem of the state, for instance, has presented itself historically in different guises even to such close neighbours as the English and the French.[3]

Even the 'perennial questions' have appeared in various shapes. What appears as a salient issue will vary according to the nature of the principal contenders, the competing social forces at work, the conflicting interests at stake. The configuration of problems arising from a struggle such as the one in early-modern England between 'improving' landlords and commoners dependent on the preservation of common and waste-land will differ from those at issue in France among peasants, seigneurs, and a tax-hungry state. Even within the same historical or national configuration, what appears as a problem to the commoner or peasant will not necessarily appear so to the gentleman-farmer, the seigneur, or the royal office-holder. We need not reduce the great political thinkers to 'prize-fighters' for this-or-that social interest in order to acknowledge the importance of identifying the particular constellation of problems that history has presented to them, or to recognise that the 'dialogue' in which they are engaged is not simply a timeless debate with rootless philosophers, but an engagement with living historical actors, both those who dominate and those who resist.

To say this is not to claim that political theorists from another time and place have nothing to say to our own. There is no inverse relation between historical contextualisation and 'relevance'. On the contrary, historical contextualisation is an essential condition for learning from the 'classics', not simply because it allows a better understanding of a thinker's meaning and intention, but also because it is in the context of history that theory emerges from the realm of pure abstraction and enters the world of human practice and social interaction.

There are, of course, commonalities of experience we share with our predecessors just by virtue of being human, and there are innumerable practices learned by humanity over the centuries in which we engage as our ancestors did. These common experiences mean that much of what great thinkers of the past have to say is readily accessible to us. But if the classics of political theory are to yield fruitful lessons, it is not enough to acknowledge these commonalities of human and historical experience or to mine the classics for certain abstract universal principles. To historicise is to humanise, and to detach ideas from their own material and practical setting is to lose our points of human contact with them.

---

3. I have discussed these differences at some length in E.M. Wood 1991.

There is a way, all-too-common, of studying the history of political theory which detaches it from the urgent human issues to which it is addressed. To think about the *politics* in political theory is, at the very least, to consider and make judgements about what it would mean to translate particular principles into actual social relationships and political arrangements. If one of the functions of political theory is to sharpen our perceptions and conceptual instruments for thinking about politics in our own time and place, that purpose is defeated by emptying historical political theories of their own political meaning.

Some years ago, for instance, I encountered an argument about Aristotle's theory of natural slavery, which seemed to me to illustrate the shortcomings of an ahistorical approach.[4] We should not, the argument went, treat the theory of natural slavery as a comment on a historically actual social condition, the relation between slaves and masters as it existed in the ancient world, because to do so is to deprive it of any significance beyond the socio-economic circumstances of its own time and place. Instead, we should recognise it as a philosophical metaphor for the universal human condition in the abstract. Yet to deny that Aristotle was defending a real social practice, the enslavement of real human-beings, or to suggest that we have more to learn about the human condition by refusing to confront his theory of slavery in its concrete historical meaning, seems a peculiar way of sensitising us to the realities of social life and politics, or indeed the human condition, in our own time or any other.

There is also another way in which the contextual analysis of political theory can illuminate our own historical moment. If we abstract a political theory from its historical context, we, in effect, assimilate it to our own. Understanding a theory historically allows us to look at our own historical condition from a critical distance, from the vantage-point of other times and other ideas. It also allows us to observe how certain assumptions, which we may now accept uncritically, came into being and how they were challenged in their formative years. Reading political theory in this way, we may be less tempted to take for granted the dominant ideas and assumptions of our own time and place.

This benefit may not be so readily available to contextual approaches in which historical processes are replaced by disconnected episodes and traditions of discourse. The Cambridge mode of contextualisation encourages us to believe that the old political thinkers have little to say in our own time and place. It invites us to think that there is nothing to learn from them, because their historical experiences have no apparent connection to our own. To discover what there is to learn from the history of political theory requires us

---

4. See Saxonhouse 1981, p. 579.

to place ourselves on the continuum of history, where we are joined to our predecessors not only by the continuities we share, but by the processes of change that intervene between us, bringing us from there to here.

Political theory in history: an overview

Born in the *polis*, this new mode of political thought would survive the *polis* and continue to set the theoretical agenda in later centuries, when very different forms of state prevailed. This longevity has not been simply a matter of tenacious intellectual legacies. The Western tradition of political theory has developed on the foundations established in ancient Greece because certain issues have remained at the centre of European political life. In varying forms, the autonomy of private property, its relative independence from the state, and the tension between these foci of social power have continued to shape the political agenda. On the one hand, appropriating classes have needed the state to maintain order, conditions for appropriation and control over producing classes. On the other hand, they have found the state a burdensome nuisance and a competitor for surplus-labour.

With a wary eye on the state, the dominant-appropriating classes have always had to turn their attention to their relations with subordinate producing classes. Indeed, their need for the state has been largely determined by those difficult relations. In particular, throughout most of Western history, peasants fed, clothed, and housed the lordly minority by means of surplus-labour extracted by payment of rents, fees, or tributes. Yet, though the aristocratic state depended on peasants, and though lords were always alive to the threat of resistance, the politically voiceless classes play little overt role in the classics of Western political theory. Their silent presence tends to be visible only in the great theoretical efforts devoted to justifying social and political hierarchies.

The relation between appropriating and producing classes was to change fundamentally with the advent of capitalism, but the history of Western political theory continued to be, in large part, the history of tensions between property and state, appropriators and producers. In general, the Western tradition of political theory has been 'history-from-above', essentially reflection on the existing state and the need for its preservation or change, written from the perspective of a member or client of the ruling classes. Yet it should be obvious that this 'history-from-above' cannot be understood without relating it to what can be learned about the 'history-from-below'. The complex three-way relation between the state, propertied classes and producers, perhaps more than anything else, sets the Western political tradition apart from others.

There is nothing unique to the West, of course, about societies in which dominant groups appropriate what others produce. But there is something distinctive about the ways in which the tensions between them have shaped political life and theory in the West. This may be precisely because the relations between appropriators and producers have never, since classical antiquity, been synonymous with the relation between rulers and subjects. To be sure, the peasant-citizen would not survive the Roman Empire, and many centuries would pass before anything comparable to the ancient-Athenian idea of democratic citizenship would re-emerge in Europe. Feudal and early-modern Europe would, in its own way, even approximate the old division between rulers and producers, as labouring classes were excluded from active political rights and the power to appropriate was typically associated with the possession of 'extra-economic' power, political, judicial or military. But even then, the relation between rulers and producers was never unambiguous, because appropriating classes confronted their labouring compatriots not, in the first instance, as a collective power organised in the state, but in a more directly personal relation as individual proprietors, in rivalry with other proprietors and even with the state.

The autonomy of property and the contradictory relations between ruling class and state meant that propertied classes in the West always had to fight on two fronts. While they would have happily subscribed to Mencius's principle about those who rule and those who feed them, they could never take for granted such a neat division between rulers and producers, because there was a much clearer division than existed elsewhere between property and state.

Although the foundations of Western political theory established in ancient Greece proved to be remarkably resilient, there have, of course, been many changes and additions to its theoretical agenda, in keeping with changing historical conditions. […] The Romans, perhaps because their aristocratic republic, did not confront challenges like those of the Athenian democracy, did not produce a tradition of political theory as fruitful as the Greek. But they did introduce other social and political innovations, especially the Roman law, which would have major implications for the development of political theory. The Empire also gave rise to Christianity, which became the imperial religion, with all its cultural consequences.

It is particularly significant that the Romans began to delineate a sharp distinction between public and private, even, perhaps, between state and society. Above all, the opposition between property and state as two distinct foci of power, which has been a constant theme throughout the history of Western political theory, was, for the first time, formally acknowledged by the Romans in their distinction between *imperium* and *dominium*, power conceived as the right to command and power in the form of ownership. This did not preclude the view – expressed already by Cicero in *On Duties* (*De Officiis*) – that the purpose of the state was to protect private property, or the conviction that the state came into being for that reason. On the contrary, the partnership of state and private property, which would continue to be a central theme of Western political theory, presupposes the separation, and the tensions, between them.

The tension between these two forms of power, which was intensified in theory and practice as Republic gave way to Empire, would[...]play a large part in the fall of the Roman Empire. With the rise of feudalism, that tension was resolved on the side of *dominium*, as the state was virtually dissolved into individual property. In contrast to the ancient division between rulers and producers, in which the state was the dominant instrument of appropriation, the feudal state scarcely had an autonomous existence apart from the hierarchical chain of individual, if conditional, property and personal lordship. Instead of a centralised public authority, the feudal state was a network of 'parcelised sovereignties', governed by a complex hierarchy of social relations and competing jurisdictions, in the hands not only of lords and kings, but also of various autonomous corporations, to say nothing of Holy-Roman emperors and popes.[5] Feudal relations – between king and lords, between lords and vassals, between lords and peasants – were both a political/military relation and a form of property. Feudal lordship meant command of property, together with control of legally dependent labour; and, at the same time, it was a piece of the state, a fragment of political and military *imperium*.

The feudal resolution of the tension between property and state could not last forever. In their relations with the peasantry, lords would inevitably turn to the state for support; and parcelised sovereignty, in turn, gave way, yet again, to state-centralisation. The new form of state that would emerge in the late middle-ages and develop in the early-modern period would forever be marked by the underlying conflict between monarchy and lordship – until capitalism completely transformed the relation between politics and property.

At each stage in this history of political practice, there were corresponding changes in theory and variations on old themes to accommodate new social

---

5. On the concept of 'parcelised sovereignty', see P. Anderson 1974, pp. 148ff. English feudalism represented a partial exception. All property was legally defined as 'feudal' and conditional; but the Anglo-Saxon state was already relatively unified, and the Normans would consolidate that unity, so that 'parcelised sovereignty' never existed in England to the extent that it did on the Continent. The distinctive development of English capitalism was not unrelated to this distinctive 'feudalism'.

tensions and political arrangements. The contradictory relations between property and state acquired new complexities, giving rise to new ideas about relations between monarchs and lords, the origins and scope of monarchical power, constitutional limits on state-power, the autonomous powers of various corporate entities, conceptions of sovereignty, the nature of obligation and the right to resist. Developments in Christianity and the rise of the Church as an independent power introduced yet more complications, raising new questions about relations between divine and civil law and about the challenge posed by the Church to secular authority. Finally, the advent of capitalism brought its own conceptual transformations, in new ideas of property and state, together with new conceptions of 'public' and 'private', political and economic, state and 'society', and a resurrection of 'democracy', not in its ancient-Greek form but in a new and distinctively capitalist meaning, which no longer represented a fundamental challenge to dominant classes.

Throughout this 'Western' history, there were also, as we shall see, significant theoretical variations among diverse European states, not just because of linguistic and cultural differences, but because social and political relations varied too. Not only were there several European feudalisms, but the dissolution of feudalism gave rise to several different transformations, producing forms as diverse as the city-states of Italy, the principalities of Germany, the absolutist state of France, and the commercial republics of the Netherlands, while the so-called 'transition from feudalism to capitalism' occurred only in England. For all the commonalities of European culture, and all the shared social issues that continued to make the Western tradition of political theory a fruitful common legacy, each of these transformations produced its own characteristic 'traditions of discourse'.

One further point is worth making. The ambiguous relation between ruling class and state gave Western political theory certain unique characteristics. Even while propertied classes could never ignore the threat from below, and even while they depended on the state to sustain their property and economic power, the tensions in their relations with the state placed a special premium on their own autonomous powers, their rights against the state, and also on conceptions of liberty – which were often indistinguishable from notions of aristocratic privilege asserted against the state. So challenges to authority could come from two directions: from resistance by subordinate classes to oppression by their overlords, and from the overlords themselves as they faced intrusions by the state. This helped to keep alive the habit of interrogating the most basic principles of authority, legitimacy and the obligation to obey, even at moments when social and political hierarchies were at their most rigid.

Plato

It is possible to look upon the dialogue *Protagoras* as the point of departure for all Plato's subsequent political theory. In this work, the crucial political questions are raised, at least in a rudimentary form, and the groundwork for their answers laid. Above all, here is perhaps the only more-or-less coherent and explicit statement of the political theory which is arguably the ultimate target of all Plato's elaborate argumentation on the nature of politics. Protagoras's long speech, the so-called 'Myth and Apology', is the most systematic expression available to us of what might be called the political theory of Greek democracy. Whether or not it specifically reflects the views of Protagoras or any other single person, it clearly represents the view of man and society which Plato associates with the democratic outlook.[6] The speech represents the democratic doctrine that constitutes the framework of Plato's own anti-democratic argument, in the sense that he appears always to be addressing himself to that doctrine implicitly – when he is not actually engaging in deliberate distortions of the democratic world-view. The *Protagoras* is, in fact, the only extant dialogue in which Plato allows his Socrates to encounter a serious democratic argument, despite the fact that assaults on democracy constitute a central and constant theme of Plato's political thought. Even in this dialogue, however, his method is not to meet the argument head-on. Neither here nor anywhere else does he actually come to grips with a democratic argument and systematically refute it. Instead, when he does not simply distort the democratic position by equating it with the amorality of a Callicles, as in the *Gorgias* [...] Plato often proceeds by simply borrowing democratic premises and ideals and manipulating them so that their meaning is magically transformed into its opposite. The most important element of this approach, the one which is the very cornerstone of Plato's anti-democratic polemic, is the argument from the arts. At a time when artisans and craftsmen formed the mainstay of the radical democracy, and were leaving their imprint on social values, Plato borrows the ethic of craftsmanship and technical skill; he does this, however, not in order to enhance the dignity and status of the ordinary artisans and craftsmen who possess such skills, but on the contrary,

---

6. On the whole, it seems more likely than not that Plato is giving a reasonably accurate account of Protagoras's views – if only because the views Plato puts in Protagoras's mouth are so different from his own and yet are surprisingly persuasive, in contrast to the ideas of Sophists in Plato's later works. After the *Protagoras*, Plato tends to make his Sophistic opponents less effective, blustering, inconsistent, ill-tempered, or completely amoral. The *Protagoras*, on the other hand, has a refreshing quality of youthful honesty about it, so that even Socrates comes off not altogether well, and Protagoras is more of a match for him than are the interlocutors supplied later by a more disingenuous Plato.

by defining politics as a specialised art, to exclude these very people – and indeed all who labour for their livelihood – from the 'craft' of politics and the right to participate in self-rule. […]

His – and probably Socrates's – attitude to craftsmen in a non-metaphorical sense is sufficiently revealed by the hierarchy of souls outlined in the *Phaedrus*, where craftsmen and farmers are placed seventh in a list of nine, superior only to sophists, demagogues, and tyrants. In fact, Plato's own hardly disguised contempt is itself one of the chief sources of the view that Athenians generally regarded the 'base' arts with disdain, as gratuitous as it is to universalise the views of an aristocrat so at odds with the mass of his compatriots. It seems more reasonable to suppose that Plato adopted the argument from the arts, not out of any personal respect, but simply because, in a democracy where 'ordinary' craftsmen and artisans had achieved a unique social and political status, respect for *technē* was more in keeping with common values than was Plato's own aristocratic disdain. Plato simply adapted to his own purposes values quite contrary to his own, using the status acquired by craftsmen to attack the democracy on which that status rested. It is not unlikely that, as he did so, Plato had always in mind Protagoras's argument about the political qualifications of shoemaker and smith, a democratic argument more in keeping with the ethic of *technē*, insofar as that ethic reflected the status of craftsmen in democratic Athens, than was Plato's effort to turn the values of craftsmanship against their real adherents.

There is also another way in which Plato elaborates his political theory by turning Protagoras on his head. In the myth at the beginning of his long speech, Protagoras suggests that civilisation was based on the technical arts and skills which are the original attributes of mankind; but, he argues, it became necessary to acquire the political virtues, justice and respect for others [*aidos*], which create a bond of friendship among men, to allow men to act together and indeed to render their technical skills useful. To establish the bonds of cooperation that would enable them to benefit from the various arts, *all* men had to share in the political virtues. […]

In the *Republic*, Plato's argument seems designed precisely to turn Protagoras's view of the arts as the foundation of society against itself. Here, too, the argument begins with an imaginary construction of society on the basis of the 'arts' and technology; but the consequence is, of course, the reverse of political equality. Plato's foundation of society on the arts becomes an argument, not for a community of equals joined in a cooperative exercise of their arts, but for a hierarchical social division of labour in which politics, like other arts, is a specialised and exclusive skill, so that there is a rigid division between rulers and ruled, instead of a self-ruling community of citizens. Paradoxically, the very proposition that the *polis* is founded on the arts – a proposition that might easily be cited by shoemaker and smith in support of their political claims – becomes the basis for excluding their practitioners from politics. [...]

It was suggested at the outset that Plato's genius lies in his attempt to 'aristocratise' the *polis* and politicise the aristocracy, to transform the notion of the *polis* in such a way as to synthesise two essentially and historically antithetical principles, the political and the aristocratic. The *Republic* should be considered in the light of this suggestion. In that work, Plato systematically reconstructs the *polis* so that its very essence becomes the subordination of the community to a ruling class that personifies the values of the Athenian aristocracy. At the same time, he formulates the modern aristocratic code in such a way that it does not entail rejection of the *polis*. As extreme as his programme may appear, however, he does not go as far as he does in the *Laws*, a seemingly more moderate and practical work. In the *Republic* he does not yet outline a complete transformation of the economic and social infrastructure of the *polis*. Instead, he simply imagines the superimposition of a new aristocratic ruling class upon the existing social structure, and addresses himself primarily to the problem of philosophically justifying its rule. In the *Laws*, he will follow up the clues provided in the *Republic* and actually propose the kind of total transformation of the social structure which would make the existence of an aristocratic ruling class possible. In the *Republic*, he is not so much outlining a programme for the new *polis*, as constructing a philosophical foundation for aristocratic rule, primarily by transforming the *idea* of the *polis*, but in part also by reformulating the code of the aristocracy so that it might contribute to its own justification by proving its truly 'political' nature. [...]

[On] the whole, his theory of education, his account of the corruption of the philosophic nature and of the decline of the state all confirm the view that the virtues – courage, temperance, justice, grace, highmindedness, and love of truth (and consequently the truly essential differences of quality among human-beings) are *created*, not simply activated, by painstaking education and an upbringing in the proper conditions, a constant exposure to the 'beautiful' and 'harmonious', a careful avoidance of the 'vulgar' and 'base'. After all, the entire system of education is obviously predicated on the assumption that the desired qualities must be laboriously inculcated. 'Grace of body and mind [...] is only to be found in one who is brought up in the right way';[7] 'courage and steadfastness may [i.e., by proper training – E.M.W.] be united in a soul that would otherwise be either unmanly or boorish',[8] and so on. If,

---

7. Plato, *The Republic*, 401e [trans. Francis M. Cornford].
8. Plato, *The Republic*, 410d–411a.

however, upbringing and education are the decisive factors, it must be understood that the upbringing and education which Plato has in mind are not
simply a kind of schooling, but a total social condition. The ultimate dividing line between the 'educated' and 'uneducated' is the line between those
who work, especially with their hands, and those who have had a 'liberal
upbringing'. The education that makes the difference between virtue and vice
is clearly an aristocratic one, unmistakably based on the traditional education
received by the upper-class youths of Athens, before the 'new education' of
the Sophists. It is clearly an education for those who have been 'set free from
all manual crafts to be the artificers of their country's freedom, with the perfect mastery which comes of working only at what conduces to that end. [...]'[9]
Just as clearly, it is an education which is possible only for a very few, quite
irrespective of the distribution of talent in the population, given the existing
conditions of the division of labour and the necessity for the majority to be
engaged in 'base and menial' ('banausic') occupations. A life prepared for
such 'banausic' occupations, moreover, is the diametrical and essential opposite of a 'liberal' upbringing. [...]

It is difficult, then, to avoid the conclusion that the essential condition for
the existence of the virtuous or philosophic few is the ensured existence of
a class of men whose livelihood does not depend on their own labour or
trade and who can command the labour of others to supply their needs and
wants. In the *Republic*, that condition is met rather fancifully by the existence
of the gentlemen-guardians, who are the non-labouring, though propertyless,
servant-rulers of the community and whose basic needs are supplied by the
labour of the community, the 'productive' classes. In the *Laws*, the condition
is met in the more obvious – though, given the historical realities, no less
utopian – form of a ruling hereditary aristocracy of landowners (of varying
degrees of wealth in movable property) possessed of land acquired not by
purchase or exchange, but only by inheritance according to the strictest rules,
and commanding the labour of a non-citizen community of slaves, artisans,
craftsmen, and traders. Despite the differences between the ruling classes of
the two works, the fundamental conditions are present in both, and, in this
sense, the ruling class of the *Laws* can be seen as the concrete form of the
principle idealised in the ruling class of the *Republic*. If, in the *Republic*, Plato
remains ambiguous about the most crucial factor determining the quality of
souls, in the *Laws* he has apparently concluded that, whatever the likelihood
of gold breeding brass or brass breeding gold, there is far greater certainty

---

9. Plato, *The Republic*, 395b–c. The word *eleutheria*, translated as 'freedom' by
Cornford, is in fact ambiguous, denoting also the qualities to be found in the life of
an aristocrat, or 'gentlemanliness'.

that labour will breed corruption; and he appears to have decided that if virtue is to survive in the world, it must be ensured that the social conditions, if not the natural qualities, for virtue be preserved and inherited. The *Republic*, however, for all its ambiguity, already points in the direction of the *Laws* in this respect, too. A central theme of the *Republic* is the doctrine that the health of a man's soul depends, first, on the total social context which surrounds him – that is, the nature of the society in which he lives – and, second, on the particular position he occupies in that social context. It is clear that, barring the rarest of accidents, even the noblest natures – like Alcibiades or Critias – possessed of native intelligence, distinguished by birth, bred in an aristocratic household, and even educated by Socrates himself, will be unable to withstand corruption by life in a democracy – that is, life in a society dominated by vulgar natures.[10] It is equally clear that whatever the nature of the society, democratic or aristocratic, the man who occupies a lowly position, the man who earns his livelihood, will possess a warped and stunted soul. A well-governed society, then, *must* be one that is ruled by men who are not subject to either form of corruption – the inherent corruption of the mob itself, or the corruption of an aristocrat led astray by the mob; it must, therefore, be a society governed by an exclusive ruling class composed of men whose livelihood does not depend on their own labour or trade, who can command the labour of others, and who, of course, share a common and exclusive kind of cultivation and refinement. A more effective philosophical basis for arguing the case of the traditional Athenian landed aristocracy can hardly be imagined than the principles established in the *Republic* and implemented in the *Laws*. [...]

Plato's proposal in the *Laws* for a radical transformation of society in many ways reverses several centuries of Athenian history, while it seeks at the same time to retain the fruits of that history – that is, to retain the *polis* as the basic principle of association, together with its cultural legacy. The proposal in a sense involves a return to the agrarian-aristocratic society of Homeric times, without a return to the *oikos*-centered primitivism of that society; and it provides an ingenious and perceptive, if utopian, account of the social and economic conditions necessary for the establishment of such an historical anomaly. The *Laws* represents a detailed programme for the establishment of a *polis* firmly grounded in the aristocratic division between non-labouring landowners and non-landowning labourers, a *polis* ruled by a hereditary landed nobility whose wealth is based on inheritance and the labour of others, which is at their command by virtue of their inheritance. The object of

---

10. Plato, *The Republic*, 496b–e.

this social transformation is to breed a virtuous citizen-body and to avoid 'the servile yoke of rule by the base' and a 'polity which will breed baser men'.[11]

The fundamental principle of the laws in the 'Magnesian' *polis*, then, is that there are certain occupations and conditions in life that are corrupting and others that are not; and that inasmuch as many will have to pursue a corrupting course in life if the society's work is to be done and if others are to be able to lead an untainted life, there must be a clear and fixed separation between the two kinds of life, and citizenship must be confined to the untainted. The citizens will be 'men whose necessities have been moderately provided for, their trades and crafts put into other hands, their lands let out to villeins who render from the produce such rent as is sufficient for sober livers'.[12] All those who supply the livelihood of these citizens, all those who engage in the necessary trades and crafts, all the 'villeins', slaves, and merchants, will be deprived of citizenship and the ownership of land on which it is based. [...]

By Plato's time [...] landed property was to a great extent alienable, and the buying and selling of land was a common practice; so that his proposed system of land-tenure is consciously archaic, perhaps modelled on Sparta, or possibly on traditions about aristocratic Athens, and clearly opposed to the system of property that existed in the Athens of his day. The fact that he proposes it and regards it as fundamental to his utopia demonstrates his understanding of the economic conditions that underlie the social, cultural, and moral developments he deplores and the weight he attaches to those economic conditions. In order to reverse the 'corruption' of democratic Athens, Plato proposes a reversion to a system of land-tenure appropriate to a pre-political, almost feudal aristocracy, but now enforced by well-developed political institutions. His stated object in reverting to such a system of land-tenure is, of course, to stave off commercialism and materialism; but it is not out of any concern about the possibilities of exploitation inherent in a system of free private property. On the contrary, his aim is to recreate an all-powerful aristocratic class with undisputed power based on hereditary inalienable and indivisible land with a command of labour even more complete than that of the early Attic aristocracy. He proposes to achieve this aim by rigidly fixing the positions of the classes and drawing more clearly than ever the line between landowning aristocracy and non-landowning commons, between appropriators and producers, eliminating the grey areas, freezing the position of each class as never before in explicit and enforceable statutory law, with the whole institutional apparatus of the *polis* to support it. His society is, without qualification,

---

11. Plato, *Laws*, 770e [trans. A.E. Taylor].
12. Plato, *Laws*, 806d.

divided between a landowning citizenry and everyone else – slave, labourer, artisan, or metic-merchant – whose primary purpose is to serve the landowning citizenry; and, as never before, the institutions of the *polis* are available to enforce and perpetuate the very social structure that the historical *polis* had helped to undermine.

The Greek concept of freedom

The peasant-utopia has, of course, never existed. There has never been a peasant-community completely free of taxes, rents, fees, tithes or labour-services, a 'free village' in which smallholders have had absolute security of tenure and freedom from subjection to a higher authority in the shape of a landlord or state. The aspirations of peasants for this kind of independence have, however, made themselves felt in various ways – in peasant-rebellions, in political and religious movements, and in cultural traditions.

Many of the most cherished ideals of Athenian culture, and even some of the most exalted notions of Greek philosophy, may owe their origins to the experience and aspirations of the Attic peasantry. If, as Robin Osborne maintains, Attic smallholders cannot properly be called peasants 'in any strong sense of that word', on the grounds that they were not clearly dominated or exploited by 'outsiders', and that 'there is no evidence at all for their possessing a distinct cultural tradition',[13] it may be because the whole of Athenian culture was so thoroughly imbued with the values of the peasant-citizen that the cultural traditions of the smallholder are not visibly distinct.

While even the most democratic *polis* was far from a peasant-utopia, the peasant-citizen came as close as any peasant ever has to the freedom described by Wolf,[14] and his deme as close as any peasant-community ever has to the ideal of the 'free village' – not as a 'homemade' social order divorced from the state, but precisely as the basic constituent unit of the state through which the peasant, for the first time, had access to this formerly alien 'negative quantity'. But even short of the democratic *polis*, the experience of the

---

13. Osborne 1985, p. 142. In Osborne 1987 he writes of the 'concealment of agriculture', remarking on the paradox that: 'On the one hand the productive countryside was of fundamental importance. On the other the arts and literature of Classical Greece largely ignore it' (p. 16). The book as a whole is devoted to demonstrating how completely the social life of Greek cities was determined by the countryside and 'the peasant basis of society' (p. 13). And nowhere was this more true than in Athens, with its 'radical recognition of the countryside as integral to the political machine of the city' (p. 130). In other words, the 'peasant basis of society', and a peasant-'culture', may have been invisible because they were ubiquitous.
14. Wolf 1971, p. 272.

peasant-citizen even in more limited forms was distinctive enough to produce unprecedented cultural patterns and ideas.

An example of how the aspirations of peasants, the striving for a particular kind of independence, autonomy and self-sufficiency motivated by the particular experience of peasant-dependence, might be diffused throughout society and become part of a more general cultural ideal, is suggested by Rodney Hilton's observation that 'it might be said that the concept of the freeman, owing no obligation, not even deference, to an overlord, is one of the most important if intangible legacies of mediaeval peasants to the modern world'.[15] Hilton is surely wrong to credit the medieval peasant with inventing the concept of the freeman. A strong case can be made that the credit belongs to the ancient Greeks. As the chorus of Persian elders tells the king's mother in Aeschylus's play *The Persians*,[16] to be an Athenian citizen is to be masterless, a servant to no mortal man. It has often been remarked that the Greek and Roman ideas of freedom, referring both to states and to individuals, have no parallel elsewhere in the ancient world: 'it is impossible,' writes M.I. Finley, 'to translate the word "freedom", *eleutheria* in Greek, *libertas* in Latin, or "free man", into any ancient Near Eastern language, including Hebrew, or into any ancient Far Eastern language either, for that matter'.[17] It seems undeniable that this apparently unprecedented idea was one of the most important cultural legacies of the Greco-Roman world. But Hilton's comment is suggestive because it locates the impetus for the invention of this far-reaching idea in the experience of the peasant. It is worth considering how the ideals of autonomy and self-sufficiency so central to Greek, and especially Athenian, culture might be traceable to the peasant-experience.

The uniqueness of the Greek and Roman concepts is often attributed to the importance of slavery in these societies, on the grounds that the absolute servility of the slave brought out in sharp relief the freedom of the citizen and evoked an unprecedented consciousness of individual liberty. There can be no doubt that the uniquely sharp and dichotomous contrast of freedom and servility in Greek and Roman systems of ideas is in some way related to the inseparable nexus of citizen and slave; but just as the latter itself cannot simply be explained by the proposition that the bondage of the slave produced the freedom of the citizen, neither is it convincing to treat slavery as the condition for the concept of freedom. Nor is it enough to say that the two ideas have been inseparable from the start. While it is no doubt true that the juridical clarity of the servile condition and that of the citizen's freedom defined

---

15. Hilton 1973, p. 235.
16. Aeschylus, *The Persians*, 241 ff.
17. Finley 1973, p. 28.

one another, we should not allow the conceptual unity of this dichotomy in its fully developed juridical form to obscure the possibility that the idea of freedom preceded the unusual expansion of slavery; that it was born of the unique experience of the peasantry in relation to landlord and state; and that, although the idea may have awaited the growth of slavery in order to reach its fullest conceptual clarity, the autonomy of the peasant and its conceptual recognition were preconditions to the juridical definition of the slave. Or, to put it another way, it was not until the peasant was liberated that the concept of slavery could be separated out with any clarity from more general and inclusive notions of servitude. In other civilisations where there existed no concept comparable to the Greek and Roman notions of freedom, there was certainly no lack of servile and dependent conditions, including slavery; what was missing was a stark contrast between servility and freedom. It was only when the whole spectrum of dependence between slavery and freedom was wiped out – a spectrum largely occupied by peasants in various conditions of juridical and political subordination – that the gap widened to permit a dichotomous conceptual distinction. [...]

Although *eleutheria* would always retain the element of privilege and belonging to an exclusive community, it acquired another dimension once the *angle of vision* changed, when freedom was seen from the vantage-point of the *un*privileged, those who needed to be *made* free. In Solon, we see the first explicit evidence of this new perspective, from the viewpoint of the liberator: he *freed* what had been *enslaved* – land and people; the peasants who had served aristocratic landlords were now *eleutheroi* – free from obligations of tribute and service to their aristocratic compatriots.[18]

At this critical moment, and at this angle of vision, *eleutheria* derives its meaning from an opposition not to chattel-slavery, but to the formerly dependent condition of the peasantry. If the *eleutheria* of the peasants is defined by contrast to their former *douleia*, it is not *douleia* in the sense of chattel-slavery, but in the older sense of a 'non-belonging' tributary population. Indeed it is perhaps only now that *doulos* begins to refer unambiguously to the chattel-slave, as the spectrum of servile conditions disappears and slaves alone remain in the (literal) condition of *douleia*, as unprivileged outsiders bound to the service of their masters. It is only now that they become, by default, exclusive claimants to the title of *douloi*. On the one hand, *doulos* as a category

---

18. See Beringer 1985, pp. 51–2, where it is suggested that there is nothing metaphorical or imprecise about Aristotle's usage of the verb *douleuein* in the *Constitution of Athens* to describe the condition of the peasants liberated by Solon, as long as we understand that words of the root *doul-* referred not to chattel-slavery, but to 'non-belongingness', 'rightlessness', and 'subjectedness'.

of persons seems to have predated the category of *eleutheros*, whose 'freedom' could be taken for granted; on the other hand, though slaves existed, *douloi* could not become clearly and exclusively identified with chattel-slaves until it was no longer possible for peasants to be *douloi*, that is, when *personal* dependence completely absorbed the ancient division between ruling and subject communities. The sharp *eleutheria/douleia* dichotomy of classical times – and probably the massive growth of slavery itself – presupposed the liberation of the peasantry.

The Greek concept of freedom cannot be adequately defined either as an appropriation of aristocratic privilege, nor as the antithesis to chattel-slavery, even if each of these definitions contains an element of historical truth. It is the status of 'the multitude [*to plethos*]' in relation to their erstwhile lords, and to those who still aspire to lordship over them, that gives the concept its distinctive emphasis on individual autonomy and masterlessness, the quality which for Aeschylus distinguished Athens so radically from states with *subjects* and no *citizens*. The Athenian citizen is the man who, like Hilton's free man, owes no service or deference to any man. It is only from this vantage-point that it makes sense to say, as Aristotle does, that freedom and equality (*eleutheria* and *isonomia*) are the essential characteristics of democracy, as distinct from other types of *polis*.[19]

Once the democratic meaning of *eleutheria* had firmly established itself, two conceptual strategies were available to opponents of democracy. They could redefine *eleutheria* to exclude *to plethos*, or they could give it – the *eleutheria* of peasants and craftsmen – a pejorative meaning. Both of these strategies were adopted by the great anti-democratic philosophers of classical times. A new aristocratic concept of *eleutheria* was invoked as a way of excluding the *demos* from the life of true citizenship by defining freedom to exclude the condition of those who must labour for a livelihood. This exclusive conception, however, required a departure from conventional usage. When, for example, Aristotle identifies the *eleutheros* with the gentleman who does not live 'at another's beck and call' because he practises no 'sordid' or 'menial' craft,[20] and when in his outline of the ideal state in the *Politics* he treats all working farmers, craftsmen and shopkeepers as servile 'conditions' of the *polis*, whose services make possible the life of true citizenship for the few who are integral 'parts' of the state, he is clearly redefining the dichotomy of freedom and servility as understood by the ordinary Athenian, the peasant or artisan who regarded himself as free. He is also departing from the usage which goes back at least to

19. Aristotle, *Politics*, 1291b, 1310a, 1317a–b (trans. Ernest Barker).
20. Aristotle, *Rhetoric*, 1367a 28–32 (trans. W. Rhys Roberts).

Solon, who applied the concept both to the land and to the men whom he had freed in his *seisachtheia*, referring to the liberated peasants as *eleutheroi*.[21]

Insofar as there existed in classical Athens a distinctively aristocratic conception of freedom, then, it was, in a sense, derivative. It is as if aristocratic opponents of democracy responded to the *eleutheria* of the *demos* by appropriating and narrowing the conception of freedom. For ordinary Athenians, the peasants and craftsmen who constituted the bulk of the citizen-body, *eleutheria* meant freedom from subjection to another, whether as a slave or in some other condition of dependence. It was only for those of aristocratic persuasion, who opposed the democracy precisely because it treated peasants and craftsmen as *eleutheroi*, that the notion of servility might be expanded to include anyone who was obliged to labour for a livelihood. For one type of citizen, *eleutheria* meant the freedom *of* labour; for the other, it meant the freedom *from* labour. To conflate these two meanings by tracing the Greek concept of freedom to the 'confiscation' of aristocratic values is perhaps to reproduce the confusion created by Jacob Burckhardt when he attributes to the *demos* an aversion to labour traceable to the anti-banausic attitude of their aristocratic forebears, or when he, like so many others, speaks of the *demos*'s idleness when he means their freedom from servitude.[22] The association of *eleutheria* with a contempt for necessary or even useful labour is an aristocratic accretion, and perhaps the best indication that the aristocratic concept of freedom was largely a negative one – *anti*-banausic – defined against the freedom of the *demos*. The aristocratic redefinition of freedom was, as it were, a way of raising the stakes.

An alternative way of turning the concept of *eleutheria* against the democracy was to use it as a term of abuse. Given the tendency to associate freedom with democracy in Athenian culture, it might seem inappropriate for an opponent of democracy to treat *eleutheria* as a virtue. Plato's definition of *eleutheria* as *licence* is the most familiar example of this reconceptualisation.[23] Aristotle may also be tending towards this view of democratic freedom as indistinguishable from licence or anarchy when he defines it as 'living as you like'.[24] And it is, certainly, the intention of the pseudo-Xenophontic account of the Athenian constitution, commonly known as the 'Old Oligarch', to depict democratic freedom as synonymous with licence and indiscipline, so much so, he maintains, that even metics and slaves in Athens lead 'singularly undisciplined' lives.[25]

---

21. Solon, fr. 36.
22. Burckhardt 1929, pp. 254–5.
23. Plato, *The Republic*, 557b ff.
24. Aristotle, *Politics*, 1317b.
25. *The Constitution of the Athenians*, I. 11–12.

In fact, as we shall see, there is much else in Athenian culture and philoso-phy that can be interpreted as a reactive adaptation of concepts which were demotic in inspiration or had acquired a democratic meaning, an attempt to redefine these concepts to deprive them of their democratic implications. In any case, the Greek concept of freedom was neither simply a response to slav-ery, nor an extension of aristocratic values, but an expression of the peasant-experience, sharpened and refined by the interaction of citizens and slaves and by the refraction of peasant-values through aristocratic opposition.

The Greek concepts of freedom and autonomy, then, may have their roots in the experience of a free peasantry, a distinctive phenomenon which existed not only in the democracy, where the last vestiges of peasant-dependence dis-appeared with the abolition of debt-bondage and clientship in the reforms of Solon, but perhaps even before those reforms and in any *polis* in which peasants were not serfs or helots, permanently subjected to an alien ruling community. In fact, it is worth noting the extent to which all three aspects of freedom – the individual freedom of the masterless citizen, the freedom of the citizen community from subjection to a ruler or despot (*despotēs* is the word which describes the master of slaves), and the autonomy of the *polis* in rela-tion to other states – were conceived in terms of freedom from the necessity to work for another. So, for example, Herodotus,[26] in his famous explanation of Athenian strength in the Persian Wars, attributes the unique courage and zeal of the Athenians to the fact that, having become a free people by overthrow-ing the tyrants, they no longer 'worked for a master', but for themselves. And just as the free peasant is one who is not subject to a juridically determined and politically enforced extraction of surplus-labour by virtue of a depen-dent status, so the truly free and autonomous state is one that not only gov-erns itself by its own laws, but also owes no tribute to another state.[27] For the Greeks, to be the subject of a king was also to labour for him, perhaps even to be looked upon as part of his *household* (like the tax- and tribute-paying sub-jects of the 'redistributive' kingdoms?). In an admirable description of a free people, a speech in Euripides's *Suppliants*[28] counts among the blessings of a free city not only the fact that the rule of law allows equal justice to rich and poor, strong and weak, alike, and that anyone who has something useful to say has the right to speak before the public, but also that here the labours of

26. Herodotus, *Histories*, V. 78.
27. It is worth noting that in Rome, too, 'the relation between king and people is considered to be analogous to the relation between master and slaves. Consequently monarchy is called dominatio; and subjection to monarchy servitus'. Wirszubski 1950, p. 5. On similar principles, a *populus liber*, an autonomous people or state, is opposed to a *populus stipendiarius*, a people subject to tribute (Wirszubski 1950, p. 4).
28. Euripides, *The Suppliants*, 429 ff.

a free citizen are not wasted, in contrast to despotic states, where one labours simply in order to enrich the tyrant by one's toil.

All these conceptions reflect the close connection which existed in antiquity between political power and the right of appropriation. As in medieval Europe, where the peasants' demand for freedom also gave rise to a conception of the freeman who owed nothing to an overlord, the Greek conception of freedom was conditioned by the unity of political and economic power. In the medieval case, that unity was embodied in the concept of *lordship*, which entailed a juridical status, a political authority, and an economic power, all at once and inseparably. And it is significant that, as Hilton points out, the medieval peasants' demand for freedom was, above all, a demand for an end to lordship. It is, however, worth noting that the famous rebel-leader, Wat Tyler, expressed the demand for the abolition of lordship by proposing that it be distributed among all men. 'This would mean the liquidation of lordship,' writes Hilton, 'but it is an interesting indication of the power of the notion of lordship that its equal partition rather than its abolition was proposed.'[29] The Greek conception of *citizenship*, which can be regarded as a 'confiscation' or equal distribution of aristocratic powers and privileges, has something in common with this perception of what freedom for the peasant would entail. In both cases, as is typically true in precapitalist societies, the traditional power of the aristocracy to appropriate the labour of peasants had been inseparable from a privileged juridical and political status; and in both cases, the freedom of the peasant could be perceived as depending upon his appropriation of that status. [...]

If a disdain for dependent labour can be regarded as a universal cultural norm in Athens, and if few Athenians were likely to dissent from the view that labouring for a livelihood could be arduous and painful, the same universality cannot be attributed to the outright contempt for labour and labourers displayed by Plato or Xenophon. In fact, the attitudes of anti-democrats like Plato, Xenophon, or Aristotle themselves constitute convincing evidence that the prevailing cultural ideal was very different from the one they espoused. Their complaint against the democracy was, after all, that the 'banausic' multitude was in command and that its servile mentality had placed its stamp on the *polis*. In other words, those who were most vociferous in their expressions of contempt for labour were clearly not *reflecting* but *attacking* the dominant world-view.

The suggestion that the pejorative judgement of labour – as distinct from the disdain for dependence or the failure positively to glorify work – derives from

---

29. Hilton 1973, p. 225.

its association with slavery obscures the most important facts about this attitude: that it was a class-prejudice more than a universal cultural ideal, and that its principal inspiration was not the existence of slaves, but the predominance of labouring *citizens*. The denigration of labour and labourers to be found in Greek literature, while perhaps especially emphatic precisely because of the unusual status enjoyed by free producers in the democracy, is certainly not uniquely characteristic of slave-societies, but can be found among propertied classes in other times and places, especially at moments when the interests and power of the privileged few have been challenged by classes engaged in the despised activities. Indeed, it is difficult to think of a more common defence of class-privilege than the idea that the 'mechanic' multitude, enslaved in body and mind by the vulgar concerns of subsistence, cannot rise above its base preoccupations and, if admitted to the public councils, must bring to them only 'confusion and tumult, or servility and corruption'.[30]

Jean-Jacques Rousseau

A word, first, about Rousseau's argument itself. The general will is usually treated by commentators – whether hostile or sympathetic to Rousseau – as simply a principle governing the conduct of *citizens*. In the 'Political Economy', however, Rousseau's general will has a different object. Here, Rousseau's argument is, in the first instance, directed not at the individual citizen, but at the 'magistrate', or rulers. His purpose in attacking the household/state analogy is to demonstrate that the magistrate cannot legitimately act in accordance with principles appropriate to the head of a household. 'The principal object of the efforts of the whole house', argues Rousseau, 'is to conserve and increase the patrimony of the father [...]'.[31] This principle of private, domestic 'economy', if applied to the state – treating the state as a means of increasing the 'patrimony' of the magistrate – is fatal to the public interest. The magistrate, therefore, unlike the father who governs the household, cannot rely on his personal, natural inclinations and passions as a standard for governing the state, but must follow 'no other rule but public reason, which is the law'.[32] The concept of the *general will* is introduced to express the uniquely public principle that should regulate the governance of the 'political economy', the management of the state. It is the principle to be followed by the magistrate,

---

30. See Ferguson 1978, p. 187.
31. Rousseau 1964b, p. 242.
32. Rousseau 1964b, p. 243.

the government, whose function is simply to execute the public 'will' which expresses the interests of the community.

At this stage in Rousseau's argument, then, the concept of the general will represents an attempt to define the state as a truly *public* thing, not a form of private property, and to locate the legitimacy of government in its adherence to the public will and interests of the people and not the private will and interests of the magistrate. We shall see later how Rousseau extends the principle of the general will to the community of citizens, especially in the *Social Contract*; but to appreciate fully the significance of his argument and his reasons for formulating it in this way, one needs to know what *problems* he was addressing and why these problems presented themselves to him precisely as they did. [...]

Like Bodin and Montchrétien, for example, Rousseau approaches the issue of the French state by first considering the household/state analogy; and he effectively declares his opposition to the prevailing principles of that state by immediately attacking the analogy. Both Bodin, and even the less 'absolutist' Montchrétien, construct the analogy on the assumption that the king, with the help of his officers, is the appropriate agent of the common good, the representative of universality and the general or public interest, as against the particular and partial interests which comprise the body-politic. It is precisely this assumption, as we have seen, that Rousseau rejects when he attacks the household/state-analogy. His own argument is based on the contrary assumption that rulers are just as likely as are their subjects – indeed, even more likely – to represent a particular or partial interest. The household/state-analogy – in which the state is treated, in effect, as a private estate – for Rousseau, simply confirms the reality of the French state and the use of public office, including the office of king, as private property. He therefore insists that a completely different principle – opposed to the private motivations of household-management, with its goal of increasing the patrimony of the master – must guide the management of the state.

Having criticised the analogy on which the notion of 'political economy' is based, he must then go on to redefine 'political economy' itself accordingly, in keeping with the uniquely public purpose of the state. It is here that he introduces the distinction between sovereignty, the supreme legislative power, and government or 'public economy', which merely executes the will of the sovereign.[33] Rousseau was not the first to draw a distinction between sovereignty and government. Significantly, the credit for this distinction must go to Bodin. The differences between Bodin and Rousseau on this score, however, are even

---

33. Rousseau 1964b, p. 244.

more striking than the similarities. Bodin distinguishes between the form of state, based on the location of sovereignty, and the form of government, based on the principle by which lands, offices, and honours are distributed – so that a monarchy, for example, can be governed aristocratically or democratically, according to how the sovereign monarch chooses to grant honours and pre-ferments. His purpose is clearly to demonstrate that, however powers and offices may be distributed, these powers are ultimately vested in the sover-eign, and that it is in effect by the will of the sovereign that they are so distrib-uted. The powers of officeholders or nobles are not held by proprietary right, but by virtue of delegation from the sovereign – ideally, the sovereign in the person of a monarch. In this respect, the distinction between state and gov-ernment, and the implied distinction between the sovereign legislative power and the subordinate power of execution, serves to reinforce Bodin's attack on feudal prerogatives and baronial anarchy, as well as on any other proprietary claims to political power apart from those of the sovereign. This feudal 'par-celisation' of power, rather than 'divided sovereignty' in the English parlia-mentary sense, is, again, the main target of his insistence on the indivisibility of sovereignty. His practical object in distinguishing the form of government from the form of state, therefore, is to sustain and enhance the authority of the monarchy against other particularistic claims to political power.

Rousseau's purpose in adopting a similar conceptual device is precisely the opposite of Bodin's. Although, like Bodin, he identifies sovereignty with the power of legislation and maintains the indivisibility of sovereign power, his object in doing so is quite different. Where Bodin's argument is a defence of royal absolutism, Rousseau's is an attack upon it. Rousseau's distinction – again, in a sense, like Bodin's – is intended to relegate the functions of the magistrate or government to a subordinate position, subject to and dependent upon a higher principle or 'general will'. His intention, however, is not to consolidate, but to undermine, the power of rulers. The 'magistrate' stands not only for lesser officials, but for all rulers, including kings; and the general will becomes not the will of the ruler, not an expression of his supremacy, but a token of his subordination to the community. In a sense, where Bodin subordinates the particularity of the people to the universality of the ruler, Rousseau subordinates the particularity of the ruler to the universality of the people. For Rousseau, the sovereign will is not something that constitutes a community out of particular and partial interests by imposing itself from without through royal legislation and the art of public management or 'polit-ical economy'. Instead, it is something that emanates from the community itself, expressing its actual common interests, and is imposed on those – the magistrate, the government, the agents of 'public economy' – whose function is merely to execute that will. The logic of this argument demands that it culminate in a radical theory of popular sovereignty, giving full effect to the principle that the sovereign will emanates from the community by actually vesting the sovereign legislative power in a popular assembly. Whether or not in the 'Political Economy' Rousseau was already prepared to pursue that logic to its conclusion, he certainly did so in the *Social Contract*.

If Rousseau's argument owes a great deal in its form to the idiom of absolutism (as commentators have suggested)[34] and to the language of a single, supreme and indivisible public will, he turns that idiom against itself. As many theorists have done, he adopts the form of his adversary's argument to attack its substance. There may be an element of truth in the proposition that the only French 'tradition of discourse' to which Rousseau was 'not much indebted' was constitutionalism and that, while 'he was one of the great proponents of the rule of law [...] his dedication to that principle was distinct from that of French constitutionalists such as Domat or Montesquieu.' In particular:

> In Rousseau's theory, law is identified with the sovereign will, as it was in the absolutist tradition, rather than an external bridle on that will, as it was in the constitutive laws of the French polity. His hostility to intermediate bodies in the state and scorn for representative assemblies, set him off clearly from the constitutionalist tradition.[35]

If Rousseau departed from the constitutionalist tradition, however, it is in part because the mainstream of French constitutionalism (and arguably even its radical Huguenot form) did not imply – as did English constitutionalism – a transfer of sovereign legislative power to the 'people' even as embodied in representative institutions.[36] To 'bridle' the sovereign will meant to guide or direct it, not to limit or check the power of the sovereign by appropriating a piece of his sovereignty. Rousseau's concern is not merely to 'bridle' the absolutist monarchy, but to overturn it, not simply to guide sovereign power, but to transfer it. In this respect, one might argue that, despite his dismissal of English representative institutions no less than French, Rousseau has something in common with the mainstream of English constitutionalism, if not French, to the extent that the English conception of limited, constitutional government has identified – in theory and practice – the limitation of royal power not simply with juristic 'bridles', but with the actual transfer of

34. See, for example, Keohane 1980, pp. 442–9.
35. Keohane 1980, p. 442.
36. Even the Huguenot tracts speak of the fiscal powers of the Estates and their right to be regularly *consulted*, but it is not clear that representative institutions are conceived as *legislative* bodies.

legislative authority. There is, however, another sense in which Rousseau's argument is, after all, best understood in relation to French constitutionalism, at least in its more radical form as exemplified by the Huguenot resistance-movement.[37]

The ideological strategy adopted by the Huguenot constitutionalists in their assault on absolutism was [...] to confront absolutism on its own ground by stressing the particularity of the monarch, attacking his treatment of the state as private property. They insisted, instead, on the 'people's' proprietary right in the state, asserting that the 'people' constitute the 'majesty' of the king, and transferred the public 'mind' from the king to the 'people' embodied in their officers and representative institutions – 'one mind compounded out of many'. Rousseau's strategy is strikingly similar – except in one decisive respect. He also proceeds by attacking the proprietary character of the absolutist state and the particularity of the ruler, and counterposes to them a common public will residing in the community; and he also maintains that the ruler is constituted by the people. However, he perceives a threat not only in the particularity of the monarch but in that of the 'magistrate' in general. He therefore locates the public will not in the 'public council', in officials and 'intermediate bodies', or in assemblies of Estates, but in the people themselves.

Rousseau's attitude towards 'intermediate bodies' is often regarded as one of the more alarming aspects of his thought, an attack on the most cherished principles of liberalism, checks on state-power, the freedom of association and opinion, of individual dissent and minority-rights, and so on. This is, again, to misread Rousseau's meaning by extracting his argument from its historical setting. Rousseau's refusal to lodge the public will in intermediate institutions does, indeed, cut him off from the French constitutionalist tradition, even in its most radical forms. His rejection of these institutions, however, should not be understood as a ('totalitarian') violation of constitutionalist principles, but rather as an attempt to extend and democratise them. Rousseau shares with the radical constitutionalists their concern for transforming the state into a truly 'public' thing which derives its public or general character from the people. That is precisely the message of the 'Political Economy'. In the *Social Contract*, if not so unequivocally in the earlier article, he advances from the creation of a truly public magistrate – a magistrate answerable in some unspecified way to the demands of the common good, the 'general will' – to the actual embodiment of that common good and the general will in a functioning popular sovereign. If, in the process, he resumes the language of absolutism, in order to

---

37. Rousseau's own association with Geneva and Calvinism should, of course, not be forgotten.

vest in the people the powers hitherto lodged in the absolute monarchy, he travels that route not past, but through, the concerns of constitutionalism and the tradition of popular resistance.

It is again a question of historical perspective. The 'intermediate bodies' that concern the French constitutionalists are not the 'voluntary associations' so dear to the heart of English liberals, organisations in the private sphere as distinct from – and, at least potentially, against – organs of the state.[38] The French 'intermediate bodies' are the corporate and representative institutions – Estates, *parlements*, municipalities, and colleges – which constituted part of '*la police*', organs of the polity. It is these institutions whose role in the state constitutionalists proposed to increase – in varying degrees and with varying preferences for some over others. Neither, however, are these 'bodies' legislative assemblies on the model of the English Parliament. These institutions were, in effect, feudal remnants, fragments of the feudal 'parcelised' state. They were recognised – and defended – as such by constitutionalists even as late as Montesquieu, who regarded these elements of 'Gothic' government as essential to the 'moderation' and legitimacy of the French monarchy. This implied, too, that the notion of intermediate bodies was – in the eighteenth century, as before – often closely associated with the defence of *aristocratic* power and might be not only undemocratic, but anti-democratic, in spirit. In the eighteenth century, even more explicitly than before, the principle of 'particular' or intermediate powers interposed between king and people was invoked to support the enlargement of power for the nobility, as in the so-called '*thèse nobiliaire*'. In these formulations, moreover, the claims of the nobility against the absolutist monarchy were likely to be equally claims against the Third Estate. The notion of constitutional checks and balances thus assumed a clearly aristocratic cast. The theory of intermediate powers was opposed to popular power more unequivocally than were English theories of representation, however undemocratic the intentions of the latter might be. Those who, like Montesquieu, preferred the *parlements* as the model of intermediate powers only partly modified the aristocratic character of the principle by extending it to include the *noblesse de robe*. Even in more radical and anti-absolutist or constitutionalist formulations, as [...] in the case of the

---

38. As for Rousseau's views on voluntary associations, it is worth considering his remarks on the *cercles* of Geneva in the *Lettre à d'Alembert* and his answers to criticisms of these remarks voiced by his friends among the burghers of Geneva who felt that the *cercles* corrupted the republic's artisans and gave them an excessive taste for independence. Rousseau suggests in reply that these *cercles* provide the appropriate education for free citizens, midway between the public education of Greece and the domestic education of monarchies 'where all subjects must remain isolated and must have nothing in common but obedience.' See Rousseau 1965–98, p. 743.

Huguenots, the insistence on intermediate bodies had the deliberate effect of limiting not only monarchical, but also popular power – for example, by stressing that the right of resistance belonged to the 'people' only as embodied in their officers and corporate representatives. Given the historical meaning and ideological function of these institutions in French political experience, the defence of intermediate bodies did not lend itself so easily to democratic extrapolation and extension – not even to the extent permitted by English theories of parliamentary representation.[39] A democratic argument such as Rousseau's would, in that context, almost inevitably be formulated as an attack on intermediate institutions.

In the end, the question comes down to the particular social interests at stake. For those who felt aggrieved at their inadequate access to the means of extra-economic appropriation provided by the state, for those who – even when they were subject to the state's appropriation through taxation – themselves appropriated the labour of others, constitutional reforms designed to give them a piece of the state might serve very well. But these were not the interests represented by Rousseau. His concern – clearly expressed in the article on 'Political Economy' – was for those on whose labour the whole structure of privilege, office, and taxation rested: small producers, and notably peasants. Much of the 'Political Economy' is devoted to the problem of taxation, and Rousseau's proposals for reforming the fiscal system are explicitly designed to relieve the peasants who bear its brunt. It is here that he provides the clearest insight into his view of the existing state as a system of private appropriation and exploitation – and this is the specific target of his proposals for reform:

> Are not all advantages of society for the powerful and rich? Do they not fill all lucrative posts? Are not all privileges and exemptions reserved for them?[40]

> [...] [W]hatever the poor pay is lost to them forever, and remains in or returns to the hands of the rich; and, as it is precisely to those men who take part in government, or to their connections, that the proceeds of taxation sooner or later pass, even when they pay their share they have a keen interest in increasing taxes.'[41]

---

39. John Locke, for example, vests a right of resistance not in intermediate bodies or 'magistrates', but in the 'people' themselves *against* 'magistrates'. While his conception of the 'people' is certainly exclusive and restrictive, the category 'people' is, as it were, more fluid, less easily controlled, and more readily expanded by democrats than the category 'magistrates' which figures in Huguenot-resistance doctrine.

40. Rousseau 1964b, p. 271.

41. Rousseau 1964b, p. 272.

Thus, suggests Rousseau, the terms of the social contract between the two conditions of men can be summed up as follows: 'You need me, because I am rich and you are poor; let us therefore make an agreement: I will permit you the honour of serving me, on the condition that you give me the little that remains to you for the pains I shall take to command you.'[42] This, then, is the principle on which taxation is now based. Rousseau proposes a system of taxation based on opposing principles, by reforming the state to eliminate the use of taxation as a means of private appropriation, and by transferring the tax-burden for clearly public purposes to those more able to bear it, in a system of progressive taxation. He dismisses with contempt the idea that the peasant will lapse into idleness if not compelled to work by the demands of taxation: 'Because for him who loses the fruits of his labour, to do nothing is to gain something; and to impose a fine on labour is a very odd way of banishing idleness.'[43]

Rousseau was not, of course, alone in proposing to reform the system of taxation, privilege, and exemption, corrupt administration and venal offices. Similar reforms were part of the Enlightenment-agenda in general, with its demands for rationalisation of the state and the fiscal apparatus, the unification of law and administration, and a system of office open to merit. All these proposals for reform were, in one way or another, directly or indirectly, conditioned by the function of the state as an instrument of appropriation, a private resource – even if some reformers wanted only to extend access to its fruits. And many reformers were convinced of the need to redistribute the burden of taxation in order to stop the drain on the countryside which fed the luxuries of city and court. Rousseau, however, was alone among the great Enlightenment-thinkers to focus on the political structure specifically as a system of exploitation, and to do so not simply from the paternalistic vantage-point of enlightened appropriators, but from the perspective of the petty producers whose labour was exploited. He could not, therefore, be content with reforms that would merely rationalise the apparatus of exploitation, giving greater equality or more political representation to the appropriators themselves. To the extent that his political reforms were intended to attack the state not simply as an inefficient, unequal, or illiberal system of administration and representation, but as a system of exploitation, he had eventually to conclude that only absolute popular sovereignty, as the sole means of displacing altogether the proprietary state, would suffice.

---

42. Rousseau 1964b, p. 273.
43. Ibid.

Once Rousseau had decided on the necessity of true popular sovereignty if the state and its officers were, indeed, to be subject to 'public reason', he was obliged to consider how the 'general will' could actually operate – not merely as a notional standard for the behaviour of rulers and citizens, but as a real and active principle of political organisation, a 'will' actually emanating from the people and expressed in practice as law. His answer was, again, shaped by the particular conditions of the existing French state and by the particular ways in which his adopted countrymen had formulated their own responses to the 'durable' questions about the common good, how it is to be determined and implemented. The typical French solution, as we have seen, conjured up a single public will, usually embodied in the monarch, or a collection of partial and selfish interests woven together by the king and the officers of the state. None of these solutions – not even those which replaced the monarchical will with 'one mind compounded out of many' – simply redefined the common good as a public interest constituted by private interests which would magically coalesce by the workings of an invisible hand, or aggregate themselves in the process of deliberation and legislation by a parliament representing private interests. [...]

Though Rousseau is never unequivocally clear about the social preconditions for such a political order, his social criticism – especially in the first and second 'Discourses' – suggests very strongly that a complete transformation of society would be required. Elsewhere, he gives indications of how his ideal society might be constituted: a small community of independent petty producers, more or less self-sufficient peasants and artisans.[44] However utopian this picture may be, it expresses clearly the principle which, for Rousseau, is the basis of a free society: that no one should be able to appropriate the labour of others or be forced to alienate his own. In the *Social Contract*, he suggests that the fundamental principles of the common good are liberty – the absence of individual dependence – and equality, which is the condition of liberty. These require a distribution of power and wealth in which no citizen can do violence to another and 'no citizen is rich enough to buy another, and none poor enough to be forced to sell himself'.[45] These, then, appear to be the conditions which make possible the general will. In order to will the general will as an expression – not an unnaturally (and impossibly) virtuous or forcible violation – of their own self-interest, people must actually, objectively, have interests in common. The common ground shared by interests in society as it

---

44. For example, in Rousseau 1967.
45. Rousseau 1964c, pp. 391–2.

is actually constituted is simply too narrow. To widen the scope of commonality requires the removal of those social relations and institutions – most especially, inequality – that render people, in reality and necessarily, enemies by interest. Democracy, it appears, is the necessary condition for a state based on 'public reason', rather than on the private interest of the magistrate; and social equality, the breakdown of the division between appropriators and producers, is the condition of democracy.

Rousseau's controversial concept of the 'general will', therefore, must be treated not as an idiosyncrasy, but as an innovation on an old French theme; not as a disturbingly illiberal answer to English questions about the relation between private rights and public interests, but as a radically democratic answer to French questions about the source of universality and the public will. [...]

John Locke

Although the chapter on property seems to have been added to the *Second Treatise* after its original completion, it certainly plays a significant part in Locke's political theory. It is here that he fleshes out the theory of natural right which forms the basis of his anti-absolutist argument. He does so by elaborating the principle that every man has a property in his own person, from which other rights follow. But if, for Locke as for the Levellers, the property that men have in their persons entails certain inalienable natural rights, it does not [...] necessarily entail all those political rights envisaged by the Levellers. A closer look at Locke's distinctive elaboration of 'self-propriety' and how it differs from that of the Levellers reveals a great deal about both his theory of property and his politics.

Locke begins his discussion of property with an observation that sounds very much like Gerrard Winstanley: God, says Locke, 'hath given the World to Men in common'.[46] Yet instead of concluding, as Winstanley did, that this common possession invalidates the institution of private property, Locke sets out to demonstrate not only that men's common ownership of the earth is compatible with private property, but that such property is grounded in natural right. Here, he puts to brilliant use the idea of 'self-propriety'. 'Though the Earth, and all inferior Creatures be common to all Men', Locke begins, 'yet every Man has a *Property* in his own Person. This no Body has any Right to but himself. The *Labour* of his Body and the *Work* of his Hands, we may

---

46. Locke, *Two Treatises of Government*, II. 26.

say, are properly his'.[47] Self-ownership, and the property that every man has in his own labour, then become the source of property in things and land. Anything in which a man 'mixes his labour', anything which, through his labour, he removes or changes from its natural state, anything to which he has added something by his labour, becomes his property and excludes the rights of other men. This is how private property grows out of common ownership, not by common consent, but by natural right – as an extension of a man's person and his labour, in which he has an exclusive right by nature. In any case, although God did give the Earth to men in common, he did not give it to them in order to waste it. He gave it to the 'industrious and rational' for the sake of 'improvement', to add to its value, usefulness and productivity by means of labour.

Are there, then, any limits to the amount of property a man is entitled to accumulate by means of his own labour? And how is it that some men have so much and some so little? Is the industry of some and the laziness of others enough to account for these differences, and can inequalities that go beyond such differences be justified? Locke maintains that there are certain limits on accumulation established by natural law. The most obvious – apart from the physical limits of the capacity to labour – is that no man should accumulate so much that he cannot consume it and lets it go to waste or spoil. Nor should he accumulate so much that he damages the interests of his fellows. He must leave enough, and good enough, to respect everyone else's right to subsistence. These 'spoilage'- and 'sufficiency'-limitations seem to mean, then, that a man's own capacity for labour together with that of his family, and his own capacity for consumption together with that of his household, set strict natural – and moral – limits on what he can accumulate. So it is hard to imagine how large accumulations and vast inequalities of wealth can be consistent with natural law.

Locke, however, has a simple answer. There is one development in human society that changes everything: the invention of money. To put it simply, money makes it possible for people to accumulate more than they themselves can consume without violating the natural-law prohibition against spoilage. The decision to attach some kind of value to gold or silver as a medium of exchange means that wealth can be accumulated in a form that keeps indefinitely. It also permits exchange and profitable commerce, which in turn create an incentive for increasing productivity and wealth. Without money and commerce, there would be neither possibility nor motivation for 'improvement' and accumulation.

---

47. Locke, *Two Treatises of Government*, II. 27.

The improvement of land encouraged by money and commerce also means that less land can support more people. On the one hand, this might be taken to mean that, although people now can accumulate more without violating the spoilage-limitation, they have no need to do so in order to live well. They can produce more wealth, and they can therefore leave more for others. Locke has, indeed, been interpreted as opposing large concentrations of property in this way. On the other hand, Locke suggests that money, commerce and 'improvement', by making land more productive and giving it more value, actually add to the 'common stock' of humanity. This means that people can accumulate more without depriving others and without violating the 'sufficiency'-limitation. In fact, a man who accumulates and improves large holdings, far from violating the rights of others, actually enhances their well-being.

In such conditions, furthermore, many people can even live without any property at all, because they can exchange their labour for a wage. It turns out that the labour which gives a man a right to property may be someone else's labour. Locke clearly takes for granted that some will have large properties and others none at all. Indeed some will create the wealth of others by work-ing for them. '*Master* and *Servant*', he writes, 'are Names as old as History',[48] and servants (a term that, in the seventeenth century, included many wage-labourers) can sell their labour without losing their natural liberty, as long as the relation between master and servant is a contractual one: not an uncondi-tional and permanent alienation, but a sale of labour for a certain time. (Locke also justifies slavery, but on different grounds: a man who loses his liberty by conquest in a lawful war may be spared his life in exchange for his permanent servitude.) And where land is 'improved' and profitably utilised, even the servant may be better off than the owners of unimproved land.

Nor does Locke stop there, for the invention of money has yet another impli-cation. Since money has value only because men have consented to it, it also implies that they have consented to its consequences: 'it is plain, that Men have agreed to disproportionate and unequal Possession of the Earth, they having by a tacit and voluntary consent found out a way, how a man may fairly pos-sess more land than he himself can use the product of [...]'.[49] Although specific laws and constitutions regulate specific systems of property, the inequality to which men have consented is not dependent on any such specific laws. It applies wherever money exists. This appears to mean that no government can override that agreement by seeking to alter the conditions of inequality to

---

48. Locke, *Two Treatises of Government*, II. 85.
49. Locke, *Two Treatises of Government*, II. 50.

which men have agreed. So the invention of money and everything that follows from it changes conditions so radically that natural law, together with man's natural freedom, equality and common possession of the earth, become consistent not only with private property but also with gross inequalities. And all of this has the legitimacy that comes from free consent. [...]

[T]he chapter on property has an important political meaning for Locke, but it also has implications that go far beyond its consequences for his theory of politics. The chapter represents a major rethinking of the whole idea of property; and this redefinition tells us something about real historical processes that were taking place in England, the development of capitalism and its distinctive property-relations.

Locke's whole argument on property turns on the notion of 'improvement'. The theme running throughout the chapter is that the Earth is there to be made productive, and that this is why private property, which emanates from labour, trumps common possession. Locke repeatedly insists that most of the value inherent in land comes not from nature, but from labour and improvement: 'tis *Labour* indeed that *puts the difference of value* on everything'.[50] It is clear, too, that the 'value' he has in mind is exchange- or commercial value. He even offers specific calculations of value contributed by labour as against nature. 'I think', he suggests, 'it will be but a very modest Computation to say, that of the *Products* of the Earth useful to the Life of Man, 9/10 are the *effects of labour*', and then immediately corrects himself: it would be more accurate to say that 99 percent should be attributed to labour rather than to nature.[51] An acre of land in unimproved America, which may be as naturally fertile as an acre in England, is not worth one-thousandth of the English acre, 'if all the Profit an *Indian* received from it were to be valued and sold here'.[52] Unimproved land is *waste*, so that a man who takes it out of common ownership and appropriates it to himself – he who removes land from the common and encloses it – in order to improve it has *given* something to humanity, not taken it away.

There is, of course, something attractive about Locke's idea that labour is the source of value and the basis of property, but it should be clear by now that there is something odd about it too. We already know, for example, that there is no direct correspondence between labour and property, because one man can appropriate the labour of another. It now appears that the issue for Locke has less to do with the activity of labour *as such* than with its profitable use. In calculating the value of the acre in America, for instance, he does not

---

50. Locke, *Two Treatises of Government*, II. 40.
51. Ibid.
52. Locke, *Two Treatises of Government*, II. 43.

talk about the Indian's labour, his expenditure of effort, but about the (lack of) profit he receives. The issue, in other words, is not the labour of a human-being, but the *productivity of property* and its application to commercial profit.

In a famous and much-debated passage, Locke writes that 'the Grass my Horse has bit; the Turfs my Servant has cut; and the Ore I have digg'd in any place where I have a right to them in common with others, become my *Property* [...]'.[53] Much ink has been spilt on this passage and what it tells us, for example, about Locke's views on wage-labour (the labour of the servant who cuts the turfs). But what is truly striking about this 'turfs'-passage is that Locke treats 'the Turfs my Servant has cut' as equivalent to 'the Ore I have digg'd'. This means not only that I, the master, have appropriated the labour of my servant, but that this appropriation is in principle no different from the servant's labouring activity itself. My own digging and my appropriat-ing the fruits of my servant's cutting are, for all intents and purposes, the same. But Locke is not interested in simply *passive* appropriation. The point is, rather, that the landlord who puts his land to productive use, who improves it, even if it is by means of someone else's labour, is being *industrious*, no less – perhaps more – than the labouring servant.

This is a point worth dwelling on. One way of understanding what Locke is driving at is to consider common usage today. When the financial pages of the daily newspaper speak of 'producers', they do not normally mean *workers*. In fact, they are likely to talk about conflicts, for example, between automo-bile 'producers' and trade-unions. The employers of labour, in other words, are being credited with 'production'. We have become so accustomed to this usage that we fail to see its implications, but it is important to keep in mind that certain very specific historical conditions were required to make it pos-sible. Traditional ruling classes, in a precapitalist society, passively appro-priating rents from dependent peasants, would never think of themselves as 'producers'. The kind of appropriation that can be called 'productive' is distinctively capitalist. It implies that property is used *actively*, not for 'con-spicuous consumption' but for investment and increasing profit. Wealth is acquired not simply by using coercive force to extract more surplus-labour from direct producers, in the manner of rentier-aristocrats, nor by 'buying cheap and selling dear' like precapitalist merchants, but by increasing labour-productivity (output per unit of work).

By conflating 'labour' with the production of profit, Locke becomes per-haps the first thinker to construct a systematic theory of property based on something like these capitalist principles. He is certainly not a theorist of a

---

53. Locke, *Two Treatises of Government*, II. 28.

mature, industrial capitalism; but his view of property, with its emphasis on productivity, already sets him apart from his predecessors. His idea that value is actively created in production is already vastly different from traditional views which focus simply on the process of exchange, the 'sphere of circula-tion'. (Only William Petty, often called the founder of political economy, had suggested anything like this 'labour-theory of value' in the seventeenth cen-tury.) Locke in his economic works is critical of those landed aristocrats who sit back and collect rents without improving their land, and he is equally criti-cal of merchants who simply act as middlemen, buying cheap in one market and selling at a higher price in another, hoarding goods to raise their price, or cornering a market to increase the profits of sale. Both types of proprietor are, in his view, parasitic. Yet his attack on proprietors of this kind should not be misread as a defence of working people against the dominant classes. He certainly has good things to say about industrious artisans and tradesmen, but his ideal seems to be the great improving landlord, whom he regards as the ultimate source of wealth in the community, what he calls the 'first pro-ducer' – a man like Shaftesbury, capitalist landlord and investor in colonial trade, a man who is not only 'industrious', but whose vast property contrib-utes greatly to the wealth of the community.

Locke's view of property is very well suited to the conditions of England in the early days of agrarian capitalism, described in Chapter One. It clearly reflects a condition in which highly concentrated land-ownership and large holdings were associated with a uniquely productive agriculture (productive not just in the sense of total output, but output per unit of work). His language of 'improvement' echoes the scientific literature devoted to the techniques of agriculture which flourished in England at this time, especially emanat-ing from the Royal Society and the groups of learned men with whom Locke and Shaftesbury were closely connected. More particularly, his constant ref-erences to common land as *waste*, his praise for the removal of land from the common, and indeed for enclosure, had very powerful resonance in that time and place.

We need to be reminded that the definition of property was, in Locke's day, not just a philosophical issue, but a very immediate practical one. A new, capitalist definition of property was in the process of establishing itself, chal-lenging traditional forms not just in theory, but in practice. For example, the idea of overlapping use-rights in the same piece of land (common lands with rights of pasturage, or privately-owned land where others had the right to collect wood or the residue of harvests, and so on) was giving way in England to *exclusive* ownership; and from the sixteenth to the eighteenth century, there were constant disputes over common and customary rights. Increasingly, the principle of 'improvement' for profitable exchange was taking precedence over other principles and other claims to property, whether those claims were based on custom or on some fundamental right of subsistence. Enhancing productivity itself became a reason for excluding other rights.

What better argument than Locke's could be found to support the landlord seeking to extinguish the customary rights of commoners, to exclude them from common land, to turn common land into exclusive private property by means of enclosure? What better argument than that enclosure, exclusion and improvement enhanced the wealth of the community and added more to the 'common stock' than it subtracted? And indeed, there are in the seventeenth century already examples of legal decisions, in conflicts over land, where judges invoke principles very much like those outlined by Locke, in order to give exclusive property precedence over common and customary rights. In the eighteenth century, when enclosure would accelerate rapidly with the active involvement of Parliament, reasons of 'improvement' would be cited systematically as the basis of title to property and as grounds for extinguishing traditional rights.

Revolution and tradition, c. 1640–1790

This is the period when ideologues of the ruling class gave a new lease of life to tradition. The trajectory of this idea from the Civil War to the revolutionary age of the eighteenth century is revealing. When Cromwell faced the Levellers and sought to defend the supremacy of men of property against the radical claim to equality of rights, he invoked convention, tradition and the historic constitution of England as the foundations of property and the unequal distribution of political rights. The principle of natural rights, he argued together with his son-in-law Ireton, endangered property itself. Some decades later, with the threat from below safely suppressed, John Locke was able to recruit the doctrine of natural right to the defence of property and the supremacy of the propertied class against the monarchy, with less fear of its subversive implications – though he did take the precaution of constructing his argument in such a way as to justify unequal distribution, concentrations of property, enclosure, and so on.[54] Even with these precautions, Locke's appeal to natural right appeared unduly risky; and in the age of revolution, it became transparently clear that this 'discursive practice' was no longer safe. It was in this spirit that Edmund Burke deployed the old argument from convention and tradition against the French-revolutionary invocation of the

---

54. See N. Wood 1984 and McNally 1989.

basic 'rights of man'. This, then, was a climate in which traditions could be revived or even invented in support of the prevailing social order.

There is, of course, a striking contrast between the British ideology of tradition (from which the *revolutionary* tradition has been expunged) and the French ideology of revolution; but this dramatic difference ought not to be misread. It is misleading to suggest that the emphasis on tradition reflects the persistence of 'pre-modern' remnants in the British state, while the French celebration of the Revolution expresses the sharp discontinuities between the absolutist state and post-revolutionary France. In a sense, the reverse is true. The English ruling class was able to invoke the traditions of the monarchy because of the distance that had long since separated the state from its precapitalist antecedents, producing a monarchy without absolutism which represented no real challenge to the propertied class and its dominant modes of appropriation. The monarchy could be endowed with great ideological value because it represented no structural threat. In France, despite the violent rupture of the Revolution and its wide-ranging effects on world-history, there were deep structural continuities between absolutism and the post-revolutionary state, continuities that the cult of Revolution served to mask. The parasitism of the Bonapartist bureaucratic state could indeed enhance its legitimacy by stressing the rupture with the predatory absolutist monarchy. In that sense, the French tradition of republicanism was perhaps rooted not so much in the emergence of an 'impersonal' bureaucratic state, as Tom Nairn suggests,[55] as, on the contrary, the persistence of old absolutist principles.

This is not to deny the radical impulses of the Revolution, the power of the libertarian and egalitarian ideas which it spawned, or its world-historic influences. On the contrary, the very tenacity of the *ancien régime* generated a correspondingly fierce opposition. It is difficult to overestimate the effects of this historic drama, not just as the source of so many modern ideas and institutions, but as a spectacle of human agency and its transformative capacities. Yet however radical this legacy of revolution may have been, it is misleading to say (as is suggested in some of the most persuasive Nairn-Anderson formulae)[56] that the necessity of a more direct and violent confrontation with the *ancien régime* called forth more powerfully modernising forces and a more thorough 'bourgeois' transformation. The tenacity of the *ancien régime* was expressed not only in the violence of opposition to it, but also in its continuing grip on French society beyond the Revolution.

55. See Nairn 1988.
56. For a discussion of the 'Nairn-Anderson theses', a series of ideas associated with the works of Tom Nairn and Perry Anderson, see E.M. Wood 1991.

The structural transformations brought about by the Revolution in France were not commensurate with its ideological power: the Revolution did little immediately to transform the social relations of production, and even the redistribution of property between classes was limited; indeed, most of the old aristocracy held on to their lands throughout the Revolution and even the Terror. Those transformations of property-relations that did occur – notably the consolidation of certain peasant-rights – moved in a direction away from capitalist development, as, in the first instance, did the 'rationalisation' of the state which expanded bourgeois access to the traditionally lucrative resource of office in the state and the army, as well as the Church, instead of encouraging more 'modern', capitalist careers. No doubt, the transformations effected by the Revolution and Napoleon served, in the end, to facilitate the development of a capitalist economy, but to say this is not to suppose that the transformation itself was set in train by mature capitalist forces breaking through the shackles of a backward state.

There is also another, more complicated reason for modifying the Nairn-Anderson formula. The specific character of the most powerful revolutionary principles – liberty, equality, fraternity – was determined by the régime to which they were opposed. In particular, the egalitarian idea was constituted in opposition to the ancient principle of *privilege*. This revolutionary impulse was, of course, to become a powerfully positive force in other, later struggles, and immediately, for example, in the battle against slavery.[57] The socialist parties of the late-nineteenth century were to be seen as the carriers of the old egalitarian and democratic political aspirations, 'the standard-bearers of that fight against inequality and "privilege" which had been central to political radicalism since the American and French revolutions'.[58]

But it is significant that this political tradition was most powerful where the proletariat was not sufficient to constitute a mass-base and where socialist parties were forced to appeal to other classes, especially those for whom landlordism, privilege and state-oppression loomed large as sources of grievance. The most revolutionary movements have tended to be those in which militantly anti-capitalist working-class struggles have been grafted on to precapitalist struggles, especially those involving the state, and where traditional 'real communities' have still been strong and collective loyalties of a kind increasingly destroyed by capitalism have still been available to reinforce new class-solidarities.

---

57. See Blackburn 1988.
58. Hobsbawm 1987, p. 138.

In Britain, the revolutionary tradition was supplanted by the infamous phenomenon of 'labourism'. For Anderson and Nairn, this represents yet another index of British backwardness, an underdeveloped proletarian class-consciousness, the corollary of an immature bourgeoisie, still carrying the traces of pre-modern class-relations rooted in old forms of agrarian capitalism. Yet it is difficult to avoid the conclusion that this distinctive pattern had something to do with the fact that Britain, alone in Europe, had a relatively advanced-capitalist class-structure and a population whose majority was working-class. This, to put it simply, was a class for which 'privilege', and even 'inequality', were no longer the dominant issues. It was a class for which grievances were no longer immediately definable in political terms. Old conflicts between absolutist states and aspiring classes, between usurping landlords and peasants defending customary rights, or between privilege and civil equality, had been displaced by 'purely economic' class-conflicts between capital and labour, and especially in the workplace. Industrial organisation and disputes over the terms and conditions of work overtook political movements and struggles.

Here, [...] a comparison with the United States is instructive. No explanations based on antique survivals or on premature development can account for the political limitations of the labour-movement in this case, in a country without ancient impediments, with a revolutionary tradition at least as central to its national mythology as that of France, and a proletariat late enough in its development to benefit from the availability of mature socialist theory in Europe.[59] But what this paragon of modernity has for some time had in common with antiquated Britain is a predominantly proletarian subordinate class, without precapitalist residues, and social antagonisms unambiguously rooted in capitalism.

The attractions of the old revolutionary tradition, and the loss sustained by the labour-movement in its detachment from the old political aspirations, should not disguise the fact that these revolutionary principles may – unfortunately? – be less 'modern' than is 'labourism'; that the development of capitalism *checked*, rather than enhanced, these revolutionary ideological tendencies; that the more proletarian the population. the more these traditional egalitarian and 'democratic' issues have receded, in part resolved by the triumph of formal democracy, in part pushed aside by issues generated in the direct class-confrontation between capital and labour and requiring the construc-

---

59. Perry Anderson wrote that 'England experienced the first industrial revolution, in a period of international counter-revolutionary war, producing the earliest proletariat when socialist theory was least formed and available [...]' (P. Anderson 1964, p. 31).

tion of wholly new revolutionary principles, which modern labour-movements have not yet successfully elaborated. If the modern French bourgeoisie seems very remote from its revolutionary past, socialist parties in advanced capitalist Europe are now hardly more recognisable as heirs to the legacy of revolution. And for socialists of more revolutionary inclinations, principles of mobilisation against capitalism as effective as the old principles of 'liberty' and 'equality' were against absolutism and privilege have proved elusive.

It would perhaps be more comforting to think that the weaknesses of the British labour-movement are largely attributable to Britain's imperfect modernity, and the effects of its 'prematurity' are undeniable; but it would probably be more accurate, more challenging – and even ultimately more encouraging – to acknowledge that this movement, more than any other in Europe, has been shaped from the beginning by the dominant class-relations of capitalismc. A preoccupation with issues directly generated by capitalism must, in the end, be the strength of such movements as much as it often seems to be their weakness. The *ancien régime* is, after all, no longer available as a major target of emancipatory struggles.

Chapter Five

Democracy, Citizenship, Liberalism, and Civil Society

Labour and democracy, ancient and modern

In modern capitalist democracy, socio-economic inequality and exploitation coexist with civic freedom and equality. Primary producers are not juridically dependent or politically disfranchised. In ancient democracy too, civic identity was dissociated from socio-economic status, and here too political equality coexisted with class-inequality. But there remains a fundamental difference. In capitalist society, primary producers are subject to economic compulsions which are independent of their political status. The power of the capitalist to appropriate the surplus-labour of workers is not dependent on a privileged juridical or civic status, but on the workers' propertylessness, which obliges them to exchange their labour-power for a wage in order to gain access to the means of labour and subsistence. Workers are subject both to the power of capital and to the imperatives of competition and profit-maximisation. The separation of civic status and class-position in capitalist societies thus has two sides: on the one hand, the right of citizenship is not determined by socio-economic position – and in this sense, capitalism can coexist with formal democracy – on the other hand, civic equality does not directly affect class-inequality, and formal democracy leaves class-exploitation fundamentally intact.

By contrast, in ancient democracy there existed a class of primary producers who were juridically free and politically privileged, and who were at the same time largely free of the necessity to enter the market to secure access to the conditions of labour and subsistence. Their civic freedom was not, like that of the modern wage-labourer, offset by the economic compulsions of capitalism. As in capitalism, the right to citizenship was not determined by socio-economic status; but, unlike capitalism, relations between classes were directly and profoundly affected by civic status. The most obvious example is the division between citizens and slaves. But citizenship directly determined economic relations in other ways too.

Democratic citizenship in Athens meant that small producers were, to a great extent, free of the extra-economic exactions to which direct producers in precapitalist societies have always been subject. They were free, for example, from the depredations of Hesiod's 'gift-devouring' lords, using jurisdictional powers to milk the peasantry; or from the direct coercion of the Spartan ruling class, exploiting helots by means of what amounted to a military occupation; or from the feudal obligations of the medieval peasant, subject to the military and jurisdictional powers of the lords; or from the taxation of European absolutism, in which public office was a primary instrument of private appropriation; and so on. As long as direct producers remained free of purely 'economic' imperatives, politically-constituted property would remain a lucrative resource, as an instrument of private appropriation or, conversely, a protection against exploitation; and, in that context, the civic status of the Athenian citizen was a valuable asset which had direct economic implications. Political equality not only coexisted with, but substantially modified socio-economic inequality, and democracy was more substantive than 'formal'.

In ancient Athens, citizenship had profound consequences for peasants and craftsmen; and, of course, a change in the juridical status of slaves – and, indeed, women – would have transformed the society entirely. In feudalism, juridical privilege and political rights could not have been redistributed without transforming the prevailing social-property relations. Only in capitalism has it become possible to leave the property-relations between capital and labour fundamentally intact while permitting the democratisation of civic and political rights.

That capitalism could survive democracy, at least in this 'formal' sense, was not, however, always obvious. As the growth of capitalist property-relations began to separate property from privilege, and especially while free labour was not yet subject to the new disciplines of industrial capitalism and complete propertylessness, the ruling classes of Europe were deeply preoccupied with the dangers posed by the labouring multitude. For a long time, it seemed that the only solution was the preservation of some kind of division between rulers and producers, between a politically privileged propertied élite and a disfranchised labouring multitude. Nor were political rights, needless to say, freely given when they were finally granted to the working classes, after prolonged and much-resisted popular struggles.

In the meantime, a wholly new conception of democracy had pushed aside the ancient-Greek idea. The critical moment in this redefinition, which had the effect (and the intention) of *diluting* the meaning of democracy, was the foundation of the United States, which I shall take up in the [...] [following sections]. Yet, however much the ruling classes of Europe and America may have feared the extension of political rights to the labouring multitude, it turned out that political rights in capitalist society no longer had the salience of citizenship in ancient democracy. The achievement of formal democracy and universal suffrage certainly represented tremendous historic advances, but it turned out that capitalism offered a new solution to the age-old problem of rulers and producers. It was no longer necessary to embody the division between privilege and labour in a political division between appropriating rulers and labouring subjects, now that democracy could be confined to a formally separate 'political' sphere while the 'economy' followed rules of its own. If the extent of the citizen-body could no longer be restricted, the scope of citizenship could now be narrowly contained, even without constitutional limits.

The contrast between the status of labour in ancient democracy and modern capitalism invites some very large questions: in a system where purely 'economic' power has replaced political privilege, what is the meaning of citizenship? What would be required to recover, in a very different context, the salience of citizenship in ancient democracy and the status of the labouring citizen?

From ancient to modern conceptions of citizenship

The ancient concept of democracy grew out of a historical experience which had conferred a unique civic status on subordinate classes, creating in particular that unprecedented formation, the peasant-citizen. In all – or at least a great deal – but name, the modern concept belongs to a different historical trajectory, most vividly exemplified in the Anglo-American tradition. The landmarks along the road to the ancient democracy, such as the reforms of Solon and Cleisthenes, represent pivotal moments in the elevation of the *demos* to citizenship. In the other history – originating not in Athenian democracy, but in European feudalism, and culminating in liberal capitalism – the major milestones, like *Magna Carta* and 1688, mark the ascent of the proper-tied classes. In this case, it is not a question of peasants liberating themselves from the political domination of their overlords, but lords themselves assert-ing their independent powers against the claims of monarchy. This is the origin of modern constitutional principles, ideas of limited government, the separation of powers, and so on: principles which have displaced the social implications of 'rule by the *demos*' – such as the balance of power between rich and poor – as the central criterion of democracy. If the peasant-citizen is the most representative figure of the first historical drama, in the second it is the feudal baron and the Whig aristocrat.

If *citizenship* is the constitutive concept of ancient democracy, the found-ing principle of the other variety is, perhaps, *lordship*. The Athenian citizen claimed to be *masterless*, a servant to no mortal man. He owed no service or deference to any lord, nor did he waste his labour to enrich a tyrant by his toil. The freedom, *eleutheria*, entailed by his citizenship was the freedom of the *demos from* lordship. *Magna Carta*, in contrast, was a charter not of a masterless *demos*, but of masters themselves, asserting feudal privileges and the freedom *of* lordship against both Crown and popular multitude, just as the *liberty* of 1688 represented the privilege of propertied gentlemen, their freedom to dis-pose of their property and servants at will.

Certainly, the assertion of aristocratic privilege against encroaching mon-archies produced the tradition of 'popular sovereignty' from which the mod-ern conception of democracy derives; yet the 'people' in question was not the *demos*, but a privileged stratum constituting an exclusive political nation situated in a public realm between the monarch and the multitude. While Athenian democracy had the effect of breaking down the age-old opposition between rulers and producers by turning peasants into citizens, the division between ruling landlords and subject-peasants was a constitutive condition of 'popular sovereignty' as it emerged in early-modern Europe. On the one hand, the fragmentation of sovereignty and the power of lordship which con-stituted European feudalism, the check on monarchy and state-centralisation exercised by these feudal principles, were to be the basis of a new kind of 'limited' state-power, the source of what were later to be called democratic principles, such as constitutionalism, representation and civil liberties. On the other hand, the obverse side of feudal lordship was a dependent peas-antry, while the 'political nation' which grew out of the community of feudal lords retained its exclusiveness and the political subordination of producing classes.

In England, the exclusive political nation found its embodiment in Parlia-ment, which, as Sir Thomas Smith wrote in the 1560s, 'hath the power of the whole realme both the head and the bodie. For everie Englishman is entended to bee there present, either in person or by procuration and attornies, of what preheminence, state dignitie, or qualitie soever he be, from the Prince (be he King or Queene) to the lowest person of England. And the consent of the Parliament is taken to be everie man's consent.'[1] It is worth noting that a man was deemed to be 'present' in Parliament even if he had no right to vote for his representative. Thomas Smith, like others before and after him, took it for granted that a propertied minority would stand for the population as a whole.

The doctrine of parliamentary supremacy was to operate against popular power, even when the political nation was no longer restricted to a relatively small community of property-holders and when the 'people' was extended to include the 'popular multitude'. In Britain today, for example, politics is the special preserve of a sovereign Parliament. Parliament may be ultimately accountable to its electorate, but the 'people' are not truly *sovereign*. For all intents and purposes, there is no *politics* – or at least no legitimate politics – outside Parliament. Indeed, the more inclusive the 'people' has become, the more the dominant political ideologies – from Conservative to mainstream Labour – have insisted on depoliticising the world outside Parliament and delegitimating 'extra-parliamentary' politics. Running parallel with this process has been a growing centralisation of parliamentary power itself in the executive, producing something very much like Cabinet, or even prime-ministerial, sovereignty.

There did emerge, in early-modern England, a body of political thought – especially in the work of James Harrington, Algernon Sidney and Henry Neville – which, on the face of it, appears to run counter to this domi-nant parliamentary tradition. This school of political theory, which has come to be known as classical republicanism, had, or seemed to have, as its central organising principle a concept of citizenship, implying not simply the pas-sive enjoyment of individual rights which we have come to associate with 'liberal democracy', but a community of active citizens in pursuit of a com-mon good. Yet there is one fundamental point on which early modern repub-licans like James Harrington agreed with their 'liberal' contemporaries: the exclusivity of the political nation.[2] Active citizenship was to be reserved for men of property, and must exclude not only women, but also those men who lacked, as Harrington put it, the 'wherewithal to live of themselves' – that is,

---

1. Smith 1982, p. 79.
2. The practical differences between republicans and Whigs, or at least the more radical wing, in the politics of the seventeenth century were not always clear.

those whose livelihood depended on working for others. This conception of citizenship had at its core a division between propertied élite and labouring multitude. It is not surprising that republicans of this variety, when seeking models in antiquity, chose the aristocratic ('mixed') constitution of Sparta or Rome, instead of democratic Athens.

In fact, such a division between propertied élite and labouring multitude may have belonged to the essence of English classical republicanism even more absolutely and irreducibly than to, say, Lockean liberalism. When Harrington set out to construct political principles appropriate to a society where feudal lordship no longer prevailed, he did not altogether jettison the principles of feudalism. It is even possible to say that his conception of citizenship was modelled in certain important respects on feudal principles. On the one hand, there was no longer to be a category of dependent property, a juridical and political division between different forms of landed property, as there had been between feudal lords and their dependants. All landed property was to be juridically and politically privileged. On the other hand, property itself was still defined as a political and military status; it was, in other words, still characterised by the inextricable unity of economic and political/military power which had constituted feudal lordship.

In this, classical republicanism was already an anachronism at the moment of its conception. Landed property in England was already assuming a *capitalist* form, in which economic power was no longer inextricably bound up with juridical, political and military status, and wealth depended increasingly on 'improvement' or the *productive* use of property subject to the imperatives of a competitive market. Here, John Locke's conception of property and agricultural 'improvement' was more in keeping with current realities.[3] And, while Locke himself was no democrat, it is arguable that a conception of property such as his was ultimately more amenable to relaxing the restrictions on membership in the political nation.[4] To put it simply, once the economic power of the propertied classes no longer depended upon 'extra-economic' status, on the juridical, political and military powers of lordship, a monopoly on politics was no longer indispensable to the élite. By contrast, within a framework dominated by an essentially precapitalist conception of property, with all its juridical and political 'embellishments' (as Marx once called them), the 'formal' equality made possible by the capitalist separation of the 'economic' and the 'political' was not even *thinkable* (literally), let alone desirable.

---

3. See N. Wood 1984.
4. For a powerful critique of attempts to portray Locke as a democrat, see McNally 1989. I have also argued against such interpretations in E.M. Wood 1992b and 1994a.

Capitalism and democratic citizenship

Capitalism, by shifting the locus of power from *lordship* to *property*, made civic status less salient, as the benefits of political privilege gave way to purely 'economic' advantage. This eventually made possible a new form of democracy. Where classical republicanism had solved the problem of a propertied élite and a labouring multitude by restricting the extent of the citizen-body (as Athenian oligarchs would have liked to do), capitalist or liberal democracy would permit the extension of citizenship by restricting its powers (as the Romans did). Where one proposed an active but exclusive citizen-body, in which the propertied classes ruled the labouring multitude, the other could – eventually – envisage an inclusive but largely passive citizen-body, embracing both elite and multitude, but whose citizenship would be limited in scope.

Capitalism transformed the political sphere in other ways too. The relation between capital and labour presupposes formally free and equal individuals, without prescriptive rights or obligations, juridical privileges or disabilities. The detachment of the individual from corporate institutions and identities began very early in England (it is, for example, reflected in Sir Thomas Smith's definition of a commonwealth as 'a societie or common doing of a multitude of free men collected together and united by common accords and covenauntes among themselves',[5] and in the individualistic psychologism that runs through the tradition of British social thought from Hobbes and Locke to Hume and beyond); and the rise of capitalism was marked by the increasing detachment of the individual (not to mention individual property) from customary, corporate, prescriptive and communal identities and obligations.

The emergence of this isolated individual did, needless to say, have its positive side, the emancipatory implications of which are emphasised by liberal doctrine, with its constitutive concept (myth?) of the sovereign individual. But there was also another side. In a sense, the creation of the sovereign individual was the price paid by the 'labouring multitude' for entry into the political community; or, to be more precise, the historical process which gave rise to capitalism, and to the modern 'free and equal' wage labourer who would eventually join the body of citizens, was the same process in which the peasant was dispossessed and deracinated, detached from both his property and his community, together with its common and customary rights.

---

5. Smith 1982 p. 57. It is interesting in this connection to compare Smith's definition with that of his contemporary, Jean Bodin, who treats 'families, colleges, or corporate bodies', not individual free men, as the constituent units of the commonwealth, reflecting the realities of France, where corporate institutions and identities continued to play a prominent role in political life (Bodin 1955).

Let us consider briefly what this means. The peasant in precapitalist societies, unlike the modern wage-labourer, remained in possession of property, in this case land, the means of labour and subsistence. This meant that the capacity of landlord or state to appropriate labour from him depended on a superior coercive power, in the form of juridical, political and military status. The principal modes of surplus-extraction to which peasants were subject – rent and tax – typically took the form of various kinds of juridical and political dependence: debt-bondage, serfdom, tributary relations, obligations to perform corvée-labour, and so on. By the same token, the capacity of peasants to resist or limit their exploitation by landlords and states depended in great measure on the strength of their own political organisation, notably the village-community. To the extent that peasants were able to achieve a degree of political independence by extending the jurisdiction of the village-community – for example, imposing their own local charters or replacing landlord-representatives with their own local magistrates – they also extended their economic powers of appropriation and resistance to exploitation. But, however strong the village-community became from time to time, there generally remained one insurmountable barrier to peasant-autonomy: the state. The peasant-village almost universally remained, as it were, outside the state, and subject to its alien power, as the peasant was excluded from the community of citizens.

It is here that Athenian democracy represents a radically unique exception. Only here was the barrier between state and village breached, as the village effectively became the constitutive unit of the state, and peasants became citizens. The Athenian citizen acquired his civic status by virtue of his membership in a deme, a geographical unit generally based on existing villages. The establishment by Cleisthenes of the deme as the constituent unit of the *polis* was, in a critical sense, the foundation of the democracy. It created a civic identity abstracted from differences of birth, an identity common to aristocracy and *demos*, symbolised by the adoption by Athenian citizens of a *demotikon*, a deme-name, as distinct from (though in practice never replacing, especially in the case of the aristocracy) the patronymic. But, even more fundamentally, Cleisthenes's reforms 'politicised the Attic countryside and rooted political identity there'.[6] They represented, in other words, the incorporation of the village into the state, and the peasant into the civic community. The economic corollary of this political status was an exceptional degree of freedom for the peasant from 'extra-economic' exactions in the form of rent or tax.[7]

---

6. Osborne 1985, p. 189.
7. For more on these points, see E.M. Wood 1988, pp. 101–7.

The medieval peasant, in contrast, remained firmly excluded from the state and correspondingly more subject to extra-economic surplus-extraction. The institutions and solidarities of the village-community could afford him some protection against landlords and states (though it could also serve as a medium of lordly control – as, for example, in manorial courts), but the state itself was alien, the exclusive preserve of feudal lords. And as the feudal 'parcelisation of sovereignty' gave way to more centralised states, the exclusivity of this political sphere survived in the privileged political nation.[8] Finally, as feudal relations gave way to capitalism, specifically in England, even the mediation of the village-community, which had stood between peasant and landlord, was lost. The individual and his property were detached from the community, as production increasingly fell outside communal regulation, whether by manorial courts or village-community (the most obvious example of this process is the replacement of the English open-field system by enclosure); customary tenures became economic leaseholds subject to the impersonal competitive pressures of the market; smallholders lost their customary use-rights to common land; increasingly, they were dispossessed, whether by coercive eviction or the economic pressures of competition. Eventually, as landholding became increasingly concentrated, the peasantry gave way to large landholders, on the one hand, and propertyless wage-labourers, on the other. In the end, the 'liberation' of the individual was complete, as capitalism, with its indifference to the 'extra-economic' identities of the labouring multitude, dissipated prescriptive attributes and 'extra-economic' differences in the solvent of the labour-market, where individuals become interchangeable units of labour abstracted from any specific personal or social identity.

It is as an aggregate of such isolated individuals, without property and abstracted from communal solidarities, that the 'labouring multitude' finally entered the community of citizens. Of course, the dissolution of traditional prescriptive identities and juridical inequalities represented an advance for these now 'free and equal' individuals; and the acquisition of citizenship conferred upon them new powers, rights, and entitlements. But we cannot take the measure of their gains and losses without remembering that the historical presupposition of their citizenship was the *devaluation* of the political sphere, the new relation between the 'economic' and the 'political' which had reduced the salience of citizenship and transferred some of its formerly exclusive powers to the purely economic domain of private property and the market, where purely economic advantage takes the place of juridical privilege and

---

8. For a discussion of the relation between peasants, lords, and the state in medieval and early-modern Europe, see Brenner 1985b.

political monopoly. The devaluation of citizenship entailed by capitalist social relations is an essential attribute of modern democracy. For that reason, the tendency of liberal doctrine to represent the historical developments which produced formal citizenship as nothing other than an enhancement of individual liberty – the freeing of the individual from an arbitrary state, as well as from the constraints of tradition and prescriptive hierarchies, from communal repressions or the demands of civic virtue – is inexcusably one-sided.

Nor can we assess the ideological effects of the modern relation between individual citizen and civic community or *nation*, without considering the degree to which that 'imagined community' is a fiction, a mythical abstraction, in conflict with the experience of the citizen's daily life.[9] The nation can, certainly, be real enough to inspire individuals to die for their country; but we must consider the extent to which this abstraction is also capable of serving as an ideological device to deny or disguise the more immediate experience of individuals, to disaggregate and delegitimate, or at least to depoliticise, the solidarities that stand between the levels of individual and nation, such as those forged in the workplace, the local community, or in a common class-experience. When the political nation was privileged and exclusive, the 'commonwealth' in large part corresponded to a real community of interest among the landed aristocracy. In modern democracies, where the civic community unites extremes of social inequality and conflicting interests, the 'common good' shared by citizens must be a much more tenuously abstract notion. [...]

In capitalist democracy, the separation between civic status and class-position operates in both directions: socio-economic position does not determine the right to citizenship – and that is what is *democratic* in capitalist democracy – but, since the power of the capitalist to appropriate the surplus-labour of workers is not dependent on a privileged juridical or civic status, civic equality does not directly affect or significantly modify class-inequality – and that is what limits democracy in capitalism. Class-relations between capital and labour can survive even with juridical equality and universal suffrage. In that sense, political equality in capitalist democracy not only coexists with socio-economic inequality, but leaves it fundamentally intact.

The American redefinition of democracy

Capitalism, then, made it possible to conceive of 'formal democracy', a form of civic equality which could coexist with social inequality and leave eco-

---

9. On the nation as an 'imagined community', see B. Anderson 1983.

nomic relations between 'élite' and 'labouring multitude' in place. Needless to say, however, the conceptual *possibility* of 'formal democracy' did not make it a historical actuality. There were to be many long and arduous struggles before the 'people' grew to encompass the labouring multitude, let alone women. It is a curious fact that in the dominant ideologies of Anglo-American political culture, these struggles have not achieved the status of principal milestones in the history of democracy. In the canons of English-speaking liberalism, the main road to modern democracy runs through Rome, *Magna Carta*, the Petition of Right and the Glorious Revolution, not Athens, the Levellers, Diggers and Chartism. Nor is it simply that the historical record belongs to the victors; for if 1688, not Levellers and Diggers, represents the winners, should not history record that democracy was on the losing side?

It is here that the American experience was decisive. English Whiggery could have long remained content to celebrate the forward march of Parliament without proclaiming it a victory for *democracy*. The Americans had no such option. Despite the fact that, in the struggle to determine the shape of the new republic, it was the anti-democrats who won, even at the moment of foundation the impulse towards mass-democracy was already too strong for that victory to be complete. Here, too, the dominant ideology divided governing élite from governed multitude; and the Federalists might have wished, had it been possible, to create an exclusive political nation, an aristocracy of propertied citizens, in which property – and specifically, landed property – remained a privileged juridical/political/military status. But economic and political realities in the colonies had already foreclosed that option. Property had irrevocably discarded its extra-economic 'embellishments', in an economy based on commodity-exchange and purely 'economic' modes of appropriation, which undermined the neat division between politically privileged property and disenfranchised labouring multitude. And the colonial experience, culminating in revolution, had created a politically active populace.

The Federalists thus faced the unprecedented task of preserving what they could of the division between mass and élite in the context of an increasingly democratic franchise and an increasingly active citizenry. It is now more generally acknowledged than it was not very long ago that US democracy was deeply flawed in its very foundations by the exclusion of women, the oppression of slaves and a genocidal colonialism in relation to indigenous peoples. What may not be quite so self-evident are the anti-democratic principles contained in the idea of democratic citizenship itself, as it was defined by the 'Founding Fathers'. The framers of the Constitution embarked on the first experiment in designing a set of political institutions that would both embody and at the same time curtail popular power, in a context where it was no longer possible to maintain an exclusive citizen-body. Where the option of an active but exclusive citizenry was unavailable, it would be necessary to create an inclusive but passive citizen-body, with limited scope for its political powers.

The Federalist ideal may have been to create an aristocracy combining wealth with republican virtue (an ideal that would inevitably give way to the dominance of wealth alone); but their practical task was to sustain a propertied oligarchy with the electoral support of a popular multitude. This also required the Federalists to produce an ideology, and specifically a redefinition of democracy, which would disguise the ambiguities in their oligarchic project. It was the anti-democratic victors in the USA who gave the modern world its definition of democracy, a definition in which the dilution of popular power is an essential ingredient. If American political institutions have not been imitated everywhere, the American experiment has nonetheless left this universal legacy.[10] [...]

The concept of *isegoria* is arguably the most distinctive concept associated with Athenian democracy, the one most distant from any analogue in modern liberal democracy – including its closest approximation, the modern concept of free speech. Alexander Hamilton was, no doubt, an advocate of free speech in the modern liberal-democratic sense, having to do with protecting the right of citizens to express themselves without interference, especially by the state. But there is in Hamilton's conception no incompatibility between advocating civil liberties, among which the freedom of expression is paramount, and the view that in the political domain the wealthy merchant is the natural representative of the humble craftsman. The man of property will speak politically for the shoemaker or blacksmith. Hamilton does not, of course, propose to silence these demotic voices. Nor does he intend to deprive them of the right to choose their representatives. He is, evidently with some reluctance, obliged to accept a fairly wide and socially inclusive or 'democratic' franchise. But like many *anti*-democrats before him, he makes certain assumptions about representation according to which the labouring multitude, like Sir Thomas Smith's 'lowest person', must find its political voice in its social superiors.

These assumptions also have to be placed in the context of the Federalist view that representation is not a way of implementing, but of *avoiding* or at least partially circumventing democracy. Their argument was not that representation is necessary in a large republic, but, on the contrary, that a large republic is desirable so that representation is unavoidable – and the smaller the

---

10. For an illuminating discussion of this model and its implications, see Manicas 1988. On the Federalists in the context of the debates leading up to and surrounding the Constitution, see G. Wood 1972.

proportion of representatives to represented, the greater the distance between them, the better. As Madison put it in 'Federalist No. 10', the effect of representation is 'to refine and enlarge the public views, by passing them through the medium of a chosen body of citizens [...]'. And an extensive republic is clearly preferable to a small one, 'more favorable to the election of proper guardians of the public weal', on the grounds of 'two obvious considerations': that there would be a smaller proportion of representatives to represented, and that each representative would be chosen by a larger electorate.[11] Representation, in other words, is intended to act as a *filter*. In these respects, the Federalist conception of representation – and especially Hamilton's – is the very antithesis of *isegoria*.

We have become so accustomed to the formula 'representative democracy' that we tend to forget the novelty of the American idea. In its Federalist form, at any rate, it meant that something hitherto perceived as the *antithesis* of democratic self-government was now not only compatible with, but constitutive of, democracy: not the *exercise* of political power, but its *relinquishment*, its *transfer* to others, its *alienation*.

The alienation of political power was so foreign to the Greek conception of democracy that even election could be regarded as an oligarchic practice, which democracies might adopt for certain specific purposes but which did not belong to the essence of the democratic constitution. Thus Aristotle, outlining how a 'mixed' constitution might be constructed out of elements from the main constitutional types, such as oligarchy and democracy, suggests the inclusion of election as an oligarchic feature. It was oligarchic because it tended to favour the *gnorimoi*, the notables, the rich and well-born who were less likely to be sympathetic to democracy. Athenians might resort to election in the case of offices requiring a narrowly technical expertise, notably the top financial and military posts (such as the military office of *strategos* to which Pericles was elected); but such offices were hedged about with stringent measures for ensuring accountability, and they were clearly understood as exceptions to the rule that all citizens could be assumed to possess the kind of civic wisdom required for general political functions. The quintessentially democratic method was selection by lot, a practice which, while acknowledging the practical constraints imposed by the size of a state and the number of its citizens, embodies a criterion of selection in principle opposed to the alienation of citizenship and to the assumption that the *demos* is politically incompetent.

---

11. Kramnick (ed.) 1987, pp. 126, 127.

The American republic firmly established a definition of democracy in which the transfer of power to 'representatives of the people' constituted not just a necessary concession to size and complexity, but rather the very essence of democracy itself. The Americans, then, though they did not invent representation, can be credited with establishing an essential constitutive idea of modern democracy: its identification with the alienation of power. But, again, the critical point here is not simply the substitution of representative for direct democracy. There are undoubtedly many reasons for favouring representation, even in the most democratic polity. The issue here is, rather, the assumptions on which the Federalist conception of representation was based. Not only did the 'Founding Fathers' conceive representation as a means of *distancing* the people from politics, but they advocated it for the same reason that Athenian democrats were suspicious of election: that it favoured the propertied classes. 'Representative democracy', like one of Aristotle's mixtures, is civilised democracy with a touch of oligarchy.

A democracy devoid of social content

In the Greek context, the political definition of the *demos* itself had a social meaning, because it was deliberately set against the exclusion of the lower classes, shoemakers and blacksmiths, from politics. It was an assertion of democracy against non-democratic definitions of the *polis* and citizenship. By contrast, when the Federalists invoked the 'people' as a political category, it was not for the purpose of asserting the rights of 'mechanics' against those who would exclude them from the public sphere. On the contrary, there is ample evidence, not least in explicit pronouncements by Federalist leaders, that their purpose – and the purpose of many provisions in the Constitution – was to dilute the power of the popular multitude, most particularly in defence of property.[12] Here, the 'people' were being invoked in support of *less* against *more* democratic principles.

In Federalist usage the 'people' was, as in Greek, an inclusive, political category; but here, the point of the political definition was not to stress the political equality of social non-equals. It had more to do with enhancing the power of the federal government; and, if the criterion of social class was to have no political relevance, it was not only in the sense that poverty or undistinguished rank was to be no formal bar to public office, but more especially in the sense that the balance of class-power would in no way represent a cri-

---

12. Hamilton's views are fairly unambiguous, but even the more 'Jeffersonian' Madison felt the need to dilute the powers of the popular multitude for the protection of property. See, for example, G. Wood 1972, pp. 221, 410–11, 503–4.

terion of democracy. There would, in effect, be no incompatibility between democracy and rule by the rich. It is in this sense that social criteria continue to be politically irrelevant today; and the modern definition of democracy is hardly less compatible with rule by the rich than it was for Alexander Hamilton.

There was a structural foundation underlying these differences in the relation between political and social meanings of the 'people', as conceived respectively in Athens and post-revolutionary America. The Federalists, what-ever their inclinations, no longer had the option, available to ruling classes elsewhere, of defining the 'people' narrowly, as synonymous with an exclu-sive political nation. The political experience of the colonies and the Revolu-tion precluded it (though, of course, women and slaves were, by definition, excluded from the political nation). But another possibility existed for Ameri-cans which had not existed for the Greeks: to displace democracy to a purely political sphere, distinct and separate from 'civil society' or the 'economy'. In Athens, there was no such clear division between 'state' and 'civil society', no distinct and autonomous 'economy', not even a conception of the state as distinct from the community of citizens – no state of 'Athens' or 'Attica', only 'the Athenians'.

Political and economic powers and rights, in other words, were not as eas-ily separated in Athens as in the USA, where property was already achieving a purely 'economic' definition, detached from juridical privilege or political power, and where the 'economy' was acquiring a life of its own. Large seg-ments of human experience and activity, and many varieties of oppression and indignity, were left untouched by political equality. If citizenship was taking precedence over other more particularistic social identities, it was at the same time becoming in many ways inconsequential.

The possibility of a democracy devoid of social content – and the absence of any such possibility in ancient Greece – has, again, to do with the vast differences in social-property relations between ancient Greece and modern capitalism. I have suggested that the social structure of capitalism changes the meaning of citizenship, so that the universality of political rights – in par-ticular, universal adult suffrage – leaves property-relations and the power of appropriation intact in a way that was never true before. It is capitalism that makes possible a form of democracy in which formal equality of politi-cal rights has a minimal effect on inequalities or relations of domination and exploitation in other spheres. These developments were sufficiently advanced in late eighteenth-century America to make possible a redefinition of democ-racy devoid of social content, the invention of 'formal democracy', the sup-pression of social criteria in the definition of democracy and in the conception of liberty associated with it. It was therefore possible for the Federalists to lay

claim to the language of democracy, while emphatically dissociating themselves from rule by the *demos* in its original Greek meaning. For the first time,
'democracy' could mean something entirely different from what it meant for
the Greeks.

For the Federalists in particular, ancient democracy was a model explicitly
to be avoided – mob-rule, the tyranny of the majority, and so on. But what
made this such an interesting conceptual problem was that, in the conditions
of post-revolutionary America, they had to reject the ancient democracy not
in the name of an opposing political ideal, not in the name of oligarchy, but
in the name of democracy itself. The colonial and revolutionary experience
had already made it impossible just to reject democracy outright, as ruling
and propertied classes had been doing unashamedly for centuries and as they
would continue to do for some time elsewhere. Political realities in the USA
were already forcing people to do what has now become conventional and
universal, when all good political things are 'democratic' and everything we
dislike in politics is undemocratic: everyone had to claim to be a democrat.
The problem, then, was to construct a conception of democracy which would,
by definition, exclude the ancient model.

The constitutional debates represent a unique historical moment, with no
parallel that I know of, in which there is a visible transition from the traditional indictment of democracy to the modern rhetorical naturalisation of
democracy for all political purposes, including those that would have been
regarded as *anti*-democratic according to the old definition. Here, we can
even watch the process of redefinition as it happens. The Federalists alternate
between sharply contrasting democracy to the republican form of government they advocate, and calling that very same republican form a 'representative democracy'. This ideological transformation takes place not only in
the sphere of political theory, but in the symbolism of the new republic. Just
consider the significance of the appeal to *Roman* symbols – the Roman pseud-
onyms adopted by the Federalists, the name of the Senate, and so on. And
consider the Roman eagle as an American icon. Not Athens, but Rome. Not
Pericles, but Cicero as role-model. Not the rule of the *demos*, but SPQR, the
'mixed constitution' of the Senate and the Roman people, the *populus* or *demos*
with rights of citizenship, but governed by an aristocracy.

From democracy to liberalism

In earlier times, democracy had meant what it said, yet its critics showed no
hesitation in denouncing the stupidity, ignorance, and unreliability of the
'common herd'. Adam Ferguson was speaking in the eighteenth century for

a long and unembarrassed tradition of anti-democrats when he asked, 'How can he who has confined his views to his own subsistence or preservation, be intrusted with the conduct of nations? Such men, when admitted to deliberate on matters of state, bring to its councils confusion and tumult, or servility and corruption; and seldom suffer it to repose from ruinous factions, or the effects of resolutions ill formed and ill conducted.'[13]

This kind of transparency was no longer possible in the late nineteenth century. Just as the ruling classes sought various ways to limit mass-democracy in practice, they adopted ideological strategies to place limits on democracy in theory. And just as revolutionary theories were 'domesticated' – for example, by French, American, and even English ruling classes[14] – so too they appropriated and naturalised democracy, assimilating its meaning to whatever political goods their particular interests could tolerate. The reconceptualisation of democracy belongs, it might be said, to the new climate of political hypocrisy and duplicity.

In an age of mass-mobilisation, then, the concept of democracy was subjected to new ideological pressures from dominant classes, demanding not only the alienation of 'democratic' power, but a clear dissociation of 'democracy' from the *'demos'* – or, at least, a decisive shift away from popular power as the principal criterion of democratic values. The effect was to shift the focus of 'democracy' away from the active exercise of popular power to the passive enjoyment of constitutional and procedural safeguards and rights, and away from the collective power of subordinate classes to the privacy and isolation of the individual citizen. More and more, the concept of 'democracy' came to be identified with *liberalism*. (The meaning of the word 'liberalism' is notoriously elusive and variable. I am using it here to refer to a body of commonly related principles having to do with 'limited' government, civil liberties, toleration, and the protection of a sphere of privacy against intrusion by the state, together with an emphasis on individuality, diversity and pluralism.)

The moment of this transvaluation is difficult to isolate, associated as it was with protracted and arduous political and ideological struggles. But hints can be found in the unresolved tensions and contradictions in the theory and practice of nineteenth-century liberalism, torn between a distaste for mass-democracy and a recognition of its inevitability, perhaps even its necessity and justice, or at any rate the advantages of mass-mobilisation in promoting programmes of reform and the wisdom of domesticating the 'many-headed hydra', the turbulent multitude, by drawing it into the civic community.

---

13. Ferguson 1978, p. 187.
14. Hobsbawm 1987, pp. 93–4.

John Stuart Mill is, perhaps, only the most extreme example of the contradictions that constituted nineteenth-century liberalism. On the one hand, he showed a strong distaste for the 'levelling' tendencies and 'collective mediocrity' of mass-democracy (nowhere more than in the *locus classicus* of modern liberalism, his essay 'On Liberty'), his Platonism, his élitism, his imperialist conviction that colonial peoples would benefit from a period of tutelage under the rule of their colonial masters; and, on the other hand, his advocacy of the rights of women, of universal suffrage (which could be made compatible with a kind of *class*-tutelage by maintaining weighted voting, as he proposes in *Considerations on Representative Government*); and he even flirted with socialist ideas (always on the condition that capitalism be preserved until 'better minds' had lifted the multitude out of its need for 'coarse stimuli', the motivations of material gain and subjection to the lower appetites). Mill never resolved this systematic ambivalence towards democracy, but we can perhaps find some hint of a possible resolution in a rather curious place, in his judgment on the original democracy of ancient Athens.

What is striking about Mill's judgment is his identification of Athenian democracy with its encouragement of variety and individuality, in contrast to the narrow and stultifying conservatism of the Spartans – whom Mill [...] even called the Tories of Greece. This characterisation of ancient Athens contrasts sharply, of course, with Mill's account of modern democracy and the threat he perceives in it to individuality and excellence. The very different assessment of democracy in its ancient form was, however, made possible only by a conspicuous evasiveness about the one literally *democratic* feature of Athenian democracy, its extension of citizenship to labouring, 'base' and 'mechanic' classes. While Mill advocated a (qualified) extension of the suffrage to the 'multitude', he evinced a notable lack of enthusiasm for rule by the *demos*, and was not inclined to dwell on its role in the ancient democracy. Far better to invoke the *liberal* values of classical Athens.

And so we come to 'liberal democracy'. The familiarity of this formula may disguise everything that is historically and ideologically problematic in this distinctively modern coupling, and it could do with some critical unpacking. There is more to this formula than the expansion of 'liberalism' to 'liberal democracy' – that is, the addition of democratic principles like universal suffrage to the pre-democratic values of constitutionalism and 'limited government'. Rather more difficult questions are raised by the *contraction* of democracy to liberalism. There is a long-standing convention that political progress or 'modernisation' has taken the form of a movement from monarchy to 'limited' or constitutional government to democracy, and more particularly from absolutism to 'liberalism' to 'liberal democracy'. In a sense, the process I am describing here reverses the conventional sequence: democracy has been overtaken by liberalism.

There was no 'liberalism' – no constitutionalism, limited government, 'individual rights' and 'civil liberties' – in classical antiquity. Ancient democracy, where the 'state' had no separate existence as a corporate entity apart from the community of citizens, produced no clear conception of a separation between 'state' and 'civil society' and no set of ideas or institutions to check the power of the state or to protect 'civil society' and the individual citizen from its intrusions. 'Liberalism' had as its fundamental pre-condition the development of a centralised state separate from, and superior to, other, more particularistic jurisdictions.

But, although 'liberalism' is a modern coinage which presupposes the 'modern' state (at least early modern absolutism), its central conceptions of liberty and constitutional limits have an earlier provenance. Liberal conceptions of limited or constitutional government, and of inviolable liberties asserted against the state, have their origins, in the late-medieval and early-modern periods, in the assertion of independent powers of *lordship* by European aristocracies against encroachment by centralising monarchies. These conceptions, in other words, at the outset represented an attempt to safeguard feudal liberties, powers and privileges. They were not democratic in their intent or in their consequences, representing backward-looking claims to a piece of the old parcelised sovereignty of feudalism, not looking forwards to a more modern democratic political order. And the association of these ideas with lordship persisted for a long time, well beyond the demise of feudalism.

There is no doubt that these essentially feudal principles were later appropriated for more democratic purposes by more 'modern' or progressive forces. Since the seventeenth century, they have been expanded from the privileges of lordship to more universal civil liberties and human rights; and they have been enriched by the values of religious and intellectual toleration. But the original principles of liberalism are derived from a system of social relations very different from the one to which they have been adapted. They were not conceived to deal with the wholly new disposition of social power that emerged with modern capitalism. This inherent limitation (about which, more in a moment) is compounded by the fact that the idea of liberalism has been made to serve much larger purposes than its basic principles were ever intended to do. Liberalism has entered modern political discourse not only as a set of ideas and institutions designed to limit state-power, but also as a *substitute* for democracy.

The original, aristocratic idea of constitutional checks on monarchical power had no associations with the idea of democracy. Its identification with 'democracy' was a much later development, which had more to do with an assertion of ruling-class powers *against* the people. The unquestionable benefits of this 'liberal' idea should not obscure the fact that its *substitution* for democracy was a *counter-revolutionary* project – or at least a means of containing revolutions already underway, stopping them short of exceeding acceptable boundaries.

Capitalism and 'liberal democracy'

Liberties that meant a great deal to early-modern aristocracies, and whose extension to the multitude *then* would have completely transformed society, cannot mean the same thing now – not least because the so-called economy has acquired a life of its own, completely outside the ambit of citizenship, political freedom, or democratic accountability. The essence of modern 'democracy' is not so much that it has *abolished* privilege, or, alternatively, that it has *extended* traditional privileges to the multitude, but rather that it has borrowed a conception of freedom designed for a world where privilege was the relevant category, and applied it to a world where privilege is not the problem. In a world where juridical or political status is not the primary determinant of our life chances, where our activities and experiences lie largely outside the reach of our legal or political identities, freedom defined in these terms leaves too much out of account.

There is, here, a paradox. Liberalism is a modern idea based on premodern, precapitalist forms of power. At the same time, if the basic principles of liberalism pre-date capitalism, what makes it possible to identify *democracy* with liberalism is capitalism itself. The idea of 'liberal democracy' became thinkable – and I mean literally thinkable – only with the emergence of capitalist social property-relations. Capitalism made possible the *redefinition* of democracy, its reduction to liberalism. On the one hand, there was now a separate political sphere, in which 'extra-economic' – political, juridical or military – status had no direct implications for economic power, the power of appropriation, exploitation and distribution. On the other hand, there now existed an economic sphere with its own power-relations, not dependent on juridical or political privilege.

So the very conditions that make liberal democracy possible also narrowly limit the scope of democratic accountability. Liberal democracy leaves untouched the whole new sphere of domination and coercion created by capitalism, its relocation of substantial powers from the state to civil society, to private property and the compulsions of the market. It leaves untouched vast areas of our daily lives – in the workplace, in the distribution of labour and resources – which are not subject to democratic accountability, but are governed by the powers of property and the 'laws' of the market, the imperatives of profit-maximisation. This would remain true even in the unlikely event that our 'formal democracy' were perfected so that wealth and economic power no longer meant the gross inequality of access to state-power which now characterises the reality, if not the ideal, of modern capitalist democracy.

The characteristic way in which liberal democracy deals with this new sphere of power is not to check, but to liberate it. In fact, liberalism does not even recognise it as a sphere of power or coercion at all. This, of course, is especially true of the market, which tends to be conceived as an opportunity, not a compulsion. The market is conceived as a sphere of freedom, choice, even by those who see the need to regulate it. Any limits that may be necessary to correct the harmful effects of this freedom are perceived as just that, limits. As with most kinds of freedom, there may have to be certain restrictions or regulations imposed on it to maintain social order; but it is still a kind of freedom. In other words, in the conceptual framework of liberal democracy, we cannot really talk, or even *think*, about freedom *from* the market. We cannot think of freedom from the market as a kind of empowerment, a liberation from compulsion, an emancipation from coercion and domination.

What about the current tendency to *identify* democracy with the 'free market'? What about this new definition, according to which the 'new democracies' of Eastern Europe are 'democratic' in proportion to their progress in 'marketisation', President Yeltsin's accretion of power to the presidency is 'democratic' because it is conducted in the name of 'privatisation' and 'the market', or General Pinochet was more 'democratic' than a freely-elected Salvador Allende? Does this usage represent a subversion or distortion of liberal democracy?

The balance has certainly been tilted too far, but it is not completely inconsistent with the fundamental principles of liberal democracy. The very condition that makes it possible to define democracy as we do in modern liberal-capitalist societies is the separation and enclosure of the economic sphere and its invulnerability to democratic power. Protecting that invulnerability has even become an essential criterion of democracy. This definition allows us to invoke democracy *against* the empowerment of the people in the economic sphere. It even makes it possible to invoke democracy in defence of a *curtailment* of democratic rights in other parts of 'civil society' or even in the political domain, if that is what is needed to protect property and the market against democratic power.

The sphere of economic power in capitalism has expanded far beyond the capacities of 'democracy' to cope with it; and liberal democracy, whether as a set of institutions or a system of ideas, is not designed to extend its reach into that domain. If we are confronting the 'end of History', it may not be in the sense that liberal democracy has triumphed, but rather in the sense that it has very nearly reached its limits. There is much good in liberalism that needs to be preserved, protected and improved, not only in parts of the world where it scarcely exists but even in capitalist democracies where it is still imperfect and often under threat. Yet the scope for further historical development may belong to the *other* tradition of democracy, the tradition overshadowed by liberal democracy, the idea of democracy in its literal meaning as popular power.

Although we have found new ways of protecting 'civil society' from the 'state', and the 'private' from intrusions by the 'public', we have yet to find new, modern ways to match the depth of freedom and democracy enjoyed by the Athenian citizen in other respects. In *The Persians*, Aeschylus has a chorus of Persian elders tell us that to be an Athenian citizen is to be masterless, a servant to no mortal man.[15] Or recall the speech in Euripides' *The Suppliants*[16] describing a free *polis* as one in which the rule of law allows equal justice to rich and poor, strong and weak alike, where anyone who has something useful to say has the right to speak before the public – that is, where there is *isegoria* – but also where the free citizen does not labour just in order to enrich a tyrant by his toil. There is something, here, which is completely absent from, and even antithetical to, the later European concept of liberty. It is the free-dom of the *demos from* masters, not the freedom of the masters themselves. It is not the oligarch's *eleutheria*, in which freedom *from* labour is the ideal qualification for citizenship, but the *eleutheria* of the labouring *demos* and the freedom *of* labour.

In practice, Athenian democracy was, certainly, exclusive, so much so that it may seem odd to call it a democracy at all. The majority of the population – women, slaves, and resident aliens (metics) – did not enjoy the privileges of citizenship. But the necessity of working for a living and even lack of prop-erty were not grounds for exclusion from full political rights. In this respect, Athens exceeded the criteria of all but the most visionary democrats for many centuries thereafter.

Nor is it self-evident that even the most democratic polity today confers on its propertyless and working classes powers equal to those enjoyed by 'banausic' citizens in Athens. Modern democracy has become more inclusive, finally abolishing slavery and granting citizenship to women as well as to

---

15. Aeschylus, *The Persians*, 242.
16. Euripides, *The Suppliants*, 429 ff.

working men. It has also gained much from the absorption of 'liberal' principles, respect for civil liberties and 'human rights'. But the progress of modern democracy has been far from unambiguous, for as political rights have become less exclusive, they have also lost much of their power.

We are, then, left with more questions than answers. How might citizenship, in modern conditions and with an inclusive citizen-body, regain the salience it once had? What would it mean, in a modern capitalist democracy, not only to preserve the gains of liberalism, civil liberties and the protection of 'civil society', nor even just to invent more democratic conceptions of representation and new modes of local autonomy, but also to recover powers lost to the 'economy'? What would it take to recover democracy from the formal separation of the 'political' and the 'economic', when political privilege has been replaced by economic coercion, exerted not just by capitalist property directly, but also through the medium of the market? If capitalism has replaced political privilege with the powers of economic coercion, what would it mean to extend citizenship – and this means not just a greater equality of 'opportunity', or the passive entitlements of welfare-provision, but democratic accountability or active self-government – into the economic sphere?

Is it possible to conceive of a form of democratic citizenship that reaches into the domain sealed off by modern capitalism? Could capitalism survive such an extension of democracy? Is capitalism compatible with democracy in its literal sense? If its current malaise proves still more protracted, will it even remain compatible with liberalism? Can capitalism still rely on its capacity to deliver material prosperity, and will it triumph together with liberal democracy, or will its survival in hard times increasingly depend on a curtailment of democratic rights?

Is liberal democracy, in theory and practice, adequate to deal even with the conditions of modern capitalism, let alone whatever may lie outside or beyond it? Does liberal democracy look like the 'end of History' because it has surpassed all conceivable alternatives, or because it has exhausted its own capacities, while concealing other possibilities? Has it really overcome all rivals, or simply obscured them temporarily from view?

The task that liberalism sets for itself is, and will always remain, indispensable. As long as there are states, there will be a need to check their power and to safeguard independent powers and organisations outside the state. For that matter, any kind of social power needs to be hedged around with protections for freedom of association, communication, diversity of opinion, an inviolable private sphere, and so on. On these scores, any future democracy will continue to have lessons to learn from the liberal tradition in theory and in practice. But liberalism – even as an ideal, let alone as a deeply flawed actuality – is not equipped to cope with the realities of power in a capitalist society, and even less to encompass a more inclusive kind of democracy than now exists.

Liberal democracy and capitalist hegemony

Something more needs to be said about the role of liberal democracy in sustaining the hegemony of capitalism. The question is not an easy one; and if it is important not to fall into the very mystifications that sustain that hegemony, it is no less important to avoid dismissing liberal democracy as nothing more than a mystification. In what follows, therefore, the term 'liberal democracy' will continue to be used instead of, say, 'bourgeois' or 'capitalist democracy', if only because these terms in a sense prejudge the issues in dispute. We are not quite ready to conflate 'liberalism' entirely with capitalism.

The first question that should be raised has to do with the nature of capitalist relations of production and the sense in which they form the kernel of liberal-democratic principles. This question has important strategic implications. One could [...] begin by assuming not only that the relation of liberal democracy to capitalism is tangential and contingent, but even that liberal-democratic 'freedom' and 'equality' are somehow *antithetical* to capitalist domination and inequality. Social-democratic revisionism seems to have been based on such an assumption, with its strategy of 'patchwork-reform' and passive faith in some 'peaceful process of dissolution'[17] which would eventually and more-or-less automatically transform capitalism into socialism. This strategy seems to have been based on the premise that the liberty and equality of bourgeois democracy were so antithetical to capitalism that the mere maintenance of bourgeois juridical and political institutions, assisted by reform, would produce a tension between freedom and equality at this level and unfreedom and inequality at other levels of society.[18] This tension would, in a sense, replace class-struggle as the motor of social transformation. At the other extreme might be a position that regards liberal democracy as so completely a mere reflection of capitalism that it must be regarded as simply a deception, a mystification. This is, roughly, the position of various ultra-left groups. Liberal-democratic capitalist states, according to this view, are not

---

17. This is how Marx describes the principles of German Social Democracy in 'Circular Letter to Bebel, Liebknecht, Bracke, and Others, 17-18 September 1879' (Marx 1978).
18. See Colletti 1972, pp. 92–7.

substantially different from authoritarian, or even fascist, forms of capitalism. If such radically divergent programmes are associated with different assessments of liberalism and its relation to capitalism, an attempt to situate liberalism in the capitalist mode of production cannot be an insignificant task for socialist political theory. […]

[…] A proper evaluation of liberal democracy, then, implies an appreciation of the ways in which the capitalist state is an active agent in class-struggle, the ways in which political powers are deployed in the interests of the dominant class, how the state enters directly into the relations of production – not only on the higher planes of class-struggle, but in the immediate confrontation between capital and labour in the workplace itself; the ways in which, for example, the legal apparatus and police-functions of the state are the necessary foundations of the contractual relation among 'equals' which constitutes the domination of the working class by the capitalists. An analysis of the link between liberalism and capitalism must recognise that the 'autonomy' and 'universality' of the capitalist state are precisely the essence of its perfection as a *class*-state; that this 'autonomy' and 'universality' (which are not merely apparent, but to a significant extent real), and the appearance of class-neutrality which is the special characteristic of the capitalist state, are all made possible and necessary by precisely that condition which also makes capitalism an effective form of class-exploitation: the complete separation of the producers from the means of production and the concentration in private hands of the capacity for direct surplus-extraction. It must be acknowledged that the clear separation of class and state in capitalism – expressed, for example, in the state's monopoly of force, which can be turned against members of the dominant class itself – is not merely a separation, but a more perfect symbiosis, in effect a cooperative division of labour between class and state which allocates to them separately the essential functions of an exploiting class: surplus-extraction and the coercive power that sustains it.

At the same time, liberal democracy, while grounded in the juridical principles of capitalist productive relations, cannot be reduced to them. The minimal form of freedom and equality intrinsic to capitalism *need* not give rise to the most developed form. If equality and freedom of a very limited and ambiguous kind are essential and common to *all* capitalist social formations, liberal-democratic political institutions have *not* been equally common and are certainly not essential to capitalism, even if they have been most conducive to capitalist development under certain historic conditions. The nature of the relation between capitalism and liberal democracy must, therefore, be further specified, with due consideration not only to general structural links, but to the particular realities of history. One must go beyond the function of

juridical and political freedom and equality in sustaining capitalist relations
of production and the position of the dominant class, and take account of
the value liberal-democratic political forms have had for subordinate classes,
indeed, the degree to which these political and legal forms are the legacy of
historic struggles by subordinate classes. The role of liberal democracy in
civilising capitalist exploitation must be acknowledged; and this acknowledgement entails a recognition of the crucial differences among forms of capitalist state. There is a massive difference between capitalism with a liberal face
and capitalism in a fascist guise. Not the least difference concerns the position
of subordinate classes, their freedom to organise and to resist. The seduction
of working-class movements by liberal-democratic political forms cannot be
lightly dismissed as a failure of class-consciousness or a betrayal of the revolution. The attractions of these institutions have been very real in countries
where the tradition has been strongest. In those countries where the tradition
has been weak, recent history has surely demonstrated as dramatically as possible that the absence of these forms has serious consequences and that their
acquisition and retention are worthy goals for a working-class movement.
Any socialist strategy ignores at its peril the hold exercised by these political
principles and institutions, or underestimates the legitimacy of their claims.

To sum up, liberal democracy can neither be completely separated from,
nor reduced to the principles of capitalist exploitation. Any reasonable analysis must consider both the foundations of liberal democracy in capitalist relations of production and its historic role in checking the excesses of capitalism.
At the same time, it must be acknowledged that the particular effectiveness of
liberal-democratic institutions rests not only on their performance – in common with other forms of state-power – as coercive instruments, but also on
their uniquely powerful *hegemonic* functions.

The legal and political institutions of liberal democracy may be the most
potent ideological force available to the capitalist class – in some respects even
more powerful than the material advances achieved under the auspices of
capitalism. The very form of the state itself, and not simply the ideological
or cultural apparatus that sustains it, is persuasive. What gives this political
form its peculiar hegemonic power, as Perry Anderson has argued, is that
the consent it commands from the dominated classes does not simply rest on
their submission to an acknowledged ruling class or their acceptance of its
right to rule. The parliamentary-democratic state is a unique form of class-
rule because it casts doubt on the very existence of a ruling class.[19] It does not,
however, achieve this effect by pure mystification. As always, hegemony has

---

19. P. Anderson 1976–7, p. 30.

two sides. It is not possible if it is not plausible.[20] Liberal democracy is the outcome of long and painful struggles. It has conferred genuine benefits on subordinate classes and given them real strengths, new possibilities of organisation and resistance which cannot be abandoned to the enemy as mere sham. To say that liberal democracy is 'hegemonic' is to say both that it serves the particular interests of the capitalist class, and that its claims to universality have an element of truth.

The point is not that people are necessarily duped into believing that they are truly sovereign when they are not; it is, rather, that with the triumph of representative institutions and finally the achievement of universal suffrage, the outer limits of popular sovereignty on a purely *political* plane really have been reached. Thus, the severe restrictions imposed upon popular power by the character of parliamentary democracy as a *class*-state may appear as the limitations of democracy itself.[21] At least, the full development of liberal democracy means that the further extension of popular power requires not simply the perfection of existing political institutions, but a radical transformation of social arrangements in general, in ways that are as yet unknown. This also means putting at risk hard-won gains for the sake of uncertain benefits. A major obstacle to the socialist project is that it requires not merely a quantitative change, not simply another extension of suffrage or a further incursion by representative institutions upon executive power, but a qualitative leap to new forms of democracy with no successful historical precedent.

Capitalist hegemony, then, rests to a significant extent on a formal separation of 'political' and 'economic' spheres, which makes possible the maximum development of purely juridical and political freedom and equality without fundamentally endangering economic exploitation.[22] Liberal-democratic legal and political forms are compatible with, indeed grounded in, capitalist relations of production because, with the complete separation of the producer from the means of production, surplus-extraction no longer requires direct 'extra-economic' coercion or the producer's juridical dependence. The coercive power on which capitalist property ultimately rests can thus appear in the form of a 'neutral' and 'autonomous' state. Not surprisingly, therefore, the separation of political and economic spheres that characterises the liberal state in *practice* has also been enshrined in *theory*, particularly in the English-speaking

---

20. For a very fine discussion of this aspect of class-hegemony, see Thompson 1975 on the rule of law as the expression of ruling-class hegemony in eighteenth-century England, especially pp. 262–3.

21. P. Anderson 1976–7, p. 30 and n. 53.

22. These points are discussed in greater detail in my article E.M. Wood 1981a. A modified version of this article is included as Chapter One of E.M. Wood 1995a.

world, where the liberal tradition has been especially strong. The effect has
been to produce various modes of political analysis that abstract 'politics'
from its social foundations: for example, in political philosophy, where concepts like 'freedom', 'equality', and 'justice' are subjected to intricately formalistic analysis deliberately divorced from social implications; or 'political
science', which scrutinises political 'behaviour' or political 'systems' as if they
were devoid of social content. These procedures give theoretical expression to
the abstraction of 'politics' in the liberal-democratic state and to the appearance of 'universality' or 'neutrality' on which its hegemony rests; and they
urge us to accept formal equality and freedom without looking too closely at
the substance enveloped in the form. [...]

To counter the ideological hegemony of the capitalist class, therefore, the
task of the theorist is *not* to demonstrate that what *appears* universal in bourgeois ideology really *is* universal, having 'no precise class-connotations' –
which is, in effect, precisely to accept the hegemonic claims of the dominant
class – but rather, to explain how what appears universal is, in fact, particular;
not simply to extract from liberal-democratic forms a sense in which they do
not express capitalist class-interests, but also to understand clearly the sense
in which they *do*; not to empty ideological formulae of their specific social content, but to explicate the specificity and particularity of meaning in them; not
to abstract ideology from its historic conditions in order to convert particular
class-interests into universal principles available for 're-articulation', but to
explore the historic conditions that have made possible the generalisation of a
particular class-interest and conferred 'universality' on the capitalist class.

This is, again, not to say that socialist political theory must, by reducing
liberal democracy to class-ideology, dismiss it as pure mystification or sham.
The point is simply that an account must be given of liberal democracy which
makes clearly visible not only its limitations, but also the *discontinuity*, the
radical break, between liberalism and socialism. If the defeat of capitalist
hegemony rests on the reclamation of democracy by socialism (and insofar as
that reclamation can be assisted by theoretical means), it cannot be achieved
simply by 'disarticulating' democracy from bourgeois class-ideology. New,
socialist, forms of democracy must be defined whose specificity is clear and
which represent an unmistakable challenge to the claims of bourgeois democracy that its particular form of 'popular sovereignty' is universal and final.

The idea of 'civil society'

At a time when a critique of capitalism is more urgent than ever, the dominant
theoretical trends on the Left are busy conceptualising away the very idea of

capitalism. The 'postmodern' world, we are told, is a pastiche of fragments and 'difference'. The systemic unity of capitalism, its 'objective structures' and totalising imperatives, have given way (if they ever existed) to a brico-lage of multiple social realities, a pluralistic structure so diverse and flexible that it can be rearranged by discursive construction. The traditional capitalist economy has been replaced by a 'post-Fordist' fragmentation, where every fragment opens up a space for emancipatory struggles. The constitutive class-relations of capitalism represent only one personal 'identity' among many others, no longer 'privileged' by its historic centrality. And so on.

However diverse the methods of conceptually dissolving capitalism – including everything from the theory of post-Fordism to postmodern 'cul-tural studies' and the 'politics of identity' – they often share one especially serviceable concept: 'civil society'. After a long and somewhat tortuous his-tory, after a series of milestones in the works of Hegel, Marx and Gramsci, this versatile idea has become an all-purpose catchword for the Left, embracing a wide range of emancipatory aspirations, as well – it must be said – as a whole set of excuses for political retreat. However constructive this idea may be in defending human liberties against state-oppression, or in marking out a ter-rain of social practices, institutions and relations neglected by the 'old' Marx-ist left, 'civil society' is now in danger of becoming an alibi for capitalism.

There has been a long intellectual tradition in the West, even reaching back to classical antiquity, which has in various ways delineated a terrain of human association, some notion of 'society', distinct from the body-politic and with moral claims independent of, and sometimes opposed to, the state's author-ity. Whatever other factors have been at work in producing such concepts, their evolution has been from the beginning bound up with the development of private property as a distinct and autonomous locus of social power. For example, although the ancient Romans, like the Greeks, still tended to iden-tify the state with the community of citizens, the 'Roman people', they did produce some major advances in the conceptual separation of state and 'soci-ety', especially in the Roman law, which distinguished between public and private spheres and gave private property a legal status and clarity it had never enjoyed before.[23]

In that sense, although the modern concept of 'civil society' is associated with the specific property-relations of capitalism, it is a variation on an old theme. Nevertheless, the variation is a critical one; and any attempt to dilute the specificity of this 'civil society', to obscure its differentiation from earlier

---

23. For an argument that the Romans, specifically in the person of Cicero, had a concept of 'society', see N. Wood 1988, especially pp. 136–42.

conceptions of 'society', risks disguising the particularity of capitalism itself as a distinct social form with its own characteristic social relations, its own modes of appropriation and exploitation, its own rules of reproduction, its own systemic imperatives.[24]

The very particular modern conception of 'civil society' – a conception that appeared systematically for the first time in the eighteenth century – is something quite distinct from earlier notions of 'society': civil society represents a separate sphere of human relations and activity, differentiated from the state but neither public nor private, or perhaps both at once, embodying not only a whole range of social interactions apart from the private sphere of the household and the public sphere of the state, but more specifically a network of distinctively economic relations, the sphere of the market-place, the arena of production, distribution and exchange. A necessary but not sufficient precondition for this conception of civil society was the modern idea of the state as an abstract entity with its own corporate identity, which evolved with the rise of European absolutism; but the full conceptual differentiation of 'civil society' required the emergence of an autonomous 'economy', separated out from the unity of the 'political' and 'economic' which still characterised the absolutist state.

Paradoxically – or perhaps not so paradoxically – the early usages of the term 'civil society' in the birthplace of capitalism, in early-modern England, far from establishing an opposition between civil society and the state, conflated the two. In sixteenth- and seventeenth-century English political thought, 'civil society' was typically synonymous with the 'commonwealth' or 'political society'. This conflation of state and 'society' represented the subordination of the state to the community of private-property holders (as against both monarch and 'multitude') which constituted the political nation. It reflected a unique political dispensation, in which the dominant class depended for its wealth and power increasingly on purely 'economic' modes of appropriation, instead of on directly coercive 'extra-economic' modes of accumulation by political and military means, like feudal rent-taking or absolutist taxation and office-holding as primary instruments of private appropriation.

But, if English usage tended to blur the distinction between state and civil society, it was English conditions – the very same system of property-relations and capitalist appropriation, but now more advanced and with a more highly

---

24. Much of John Keane's argument is, for example, predicated on a criticism of Marxism for its identification of 'civil society' with capitalism, which he opposes by invoking the long tradition of conceptions of 'society' in the West, reaching much further back than the advent of capitalism. See Keane 1988a.

developed market-mechanism – that made possible the modern conceptual opposition between the two. [...]

The civil-society argument

The concept of 'civil society' is being mobilised to serve so many varied purposes that it is impossible to isolate a single school of thought associated with it; but some common themes have emerged. 'Civil society' is generally intended to identify an arena of (at least potential) freedom outside the state, a space for autonomy, voluntary association and plurality or even conflict, guaranteed by the kind of 'formal democracy' that has evolved in the West. The concept is also meant to reduce the capitalist system (or the 'economy') to one of many spheres in the plural and heterogeneous complexity of modern society. The concept of 'civil society' can achieve this effect in one of two principal ways. It can be made to designate that multiplicity itself as against the coercions of both state and capitalist economy; or, more commonly, it can encompass the 'economy' within a larger sphere of multiple non-state institutions and relations.[25] In either case, the emphasis is on the plurality of social relations and practices among which the capitalist economy takes its place as one of many.

The principal current usages proceed from the distinction between civil society and state. 'Civil society' is defined by the advocates of this distinction in terms of a few simple oppositions: for example, 'the state (and its military, policing, legal, administrative, productive, and cultural organs) and the non-state (market-regulated, privately controlled or voluntarily organised) realm of civil society';[26] or 'political' versus 'social' power, 'public' versus 'private' law, 'state-sanctioned (dis)information and propaganda' versus 'freely circulated public opinion'.[27] In this definition, 'civil society' encompasses a very wide range of institutions and relations, from households, trade-unions, voluntary associations, hospitals, churches, to the market, capitalist enterprises, indeed, the whole capitalist economy. The significant antitheses are simply state and non-state, or perhaps political and social.

This dichotomy apparently corresponds to the opposition between coercion, as embodied in the state, and freedom or voluntary action, which belongs in principle, if not necessarily in practice, to civil society. Civil society may be

25. Something like the first conception can, for example, be extracted from Cohen 1982. The second view is elaborated by Keane 1988a. For his criticism of Cohen's conception, see p. 86 n.
26. Keane 1988b, p. 1.
27. Keane 1988b, p. 2.

in various ways and degrees submerged or eclipsed by the state, and different political systems or whole 'historical regions' may vary according to the degree of 'autonomy' which they accord to the non-state sphere. It is a special characteristic of the West, for example, that it has given rise to a uniquely well-developed separation of state and civil society, and hence a particularly advanced form of political freedom.

The advocates of this state/civil-society distinction generally ascribe to it two principal benefits. First, it focuses our attention on the dangers of state-oppression and on the need to set proper limits on the actions of the state, by organising and reinforcing the pressures against it within society. In other words, it revives the liberal concern with the limitation and legitimation of political power, and especially the control of such power by freedom of association and autonomous organisation within society, too often neglected by the Left in theory and practice. Second, the concept of civil society recognises and celebrates difference and diversity. Its advocates make pluralism a primary good, in contrast, it is claimed, to Marxism, which is, they say, essentially monistic, reductionist, economistic.[28] This new pluralism invites us to appreciate a whole range of institutions and relations neglected by traditional socialism in its preoccupation with the economy and class.

The impetus to the revival of this conceptual dichotomy has come from several directions. The strongest impulse undoubtedly came from Eastern Europe, where 'civil society' was a major weapon in the ideological arsenal of opposition-forces against state-oppression. Here, the issues were fairly clear: the state – including both its political and economic apparatuses of domination – could be more-or-less unambiguously set against a (potentially) free space outside the state. The civil-society/state antithesis could, for example, be said to correspond neatly to the opposition of Solidarity to Party and state.[29]

The crisis of the Communist states has, needless to say, also left a deep impression on the Western Left, converging with other influences: the limitations of social democracy, with its unbounded faith in the state as the agent of social improvement, as well as the emergence of emancipatory struggles by social movements not based on class, with a sensitivity to dimensions of human experience all-too-often neglected by the traditional socialist Left. These heightened sensitivities to the dangers posed by the state and to the complexities of human experience have been associated with a wide range of activisms, taking in everything from feminism, ecology and peace, to consti-

---

28. Norman Geras debunks such myths about Marxism in Geras 1990.
29. For the application of 'civil society' to events in Poland, see Arato 1981 and 1981–2.

tutional reform. Each of these projects has often drawn upon the concept of civil society.

No socialist can doubt the value of these new sensitivities, but there must be serious misgivings about this particular method of focusing our attention on them. We are being asked to pay a heavy price for the all-embracing concept of 'civil society'. This conceptual portmanteau, which indiscriminately lumps together everything from households and voluntary associations to the economic system of capitalism, confuses and disguises as much as it reveals. In Eastern Europe, it can be made to apprehend everything from the defence of political rights and cultural freedoms to the marketisation of post-Communist economies and the restoration of capitalism. 'Civil society' can serve as a code-word or cover for capitalism, and the market can be lumped together with other less ambiguous goods, like political and intellectual liberties, as an unequivocally desirable goal.

But if the dangers of this conceptual strategy and of assigning the market to the free space of 'civil society' appear to pale before the enormity of Stalinist oppression in the East, problems of an altogether different order arise in the West, where a fully developed capitalism does actually exist, and where state-oppression is not an immediate and massive evil which overwhelms all other social ills. Since, in this case, 'civil society' is made to encompass a whole layer of social reality that did not exist in Communist societies, the implications of its usage are, in some important respects, even more problematic.

Here, the danger lies in the fact that the totalising logic and the coercive power of capitalism become invisible, when the whole social system of capitalism is reduced to one set of institutions and relations among many others, on a conceptual par with households or voluntary associations. Such a reduction is, in fact, the principal distinctive feature of 'civil society' in its new incarnation. Its effect is to conceptualise away the problem of capitalism, by disaggregating society into fragments, with no overarching power-structure, no totalising unity, no systemic coercions – in other words, no capitalist system, with its expansionary drive and its capacity to penetrate every aspect of social life.

It is a typical strategy of the 'civil society' argument – indeed, its *raison d'être* – to attack Marxist 'reductionism' or 'economism'. Marxism, it is said, reduces civil society to the 'mode of production', the capitalist economy. 'The importance of other institutions of civil society – such as households, churches, scientific and literary associations, prisons and hospitals – is devalued'.[30]

---

30. Keane 1988a, p. 32.

Whether or not Marxists have habitually paid too little attention to these 'other' institutions, the weakness of this juxtaposition (the capitalist economy and 'other institutions' like hospitals?) should be immediately apparent. It must, surely, be possible even for non-Marxists to acknowledge, for example, the very simple truth that in the West hospitals are situated within a capitalist economy which has profoundly affected the organisation of health-care and the nature of medical institutions. But is it possible to conceive of an analogous proposition about the effects of hospitals on capitalism? Does this observation about 'other institutions' mean that Marx did not value households and hospitals, or is it, rather, that he did not attribute to them the same historically determinative force? Is there no basis for distinguishing among these various 'institutions' on all sorts of quantitative and qualitative grounds, from size and scope to social power and historical efficacy? Typically, the current usage of 'civil society' evades questions like this. It also has the effect of confusing the moral claims of 'other' institutions with their determinative power, or rather of dismissing altogether the essentially empirical question of historical and social determinations.

There is another version of the argument which, instead of simply evading the systemic totality of capitalism, explicitly denies it. The very existence of other modes of domination than class-relations, other principles of stratification than class-inequality, other social struggles than class-struggle, is taken to demonstrate that capitalism, whose constitutive relation is class, is not a totalising system. The Marxist preoccupation with 'economic' relations and class at the expense of other social relations and identities is understood to demonstrate that the attempt to 'totalize all society from the standpoint of one sphere, the economy or the mode of production', is misconceived for the simple reason that other 'spheres' self-evidently exist.[31]

This argument is circular and question-begging. To deny the totalising logic of capitalism, it is not enough merely to indicate the plurality of social identities and relations. The class-relation that constitutes capitalism is not, after all, just a personal identity, nor even just a principle of 'stratification' or inequality. It is not only a specific system of power-relations, but also the constitutive relation of a distinctive social process, the dynamic of accumulation and the self-expansion of capital. Of course, it can be easily – self-evidently – shown that class is not the only principle of 'stratification', the only form of inequality and domination. But this tells us virtually nothing about the totalising logic of capitalism.

31. Cohen 1982, p. 192.

To deny the totalising logic of capitalism, it would have to be convincingly demonstrated that these other spheres and identities do not come – or not in any significant way – within the determinative force of capitalism, its system of social-property relations, its expansionary imperatives, its drive for accumulation, its commodification of all social life, its creation of the market as a necessity, a compulsive mechanism of competition and self-sustaining 'growth', and so on. But 'civil-society' arguments (or, indeed, 'post-Marxist' arguments in general) do not typically take the form of historically and empirically refuting the determinative effects of capitalist relations. Instead (when they do not take the simple circular form: capitalism is not a totalising system because spheres other than the economy exist) they tend to proceed as abstract philosophical arguments, as internal critiques of Marxist theory, or, most commonly, as moral prescriptions about the dangers of devaluing 'other' spheres of human experience.

In one form or another, capitalism is cut down to the size and weight of 'other' singular and specific institutions and disappears into a conceptual night where all cats are grey. The strategy of dissolving capitalism into an unstructured and undifferentiated plurality of social institutions and relations cannot help but weaken both the analytical and the normative force of 'civil society', its capacity to deal with the limitation and legitimation of power, as well as its usefulness in guiding emancipatory projects. The current theories occlude 'civil society' in its distinctive sense as a social form specific to capitalism, a systemic totality within which all 'other' institutions are situated and all social forces must find their way, a specific and unprecedented sphere of social power, which poses wholly new problems of legitimation and control, problems not addressed by traditional theories of the state nor by contemporary liberalism.

'Civil society' and the devaluation of democracy

It is not, then, enough to say that democracy can be expanded by detaching the principles of 'formal democracy' from any association with capitalism. Nor is it enough to say that capitalist democracy is incomplete, one stage in an unambiguously progressive development which must be perfected by socialism and advanced beyond the limitations of 'formal democracy'. The point is, rather, that the association of capitalism with 'formal democracy' represents a contradictory unity of advance and retreat, both an enhancement and a devaluation of democracy. 'Formal democracy' certainly is an improvement on political forms lacking civil liberties, the rule of law and the principle of representation. But it is also, equally and at the same time, a subtraction from the substance of the democratic idea, and one which is historically and structurally associated with capitalism.[32]

I have already elaborated on some of these themes in previous chapters. Here, it is enough to note a certain paradox in the insistence that we should not allow our conception of human emancipation to be constrained by the identification of 'formal democracy' with capitalism. If we think of human emancipation as little more than an extension of liberal democracy, then we may, in the end, be persuaded to believe that capitalism is, after all, its surest guarantee.

The separation of the state and civil society in the West has, certainly, given rise to new forms of freedom and equality, but it has also created new modes

---

32. The defence of formal democracy is sometimes explicitly accompanied by an attack on 'substantive' democracy. Agnes Heller writes: 'The statement of Aristotle, a highly realistic analyst, that all democracies are immediately transformed into anarchy, the latter into tyranny, was a statement of fact, not an aristocratic slandering by an anti-democrat. The Roman republic was not for a moment democratic. And I should like to add to all this that even if the degradation of modern democracies into tyrannies is far from being excluded (we were witnesses to it in the cases of German and Italian Fascism), the endurance of modern democracies is due precisely to their formal character' (Heller 1988, p. 130).

Let us take each sentence in turn. The denunciation of ancient democracy as the inevitable forerunner of anarchy and tyranny (which is, incidentally, more typical of Plato or Polybius than Aristotle) is, precisely, an anti-democratic slander. For one thing, it bears no relation to real historical sequences, causal or even chronological. Athenian democracy brought an end to the institution of tyranny, and went on to survive nearly two centuries, only to be defeated not by anarchy, but by a superior military power. During those centuries, of course, Athens produced an astonishingly fruitful and influential culture which survived its defeat and also laid the foundation for Western conceptions of citizenship and the rule of law. The Roman Republic was indeed 'not for a moment democratic', and the most notable result of its aristocratic régime was the demise of the Republic and its replacement by autocratic imperial rule. (The undemocratic Republic was, incidentally, a major inspiration for what Heller calls a 'constitutive' document of modern democracy, the US constitution.) To say that the 'degradation of modern democracies into tyrannies is far from being excluded' seems a bit coy in conjunction with a (parenthetical) reference to fascism – not to mention the history of war and imperialism which has been inextricably associated with the régime of 'formal democracy'. As for endurance, it is surely worth mentioning that there does not yet exist a 'formal democracy' whose life-span equals, let alone exceeds, the duration of the Athenian democracy. No European 'democracy', by Heller's criteria, is even a century old (in Britain, for example, plural voting survived until 1948); and the American republic, which she credits with the 'constitutive idea' of formal democracy, took a long time to improve on the Athenian exclusion of women and slaves, while free working men – full citizens in the Athenian democracy – cannot be said to have gained full admission even to 'formal' citizenship until the last state property-qualifications were removed in the nineteenth century (not to mention the variety of stratagems to discourage voting by the poor in general and blacks in particular, which have not been exhausted to this day). Thus, at best (and for white men only), an endurance-record of perhaps one century and a half exists for modern 'formal democracies'.

of domination and coercion. One way of characterising the specificity of 'civil society' as a particular social form unique to the modern world – the particular historical conditions that made possible the modern distinction between state and civil society – is to say that it constituted a new form of social power, in which many coercive functions that once belonged to the state were relocated in the 'private' sphere, in private property, class-exploitation, and market-imperatives. It is, in a sense, this 'privatisation' of public power that has created the historically novel realm of 'civil society'.

'Civil society' constitutes not only a wholly new relation between 'public' and 'private', but more precisely a wholly new 'private' realm, with a distinctive 'public' presence and oppressions of its own, a unique structure of power and domination, and a ruthless systemic logic. It represents a particular network of social relations that does not simply stand in opposition to the coercive, 'policing' and 'administrative' functions of the state, but represents the *relocation* of these functions, or at least some significant part of them. It entails a new division of labour between the 'public' sphere of the state and the 'private' sphere of capitalist property and the imperatives of the market, in which appropriation, exploitation and domination are detached from public authority and social responsibility; while these new private powers rely on the state to sustain them, by means of a more thoroughly concentrated power of enforcement than has ever existed before.

'Civil society' has given private property and its possessors a command over people and their daily lives, a power enforced by the state but accountable to no one, which many an old tyrannical state would have envied. Even those activities and experiences that fall outside the immediate command-structure of the capitalist enterprise, or outside the very great political power of capital, are regulated by the dictates of the market, the necessities of competition and profitability. Even when the market is not, as it commonly is in advanced capitalist societies, merely an instrument of power for giant conglomerates and multinational corporations, it is still a coercive force, capable of subjecting all human values, activities and relationships to its imperatives. No ancient despot could have hoped to penetrate the personal lives of his subjects – their life-chances, choices, preferences, opinions and relationships – in the same comprehensive and minute detail, not only in the workplace, but in every corner of their lives. And the market has created new instruments of power to be manipulated not only by multinational capital, but by advanced capitalist states, which can act to impose draconian 'market-disciplines' on other economies while often sheltering their own domestic capital. Coercion, in other words, has been not just a disorder of 'civil society', but one of its constitutive principles. For that matter, the coercive functions of the state have in large part been occupied with the enforcement of domination in civil society.

This historical reality tends to undermine the neat distinctions required by current theories which ask us to treat civil society as, at least in principle, the sphere of freedom and voluntary action, the antithesis of the irreducibly coercive principle which intrinsically belongs to the state. It is certainly true that in capitalist society, with its separation of 'political' and 'economic' spheres, or the state and civil society, coercive public power is centralised and concentrated to a greater degree than ever before, but this simply means that one of the principal functions of 'public' coercion by the state is to sustain 'private' power in civil society.

One of the most obvious examples of the distorted vision produced by the simple dichotomy between the state as the site of coercion and 'civil society' as a free space is the extent to which civil liberties like freedom of expression or the press in capitalist societies are measured not by the breadth of opinion and debate available in the media, but the extent to which the media are private property and capital is free to profit from them. The press is 'free' when it is private, however much it may 'manufacture consent'.

The current theories of civil society do, of course, acknowledge that civil society is not a realm of perfect freedom or democracy. It is, for example, marred by oppression in the family, in gender-relations, in the workplace, by racist attitudes, homophobia, and so on. In fact, at least in advanced-capitalist societies, such oppressions have become the main focus of struggle, as 'politics' in the old-fashioned sense, having to do with state-power, parties and opposition to them, has become increasingly unfashionable. Yet these oppressions are treated not as constitutive of civil society, but as dysfunctions in it. In principle, coercion belongs to the state, while civil society is where freedom is rooted; and human emancipation, according to these arguments, consists in the autonomy of civil society, its expansion and enrichment, its liberation from the state, and its protection by formal democracy. What tends to disappear from view, again, is the relations of exploitation and domination which irreducibly constitute civil society, not just as some alien and correctible disorder, but as its very essence, the particular structure of domination and coercion that is specific to capitalism as a systemic totality – and which also determines the coercive functions of the state.

Chapter Six

The Enlightenment, Postmodernism, and the Post-'New Left'

Modernity vs. capitalism: France vs. England

Whatever else people mean by 'modernity', and whether they think it is good or bad or both, they usually believe it has something to do with what sociologist Max Weber called the process of *rationalisation*: the rationalisation of the state in bureaucratic organisation, the rationalisation of the economy in industrial capitalism, the rationalisation of culture in the spread of education, the decline of superstition, and the progress of science and technology. The process of rationalisation is typically associated with certain intellectual or cultural patterns that go back to the Enlightenment: rationalism and an obsession with rational planning, a fondness for 'totalising' views of the world, the standardisation of knowledge, universalism (a belief in universal truths and values), and a belief in linear progress, especially of reason and freedom.

The Enlightenment is typically conceived of as a, if not the, major turning-point in the advance of modernity, and the conflation of modernity with capitalism is most readily visible in the way theories of modernity connect the Enlightenment with capitalism. The characteristic features of the Enlightenment are supposed to be associated with the development of capitalism, either because early capitalism, in the process of unfolding itself, created them, or because the advancement of 'rationalisation' that produced the Enlightenment also brought capitalism with it. Weber, for instance, is famous for distinguishing among various meanings of rationality (formal or instrumental versus substantive, and so on), yet his argument about the historical process of rationalisation depends, of course, on *assimilating* the various meanings of reason and rationality, so that the instrumental rationality of capitalism is, by definition, related to reason in its Enlightenment-meaning. For better or worse, the process that brought us the best of Enlightenment-principles – a resistance to all arbitrary power, a commitment to universal human emancipation, and a critical stance toward all kinds of authority, whether intellectual, religious, or political – is, according to this view, the same process that brought us the capitalist organisation of production.

To unravel the conflation of capitalism and modernity, we might begin by situating the Enlightenment in its own historical setting. Much of the Enlightenment-project belongs to a distinctly *non*-capitalist – not just *pre*-capitalist – society. Many features of the Enlightenment, in other words, are rooted in non-capitalist social property-relations. They belong to a social form that is not just a transitional point on the way to capitalism, but an alternative route out of feudalism. In particular, the French Enlightenment belongs to the absolutist state in France.

The absolutist state in eighteenth-century France functioned not just as a political form, but as an economic resource for a substantial section of the ruling class. In that sense, it represents not just the political but also the economic or material context of the Enlightenment. The absolutist state was a centralised instrument of extra-economic surplus-extraction, and office in the state was a form of property that gave its possessors access to peasant-produced surpluses. There also were other, decentralised forms of extra-economic appropriation, the residues of feudalism and its so-called 'parcelised sovereignties'. These forms of extra-economic appropriation were, in other words, directly antithetical to the purely *economic* form of *capitalist* exploitation.

Now consider the fact that the principal home of the so-called 'project of modernity', eighteenth-century France, was an overwhelmingly rural society, with a limited and fragmented internal market. Its markets still operated on non-capitalist principles: not the appropriation of surplus-value from commodified labour-power, not the creation of value in production, but the age-old practices of commercial profit-taking – profit on alienation, buying cheap and selling dear, with great commercial wealth derived especially from trading in luxury goods or supplies for the state. The overwhelmingly-peasant population was the antithesis of a mass-consumer market. As for the bourgeoisie, which is supposed to be the main material source, so to speak, of the

Enlightenment, it was *not* a capitalist class. In fact, it was not, for the most part, even a traditional commercial class. The main bourgeois actors in the Enlightenment, and later in the French Revolution, were professionals, office-holders, and intellectuals. Their quarrel with the aristocracy had little to do with liberating capitalism from the fetters of feudalism.

Where, then, did the principles of so-called 'modernity' come from? Did they come out of a new but growing capitalism? Did they represent an aspiring capitalist class struggling against a feudal aristocracy? Can we at least say that capitalism was the unintended consequence of the project of bourgeois modernity? Or did that project represent something different?

Consider the class-interests of the French bourgeoisie. One way of focusing on them is to turn to the French Revolution, often treated as the culmination of the Enlightenment-project. What were the main revolutionary objectives of the bourgeoisie? At the core of its programme were civil equality, the attack on privilege, and a demand for 'careers open to talent'. This meant, for example, equal access to the highest state-offices, which tended to be monopolised by birth and wealth and which the aristocracy were threatening to close off altogether. It also meant a more equitable system of taxation, so that the burden would no longer be disproportionately carried by the Third Estate for the benefit of the privileged estates, among whose most cherished privileges were exemptions from taxation. The targets of these complaints were the aristocracy and the Church.

How did these bourgeois interests express themselves ideologically? Take the example of universalism, the belief in certain principles that apply to humanity in general at all times and places. Universalism has had a long history in the West, but it had a very special meaning and salience for the French bourgeoisie. To put it briefly, the bourgeois challenge to privilege and the privileged estates, to the nobility and the Church, expressed itself in asserting universalism against aristocratic particularism. The bourgeoisie challenged the aristocracy by invoking the universal principles of citizenship, civic equality, and the 'nation' – a universalistic identity that transcended the more particular and exclusive identities of kinship, tribe, village, status, estate, or class.

In other words, *universality* was opposed to *privilege* in its literal meaning as a special or private law. Universality stood against privilege and differential rights. It was a fairly easy step from attacking traditional privilege to attacking the principles of custom and tradition in general. And this kind of challenge easily became a theory of history, in which the bourgeoisie and its organic intellectuals were assigned a leading role as the historic agents of a rupture with the past, the embodiments of reason and freedom, the vanguard of progress.

From modernity to postmodernity

Since about the early 1970s, we are supposed to have been living in a new his-torical epoch. That epoch has been described in various ways. Some accounts emphasise cultural changes ('postmodernism'), while others focus more on economic transformations, changes in production and marketing, or in cor-porate and financial organisation ('late capitalism', 'multinational capital-ism', 'flexible accumulation', and so on). These descriptions have in common a preoccupation with new technologies, new forms of communication, the Internet, the 'information-superhighway'. Whatever else this new age is, it is the 'information-age'. And whatever other factors are supposed to have figured in this epochal shift, the new technologies have been its indispensable condition. All these factors – cultural and economic, with their technological foundations – have been brought together in the concept of 'postmodernity' and the proposition that in the past two or three decades we have witnessed a historic transition from 'modernity' to postmodernity.

I want to consider what is involved in periodising the history of capitalism into these two major phases, modernity and postmodernity. Then I shall look more closely at what seems to me wrong with the concept of modernity itself. If *that* concept falls, it should follow that there cannot be much left of *post*-modernity. My main objective is to consider whether this periodisation helps or hinders our understanding of capitalism.

I had better make one thing clear at the start. Of course it is important to analyse the never-ending changes in capitalism. But periodisation involves more than just tracking the process of change. To propose a periodisation of epochal shifts is to say something about what is essential in defining a social form like capitalism. Epochal shifts have to do with basic transformations in some essential constitutive element of the system. In other words, how we periodise capitalism depends on how we define the system in the first place. The question then is this: what do concepts like modernity and postmoder-nity tell us about the ways in which the people who use them understand capitalism?

I had better explain, too, that I shall not be talking about the ideas of those people whom we loosely call, or who call themselves, postmodern-*ists*. My main concern, here, is the political economy of what some people, including Marxists like Fredric Jameson and David Harvey, are calling postmodernity. So let me sketch out very briefly what they have in mind.[1]

---

1. See, for example, F. Jameson 1996 and Harvey 1990.

According to theorists like Jameson and Harvey, modernity and postmodernity represent two different phases of capitalism. The shift from the one to the other has not been a shift from capitalism to some postcapitalist or 'postindustrial' era, and the basic logic of capitalist accumulation still applies. But there has, nevertheless, been a 'sea-change' in the nature of capitalism, a shift from one material configuration to another, expressed in a transition from one cultural formation to a different one.

For Jameson, for instance, postmodernity corresponds to 'late capitalism' or a new multinational, 'informational', and 'consumerist' phase of capitalism. David Harvey, following the *Régulation*-school, would describe it as a transition from Fordism to flexible accumulation. A similar idea occurs in rather-less nuanced form in certain theories of 'disorganised capitalism'.[2] Postmodernity, then, corresponds to a phase of capitalism where mass-production of standardised goods, and the forms of labour associated with it, have been replaced by flexibility: new forms of production – 'lean production', the 'team-concept', 'just-in-time' production; diversification of commodities for niche-markets, a 'flexible' labour-force, mobile capital, and so on, all made possible by new informational technologies.

Corresponding to these shifts, according to these theories, there have been major cultural changes. One important way of explaining these changes, notably in Harvey's account of postmodernity, has to do with a 'time-space compression', the acceleration of time and the contraction of space made possible by new technologies, in new forms of telecommunication, in fast new methods of production and marketing, new patterns of consumption, new modes of financial organisation. The result has been a new cultural and intellectual configuration summed up in the formula 'postmodernism', which is said to have replaced the culture of modernism and the intellectual patterns associated with the 'project of modernity'.

The project of modernity, according to these accounts, had its origins in the Enlightenment, though it came to fruition in the nineteenth century. The so-called Enlightenment-project is supposed to represent rationalism, technocentrism, the standardisation of knowledge and production, a belief in linear progress, and in universal, absolute truths. *Post*-modernism is supposed to be a reaction to the project of modernity – though it can also be seen as rooted in modernism, in the scepticism, the sensitivity to change and contingency which were already present in the Enlightenment. Postmodernism sees the world as essentially fragmented and indeterminate, rejects any 'totalising'

---

2. For the theory of 'disorganised capitalism', see Lash and Urry 1987.

discourses, any so-called 'metanarratives', comprehensive and universalistic theories about the world and history. It also rejects any universalistic political projects, even universalistic emancipatory projects – in other words, projects for a general '*human* emancipation', rather than very particular struggles against very diverse and particular oppressions.

What, then, are the implications of dividing the history of capitalism into these phases, modernity and postmodernity? The first important thing to keep in mind is that modernity is identified with capitalism. This identification may seem fairly innocuous, but I shall argue that it is a fundamental mistake, that the so-called project of modernity may have little to do with capitalism.

The second point is that this periodisation seems to mean that there are really two major phases in capitalism and one major rupture. First, modernity seems to be everything from the eighteenth century until (probably) the 1970s (Harvey actually gives it a very precise date: 1972). We can subdivide the long phase of modernity into smaller phases (as both Jameson and Harvey do); but postmodernity seems to represent a distinctive kind of break. People may disagree about exactly when the break took place, or about its magnitude. But they seem to agree that this break is different from other epochal changes in the history of capitalism. It seems to be a break not just from some immediately preceding phase, but from the whole preceding history of capitalism. At least, that seems to be the inescapable implication of tracing modernity back to the Enlightenment. So there is a major interruption in the history of capitalism somewhere between modernity and postmodernity. I shall argue that this interruption, or at least this way of looking at it, is problematic too.

Modernity and the non-history of capitalism

Let us look first at the identification of modernity with capitalism. For that, we have to begin at the beginning, with the *origin* of capitalism.[3] The main point I want to make is this: in most accounts of capitalism, there really *is* no beginning. Capitalism seems always to *be* there, somewhere; and it only needs to be released from its chains – for instance, from the fetters of feudalism – to be allowed to grow and mature. Typically, these fetters are *political*: the parasitic powers of lordship, or the restrictions of an autocratic state; and these political constraints confine the free movement of 'economic' actors and the free expression of economic rationality. The 'economic' is identified with exchange or markets; and the assumption seems to be that the seeds of capitalism are contained in the most primitive acts of exchange, in any form of

---

3. I have developed some of the arguments in this section in E.M. Wood 1994d.

trade or market-activity. That assumption is typically connected with another one, namely that history has been an almost natural process of technological development. One way or another, capitalism more-or-less naturally appears when and where expanding markets and technological development reach the right level. Many Marxist explanations are fundamentally the same – with the addition of bourgeois revolutions to help break through the fetters.

The effect of these explanations is to stress the *continuity* between non-capitalist and capitalist societies, and to deny or disguise the *specificity* of capitalism. Exchange has existed since time-immemorial, and it seems that the capitalist market is just more of the same. In this kind of argument, capitalism's need to revolutionise the forces of production is just an extension and an acceleration of universal and transhistorical – almost *natural* – tendencies. So the lineage of capitalism passes naturally from the earliest merchant through the medieval burgher to the Enlightenment-bourgeois and finally to the industrial capitalist.

There is a similar logic in certain Marxist versions of this story, even though the narrative in more recent versions often shifts from the town to the countryside, and merchants are replaced by rural commodity-producers. In these versions, petty commodity-production, released from the bonds of feudalism, more-or-less naturally grows into capitalism. In other words, petty commodity-producers, given half a chance, will take the capitalist road.

What gets lost in these narratives is a perception of the capitalist market as a specific social form, the product of a dramatic historical rupture. The capitalist market looks more like an *opportunity* than an *imperative*, a *compulsion*, the imperative of accumulation and profit-maximisation, which is rooted in very specific social-property relations and which creates its own very specific drive to improve labour-productivity by technical means.

The concept of modernity, as commonly used, belongs to this standard view of history, the one that takes capitalism for granted as the outcome of already existing tendencies, even natural laws, when and where they are given a chance. In the evolutionary process leading from early forms of exchange to modern-industrial capitalism, modernity kicks in when these shackled economic forces, and the economic rationality of the bourgeois, are liberated from traditional constraints.

This concept of modernity, then, belongs to a view of history that *cuts across* the great divide between capitalist and non-capitalist societies. It treats specifically capitalist laws of motion as if they were the universal laws of history. And it lumps together various very different historical developments, capitalist and non-capitalist. At its worst, then, this view of history makes capitalism historically invisible. At the very least, it *naturalises* capitalism.

It is important to note, too, that even *anti*-modernism can have the same effect of naturalising capitalism. This effect is already visible in the sociological theories of Max Weber: modern history, he says, has been a long process of *rationalisation*, the rationalisation of the state in bureaucratic organisation and the rationalisation of the economy in industrial capitalism. The effect of this process – the progress of reason and freedom associated with the Enlightenment – has been to liberate humanity from traditional constraints; but at the same time, rationalisation produces and disguises a new oppression, the 'iron-cage' of modern organisational forms. Much of this argument depends, of course, on assimilating the various meanings of 'reason' and 'rationality' (which Weber is famous for distinguishing, though his analysis of modern history arguably relies in large part on their conflation, so that the instrumental 'rationality' of capitalism is by definition related to 'reason' in its Enlightenment-meaning). The paradoxical implication, here, is that capitalism and bureaucratic domination are just natural extensions of the progress of reason and freedom. In Weber's theory, we can already see one of the characteristic paradoxes of today's postmodernism: in anti-modernism there is often no great distance between lament and celebration.[4]

Themes of the postmodern Left

[...][The] most recent analyses of postmodernity, which combine so many features of older diagnoses of epochal decline, are remarkably unconscious of their own history. In their conviction that what they say represents a radical rupture with the past, they are sublimely oblivious to everything that has been said so many times before. Even the epistemological scepticism, the assault on universal truths and values, the questioning of self-identity, which are so much a part of the current intellectual fashions, have a history as old as philosophy. More particularly, the postmodern sense of epochal novelty depends on ignoring, or denying, one overwhelming historical reality: that all the ruptures of the twentieth century have been bound together in a single historical unity by the logic – and the internal contradictions – of capitalism, the system that dies a thousand deaths.

This brings us to the most distinctive characteristic of the new postmodernists: despite their insistence on epochal differences and specificities, despite their claim to have exposed the historicity of all values and 'knowledges' (or precisely *because* of their insistence on 'difference' and the fragmented nature of reality and human knowledge), they are remarkably insensitive to history.

---

4. See Weber 1968.

This insensitivity is revealed not least in a deafness to the reactionary echoes of their attacks on 'Enlightenment'-values and their fundamental irrationalism. Here, then, is one major difference between the current enunciations of epochal change and all the others. Earlier theories were based – by definition – on some particular conception of history, and were predicated on the importance of historical analysis. [...]

[The] current theories of postmodernity [...] effectively deny the very existence of structure or structural connections and the very possibility of 'causal analysis'. Structures and causes have been replaced by fragments and contingencies. There is no such thing as a social system (e.g. the capitalist system) with its own systemic unity and 'laws of motion'. There are only many different kinds of power, oppression, identity, and 'discourse'. Not only do we have to reject the old 'grand narratives', like Enlightenment-concepts of progress; we have to give up any idea of intelligible historical process and causality, and with it, evidently, any idea of 'making history'. There are no structured processes accessible to human knowledge (or, it must be supposed, to human action). There are only anarchic, disconnected, and inexplicable *differences*. For the first time, we have what appears to be a contradiction in terms: a theory of epochal change based on a denial of history.

There is one other especially curious thing about the new idea of postmodernity, one particularly notable paradox. On the one hand, the denial of history on which it is based is associated with a kind of political pessimism. Since there are no systems and no history susceptible to causal analysis, we cannot get to the root of the many powers that oppress us; and we certainly cannot aspire to some kind of united opposition, some kind of general *human* emancipation, or even a general contestation of capitalism, of the kind that socialists used to believe in. The most we can hope for is a lot of particular and separate resistances. On the other hand, this political pessimism appears to have its origins in a rather optimistic view of capitalist prosperity and possibility. Today's postmodernists (typically survivors of the 'sixties generation' and their students) seem to have a view of the world still rooted in the 'Golden Age' of capitalism, the dominant feature of which is 'consumerism', the multiplicity of consumption patterns, and the proliferation of 'life-styles'. Here too they reveal their fundamental ahistoricism, as the structural crises of capitalism since that 'golden' moment seem to have passed them right by, or at least to have made no significant theoretical impression. For some, this means that the opportunities for opposition to capitalism are severely limited. Others seem to be saying that, if we can't really change or even understand the system (or even *think* about it as a system at all), and if we don't, and can't, have a vantage-point from which to criticise the system, let alone oppose it, we may as well lie back and enjoy it. Exponents of these intellectual trends certainly know that all is not well; but there is very little in these fashions that helps, for example, to make sense of today's increasing poverty and homelessness, the growing class of working poor, new forms of insecure and part-time labour, and so on. Both sides of the twentieth-century's ambiguous history – both its horrors and its wonders – have, no doubt, played a part in forming the post-modernist consciousness; but the horrors that have undermined the old idea of progress are less important in defining the distinctive nature of today's postmodernism than are the wonders of modern technology and the riches of consumer capitalism. Postmodernism sometimes looks like the ambiguities of capitalism as seen from the vantage-point of those who enjoy its benefits more than they suffer its costs. [...]

It would be easy, after having said all this, to dismiss the current fashions. But for all their contradictions, their lack of historical sensitivity, their apparently unconscious repetition of old themes, and their defeatism, they are also responding to something real, to real conditions in the contemporary world in the current conditions of capitalism, with which people on the socialist Left must come to terms.

Here, first, is a list of the most important themes of the 'postmodern' Left (I shall use that term broadly to cover a variety of intellectual and political trends that have emerged in recent years, including 'post-Marxism' and 'poststructuralism'): a focus on language, culture, and 'discourse' (on the grounds that language is all we can know about the world and we have access to no other reality), to the exclusion of the Left's traditional 'economistic' concerns and the old preoccupations of political economy; a rejection of 'totalising' knowledge and of 'universalistic' values (including Western conceptions of 'rationality', general ideas of equality, whether liberal or socialist, and the Marxist conception of general human emancipation), in favour of an emphasis on 'difference', on varied particular identities such as gender, race, ethnicity, sexuality, on various particular and separate oppressions and struggles; an insistence on the fluid and fragmented nature of the human self (the 'decentered subject'), which makes our identities so variable, uncertain, and fragile that it is hard to see how we can develop the kind of consciousness that might form the basis of solidarity and collective action founded on a common social 'identity' (such as class), a common experience, and common interests – a celebration of the 'marginal'; and a repudiation of 'grand narratives', such as Western ideas of progress, including Marxist theories of history. All of these themes tend to be lumped together in a dismissal of 'essentialism', in particular Marxism, which allegedly reduces the varied complexity of human experience to a monolithic view of the world, 'privileging' the mode of production as a historical determinant and class as against other 'identities', and 'economic' or 'material' determinants as against the 'discursive construction' of reality. This denunciation of 'essentialism' tends to cover not just truly monolithic and simplistic explanations of the world (like Stalinist varieties of Marxism) but *any* kind of causal analysis.

[...] [The] main thread running through all these postmodern principles is an emphasis on the fragmented nature of the world and of human knowledge, and the impossibility of any emancipatory politics based on some kind of 'totalising' vision. Even an anti-capitalist politics is too 'totalising' or 'universalist', since capitalism as a totalising system can hardly be said to exist at all in postmodern discourse, so that even the *critique* of capitalism is precluded. In fact, 'politics', in any traditional sense of the word, having to do with the overarching power of classes or states and opposition to them, is effectively ruled out, giving way to the fractured struggles of 'identity-politics' or even the 'personal as political' – though there are some more universal projects that do hold some attractions for the postmodern Left, such as environmental politics. In short: a deep epistemological scepticism and a profound political defeatism.

Yet none of us would want to deny the importance of some of these themes. For instance, the history of the twentieth century could hardly inspire confidence in traditional notions of progress, and those of us who profess to believe in some kind of 'progressive' politics have to come to terms with all that has happened to undermine Enlightenment-optimism. And who would want to deny the importance of 'identities' other than class, of struggles against sexual and racial oppression, or the complexities of human experience in such a mobile and changeable world, with such fragile and shifting solidarities? At the same time, who can be oblivious to the resurgence of 'identities' like nationalism as powerful, and often destructive, historical forces? Do we not have to come to terms with the restructuring of capitalism, now both more global and more 'segmented' than ever before? For that matter, who is unaware of the structural changes that have transformed the nature of the working class itself? And what serious socialist has ever been unconscious of the racial or sexual divisions within the working class? Who would want to subscribe to the kind of ideological and cultural imperialism that suppresses the multiplicity of human values and cultures? And how can we possibly deny the importance of language and cultural politics in a world so dominated by symbols, images, and 'mass-communication', not to mention the 'information-superhighway?' Who would deny these things in a world of global capitalism so dependent on the manipulation of symbols and images in a culture of advertisement, where the 'media' mediate our own most personal experiences, sometimes to the point where what we see on television seems more real than our own lives, and where the terms of political debate are set – and narrowly constricted – by the dictates of capital in the most direct way, as knowledge and communication are increasingly in the hands of corporate giants?

We do not have to accept postmodernist assumptions in order to see all these things. On the contrary, these developments cry out for a materialist explanation. For that matter, there have been few cultural phenomena in human history whose material foundations are more glaringly obvious than those of postmodernism itself. There is, in fact, no better confirmation of historical materialism than the connection between postmodernist culture and a segmented, consumerist, and mobile-global capitalism. Nor does a materialist approach mean that we have to devalue or denigrate the cultural dimensions of human experience. A materialist understanding is, instead, an essential step in liberating culture from the stranglehold of commodification.

If postmodernism does tell us something, in a distorted way, about the conditions of contemporary capitalism, the real trick is to figure out exactly what those conditions are, *why* they are, and where we go from here. The trick, in other words, is to suggest historical explanations for those conditions instead of just submitting to them and indulging in ideological adaptations. The trick is to identify the real problems to which the current intellectual fashions offer false – or no – solutions, and in so doing to challenge the limits they impose on action and resistance. [...]

Enlightenment vs. capitalism: Condorcet vs. Locke

Just to introduce the comparison between these two intellectual formations we can begin with two paradigmatic examples that respectively represent key moments in the development of each ideological formation and illustrate two quite distinct conceptions of progress.

The culmination of the Enlightenment-conception of progress, in a way its last gasp, is Antoine-Nicolas de Condorcet's *Sketch for a Historical Picture of the Progress of the Human Mind* – published in 1795 and written while he was hiding from the Jacobins in fear of his life. It can, of course, be argued that Condorcet was not a representative figure; that his optimism, no less than his universalism and egalitarianism (at least in anticipation of progress), was exceptional among the great Enlightenment-thinkers. Optimism was, in any case, only one side of the Enlightenment-picture. The secular view of history that distinguishes this concept of progress from religious millennialism is necessarily two-sided: it does not simply make assumptions about human perfectibility or the historical possibilities available to human agency. It is also, and for the same reasons, shot through with pessimism about the dark side of human life; and the tension between these two is a constant theme in the Enlightenment.

But if Condorcet is exceptional, the very qualities that make him so also make him perhaps the most revealing example. His notion of progress as the universal triumph of human reason over ignorance and superstition may be more uncompromising than others of his time, but it does represent a crystallisation, without ambiguities, of the themes that bind all Enlightenment-figures together and give the concept of 'Enlightenment' whatever meaning it has. Precisely because his optimism about the beneficence of human reason is so uncompromising, because his universalism is so wide-ranging and cosmopolitan – because, in other words, he takes Enlightenment-principles to what critics would regard as their extremes – his *Sketch* provides a clear and simple measure against which to test the standard accusations levelled at the 'Enlightenment-project', about the inherent oppressiveness of its rationalism and the imperialism of its universalist principles.

Here, first, is how Condorcet sums up the goal of human progress: 'Our hopes for the future condition of the human race can be subsumed under three important heads: the abolition of inequality between nations, the progress of equality within each nation, and the true perfection of mankind'. The 'final end of the social art', Condorcet says in the most unambiguous terms, is 'real equality'.[5]

Here are his views on imperialism:

> Survey the history of our settlements and commercial undertakings in Africa or in Asia and you will see how our trade monopolies, our treachery, our murderous contempt for men of another colour or creed, the insolence of our usurpations, the intrigues or the exaggerated proselytic zeal of our priests, have destroyed the respect and goodwill that the superiority of our knowledge and the benefits of our commerce at first won for us in the eyes of the inhabitants.[6]

And sexual oppression:

> Among the causes of the progress of the human mind that are of the utmost importance to the general happiness, we must number the complete annihilation of the prejudices that have brought about an inequality of rights between the sexes, an inequality fatal even to the party in whose

5. Condorcet 1955, pp. 172, 173.
6. Condorcet 1955, pp. 175–6.

favour it works. It is vain for us to look for a justification of this principle in any differences of physical organization, intellect or moral sensibility between men and women. This inequality has its origin solely in an abuse of strength. [...][7]

Condorcet may not be typical in the degree to which he holds such views, but even postmodernist critics of the Enlightenment may have some difficulty in deconstructing this discourse of equality or transforming it into something evil and oppressive. Nor can we dismiss the many ambiguities in the Enlightenment-legacy, or the dangers inherent in excessive optimism about the perfection of humanity, not to mention the evils perpetrated in the name of progress. But it remains significant that here, in the *locus classicus* of Enlightenment-optimism, equality within and between nations, races and sexes emerges not in opposition to, or in uneasy juxtaposition with, rationalism and universalism, but as their logical conclusion, the final destination of progress.

The significance of this logic and this aspiration becomes more evident when we compare them with a pattern of thought exemplary of capitalism, which suggests a somewhat different conception of progress. Here, the most instructive example comes from John Locke. What makes Locke such a revealing object of comparison is the common ground he shares with his Enlightenment-successors, which brings their divergences into sharp relief. Locke was, certainly, a major influence on the Enlightenment, especially through his epistemology. While he never went as far as Condorcet would later go, he had some reasonably enlightened attitudes about natural equality, as well as toleration and opposition to tyrannical government. The point, however, is that he also had some very distinctive ideas which set him apart from the main figures of the French Enlightenment and which are uniquely characteristic of capitalism. In fact, it is striking that, though Locke is writing a century before Condorcet, at an early stage of capitalist development, some of his seventeenth-century attitudes have a more familiar ring to those of us living in advanced-capitalist societies.

Let us consider Locke's famous observation, in the *Second Treatise*, that 'in the beginning, all the World was *America*'.[8] This simple passage is loaded with meaning. America stands for the quintessentially primitive condition of

---

7. Condorcet 1955, p. 193.
8. John Locke, *Two Treatises of Government*, II. 49. This abbreviated account of Locke's views on property and 'improvement' has been developed in greater detail in E.M. Wood 1994a. See also Wood and Wood 1997, Chapter Six.

humanity in the continuum of human development, and it provides a standard against which to judge a more advanced condition.

Locke is here making the point that the earliest, and natural, condition of the Earth was effectively 'waste' and that human-beings have a divine obligation to remove the Earth from the waste, to make the Earth *productive*, to *improve* it ('improvement' is the word Locke uses, which was becoming increasingly conventional in his day, and increasingly important to landholders of capitalist inclinations).[9]

Locke's measure of improvement or productivity is 'profit', not in the older meaning of advantage, whether material or otherwise, but quite simply as exchange-value or commercial gain. Here, for example, is how he contrasts the value of land in unimproved America with land in England. An acre of land in America, which may be as naturally fertile as an acre in England, is not worth one thousandth of the English acre, if we calculate 'all the Profit an *Indian* received from it were it valued and sold here'.[10] This is the context in which we have to understand Locke's theory of property, which maintains that men acquire a right of property in something by mixing their labour with it. In this passage about the Indian, and in others, he makes it clear that the issue is not labour as such, but the productive – and, more particularly, the profitable – use of property. The issue, for example, is not how much effort the Indian may have exerted, but the profit – or lack of profit – he would obtain from his exertions in a commercial exchange. From Locke's point of view, the Indian has failed to do what is necessary to establish his right to property, and his land is fair game for those 'industrious' and 'rational' people who are willing and able to make it profitably productive. Of course, it is not necessarily the labourer who acquires the right of property in any case, but rather the person – notably the landlord and his capitalist tenant – who puts that labour to profitable use.

This argument has many implications – for instance, that improvement, or productivity and profit, trump any other claims, such as the customary rights of English commoners, or the rights of indigenous peoples. For all the natural equality of men, on which Locke emphatically insists, the requirements of productivity and profit trump that too. To put it bluntly, this is a warrant for capitalism: productivism, profit-maximisation, the exploitation of human-beings and resources. It is also a warrant for appropriating 'waste' land, and

---

9. For waste-land, see Locke, *Two Treatises*, II. 36, 37. For a discussion of Locke's connection with the 'improvement'-literature of seventeenth-century England, see N. Wood 1984.

10. Locke, *Two Treatises*, II. 43.

so for settler-'plantations'. Locke's productivity-principle can even provide a basis for colonialism and imperialism.

Above all, we get a fairly clear picture of what constitutes progress for Locke, and the contrast with Condorcet is striking. Consider the main axis along which each thinker divides the advanced from the undeveloped state of humanity: for Condorcet, it is rationality vs. ignorance and superstition, equality vs. inequality; for Locke it is profit vs. waste. Locke certainly identifies rationality as a superior condition, but while, for Condorcet, the progress of reason is inextricably bound up with the advance of equality, for Locke, rationality is paired with 'industriousness' and is very hard to dissociate from productivity and profit making.[11] In fact, beginning with the proposition that all men are naturally equal, he turns these principles of productivity and profit into a new and historically unprecedented kind of validation of inequality.

Enlightenment-universalism

Condorcet, for instance, called for mass-education – and he actually devised a plan for the *Académie* as the institution that would preside over a system of mass-education. The kind of egalitarianism he espoused, his insistence on defining progress in terms of increasing equality and social inclusion, was inseparable from his view of the intellectual's mission. In a sense, his egalitarianism and his elitism were two sides of one coin. For him, as for other Enlightenment-figures, the intellectuals' special claim to status and authority was their role in educating the world.

There is no intention, here, of exaggerating the Enlightenment-commitment to equality. There were obviously strict limits to the equality envisaged even by thinkers like Condorcet, let alone, say, Voltaire, and much of it was, in any case, deferred to an indefinite future. But it is still significant as an aspiration, and it is significant how, in these very particular historical conditions, the logic of intellectual elitism impelled Enlightenment-thinkers in that direction, into ideas that could be, and were, appropriated by far more radical and revolutionary forces.

---

11. Locke can even reconcile slavery with his assertion of men's natural freedom and equality, though on different grounds from the productivity-principle. Although no-one can enslave himself by contract or consent, people can be legitimately enslaved as captives in a just war. This more or less traditional justification of slavery, apparently as a punishment for violation of natural law, would apply to any time and place. See Locke, *Two Treatises*, II. 23. Here again, Locke's view contrasts sharply with Condorcet's, for whom the abolition of slavery would be a sign of progress.

No one can doubt that Enlightenment-universalism could and did have oppressive, racist and imperialist manifestations, but it is also important to keep in mind something that postmodernist critics systematically forget: the connection between Enlightenment-universalism and a critical temper that subjected European knowledge, European authority and European culture to more trenchant critique than any other. Even the conception of progress, which is supposed to be the essence of Enlightenment-Eurocentrism, had anti-imperialist implications.

The conception of progress as the progress of the human mind and knowledge takes for granted that the advance of knowledge is a very long-term cumulative process, projecting, if not into infinity, at least into the indefinite future. This conception, to be sure, implies that at some point, if not in the foreseeable future, some certain truths can and will be discovered; and it further implies that some cultures are more advanced, and therefore superior to others. But it also implies – perhaps even more fundamentally – that any given knowledge is open to question, that all authority is subject to challenge, that no one has a monopoly on truth.

The appropriation of history by intellectuals certainly evinces a far-reaching hubris. But at the same time that these intellectuals are arrogating history to themselves, they are also taking on the burden of human fallibility and the whole dark history of human error and evil. A deep pessimism is never very far away from Enlightenment-optimism. It is, in fact, just the other side of the same coin. If Enlightenment-conceptions of knowledge and progress are founded on a kind of universalism, then it is a universalism that implies open-endedness, flexibility, scepticism.

For all its dangers, Enlightenment-universalism has provided a theoretical underpinning for emancipatory projects much more effective than anything postmodernists have been able to devise. So, indeed, has the concept of progress. For that matter, it gives us something that postmodernist celebrations of diversity and difference do not and cannot: a *reason* for recognising and respecting otherness – if only on the grounds that the cumulative and open-ended quality of human knowledge and the progress of the human mind requires us to be careful about closing any doors.

Condorcet may not have been typical in the degree to which he took the emancipatory logic of the Enlightenment seriously, but it says something about the complexity of the Enlightenment – and about the vacuity of many criticisms today – that this most classic example of Enlightenment-optimism and universalism is also the one that most explicitly attacks the very evils ascribed to that Enlightenment-optimism by critics today: racism, sexism, imperialism. Nor is this an accidental or contradictory juxtaposition:

Condorcet's universalism and his optimism about human progress rest on the same foundation as his commitment to equality, his respect for the authenticity and integrity of other cultures, his attack on imperialism.

The periodisation of the Western Left

[...][Whatever] the immediate causes of the student-revolt in the 1960s and whatever deprivations may have played a part in it, the movement occurred not in the context of economic decline or stagnation, but in a moment – and as a result – of capitalist prosperity. The intricate mechanisms by which material prosperity produced widespread rebellion may not be easy to trace, but a recognition of this simple fact brings into focus the sharp generational rupture between the first New Left and those that followed it.

Greg Elliott describes the second British New Left as founded on a similar social base as their predecessors: 'the enlarged stratum of intellectual and cultural producers generated by post-war capitalism – a category swelled by the massive expansion of tertiary education in the 1960s'.[12] Without making too much of the (not insignificant) difference between the enlargement of the 'stratum of intellectual and cultural producers' before the 1960s, and the growth of the tertiary sector which occurred in that decade, I do think that (apart from various differences in age, personal experience, background and experience) some important distinctions need to be made between the first New Left's leading lights – people like E.P. Thompson, John Saville and Ralph Miliband – and the second generation: Perry Anderson, Robin Blackburn, et al.

The difference between Ralph Miliband, Edward Thompson, or John Saville and the next generation of New-Left luminaries was not just an age difference of, say, twelve to twenty years. That relatively small generational difference reflected a much larger historical shift, maybe one of the most significant epochal shifts in modern history. One clear dividing line between these generations is the Second World-War (in which Miliband, Thompson and Saville all served), preceded by the Spanish Civil War, which was the formative event for so many Western socialists. This means that the first generation, in one way or another, directly experienced the historic trauma of fascism and the struggle against it, as well as the social interactions, the contact with people of all classes, the political experience and expectations generated by the Second World-War.

---

12. Elliott 1994, p. 46.

There was no comparable formative experience in the political development of the second generation. Even the Vietnam War, opposition to which was a critical moment in the development of the second New Left, is as important for what it did *not* mean to them, as for what it did. After all, besides its geographic distance, this was a war to which students and intellectuals related largely by their absence from it. At any rate, it may help to place the differences between the two generations into perspective if we consider that the only life-experience that shaped the second generation, as the Second World-War had shaped the first, was their experience as university-students.

In some ways even more important is the fact that the first and second generations stood on different sides of the great divide between the Depression and an ascendant capitalism. The difference between those two generations is the very large difference between those who grew up in the Depression, and those who came to political consciousness in a time of rising prosperity. The historical memory of the first generation would continue to shape their conception of capitalism, its possibilities and limits, just as fascism – together with the class-divide between ruling-class appeasement and socialist resistance – would remain, for them, the most vivid expression of capitalist decline. For the second generation, capitalist productivity and growth, conjoined with 'bourgeois democracy' in advanced capitalist countries, would serve as the normative guide.

It may seem odd to make this claim about the second generation, a group of young intellectuals whose theoretical and political agenda grew out of a preoccupation with capitalist *decline*, in a country that seemed to them exempt from any rising economic tide. Perry Anderson himself has written that the new editorial group [at *New Left Review*] found its bearings, its own editorial programme, at a time when 'the national crisis of British capitalism was unmistakable', and that *NLR*'s project was to comprehend that national crisis.[13] The series of articles written by Anderson and [Tom] Nairn in 1964–5, analysing the various elements of Britain's crisis, the inadequacies of British capitalism and its attendant culture, set the agenda which established the new identity of *NLR*.[14] Yet if the dominant theme in the new *NLR* programme was capitalist decline, it is just here, in the 'Nairn-Anderson' theses, that the assumptions [...] about capitalist progress are most clearly visible. The analysis of Britain's 'present crisis' makes it clear that the defining idea of this second

---

13. P. Anderson 1980, pp. 137–8.
14. The so-called 'Nairn-Anderson theses' were elaborated in a series of texts by Perry Anderson and Tom Nairn: P. Anderson 1964, 1966 and 1968; and Nairn 1964a, 1964b, 1964c, 1970 and 1977. Both authors have more recently taken up these themes again: P. Anderson 1987 and Nairn 1988.

New Left, the idea that determined its self-proclaimed identity, was a conception of capitalism in which that 'crisis' was *exceptional*, testimony not to the inherent contradictions of capitalism in general, but to the specific *imperfections* of Britain as a capitalist economy and its *deviations* from the capitalist norm. This was combined with a view of capitalist democracy according to which Britain's failure to transform its political and cultural superstructures, and especially its failure to modernise its state by means of 'bourgeois revolution', was at the root of its economic debility.

Nothing could be further from the formative experience of the first generation. The ensemble of Depression, fascism and Second World-War surely shaped the consciousness of the first New Left as profoundly as, say, the French Revolution and Napoleonic wars had determined the intellectual life of another generation. It is hard to imagine an intellectual history of the late eighteenth and early nineteenth centuries that remains silent on the cultural and ideological effects of the latter events, but some histories of the New Left have accomplished something like a silence of that magnitude. Yet the epochal difference that divides the first and second generations of the New Left is, if anything, underlined by the failure of recent commentators to take note of it. That failure testifies to a historical amnesia so profound that it has afflicted historians and their subjects alike.

Contextual differences, then, had a great deal to do with the distinctive attitudes that set the first New Left apart from their successors. Not least among these attitudes, especially in Britain, was the first generation's continuing attachment – often organisational, but always in principle – to the labour-movement. Their conception of capitalism entailed a particular view of the agencies best-suited to transform it; and, while the realities of modern capitalism and modern means of communication had, in their view, placed cultural struggle very high on the socialist agenda, the objective was to transform, not to replace, the working class. People like Thompson (and, for that matter, Raymond Williams) remained vehemently opposed to conceptions of hegemony depicting a working class irredeemably mesmerised by consumer-capitalism and the mass-media, and requiring substitution by free-thinking intellectuals. The continuities between the cultural preoccupations of the first and second New Left should not disguise the rupture between their respective conceptions of socialist agency and the relationship between intellectuals and the working class.

It is also worth noting certain significant differences between British Marxist intellectuals and their counterparts elsewhere in Europe. If the British Communist Party never became a mass-party like others in Europe, it was nevertheless grounded in a uniquely long-established and strong labour-movement. By contrast, the mass-parties of Italy, France or Spain had less well-established traditions of organised labour. They did, however, gain a powerful impetus from the anti-fascist struggle. Perhaps because so many Communist intellectuals in these countries had been drawn to Communism not so much by any attachment to the labour-movement or even any prior ideological commitment to socialism, but by the fight against fascism – and perhaps because of other more long-standing differences in the position of intellectuals, notably in their relation to the state – their relationship to the working class was also arguably different, certainly as regards their conception of the task confronting left intellectuals in advancing the socialist cause. It is possible to argue that the intellectual's aspiration to primacy was embedded in the culture of the Continental Left much earlier, and more organically. To put the point briefly and baldly, it is hard to imagine anyone accusing, say, French left-intellectuals at *any* time of 'populism'.

This means that the autonomisation of politics and ideology, together with a detachment from the labour-movement, represented a sharper rupture for the British Left than for some others. It also means that the adoption of Continental Marxism by the second New Left, in its *NLR* incarnation, represented a significant *political* break, marking a more decisive shift away from the labour-movement and class-politics than is immediately apparent in its revival of Marxist theory. That shift was, it could be argued, right from the beginning encoded in *NLR*'s anti-'populism'; and it is one of the major paradoxes of the second New Left that this transformation took the form of a renewed commitment to revolutionary Marxism.

Left intellectuals and contemporary capitalism

The readiness with which some British left intellectuals in the eighties (most notably in *Marxism Today*) accepted the claims of Thatcher's 'people's capitalism' – its boasts about extending the benefits of consumerism, shareholding and home-ownership to the working class – illustrates how divorced the new inverted (or anti-) populism could be from the realities of capitalism as it now is, and how thoroughly unprepared it would be for the prolonged and structural crisis that was just around the corner. Even at the height of Thatcherism, this judgement seemed at best a little premature and overblown, and at worst patronising, vastly exaggerating the extent and duration of the material benefits accruing to the great majority and underestimating the very strict limits of that 'revolution'. Today, as Thatcher's chickens have come home to roost with a vengeance, that judgement seems not only naïve, but in questionable taste.

But this is only one – and not the most extreme – example of the extent to which the Left today is ill-equipped to confront the problems of the here-and-now. If a growing consumerism was the defining characteristic of earlier decades, the capitalism of the nineties, while still, of course, consumerist, has its own distinctive form. It is more specifically defined by things like structural mass-unemployment, growing poverty and homelessness, 'flexible' labour-markets, and changing patterns of work in the form of casualisation and low-paid part-time jobs, or overwork for the remaining few in 'downsized' enterprises, together with the global imposition of market-imperatives increasingly immune to cushioning by the old forms of state-intervention.

The new capitalism has its expression, too, in the altered prospects and aspirations of university-students. Lin Chun and Greg Elliott both conclude their discussions of the British New Left with a reference to Jonathan Ree's comment in 1974 that 'the socialist intellectual youngsters occupy the buildings, while the socialist intellectual oldsters occupy the chairs'.[15] For Lin Chun, this is a comment on the confinement of modern radicalism in the West to the academy, both then and now. For Greg Elliott, Ree's observation highlights the difference between then and now. 'Updated for New Times,' he nicely observes, 'Ree's verdict might read: the post-modernist intellectual oldsters occupy the chairs, while the environmentalist youngsters are preoccupied with making ends meet'.

And that about sums it up. Some of yesterday's militant youngsters are today's postmodernist chair-holding oldsters. If their high aspirations yesterday to change (if not to rule) the world have failed to materialise, their hopes of a comfortable career have, at least, been fulfilled. Their – I should say our – students today can barely hope for a decent job, never mind think about leading a cultural revolution. If there ever was a proletarianisation of students, this is it, as overcrowded and underfunded universities house students, many of whom (especially in North America) are already part-time wage-earners, and for whom a university-education has become both more economically essential and increasingly irrelevant; a necessary, but far from sufficient, condition of life-time employment.

The current theoretical fashions are very far removed from these realities. They are not about the new world-order since 1989, nor even about the long-term trends in capitalist development since the late 1970s. What passes for the very up-to-date looks less like a confrontation with the eighties and nineties, than the agenda of the sixties running its course. At the very time that capitalism exerts its totalising logic on the whole 'new world-order', the most

---

15. Chun 1993, p. 195; Elliott 1994, p. 48.

fashionable left-intellectuals, cultivating their varied and fragmented patches of discourse and difference, claim the supremacy of their discursive practices while ruling out any form of 'totalising' knowledge that might be adequate to comprehend the operations of the capitalist system. They even deny its systematic totality, its very existence as a system, while still, paradoxically, accepting, at least by default, the universality and eternity of 'the market'. As the expanding logic of that 'market' creates increasing strains along the fault-lines of class, we are enjoined to pursue the fragmented 'politics of identity', with little hope of anything more than the most particularistic and local resistances within the interstices of capitalism.

To confront today's realities requires striking out in new directions. At the same time, while the new conditions of contemporary capitalism require new analyses, we should not make the mistake, as Raymond Williams tells us the younger New Left did, of underestimating everything that has not changed in the capitalist system.[16] If, as now seems very likely, the rising tide of capitalist prosperity in the fifties and sixties proves to be an aberration, it also seems likely that in our present condition we shall get more guidance from those who remember the thirties and forties than from those whose ideas are deeply rooted in an ascendant capitalism, or from their postmodern successors who have yet to catch up with the present, let alone look to the future.

16. R. Williams 1979, pp. 361–6.

Chapter Seven

Globalisation and Imperialism

Globalisation and the nation-state

Although the world today is, more than ever before, a world of nation-states, we are constantly being told that the global expansion of capitalism has ruptured its historic association with the nation-state. The state, we are assured, is being pushed aside by 'globalisation' and transnational forces.

But, while no one would deny the global reach of capital, there is little evidence that today's 'global' capital is less in need of national states than were earlier capitalist interests. Global capital, no less than 'national' capital, relies on nation-states to maintain local conditions favourable to accumulation, as well as to help it navigate the global economy. It might, then, be more accurate to say that 'globalisation' is characterised less by the decline of the nation-state than by a growing contradiction between the global scope of capital and its persistent need for more local and national forms of 'extra-economic' support, a growing disparity between its economic reach and its political grasp.

We can make sense of this contradiction by looking more closely at the historic separation between the 'economic' and the 'political' in capitalism, in contrast to earlier forms. The precapitalist unity of economic and political powers, such as that of feudal lordship, meant, among other things, that the economic powers of the feudal lord could never extend beyond the reach of his personal ties or alliances and extra-economic powers, his military force, political rule, or judicial authority. Nor, for that matter, could the economic powers of the absolutist state or any precapitalist empire exceed its extra-economic range.

Unlike other systems of exploitation, in which appropriating classes or states extract surplus-labour from producers by direct coercion, capitalist exploitation is characterised by a division of labour between the 'economic' moment of appropriation and the 'extra-economic' or 'political' moment of coercion. Underlying this separation is the market-dependence of all economic actors, appropriators and producers, which generates economic imperatives distinct and apart from direct political coercion. This separation – which creates two distinct 'spheres', each with its own dynamics, its own temporalities, and its own spatial range – is both a source of strength and a source of contradiction.

On the one hand, the distinctive division of labour between the economic and political moments of capitalism, and between economic imperatives and political coercion, makes possible capitalism's unique capacity for universalisation and spatial expansion. Capital is not only uniquely *driven* to extend its economic reach, but also uniquely *able* to do so. The self-expansion of capital is not limited to what the capitalist can squeeze out of the direct producers by direct coercion, nor is capital-accumulation confined within the spatial range of personal domination. By means of specifically economic (market-)imperatives, capital is uniquely able to escape the limits of direct coercion and move far beyond the borders of political authority. This makes possible both its distinctive forms of class-domination, and its particular forms of imperialism.

On the other hand, while the scope of capitalist economic imperatives can far outreach direct political rule and legal authority, the same disjunction that makes this possible is the root of an irreducible contradiction. The economic imperatives of capitalism are always in need of support by extra-economic powers of regulation and coercion, to create and sustain the conditions of accumulation and maintain the system of capitalist property. The transfer of certain 'political' powers to capital can never eliminate the need to retain others in a formally separate political 'sphere', preserving the division between the moment of economic appropriation and the moment of political coercion. Nor can purely economic imperatives ever completely supplant direct political coercion, or, indeed, survive at all without political support.

In fact, capitalism, in some ways more than any other social form, needs politically-organised and legally-defined stability, regularity, and predictability in its social arrangements. Yet these are conditions of capital's existence and self-reproduction that it cannot provide for itself and that its own inherently anarchic laws of motion constantly subvert. To stabilise its constitutive social relations – between capital and labour, or capital and other capitals –

capitalism is especially reliant on legally-defined and politically-authorised regularities. Business-transactions at every level require consistency and reliable enforcement, in contractual relations, monetary standards, exchanges of property. The coercions that sustain these regularities must exist apart from capital's own powers of appropriation, if it is to preserve its capacity for self-expansion.

Capitalist transactions also require an elaborate infrastructure that its own profit-maximising imperatives are ill-equipped to provide. And, finally, in a system of market-dependence, access to the means of subsistence is subject to the vagaries of the market, especially for the propertyless majority, whose access even to the means of labour depends on selling their labour-power. A system like this, where the economy has been 'disembedded' from other social relations, will also have a distinctive need for politically-organised social provision, even just to keep people alive through times when they cannot sell their labour-power, and to ensure a 'reserve-army' of workers.

This means that capitalism remains dependent on extra-economic conditions, political and legal supports. Until now, no one has found a more effective means of supplying those supports than the political form with which capitalism has been historically, if not causally, connected: the old nation-state. As much as 'global' capital might like a corresponding 'global' state, the kind of day-to-day stability, regularity, and predictability required for capital-accumulation is inconceivable on anything like a global scale.

Nation-states, classes, and universal capitalism

[...][Throughout] all the various phases or 'régimes' of capitalism, there has been one over-arching pattern: not the decline, but, on the contrary, the persistence and even the proliferation of the nation-state. It is not just that nation-states have stubbornly held on through the universalisation of capitalism. If anything, the universalisation of capitalism has also meant, or at least been accompanied by, the universalisation of the nation-state. Global capitalism is, more than ever, a global system of national states, and the universalisation of capitalism is presided over by nation-states, especially one hegemonic superpower.

This is a point worth emphasising. The conventional view of globalisation seems to be based on the assumption that the natural tendency of capitalist development, and specifically its internationalisation, is to submerge the nation-state, even if the process is, admittedly, still far from over. The internationalisation of capital, according to that view, is apparently in an inverse relation to the development of the nation-state: the more internationalisation, the less nation-state. But the historical record suggests something different. The internationalisation of capital has been accompanied by the universalisation of capital's original political form. When capitalism was born, the world was very far from being a world of nation-states. Today, it is just that. And while new transnational institutions have certainly emerged, they have not so much displaced the nation-state, as given it new roles – in fact, in some cases, new instruments and powers.

Globalisation itself is a phenomenon of national economies and national states. It is impossible to make sense of it without taking account of both uneven development and competition among national economies and without acknowledging the constant tension (the consistently contradictory relations between the USA and Japan spring to mind) between international cooperation and struggles for dominance among national capitalisms. Much of what goes under the name of globalisation consists of national states carrying out policies to promote the international 'competitiveness' of their own national economies, to maintain or restore profitability to domestic capital, to promote the free movement of capital while controlling the movements of labour, typically by confining it within national boundaries, or at least strictly controlling its movements to coincide with the needs of capital, and always by subjecting it to disciplines enforced by nation-states. Even policies to create and sustain global markets, not to mention policies deliberately designed to forfeit national sovereignty, are conceived, implemented, and enforced by national governments. And nowhere is the nexus of global capital and nation-state more obvious than in the degree to which transnational organisations of capital like the IMF not only serve as the instruments of dominant states, but also depend on subordinate states as the conduit of globalisation.

If there has been a real movement towards transnational integration, it has tended to take the form less of globalisation, than of regionalisation. But even at the level of regional integration, the centrifugal forces of the nation-state are still at work. The global economy is constituted by regional blocs of unevenly developed and hierarchically organised national economies and nation-states. Even – or particularly – in the most ambitious, if not the only, project of transnational unification, the European Union, the tensions between cooperation and competition, or between integration and national sovereignty, are vividly on display. Real political integration, if it were possible at all, would, of course, simply create a larger state, whose purpose would be to compete with other national economies and states – and particularly the US superstate. But as it is, European integration has tended to mean growing competition among its national constituents, which is, if anything, intensified by monetary union. Nor has European integration transcended the contradictory logic of uneven development or the national exclusiveness that follows from it. In fact, the Union has brought into sharper relief the hierarchy of national economies. Major European leaders are generally quite open about the primacy of nation-states, and even those most committed to political integration persist in thinking about Europe as divided between an *'avant garde'* or 'centre of gravity' and a periphery of marginal economies.

When we speak of global economic crises or downturns, too, nation-states and national economies invariably come to the fore. To be sure, crisis is never simply an Asian or Latin-American crisis, nor is it a consequence of specific national strategies or policy-failures, or the effect of 'crony-capitalism' or any other specific and defective form of capitalism. Capitalist crisis is a consequence of systemic processes inherent in capitalism as such. At the same time, global crises are always shaped by the specific national forms of the global economy's constituent parts, each with its own history and its own internal logic, and by the relations among diverse and unevenly developed national entities.

It has been argued [...] that, despite the persistence of national economies and nation-states, there now exists a 'global'-capitalist class. Yet throughout the world of 'global capitalism', the principal economic actors and classes are still organised, above all, on a *national* basis. Each nation's working class has its own class-formations, practices, and traditions; and while no one would deny that capital is far more mobile and less place-rooted than labour, we are still a very long way from a truly global-capitalist class. No one is likely to have much trouble distinguishing US from Japanese capital, or either one from Russian or Brazilian, not only as regards their obvious cultural differences, but also the divergent and competing interests among them. National classes are likely to persist precisely because global integration itself, whatever else it may mean, has meant intensified competition among national capitals.

The indispensable state

The state, in both imperial and subordinate economies, still provides the indispensable conditions of accumulation for global capital, no less than for very local enterprises; and it is, in the final analysis, the state that has created the conditions enabling global capital to survive and to navigate the world. It would not be too much to say that the state is the *only* non-economic institution truly indispensable to capital. While we can imagine capital continuing its daily operations if the WTO were destroyed, and perhaps even welcoming the removal of obstacles placed in its way by organisations that give subordinate economies some voice, it is inconceivable that those operations would long survive the destruction of the local state.

Globalisation has, certainly, been marked by a withdrawal of the state from its social-welfare and ameliorative functions; and, for many observers, this has, perhaps more than anything else, created an impression of the state's decline. But, for all the attacks on the welfare-state launched by successive neoliberal governments, it cannot even be argued that global capital has been able to dispense with the social functions performed by nation-states since the early days of capitalism. Even while labour-movements and forces on the Left have been in retreat, with so-called social-democratic governments joining in the neoliberal assault, at least a minimal 'safety-net' of social provision has proved to be an essential condition of economic success and social stability in advanced-capitalist countries. At the same time, developing countries that may in the past have been able to rely more on traditional supports, such as extended families and village-communities, have been under pressure to shift at least some of these functions to the state, as the process of 'development' and the commodification of life have destroyed or weakened old social networks – though, ironically, this has made them even more vulnerable to the demands of imperial capital, as privatisation of public services has become a condition of investment, loans and aid.

Oppositional movements must struggle constantly to maintain anything close to decent social provision. But it is hard to see how any capitalist economy can long survive, let alone prosper, without a state that to some extent, however inadequately, balances the economic and social disruptions caused by the capitalist market and class-exploitation. Globalisation, which has further undermined traditional communities and social networks, has, if anything, made this state-function more – rather than less – necessary to the preservation of the capitalist system. This does not mean that capital will ever willingly encourage social provision. It simply means that its hostility to social programmes, as being necessarily a drag on capital-accumulation, is one of capitalism's many insoluble contradictions.

On the international plane, too, the state continues to be vital. The new imperialism, in contrast to older forms of colonial empire, depends more than ever on a system of multiple and more-or-less sovereign national states. The very fact that 'globalisation' has extended capital's purely economic powers far beyond the range of any single nation-state means that global capital requires *many* nation-states to perform the administrative and coercive functions that sustain the system of property and provide the kind of day-to-day regularity, predictability, and legal order that capitalism needs more than any other social form. No conceivable form of 'global governance' could provide the kind of daily order or the conditions of accumulation that capital requires.

The world today is more than ever a world of nation-states. The political form of globalisation is not a global state or global sovereignty. Nor does the lack of correspondence between global economy and national states simply represent some kind of time-lag in political development. The very essence of globalisation is a global economy administered by a global system of multiple states and local sovereignties, structured in a complex relation of domination and subordination.

The administration and enforcement of the new imperialism by a system of multiple states has, of course, created many problems of its own. It is not a simple matter to maintain the right kind of order among so many national entities, each with its own internal needs and pressures, to say nothing of its own coercive powers. Inevitably, to manage such a system ultimately requires a single overwhelming military power, which can keep all the others in line. At the same time, that power cannot be allowed to disrupt the orderly predictability that capital requires, nor can war be allowed to endanger vital markets and sources of capital. This is the conundrum that confronts the world's only superpower.

Precapitalist imperialism

All the major powers in sixteenth- and seventeenth-century Europe were deeply engaged in colonial ventures, conquest, plunder, and imperial oppression. Yet these ventures were associated with very different patterns of economic development, only one of which was capitalist. In fact, the one unambiguous case of capitalist development, England, was notoriously slow in embarking on overseas colonisation, or even dominating trade-routes; and the development of its distinctive social-property relations was already well underway by the time it became a major contender in the colonial race. So the connection between capitalism and imperialism is far from simple and straightforward.

A common account of the connection between imperialism and capitalism, often associated with left-versions of the commercialisation-model, suggests that European imperialist ventures in the New World, Africa, and Asia were decisive in the process of 'primitive accumulation' leading to capitalism. Imperialism permitted 'proto-capitalists' in Europe to accumulate the critical mass of wealth required to make the leap forwards that distinguished 'the West' from other societies that until then had been more advanced in commercial, technological, and cultural development. At the same time, imperialist exploitation drained the resources and halted the development of non-European economies.

Some versions of this explanation emphasise the importance of wealth amassed from the New World, in the form of gold and silver. Here, the critical – or at least emblematic – date is 1492, when Columbus sailed (inadvertently) to the Americas. Others stress the importance of the later slave-trade and the wealth derived from slave-plantations, in particular for the trade in sugar. Still others single out the importance of the British Empire in India in the process of industrialisation.[1]

Yet we cannot get very far in explaining the rise of capitalism by invoking the contribution of imperialism to 'primitive accumulation' or, indeed, by attributing to it any decisive role in the *origin* of capitalism. Not only did British overseas-colonisation lag behind the imperialist ventures of its European rivals, its acquisition of colonial wealth also lagged behind its own domestic capitalist development. By contrast, Spain, the dominant early colonial power and the leader in 'primitive accumulation' of the classical kind, which amassed huge wealth, especially from South-American mines, and was well endowed with 'capital' in the simple sense of wealth, did not develop in a capitalist direction. Instead, it expended its massive colonial wealth in essentially feudal pursuits, especially war as a means of extra-economic appropriation, and the construction of its Habsburg empire in Europe. Having overextended and overtaxed its European empire, it went into a deep and long-term decline in the seventeenth and eighteenth centuries.

Nor is it a simple matter to trace the causal connections between imperialism and the later development of industrial capitalism. Marxist historians, for instance, have forcefully argued, against many arguments to the contrary, that the greatest crime of European empire, slavery, made a major contribution to the development of industrial capitalism.[2] But here, too, we have to keep in mind that Britain was not alone in exploiting colonial slavery, and that elsewhere it had different effects. Other major European powers amassed great wealth from slavery and from the trade in sugar or in addictive goods like tobacco, which, it has been argued, fuelled the trade in living human-beings.[3] But, again, only in Britain was that wealth converted into industrial capital.

So we are still left with the question of why colonialism was associated with capitalism in one case and not another. Even those who are less interested in the origin of capitalism than in the 'Industrial Revolution', at a time when Britain really had become a pre-eminent imperial power, still have to explain why imperialism produced industrial capitalism in this case and not in others.

---

1. For recent examples, see Blaut 1993; and Frank 1998. Such 'anti-Eurocentric' arguments about the role of European imperialism are discussed in E.M. Wood 2001b.
2. The Marxist classics on this subject are the works of E. Williams 1961 and James 1989. The most recent major contribution to this debate is Blackburn 1997.
3. Blackburn 1997 makes this argument.

It is very hard to avoid the conclusion that much, if not everything, depended on the social-property relations at home in the imperial power, the particular conditions of systemic reproduction associated with those property-relations, and the particular economic processes set in motion by them. The wealth amassed from colonial exploitation may have contributed substantially to further development, even if it was not a necessary precondition of the *origin* of capitalism. And once British capitalism, especially in its industrial form, was well established, it was able to impose capitalist imperatives on other economies with different social-property relations. But no amount of colonial wealth would have had these effects without the imperatives generated by England's domestic property-relations. If wealth from the colonies and the slave-trade contributed to Britain's industrial revolution, it was because the British economy had already for a long time been structured by capitalist social-property relations. By contrast, the truly enormous wealth accumulated by Spain and Portugal had no such effect, because they were unambiguously non-capitalist economies.

We can, nevertheless, identify a specifically-capitalist form of imperialism, an imperialism that was more the result than the cause of capitalist development and stands in contrast to other European forms. So let us, first, sketch out in very broad strokes the traditional, precapitalist modes of imperialism and the way they were related to precapitalist social-property relations at home in the imperial power.

As we have seen, in precapitalist societies, appropriation – whether just to meet the material needs of society or to enhance the wealth of exploiters – took, so to speak, an absolute form: squeezing more out of direct producers, rather than enhancing the productivity of labour. That is to say, as a general rule, precapitalist exploitation took place by 'extra-economic' means, by means of direct coercion, using military, political, and juridical powers to extract surpluses from direct producers who typically remained in possession of the means of production. For that reason, too, relations of economic exploitation between classes were inseparable from 'non-economic' relations like the political relations between rulers and subjects. As for trade in these societies, it generally took the form of profit on alienation, buying cheap and selling dear, typically in separate markets, depending more on extra-economic advantages of various kinds than on competitive production.

Imperial expansion tended to follow the same logic. In some cases, it was largely an extension of coercive, extra-economic, absolute appropriation: using military power to squeeze taxes and tribute out of subject-territories; seizing more territory and resources; capturing and enslaving human-beings. In other cases, it was conducted in the interests of non-capitalist commerce, where profits were derived from a carrying trade or from arbitrage among many separate markets. In cases like this, extra-economic power might be used to secure trade-routes, to impose monopolies, to gain exclusive rights to some precious commodity, and so on.

Consider some of the typical patterns of European colonialism in the early-modern period. Much of it has to do not with the settlement of colonies by people from the metropolis, but rather with gaining control of important trade-routes or trading monopolies, or cornering the supply of some precious commodity. The Spanish empire in the Americas, long the dominant European overseas-empire, was less concerned even with commerce than with amassing bullion, extracting its wealth from the gold- and silver-mines of South America. So dependent did the Spanish economy become on this treasure, that many observers from the beginning have argued that this preoccupation at the expense of commerce or agricultural production obstructed Spain's economic development.

Where there was settlement, it tended to be for the purpose of enhancing trade, whether by establishing trading posts or by means of more wide-ranging territorial occupation. This kind of settlement might have little to do with production, or production might be for the purpose of provisioning the imperial power's merchant-ships – as was the case with the Cape Colony established by the Dutch in southern Africa.

Another example of precapitalist empire was the French colonisation of Canada, where the principal economic objective was the fur-trade. At the same time, a type of settler-colony was established that seems to have had no immediate economic function. The *seigneuries* of New France constituted a subsistence-economy, deliberately (if loosely) modelled on feudalism. Whatever purpose they may have served for the mother-country, there was nothing, here, either in the form of the settlements or in their purpose, that suggests any association with, or predisposition to, capitalist development.

In other cases, where production was developed as an adjunct to trade, it tended to be based on precapitalist modes of extra-economic exploitation: in particular, the slave-plantation, which several European powers favoured, especially in pursuit of the massive trade in sugar, or the Spanish *encomienda*-system, which amounted to the enslavement of indigenous peoples. Needless to say, capitalism did not put an end to these old imperial practices. On the contrary, it created new reasons, new needs, for pursuing some of them with even greater gusto, especially slavery. But the point is that it created a whole new logic of its own, new forms of appropriation and exploitation with their own rules and requirements, and with that came a new imperial dynamic, which affected even older forms of exploitation.

The classic age of imperialism

For all the profound disagreements among the classical-Marxist theorists of imperialism, they shared one fundamental premise: that imperialism had to do with the location of capitalism in a world that was not – and probably never would be – fully, or even predominantly, capitalist. Underlying the basic Leninist idea that imperialism represented 'the highest stage of capitalism', for instance, was the assumption that capitalism had reached a stage where the main axis of international conflict and military confrontation would run between imperialist states. But that competition was, by definition, rivalry over division and redivision of a largely non-capitalist world. The further capitalism spread (at uneven rates), the more acute would be the rivalry among the main imperialist powers. At the same time, they would face increasing resistance. The whole point – and the reason imperialism was the highest stage of capitalism – was that it was the *final* stage, which meant that capitalism would end before the non-capitalist victims of imperialism were finally and completely swallowed up by capitalism.

The point is made most explicitly by Rosa Luxemburg. The essence of her classic work in political economy, *The Accumulation of Capital*, is to offer an alternative, or supplement, to Marx's analysis of capitalism – essentially in one country – as a self-enclosed system. Her argument is that the capitalist system needs an outlet in non-capitalist formations, which is why capitalism inevitably means militarism and imperialism. Capitalist militarism, having gone through various stages, beginning with the straightforward conquest of territory, has now reached its 'final' stage, as 'a weapon in the competitive struggle between capitalist countries for areas of non-capitalist civilization'. But one of the fundamental contradictions of capitalism, she suggests, is that although 'it strives to become universal, and, indeed, on account of this tendency, it must break down – because it is immanently incapable of becoming a universal form of production'. It is the first mode of economy that tends to engulf the whole world, but it is also the first that cannot exist by itself because it 'needs other economic systems as a medium and soil'.[4]

So, in these theories of imperialism, capitalism by definition assumes a non-capitalist environment. In fact, capitalism depends for its survival not only on the existence of these non-capitalist formations, but on essentially precapitalist instruments of 'extra-economic' force, military and geopolitical coercion, and on traditional inter-state rivalries, colonial wars and territorial domination. These accounts were profoundly illuminating about the age in which they

----

4. Luxemburg 1963, p. 467.

were written; and, to this day, it has still not been demonstrated they were wrong in assuming that capitalism could not universalise its successes and the prosperity of the most advanced economies, nor that the major capitalist powers would always depend on exploiting subordinate economies. But we have yet to see a systematic theory of imperialism designed for a world in which all international relations are internal to capitalism and governed by capitalist imperatives. That, at least in part, is because a world of more-or-less universal capitalism, in which capitalist imperatives are a universal instrument of imperial domination, is a very recent development.

Europe, however advanced the development of capitalism may have been in parts of it, went into the First World-War as a continent of rival geopolitical and military empires. The United States, too, played its part in this old imperial system. Since the early days of the Monroe Doctrine, it had extended its 'sphere of influence', in the Western hemisphere and beyond, by military means, if not (or not always) for the purpose of direct colonisation, then certainly to ensure compliant régimes.

The world emerged from the War with some of the major imperial powers in shreds. But, if the classic age of imperialism effectively ended in 1918, and if the USA was already showing signs of becoming the world's first truly economic empire (not, of course, without a great deal of extra-economic force on its side and a history of direct imperial violence), several more decades would pass before a new form of empire clearly emerged. It can, in fact, hardly be said to have happened before the end of the Second World-War.

The latter may have been the last major war among capitalist powers to be driven by a quest for outright territorial expansion in pursuit of economic goals – above all, Germany's campaign, launched in compliance with its major industrial interests, for control not only of Eastern-European land and resources, but even of Caspian and Caucasian oil-fields. It was also, perhaps, the last conflict among capitalist powers in which, while pursuing economic interests, the principal aggressors relied completely on extra-economic force rather than market-imperatives, subjecting their own economies to total control by thoroughly militarised states. When the two defeated powers, Germany and Japan, emerged as the principal economic competitors to the US economy, with a great deal of help from the victors, a new age had truly begun.

This would be an age in which economic competition – in uneasy tandem with the cooperation among capitalist states required to guarantee their markets – overtook military rivalry among the major capitalist powers. The main axis of military and geo-political conflict would run not between capitalist powers, but between the capitalist and the developed non-capitalist world – until the Cold War ended with even the former Soviet Union drawn into the capitalist orbit. Yet, if this conflict was not between rival capitalist powers, it certainly had wide-ranging implications for the global capitalist order.

The conflict between the USA and USSR never issued in direct military confrontation, yet the Cold War marked a major transition in the role of imperial military power. Without seeking outright territorial expansion, the USA nevertheless became the world's most powerful military force, with a highly militarised economy. It was during this time that the purpose of military power shifted decisively away from the relatively well defined goals of imperial expansion and inter-imperialist rivalry to the open-ended objective of policing the world in the interests of (US) capital. This military pattern, and the needs that it served, would not change with the 'collapse of Communism'; and the Cold War would be replaced by other scenarios of war without end. Today's Bush Doctrine is directly descended from strategies born in the Cold War.

Relations with the less developed world were altered too. In the wake of the First World-War, as empires crumbled, nation-states proliferated. This was not only a consequence of national-liberation struggles, but also, typically, a matter of imperialist policy. In the Middle-East, for example, Western powers, notably Britain and France, began to carve up the remnants of the Ottoman Empire, not by appropriating them as direct colonial possessions, but by creating new and somewhat arbitrary states, to suit their own imperial purposes, mainly to control the oil-supply – a task later taken over by the United States.

The new imperialism that would eventually emerge from the wreckage of the old would no longer be a relationship between imperial masters and colonial subjects, but a complex interaction between more-or-less sovereign states. This capitalist imperialism, certainly, absorbed the world into its economic orbit, but it was increasingly a world of nation-states. The USA emerged from the Second World-War as the strongest economic and military power, and took command of a new imperialism governed by economic imperatives and administered by a system of multiple states – with all the contradictions and dangers this combination would present. This economic empire would be sustained by political and military hegemony over a complex state-system, consisting of enemies who had to be contained, friends who had to be kept under control, and a 'Third World' that had to be made available to Western capital.

Globalisation and war

The 'second', and more properly 'British', Empire, whose crown-jewel was India, produced its own ideological requirements. To justify imperial domination of a strong commercial power like India with complex political institutions, where the land was very much and insurmountably occupied, and where the issue was neither simply trade nor colonial settlement, but domination of one major power by another, demanded arguments other than those deployed in colonising the New World. Much of the old ideological repertoire could be adapted to suit this new conquest, but some adjustments had to be made. In particular, a modernisation, so to speak, of the old universal-society argument was called upon to bear the ideological weight of the new empire. Where the old version invoked certain universal principles of civilised order to justify imperial wars, that theme was now modified by more recent conceptions of progress. India could then be depicted as enjoying benign British tutelage, at least until its political and economic development had caught up with the imperial guardian.

But, if the new empire had different ideological requirements than the old, the theoretical innovations that had buttressed the first British Empire, in Ireland and America, remained in some respects more prescient about the future shape of capitalist imperialism. This is true not, of course, in the sense that colonial settlement was to be the dominant form of capitalist imperialism. But, in other ways, the ideological weapons forged to defend the Irish and American models were more specifically capitalist than other available theories. It is here that we begin to find a conception of empire not as conquest or even military domination and political jurisdiction, but as purely economic hegemony.

John Locke, again, best reflects this new conception of empire, in the sense that his theory of colonial appropriation by-passes altogether the question of political jurisdiction or the right of one political power to dominate another. In his theory of property, we can observe imperialism becoming a directly economic relationship, even if that relationship required brutal force to implant it. That kind of relationship could be justified not by the right to rule, but by the right, indeed the obligation, to produce exchange-value.

Capitalist imperialism eventually became almost entirely a matter of economic domination, in which market-imperatives, manipulated by the dominant capitalist powers, were made to do the work no longer done by imperial states or colonial settlers. It is a distinctive and essential characteristic of capitalist imperialism that its economic reach far exceeds its direct political and military grasp. It can rely on the economic imperatives of 'the market' to do much of its imperial work. This sharply differentiates it from earlier forms of imperialism, which depended directly on such extra-economic powers, whether territorial empires that could reach only as far as the capacity of their direct coercive powers to impose their rule, or commercial empires whose advantages depended, for example, on domination of the seas.

Once subordinate powers are made vulnerable to economic imperatives and the 'laws' of the market, direct rule by imperial states is no longer required to impose the will of capital. But, here, we encounter a paradox, or, better still, a fundamental contradiction of capitalism. Market-imperatives may reach far beyond the power of any single state, but these imperatives themselves must be enforced by coercive extra-economic power. Neither the imposition of economic imperatives, nor the everyday social order demanded by capital-accumulation and the operations of the market, can be achieved without the help of coercive powers much more local and territorially limited than the economic reach of capital.

That is why, paradoxically, the more purely economic empire has become, the more the nation-state has proliferated. Not only imperial powers, but also subordinate states, have proved necessary to the rule of global capital. It has, in fact, been a major strategy of capitalist imperialism even to create local states to act as conduits for capitalist imperatives.

Globalisation has not transcended this need. The 'globalised' world is more than ever a world of nation-states. In fact, the new imperialism we call global-isation, precisely because it depends on a wide-ranging economic hegemony that reaches far beyond any state's territorial boundaries or political domin-ion, is a form of imperialism more dependent than any other on a system of multiple states.

Subordinate states that act at the behest of global capital may be more effec-tive than the old colonial settlers who once carried capitalist imperatives throughout the world, but they also pose great risks. In particular, they are subject to their own internal pressures and oppositional forces, and their own coercive powers can fall into the wrong hands, which may oppose the will of imperial capital. In this globalised world, where the nation-state is supposed to be dying, the irony is that, because the new imperialism depends more than ever on a system of multiple states, it matters to capital more than ever who commands those local states and how. For instance, popular struggles for truly democratic states, for a transformation in the balance of class-forces in the state, with international solidarity among such democratic national strug-gles, might present a greater challenge to imperial power than ever before.

At any rate, the imperial power has acted to ensure against any risk of los-ing its hold on the global state-system. However unlikely or distant that pros-pect may seem, the USA has been ready to anticipate it by using its one most unambiguous advantage, its overwhelming military power – if only because it can do so more-or-less with impunity.

But, if military force remains an indispensable tool of the new imperialism, its nature and objectives must be different from its application in old colonial empires. The old forms of colonial imperialism required outright conquest, together with theories of war and peace to justify it. Early capitalist imperialism, while no less dependent on coercive force to take control of colonial territory, seemed able to dispense with a political defence of colonisation and to incorporate the justification of colonial settlement into a theory of property. Globalisation, the economic imperialism of capital taken to its logical conclusion, has, paradoxically, required a new doctrine of extra-economic, and especially military, coercion.

The practical and doctrinal difficulties posed by this new situation are obvious. If local states will guard the economy, who will guard the guardians? It is impossible for any single state-power, even the massive military force of the USA, to impose itself every day, everywhere, throughout the global system. Nor can any conceivable collective force impose the will of global capital all the time on a multitude of subordinate states, or maintain the predictable order required by capital's daily transactions. It is not easy to identify the role of military force in defending a borderless empire and establishing imperial control over a global economy, instead of sovereignty over a clearly bounded territory.

Since even US military power cannot be everywhere at once (it has never even aspired to more than two local wars at a time), the only option is to demonstrate, by frequent displays of military force, that it can go anywhere at any time, and do great damage. This is not to say that war will be constant. 'Operation Infinite War' is apparently intended to produce something more like Hobbes's 'state of war': 'the nature of war,' he writes in the *Leviathan*, 'consisteth not in actual fighting, but in the known disposition thereto during all the time there is no assurance to the contrary'. It is this endless possibility of war that imperial capital needs in order to sustain its hegemony over the global system of multiple states.

Hobbes understood what the new imperialists know: that power rests to a great extent on psychology and especially fear. As the right-wing commentator, Charles Krauthammer has recently said in the *Washington Post*[5] [30 November 2001], 'the elementary truth that seems to elude the experts again and again – Gulf war, Afghan war, next war – is that power is its own reward. Victory changes everything, psychology above all. The psychology in the region is now one of fear and deep respect for American power. Now is the time to use it to deter, defeat or destroy the other régimes[…]', above all, Iraq. So, while power produces fear, fear produces more power; and the purpose of

---

5. Krauthammer 2001.

a war like the one in Afghanistan is to create a psychological climate, as much as anything else, a purpose more easily served by attacking adversaries who can be defeated with relative ease (and where, perhaps, the outcome matters relatively little to the imperial power), and then moving on to bigger game, fortified by universal fear.

This does not necessarily mean that the USA, as global capital's ultimate coercive power, will wage war for no reason at all, just for the purpose of display. There are likely to be more finite goals, as in Afghanistan, though even here, the objectives probably have more to do with trying out new modes of war and, above all, creating a political climate for the open-ended 'war against terrorism' – even more than, say, ensuring access to the huge oil- and gas-reserves of Central Asia, which many commentators have suggested is the purpose of the war.

But, whatever specific objectives such wars may have, there is always something more. The larger purpose is to shape the political environment in a complex system of multiple states. In some cases, particularly in subordinate states, the object is exemplary terror, *pour encourager les autres*. In advanced-capitalist states, the political environment is shaped in other ways, by their implication in imperial alliances.[6] But, in all cases, the overriding objective is to demonstrate US hegemony.

Such purposes help to explain why there has developed a pattern of resort to military action by the US in situations ill-suited to military solutions; why massive military action is anything but a last resort; and why the connection between means and ends in these military ventures is typically so tenuous. An endless empire which has no boundaries, even no territory, requires war without end. An invisible empire requires infinite war, and a new doctrine of war to justify it.

Globalisation and imperial hegemony

There are several quite distinct dangers that may threaten this US-dominated global system, which all have to do with the state. One is the disorder engendered by the *absence* of effective state-powers – such as today's so-called 'failed' states – which endanger the stable and predictable environment that capital needs. Another is the threat from states operating outside the normal scope of the US-dominated world-order, what Washington likes to call 'rogue'-states (or 'the axis of evil') – which are distinguished from equally evil states that do remain within the US orbit.

6. See Gowan 2002, on US efforts to shape the political environment in allied capitalist powers.

Yet an even greater challenge is posed not by such marginal cases, but by states and economies that may function all-too-well and threaten to contest US supremacy. Such threats come not only from possible future competitors like China or Russia. There are more immediate challenges within the capitalist order, and even at its very core. The European Union, for instance, is potentially a stronger economic power than the USA.

But maintaining hegemony among major capitalist powers is a far more complicated business than achieving geo-political dominance, or even a 'balance of power', as old imperial states sought to do in the days of traditional inter-imperialist rivalry. It is no longer a simple matter of defeating rivals. War with major capitalist competitors, while it can never be ruled out, is likely to be self-defeating, destroying not only competition, but markets and investment-opportunities at the same time. Imperial dominance in a global-capitalist economy requires a delicate and contradictory balance between suppressing competition and maintaining conditions in competing economies that generate markets and profit. This is one of the most fundamental contradictions of the new world-order.

The contradictory relations among major capitalist states are nicely illustrated by the development of Germany and Japan after the Second World-War, and their relationship with former adversaries. Their economic success was, from the US point of view, inseparably both good and bad, supplying markets and capital, but also competitive threats. Relations among the major capitalist nations have been maintained in an uneasy balance between competition and cooperation ever since, with major disagreements regularly erupting, but without a threat of war.

Imperial hegemony in the world of global capitalism, then, means controlling rival economies and states without going to war with them. At the same time, the new military doctrine is based on the assumption that military power is an indispensable tool in maintaining the critical balance, even if its application in controlling major competitors must be indirect. This is especially true when other economies are rising in relation to the hegemonic power. It has certainly not escaped the notice of the 'only superpower' that, while its own economy was (and still is?) in decline, some other parts of the world, notably China, were experiencing historically unprecedented growth.[7] The emergence of the European Union as an economic superpower has also

---

7. On the contrasts between the long economic downturn in the West, especially in the USA, and remarkable rises elsewhere at the same time – with China, for instance, experiencing growth-rates during the West's long downturn that 'dwarfed' even those of the post-war boom in the West – see Perry Anderson's essay on Eric Hobsbawm's history of the contemporary world: P. Anderson 2002, especially p. 12.

262 • Chapter Seven

placed a special premium on military supremacy as the only reliable index of
US hegemony.

The contradictions of capitalist imperialism

My own view of the relation between economic and political power in capitalism is, in some respects, diametrically opposed to David Harvey's.[8] While he
argues that ever-expanding capital-accumulation must be accompanied by an
ever-expanding political power and command over territory, and that this is
the logic of capitalist imperialism, I argue almost the reverse: the specificity
of capitalist imperialism lies in the unique capacity of capital to impose its
hegemony *without* expanding its territorial political power. In all other forms
of empire, the scope of hegemony depended directly on the reach of geo-
political and military force. Capitalism alone has created an autonomously
economic form of domination.

So, Harvey starts from the premise that capital needs to 'expand geographic
control', preferably in the form of territorial dominion. It is true, he writes, that
the most recent imperial hegemon, the USA, has devised a distinctive form of
imperialism, which nominally recognises the independence of the countries
over which it exercises hegemony. But this brand of imperialism still con-
forms to his basic rule, because it is, in his view, largely an ideological cover,
adopted principally for domestic reasons, partly to preserve the capacities of
domestic consumption, but above all to disguise the same imperial ambitions
that drove the territorial-colonial empires of classic imperialism. By contrast,
I argue that the USA is the first truly capitalist empire, precisely because it is
the first imperial hegemon to possess the kind of economic power needed to
dispense with territorial ambitions and to sustain its hegemony through the
economic imperatives of capitalism, though [...] this has been accompanied
by new 'extra-economic' – especially military – requirements. The invention of 'open-door' imperialism was not just an ideological subterfuge or a
second-best alternative imposed on the USA by recalcitrant anti-colonial sen-
timent at home. It was the *preferred option* of a power capable of sustaining its
hegemony without incurring the costs and risks of direct political rule or territorial control. After the USA had completed its westward expansion on its
own continent, coercively displacing the indigenous population, it generally
preferred a so-called 'informal' empire, without colonial rule.

[...] [There] is another way of formulating the contradictions of capitalist
imperialism, which may or may not be consistent with Harvey's argument, but

---

8. Harvey 2003.

which, in any case, is the one I would favour. It requires us, first, to acknowledge the specificities of capitalism and its particular form of appropriation, as distinct from other social formations. This means that we would also be obliged to recognise the distinctive role of the 'political' in a system where property itself is not 'politically constituted' and appropriation takes place by 'economic' means. The specific 'political' logic of capitalist imperialism would, then, be something other than the drive for territorial expansion, the direct command of territory, or the appropriation of surpluses by extra-economic means, whether in the form of pillage, tax or tribute. Extra-economic power would, certainly, be treated as essential to capital-accumulation, but its principal functions would be the imposition, maintenance and enforcement of social property-relations conducive to the exertion of economic power; the creation of a predictable social and administrative order of the kind that capitalism needs more than any other social form; and, in general, the provision of conditions congenial to accumulation. Any contradictions between the two 'logics' of power would not take the form of a tension between two distinct imperial drives; and, while these contradictions would certainly arise from the relation between the economic powers of capital and the political powers of the territorial entities that serve them, that relation is not adequately conveyed by Hannah Arendt's rule that endless capital-accumulation requires an endless accumulation of political power. On the contrary, the contradictions would emanate from capital's unique ability to *distance itself from* political power.

I will not here repeat what I have said elsewhere about these contradictions, except to emphasise one or two essential points as they relate to capitalist imperialism. If the essential role of the state in capitalism is not to serve as an instrument of appropriation, or a form of 'politically-constituted property', but rather as a means of creating and sustaining the conditions of accumulation at arm's length, maintaining the social, legal and administrative order necessary to accumulation, this is true of the state's role not only in the domestic economy, but also in capitalist imperialism. Just as domestic capital requires order on the national plane, the global expansion of capital requires the maintenance of order and conditions of accumulation on a global scale.

But, here, wholly new problems arise, because the necessary order requires a degree of supervision incompatible with the global scope of capital-accumulation. The economic reach of capital may be global; but a truly global state, which can offer the kind of minute and reliable administration capital needs, is all but inconceivable. It is also true that global capital benefits in various ways from the unevenness of national economies and from the control of labour-mobility, which also argues in favour of territorial states to enclose and control these economic fragments. In other words, global capital *needs* a fragmentation of political space.

I should, perhaps, concede that the impossibility of a global state to match global capital is not something that can be grasped entirely on the theoretical plane. To a large extent, this proposition is a lower-level practical observation about the insurmountable difficulty of sustaining on a large geographical scale the close regulation and predictability capital needs. That said, it remains true that the very possibility of a contradiction between the global scale of capital and the territorial limits of the state is something specific to capitalism, and this can indeed be captured theoretically.

In any case, the more *global* the economy has become, the more economic circuits have been organised by territorial states and inter-state relations; and capital has come to rely more than ever on territorial states to install and enforce the conditions of accumulation on a global scale. For instance, global capital today depends on local states throughout the world to operate its neo-liberal strategies. It is, certainly true that capital has made use of new trans-national organisations to facilitate its navigation of the global economy, and territorial states themselves have also had to respond to the needs of global capital. But, if anything, the political logic of capitalism has reinforced the fragmentation of the global system into territorial entities, instead of creating some kind of global state.

So, the political form of global capitalism is not a global state but a global system of multiple territorial states; and this creates its own distinctive contradictions. We are only now beginning to see their implications. The division of labour between political and economic power, between capital and state, was more-or-less manageable, as long as the reach of economic hegemony was more-or-less the same as the reach of the national state. But, today, there is a growing distance between the economic reach of capital and the scope of political power. While it is possible to envisage a redrawing of current territorial boundaries, with increasing regionalisation on the one hand and localisation on the other, I cannot imagine any existing or conceivable form of 'global governance' providing the degree of order and regularity that capital needs.

This means that states operating on behalf of global capital have to organise not only their own domestic social order, but the international order among states. It is no longer a matter of capturing this-or-that bit of territory, dominating this-or-that subject people, defeating this-or-that imperial rival. The new imperial project depends on policing the whole global system of states and ensuring that imperial capital can safely and profitably navigate throughout that global system. But, since there is no single overarching global state with the power to transcend and control all national entities, there are, again, wholly new contradictions.

In particular, the extra-economic force required to maintain a global order congenial to capital must, in the absence of a global state, be exercised by territorial states. These territorial states must, in turn, be policed to guarantee an international order congenial to the movements of capital; but, since this cannot be done by a global *political* power, the organisation of multiple states is largely a *military* project. The military policy of the major capitalist states since the end of the Second World-War has been based on the assumption that what is required to maintain a stable and orderly system of multiple states is one overwhelmingly preponderant military power. It has been a central plank of US foreign policy since at least the 1940s, and certainly long before the [...] Bush régime, to ensure the unassailable predominance of US military power; and, in general, this principle has been accepted by its major allies among the advanced-capitalist states.

This is the setting in which a George W. Bush is possible – and at a time when the relative decline of US economic power has made its military supremacy that much more important. If Bush has mobilised this force in ways unlike his predecessors, and if his imperial project goes beyond anything envisaged by them, he has been able to pursue it only because the foundations – infrastructural and ideological – had already been laid by previous administrations. Discontinuities there certainly have been, but there are also essential underlying continuities, grounded in the fundamental contradictions of capitalist imperialism.

A single territorial power policing the whole global system for capital by military means is, from the start, a contradictory and dangerous project. The most obvious point is that the particular interests of one nation-state and its own national capitals will inevitably take precedence over all others. But perhaps the most problematic aspect of the new imperialist militarism is that its military objectives are, by nature, open-ended. Earlier imperial projects were easier to fathom because their purposes and scope were relatively well-defined, whether it was to capture territory, resources and slaves, to monopolise trade-routes, or simply to defeat a rival. In the case of the 'new' imperialism, where the object of military force is less to achieve a specific result, than to oversee the whole global system and to assert a general predominance, it is not surprising to see military adventures with no identifiable purpose, scope or exit-strategy; and since the territorial limitations of the hegemonic state mean that its military power cannot be everywhere at once, the 'demonstration-effect' becomes especially important. Bush's military policy of endless war, without any limits of time or geography, only takes to extremes the logic of the open-ended militarism already inherent in the contradictions of the new imperialism.

The madness of the war in Iraq, for instance, is probably inexplicable without reference to this distinctive military logic. Oil is not enough to explain it. As many commentators have pointed out, oil-producing countries have no interest in withholding their prize-commodity from those who can afford to buy it, and US access to Middle-Eastern oil-markets has never been in serious danger. Even if we assume that oil-reserves in the not-too-distant future will be severely limited and that, therefore, today's (and tomorrow's) major powers are seeking to establish control of strategic oil-producing regions, the US strategic position in the Gulf, or even its capacity to control the access of others to oil, did not require the invasion of Iraq or the overthrow of Saddam Hussein.[9] It is even possible that the chaos engendered by the invasion of Iraq has made matters worse for the US. But the overarching open-ended military project of the new imperialism can always make a case for war, when other, more precise objectives by themselves are not enough, and even when there are powerful arguments against it. In the light of this project, it is even possible – as I think was the case in Iraq – that the target of military force will be selected not because it represents a threat but, on the contrary, because it represents no threat at all, and hence appears a likely candidate *pour encourager les autres* at relatively little risk to the aggressor. What may seem inexplicable in relation to any specific objectives may make some kind of perverted sense when the primary purpose is to 'shock and awe' the world – even if this kind of perversion, with all the instabilities it generates, is likely to be self-defeating.

---

9. On the latter two points, see Brenner 2006b.

Chapter Eight
Socialism

The end of the welfare-state 'compact'

A surprising number of people on the Left talk, like Frances Fox Piven and Richard A. Cloward, about compacts of one kind or another between capital and labour.[1] For instance, many speak of a post-war 'accord' between the classes in the United States after the Second World-War. In that accord, 'Keynesian' state-intervention and the welfare-state combined with a settlement at the microeconomic level, in which labour conceded control of the labour-process to capital in exchange for wage-increases in keeping with productivity-gains and inflation. Some commentators seem to treat this post-war accord as if it ushered in some kind of 'golden age', while others are inclined to call it a betrayal by the 'labour-bureaucracy.' But either way, for people who think in terms of a post-war accord, the electoral triumph of neo-liberalism, in the persons of Margaret Thatcher and Ronald Reagan, is as close as we can get to a precise moment when globalisation ended that compact.

Let us, then, work back from this turning-point. In what way, if any, does it mark a watershed between a social compact and its breach? What did it bring to an end?

The decline in the labour-movement and the dismantling of the welfare-state are obviously not illusions – though they mean more in countries that

---

1. Piven and Cloward 1998a and 1998b.

have actually had a welfare-state worth talking about, which is not self-evidently true of the United States when compared to, say, the Scandinavian countries, or even Canada and Britain. In certain European cases, notably in Scandinavia, there may even be some justification for talking about the kind of 'compact' Piven and Cloward have in mind. And the post-war 'settlement' in Britain was undoubtedly driven by capital's fear of militant (and hopeful) working-class soldiers returning from the War. There is no doubt that the neoliberal programme, now adopted even by social-democratic régimes, marks a significant departure from that distinctive post-war moment. But let us put things into perspective.

Let us talk about the United States in particular. The first important point about the post-war 'golden age' is its uniqueness.[2] For the United States, the early post-war period was a historically unprecedented and almost certainly unrepeatable 'conjuncture'. What was truly remarkable was the unrivalled hegemony of the United States and its relative freedom from competition. But the economic breathing space was short (its loss only partially offset by continued military superiority and spending), as two other major players, the two defeated powers, Germany and Japan, entered their own impressive periods of growth.

What about class-relations? Was there, as is often argued, an 'accord', in which labour and capital agreed to keep both wages and prices relatively high by means of mutual concessions? There may have been a short period of *relative* calm in the war against labour while the lack of competition allowed capital to tolerate higher wages – though we should not forget that the 1940s were the years of the Red Scare, the Taft-Hartley Act, and the beginning of the Cold War. If wages continued to rise for a while (at least in some parts of the country) even when, in the context of increasing competition, they seriously threatened profits, it was primarily because of rank-and-file militancy. But capital did not sustain the squeeze on profits for long. If there was a truce in its class-war against labour, it did not last. In the late 1950s and the 1960s, class-conflict heated up. US capital, now facing renewed and intensified competition, launched a vicious and sustained attack on labour.

So, while labour certainly lost control of the labour-process (and, as some versions of the 'accord'-model point out, elements in the labour-bureaucracy certainly collaborated in US-imperialist policies), it is hard to see this as an 'accord'. We have to keep in mind that the so-called golden age was a period when capital sustained its profits not by 'accords' so much as by vicious

---

2. The following discussion of the post-war period is indebted to Brenner 2006a, especially Part Two.

class-conflict: from Taft-Hartley in the late 1940s, to union-avoidance strategies by companies like IBM or deunionisation-strategies by General Electric in
the late fifties and early sixties, to savage bouts of union-busting and 'some of
the worst storms in labour history' in the late fifties, followed by a decade of
union-unrest from the early sixties to the early seventies, with a rank-and-file
chafing against their leadership's inadequate responses to attacks by capital.
'It is generally forgotten', writes Mike Davis, 'how close American industrial
relations came to a raw re-opening of the class war in those years'.[3] Far from
representing a time of concord, or even a cease-fire, between the two classes,
the 'golden age' was a time of unrelenting assault by capital against labour.

If there was an ebb and flow in capital's war against labour during the
'golden age', it was not only a matter of changes in working-class power or
militancy. It had a great deal to do with the beginning and end of US capital's
unique moment of unchallenged ascendancy. The idea of the 'compact' makes
that moment seem too voluntary, and therefore possibly recoverable, instead
of historically specific and unrepeatable. On the one hand, this tends to lay the
blame for deteriorating conditions mainly on the failures of organised labour.
On the other hand, if some labour-leaders today still believe they can go back
to a 'golden age', the notion of the 'compact' or 'accord' may be partly responsible for that illusion.

The compact-model does not look much better if we move further back, as
Piven and Cloward seem to do, in search of the compact, to the 1930s and the
New Deal. It is certainly true that labour-organisation in the United States
reached a high point in the 1930s, and without some heroic class-struggles
there would have been no New Deal. But the correlation between the policies of the New Deal and the disposition of class-power is far from simple
and direct, and it is very hard to think of it as just a compact in which capital
conciliated labour.

I see no reason to question the often repeated observation that the New
Deal saved capitalism, and was intended to save capitalism. It was, of course,
done against the will of most (though not all) capitalists and against their
resistance at every step. In that sense, the New Deal represents a disjuncture
between the state and the capitalist class. But, as in the case of the old poor-
laws in England, it is hard to say that this disjuncture was simply determined
by the strength of labour against capital, or that it acted against the interests of
capital in favour of labour. Nor was the weakness of capital, in that moment
of extremity, in direct proportion to labour's strength. On the contrary, it
was the consequence of a deep economic crisis that profoundly affected *both*

---

3. Davis 1986, p. 123.

classes – and we surely would not want to say that the effects on labour were unambiguously empowering.

While any social and political gains for the working class, both before and after the War, were never freely given without class-struggle, there was never a simple and straightforward correlation between social provision and the disposition of class-power of the kind suggested by the compact-model.

The Second World-War marked – and basically caused – the transition from depression to boom. Economic conditions in the post-war boom were exactly the reverse of those in the 1930s. In one case depression (the weakness of capital?), and in the other case economic boom (the strength of capital?) constituted the conditions for social reform. Even if the pre-war reforms can be explained by the organisation and militancy of labour while capital was reeling from the Depression, what power-relation explains the 'golden age' after the War? It would be hard to prove that the power of labour surpassed the increasing strength of capital, and even harder to show that capital had been forced to call a truce in its war against labour. So the interplay of economic conditions and class-power is clearly more complicated than the compact-model or the theory of epochal shifts and 'power-eras' suggest.

What about the *breach* of the compact? There is no doubt that the signs of decline – in the proportion of unionised labour, in welfare-provision, and so on – have been especially dramatic since the early eighties. But, as Harry Magdoff reminds us[...]'the spirit of neoliberalism' was already present much earlier, at the height of the so-called 'age of Keynesian social democracy'.[4] Nor should we forget that, in the United States, the decline in union-density began in the fifties, and continued as new industries developed, especially in the South and Southwest, without a corresponding organisation of the new labour-force (maybe, as critics of the labour-bureaucracy will tell us, because these regions were deliberately conceded to capital – but if this is the 'accord', it means something rather different from what Piven and Cloward seem to have in mind).

There are other problems too. If we identify the breach with the electoral triumph of neoliberalism, should we say that Thatcher's election was a response to the weakness of labour or, on the contrary, to the period of labour-militancy that preceded her victory? Once again, as in the case of the poor-law reform in England in the 1830s, maybe the mobilisation of capital had less to do with labour's weakness, than with its strength. Such an explanation has flaws of its own, but it is no less, and probably more, plausible than the other. In any case, it does at least illustrate, yet again, the complexity of the relation between class-power and the welfare-state.

---

4. Magdoff 1998.

There are no social democrats now

[...]What is it, then, about this 'epochal shift' that so many people find so compelling, and what difference does it make? Its attractions for capitalist ideologues are clear enough. There is no more convincing argument for TINA (There Is No Alternative) than the insistence that history has taken some irrevocable turn, closing off options – like social democracy, let alone socialism – which may at one time have looked attractive and possible, but are now a thing of the past. The appeal of such arguments to socialists, though, is rather more mysterious.

Piven and Cloward may give us a hint. 'We are all social democrats now', they say. That, in a sense, is the main theme of their challenge to 'the emerging *MR* [*Monthly Review*] position' on globalisation. We are all, they say, nostalgic for the traditional certainties about the working class and the possibilities of class-struggle in the 'industrial era', the era of big unions, labour-parties, and mass-strikes – all those things that helped create the welfare-state but which globalisation has effectively destroyed. And we mourn the passing of all those old formations and all those old possibilities. That nostalgia is, they claim, what lies behind *MR*'s refusal to acknowledge that something fundamental has changed with globalisation, and that we on the Left have suffered a truly 'awesome' loss.

But it occurs to me that something else is going on, which I can sum up with my own aphorism: 'There are *no* social democrats now'. People are waking up to the fact that social democracy is not a viable option. For those who have tended to identify social democracy with social*ism*, there seems to be no other alternative to capitalism – in fact, no alternative to the more inhumane, neoliberal forms of capitalism. So the loss of social democracy is, for them, indeed an awesome one. It is, for them, a more cataclysmic and perhaps even final loss than for those who, while certainly supporting the welfare-state or any amelioration of capitalism's destructive consequences, have always doubted the long-term sustainability of capitalism 'with a human face'. Those who used to place all their hopes in social democracy are inclined to explain their awesome loss not by conceding that a humane capitalism was *never* sustainable in the long term, but by invoking some massive epochal shift which has destroyed the foundations of what used to be, but no longer is, a real possibility.[5]

Piven and Cloward seem to have mixed feelings about this. What they say about social democracy reads like an epitaph. Yet they hold out the hope of

---

5. I owe to John Mage this explanation of why so many on the Left feel compelled to talk about 'globalisation' as a massive historical transformation of epochal proportions, different from the changes that capitalism regularly undergoes.

a resurrection – or at least a reincarnation in another form, some new kind of compact, some new way of making capitalism tolerable. There is, though, no hint of anything more. The 'compact'-model implies that what the Left should be aiming for, and all we can hope for, is to wring concessions from capitalists – as earlier generations wrested concessions from the capitalist class on poor-relief, which they later lost, and as workers in the 'industrial' era have won and lost the welfare-state. This idea that the object of working-class power is to wring concessions from capital within a capitalist system nicely sums up the essence of social democracy – especially together with a theory of history in which changes of government may look like major epochal shifts, if only because fundamental transformations of property- and class-relations have, in effect, been ruled out.

I agree, of course, that class-power is what it is ultimately all about. And I do not want to take issue with the very useful and illuminating things Piven and Cloward say about the formation of working-class power, about the processes of organisation and ideological penetration.[6] The problem I have with their argument concerns their account of what working-class power is for, or what it can and cannot accomplish in the context of capitalism.

My point is simply this: there is no such thing as a compact between capital and labour in any meaningful sense. The system is constituted by the fundamental class-antagonism at its heart, and within the confines of the system, the capitalist class always, by definition, has the advantage. That may help to explain, among other things, how capital can mobilise in response not to the weakness of labour, but to its strength, and yet still win the day. Class-struggle is a constant necessity to ward off the worst excesses of exploitation, and the working class has had a long and heroic history of achievements in that respect. Class-struggle has, paradoxically, also been necessary to save capitalism from itself and its inherently destructive, even self-destructive, drives. But, within the confines of the system, the victories of working-class power, even at its highest points, will always be severely constrained and fragile. A strategy limited to the objective of wringing concessions from

---

6. I am not sure, by the way, why they think that I, or anyone else at *Monthly Review*, believes that there is anything automatic about the 'actualisation' of working-class power. See, for example, my argument in E.M. Wood 1986, Chapters Six and Seven. I have also consistently argued, contrary to some conventional Marxist wisdom (and contrary to the assumptions Piven and Cloward attribute to Marxism), that the development of industrial capitalism does not automatically and unambiguously promote the growth of working-class power, but that, on the contrary, the very structure of a mature industrial capitalism has a centrifugal effect on class-struggle, a fragmentation of the working class, together with a tendency to drive a wedge between 'economic' or 'industrial' struggles and political ones, which requires difficult ideological and organisational processes to overcome. See, for instance, E.M. Wood 1995a.

capital, while it may be all that is possible in certain conditions, is, in the long run, self-defeating.

Yet I believe that working-class power can do a great deal *more* than wring concessions from capital. Socialism still remains a realistic option – more realistic than capitalism with a human face. But, even short of socialism, and as part of the struggle to attain it, there is a difference between just struggling to win concessions from capital, and struggling to wrest *control* away from capital; a difference between striving for 'safety-nets' within the capitalist system, and striving, instead, to detach the conditions of life from the logic of capitalism. There is, in other words, a difference between seeking some elusive and short-term class-compact, and challenging the underlying class-relation itself.[7]

The question, then, is whether today's conditions are more or less conducive to those more ambitious goals and to the more combative methods needed to achieve them, and whether what people are calling 'globalisation' detracts from, or enhances, the possibilities of struggle.

It may be that the conditions have never yet been right for a truly socialist struggle – not just for the achievement of socialism, but even for less final challenges to capitalism: struggles not just to win concessions from capital within a capitalist system, but to oppose the system itself with an economic logic of a different kind. In an underdeveloped capitalism, the material conditions are simply not there. But, in cases where the productive forces have been sufficiently developed to make socialist alternatives possible, the very same conditions that have made them so have had a contradictory effect on working-class unity, organisation, and ideology.

There has not been the kind of unambiguous relationship between the development of industrial capitalism and the growth of a united and powerful working class which Marxists once expected. Industrial capitalism – and here, I depart from much of conventional Marxist wisdom (and from the assumptions that Piven and Cloward attribute to Marxists) – has also militated *against* working-class unity, fragmenting the working class and turning it inwards, away from the centres of capitalist power towards the individual workplace. Struggles at the point of production have, of course, been absolutely vital, and still are, but they have also had a centrifugal effect on working-class power and struggle. They have also marked a separation between 'economic' or 'industrial' struggles and political ones.

What we are seeing today may be the beginning of an era – a *real* epochal shift, maybe the first of its kind in the history of capitalism – in which the

---

7. For a discussion of socialist – as distinct from social-democratic – alternatives in societies that are still capitalist, see Albo 1996; and Gindin 1997.

material and technological conditions for a truly socialist and democratic organisation of material life are present, while, for the first time, new conditions are emerging that can overcome the centrifugal effects of industrial capitalism and reconnect economic with political struggles. Meantime, capitalism, having become a virtually universal system, no longer has the same scope for external expansion which used to save it from its internal contradictions, so it has become subject to those contradictions in historically unprecedented ways. This is what I have called the 'universalisation' of capitalism, which is, indeed, an important historical change.

Among the current contradictions is that capitalism no longer seems able to sustain maximum-profitability by means of commensurate economic growth, and seems now to be relying more and more on simply *redistributing* wealth in favour of the rich, and on increasing inequalities, within and between national economies, with the help of the neoliberal state. In advanced-capitalist countries, the most visible sign of that redistribution is the decline of the welfare-state. And, while changes in the patterns of labour towards growing insecurity may have more to do with this process of redistribution than with an absolute decline in the need for labour, the ability of capitalism to absorb a growing reserve-army of labour is, at least, open to question. The result may be to break the old pattern, to upset the long-standing balance, that has up to now repeatedly saved capitalism from itself – the balance in which the danger of social unrest and disorder has been met not only by direct coercion, but also by social provision.

Piven and Cloward conclude their piece by hinting at new possibilities. What I am saying is that those possibilities may be closer than we think – and precisely because of 'globalisation'. 'Globalisation' is not just about the power of capital. It is also about the *vulnerability* of capital subjected to the pressures of international competition and its own internal contradictions. Besides, I do not accept the premise of the 'globalisation-thesis' – which Piven and Cloward never quite contradict – that the importance of the state and political power declines in proportion to globalisation.

On the contrary, I think […] that capital now needs the state more than ever to sustain maximum-profitability in a global market – so much so, I would say, that working-class political power could now challenge capital in ways it never could before. And, with the 'globalising' state as a target of struggle – we have been seeing unprecedented examples of this kind of struggle in many parts of the world in the last few years – there now exists a focus for working-class solidarity, within and across nation-states, of a kind that has never before existed in advanced capitalist countries.

So it may indeed be the beginning of a new – a *really* new – power-era.

Market-dependence vs. market-enablement

[…]Robert Brenner gives market-dependence and subjection to competition an explanatory status distinct and apart from, even prior to, the relation between capital and labour, which Marxists generally regard as capitalism's defining characteristic[…]. While he certainly takes full account of the connections between market-dependence and relations of exploitation, he suggests that capitalism is, in the first instance, defined by market-dependence and subjection to competition, and that there is an irreducible contradiction in the relation among capitals that is independent of the relation between capital and labour.

On this foundation, Brenner has constructed an analysis of the long post-war downturn that locates the critical mechanism of economic decline in the relation among capitals, as distinct from the relations between capital and labour. Arguing against explanations of the downturn that blame it on a profit-squeeze caused by conditions too favourable to labour, he explores the irreducible contradiction in the relation among capitals, which is independent of the relation with labour. In a nutshell, the argument explains how the conditions of capitalist competition inevitably lead to overcapacity, and, finally, to economic downturn, whatever the relations between capital and labour and even when demand is reliable and rising. Investment in fixed capital allows producers to stay in the market even when lower-cost competitors enter the fray, and they can stay in even at a lower rate of profit. But the point is also that the same heavy investment means they *must* stay in, even just to recoup their costs, or, at least, it is hard to get out at the right time. So manufacturers hang on to surplus-plant instead of closing it. The end result is a declining rate of aggregate-profit across the industry, with wider effects throughout the whole economy.[8]

Many people on the Left have been put off by Brenner's insistence that the fundamental contradiction that produces economic downturn is rooted in the 'horizontal' relation of competition among capitals, as distinct from the 'vertical' class-relation between capital and labour. Surely, many would say, focusing on competition as against class is about as serious a crime as any

---

8. An account of this basic mechanism similar to Brenner 2006a can be found in 'How the Mighty Are Falling', *Financial Times*, 30 November 1998. But this is just the kernel of Brenner's analysis, which attempts to explain not only the basic mechanism of overproduction/overcapacity and the consequent fall in profitability, but also why these continued to be reproduced in the long downturn, keeping profitability from recovering for such a long time. David McNally briefly summarises the argument and elaborates on some of the ways in which the tendency to overcapacity analysed by Brenner is related to wider trends in the global economy; see McNally 1999.

Marxist could commit, and it surely has serious political implications. Some critics even suggest that this analysis marginalises class-struggle and places 'competitiveness' at the centre of left politics.

[…] In what follows, I will try to show that, if we always look at capitalism through the lens of market-dependence, much else will become clear – for instance, about the limits of 'non-transformational' politics, designed to manage capitalism, rather than to transform it. […]

Left strategies of market-enablement

Let us take a quick look at the two main economic strategies that have dominated left-thinking for quite a while. First, we have so-called counter-cyclical – or, more specifically, Keynesian – policies intended to regulate the capitalist economy, to smooth out its business-cycles by means of state-intervention. These are obviously not exclusive to the Left, but they have been most consistently attractive to left-of-centre parties. But more recently, you have many people on the Left casting doubt on that kind of policy and, instead, joining the right in adopting neoliberal globalisation-programmes. The Left has invented 'progressive competitiveness', the Third Way, or neo-liberalism with a human face.

At first glance, Keynesian and neoliberal strategies seem diametrically opposed. The first, as we all know, involve state-intervention, what right-wing critics like to call 'tax and spend', for the purpose of increasing demand: stimulating investment by stimulating consumption. The other strategy, call it left neoliberalism, assumes that it was precisely Keynesian tax-and-spend policies that destroyed productivity and profitability, and propelled the world-economy into a prolonged downturn after the post-war boom.

Both these strategies have demonstrably failed to overcome the inherent contradictions of capitalism. The exceptional post-war boom – and, make no mistake about it, it was exceptional – ended more than a quarter of a century ago, so even if we give Keynesian strategies the credit for it, we have to concede that they could not sustain it. This has led many economists, right and left, to adopt what Brenner calls the 'contradictions-of-Keynesianism' view. Reduced to its fundamentals, the 'contradictions-of-Keynesianism' view is that Keynesian demand-management produced the long post-war boom by solving the problem of underconsumption, but was self-undermining in the long run. By adopting policies to stimulate demand, this argument says, it strengthened the position of labour against capital and ended up by squeezing profits, thereby discouraging investment. The apparently inevitable response, then, was a swing of the pendulum to neoliberalism.

Brenner makes a devastating argument against explanations of the downturn that blame it on the strength of labour and its squeeze on profits. He shows in great empirical detail that the long downturn was not, and could not have been, caused by labour. He points out, among other things, that victories by labour, which tend to be relatively localised, cannot in general account for system-wide crises. They certainly cannot account for the prolonged and universal downturn that affected all economies at roughly the same time and at the same pace, in spite of all the many variations in their labour-régimes or their configurations of class-power. And he shows that, at the onset of the downturn, labour-conditions were not that great, anyway.

But neoliberalism has not provided the answer either. The neoliberal strategies that came in response to the downturn and were supposed to correct the failures of Keynesianism are now failing even more spectacularly.[9] And we still have to confront the fact that so many different economies, with so many different institutional and political configurations, have suffered the same fate.

So we seem to be driven to an odd conclusion: it begins to appear that Keynesianism and neoliberalism are simply two sides of the same coin. The 'contradictions-of-Keynesianism' view seems to suggest that both strategies, Keynesian and neoliberal, are counter-cyclical in their intentions, but each for a different phase of the cycle. On the face of it, that may seem an unhelpful conclusion. On second thoughts, though, maybe it does have the virtue of expressing some kind of reality. But, instead of saying that what was right for one period was wrong for another, or that Keynesianism fell victim to its own success, it might have been better to say that both phases – the Keynesian and the neoliberal – represent the same underlying contradiction. The successive failures of both strategies reflect the same fundamental reality, which neither is prepared, or able, to confront.

The point I want to make, then, is that these strategies have failed not for antithetical reasons, but for the same reason. However opposed these two strategies may seem in principle, the fact is that their underlying assumptions are fundamentally the same. In a way, both are based on the same false assumption: that if there is a contradiction in capitalism, it manifests itself simply at the level of the business-cycle. That means, in the final analysis, that the contradictions of capitalism are benign, or at least manageable.

---

9. Calling neoliberalism a failure will no doubt seem odd to those who regard the US economy as a brilliant success. For a corrective to that triumphalism, see Henwood 1999.

In a way, both also seem to assume that we just need to strike the right balance between classes. It is true that neoliberalism gives a one-sided advantage to capital and blames crisis on things like unreasonable wage-demands or inflexible labour-markets and practices, while Keynesianism is more generous to labour, at least to the extent that it treats high employment and decent wages as essential sources of consumer-demand. But neither this difference nor the others I have mentioned change the fact that both Keynesianism and neoliberalism are operating only at the level of the surface-contradiction, and never probe beneath it.

At bottom, the common ground of these strategies is that both are looking for ways to enhance market-opportunities, to enable the market to function at its best, or to enable people to make the most of it. Neoliberals may seek to do it by deregulating markets, while Keynesians subsidise demand. But since neither comes close to confronting the conditions that make people dependent on the market in the first place, neither touches the underlying contradiction.

The political implications of competition

[…] The fact that market-dependence and competition preceded proletarianisation tells us something about the relations of competition and their autonomy from the relations between capital and labour. It means that producers and possessors of the means of production, who are not themselves wage-labourers, can be market-dependent without employing wage-labour. In other words – and this is the basic theoretical point – market-dependence and competition give rise to the imperatives of accumulation and innovation even in the absence of exploitation of labour by capital, while, in the absence of competition, no form of exploitation will have those effects. This clearly has implications for the pressures that affect capital, even abstracted from its relation to wage-labour.

But I want to go beyond that claim. The fact that market-dependence can exist without complete dispossession of the direct producers has other implications. For instance, it tells us something about the impossibility of so-called market-socialism. I think market-socialism is impossible – I think the term market-socialism is a contradiction in terms – because, even in the absence of a class-division between capital and labour, even if the means of production are returned to the direct producers, as long as the market regulates the economy there will always be imperatives of accumulation and competition; these imperatives will take precedence over social needs and well-being; and there will always be exploitation of labour – not to mention the ecological damage that inevitably goes with a system driven by those imperatives.

Once the market becomes an economic 'discipline' or 'regulator', once economic actors become market-dependent, even workers who own the means of production, individually or collectively, will be forced to respond to the market's imperatives – to compete and accumulate, to exploit themselves, and to let so-called 'uncompetitive' enterprises and their workers go under. (Marx, by the way, suggested just this possibility in a discussion of workers' cooperatives and how they would be self-exploiting in the presence of market-imperatives.) To the extent that these competitive pressures demand the intensification of labour to maximise labour-productivity, hierarchical relations in the process of production will be generated even in the absence of vertical relations between classes. And it even seems likely that the end-result would be to reproduce the vertical relations of class. Just as market-imperatives expropriated direct producers in the early days of capitalism, so they could have a similar effect in 'market-socialism'.

If market-dependence and market-imperatives are, in some important ways, independent of the relation between capital and labour, what does this add up to politically? What political implications should we draw from the independence of horizontal relations? Does it, for instance, mean that left politics should concentrate on improving 'competitiveness', rather than on militant class-struggle?

A common view, not least on the Left today (for example, in the 'contra-dictions-of-Keynesianism' view) is that too much class-militancy is counter-productive, that by undermining the profitability of capital it undermines employment and social provision. But if there is an irreducible contradiction of market-dependence in the relation among capitals, which is independent of the relations between capital and labour, we may draw a very different conclusion. We may conclude that there is no such obvious reason for restraining militant struggle.

If the dynamics of competition can operate even in the absence of any class-division between capital and labour, it seems to follow that, where there is such a class-division, the underlying competitive dynamic will operate no matter what the configuration of class-power may be. So, if competition is the focal point, the mechanism, of a fundamental contradiction, if competition is not just the mechanism of capitalist dynamism, but, at the same time, a mechanism of stagnation and downturn, that fundamental contradiction is irreducible and it cannot be circumvented, or even significantly modified, by any kind of class-relation between capital and labour.

This is certainly not to say that class-victories and defeats have no effect on capitalist profitability. But an analysis like Brenner's suggests that the connections are weaker than the conventional view allows. The point is not that capitalist profits are not affected by class-struggle. It is that, even in the absence of a squeeze on profits by class-struggle, the contradiction in the relations among capitals will still bring about crisis, and capital will still squeeze workers.

I am sure that it is old news to socialists that there is a dual contradiction in capitalism, but I think that much of what passes for left politics these days seems to proceed on the assumption that there is nothing fundamentally contradictory or problematic in the relation among capitals. For example, pessimistic socialists seem to be giving up altogether on the grounds that there is now an increasingly unified global-capitalist class which renders states and working classes helpless. Optimistic social democrats and advocates of the 'Third Way' think they can achieve some humane kind of competitiveness, while the neo-Keynesian Left seems to be suggesting that we can avoid the contradictions of capitalism if only we can strike the right balance in the class-relation between capital and labour. What I am arguing, instead, is that if we understand how capitalist contradictions are independent of class-relations, we will also understand the critical importance, the indispensability, and the possibilities of militant class-struggle.

I am trying to emphasise both the ways in which competition and class are separate, and the ways in which they are inextricably linked. Both sides of the equation have to be kept in mind in devising our oppositional politics. On the one hand, the dependence of capital on labour, the simple fact that labour produces capital, the fact that the generalisation of market-imperatives does depend on the general commodification of labour-power – all these things mean that class-struggle will always be the basic and necessary condition of any socialist transformation. And, if anything, the independent contradictions of competition are a source of capitalist vulnerability, which increases, not decreases, the opportunities for transformational struggles.

On the other hand, there is a great deal to be done short of a socialist transformation. If we focus on the irreducible contradiction in the relations among capitals, which is there whatever the relations between capital and labour, there really is no reason to place limits on class-struggle in pursuit of social protection and workplace-advances, and they should be pursued as militantly as possible – both to achieve immediate reforms and to enhance class-consciousness and organisation for more long-term transformational struggles. The simple point is that they do not have to be constrained by the assumption that they are the ultimate source of the problem. They neither create, nor can they resolve, the contradictions in the relation among capitals.

As for what lies between protective or maintenance-strategies and real transformational struggles – well, that is the hard part. But at least a few things are pretty clear. We may not know exactly what to do, but we should at least know what *not* to do. It makes no sense at all to pursue strategies that pull the economy ever-further into the intensifying contradictions of the global economy – like deregulatory and export-led strategies beloved by the World Bank and the IMF, which simply deepen the contradictions of market-dependence.

The best that socialists can do is to aim as much as possible to detach social life from market-dependence. That means striving for the decommodification of as many spheres of life as possible, and their democratisation – not just their subjection to the political rule of 'formal' democracy, but their removal from the direct control of capital and from the 'impersonal' control of market-imperatives, which subordinate every human need and practice to the requirements of accumulation and profit-maximisation. If that seems utopian, just consider how unrealistic it is to adopt a strategy of export-oriented competitiveness in a crisis-ridden global economy with an irreducible structural tendency to overcapacity.

But it is not my objective to outline policy-solutions. My main point is simply that there can be struggles and objectives short of a socialist transformation, but there cannot be such a thing as a Third Way. There really is no middle-ground between capitalism and socialism.

That is not a paradox. It simply means that all oppositional struggles – both day-to-day struggles to improve the conditions of life and work, and struggles for real social change – should be informed by one basic perception: that class-struggle cannot, either by its presence or by its absence, eliminate the contradictions in the capitalist system, even though it can ultimately eliminate the system itself. This means struggling for every possible gain within capitalism, without falling into the hopeless trap of believing that the Left can do a better job of managing capitalism. Managing capitalism is not the job of socialists, but, more particularly, it is not a job that can be done at all.

The working class and the struggle for socialism

[…][The] reconceptualisation of the revolutionary project by [post-Marxists] has served to reinforce a tendency that has come from other directions as well: the displacement of the working class from the centre of Marxist theory and practice.[10] Whether that displacement has been determined by the exigencies

10. [Most of the excerpts in the rest of this chapter are part of an engagement with a series of writings in the early 1980s, dubbed by Wood as the 'new "true" socialism' (NTS). The expression 'true socialism' was used by Marx and Engels in the 1840s to describe a group of writers; in the 1980s, Wood argued, 'we seem to be witnessing a revival of "true" socialism'. She noted, among other things, that the 'most distinctive feature of this [NTS] current is the autonomization of ideology and politics from any social basis, and more specifically, from any class foundation'. These theories, while claiming to be part of the Marxist tradition, 'effectively expel the working class from

of the power-struggle, by despair in the face of a non-revolutionary working class in the West, or simply by conservative and anti-democratic impulses, the search for revolutionary surrogates has been a hallmark of contemporary socialism. Whatever the reasons for this tendency, and whether or not it is accompanied by an explicit reformulation of Marxism and its whole conception of the revolutionary process, to dislodge the working class is necessarily to redefine the socialist project, both in its means and its ends.

Revolutionary socialism has traditionally placed the working class and its struggles at the heart of social transformation and the building of socialism, not simply as an act of faith, but as a conclusion based upon a comprehensive analysis of social relations and power. In the first place, this conclusion is based on the historical-materialist principle which places the relations of production at the centre of social life and regards their exploitative character as the root of social and political oppression. The proposition that the working class is potentially *the* revolutionary class is not some metaphysical abstraction, but an extension of these materialist principles, suggesting that, given the centrality of production and exploitation in human social life, and given the particular nature of production and exploitation in capitalist society, certain other propositions follow: (1) the working class is the social group with the most direct objective interest in bringing about the transition to socialism; (2) the working class, as the direct object of the most fundamental and determinative – though certainly not the only – form of oppression, and the one class whose interests do not rest on the oppression of other classes, can create the conditions for liberating all human-beings in the struggle to liberate itself; (3) given the fundamental and ultimately unresolvable opposition between exploiting and exploited classes that lies at the heart of the structure of oppression, *class-struggle* must be the principal motor of this emancipatory transformation; and (4) the working class is the one social force that has a strategic social power sufficient to permit its development into a revolutionary force. Underlying this analysis is an emancipatory vision that looks forwards to the *disalienation of power* at every level of human endeavour, from the creative power of labour to the political power of the state.

To displace the working class from its position in the struggle for socialism is either to make a gross strategic error or to challenge this analysis of social relations and power, and at least implicitly to redefine the nature of the liberation which socialism offers. It is significant, however, that the

the centre of the socialist project and displace class antagonisms by cleavages of ideology or "discourse"'. Despite differences within the NTS, these writers 'all have one premise in common: the working class has no privileged position in the struggle for socialism'. See E.M. Wood 1986, especially pp. 1–11.]

traditional view of the working class as the primary agent of revolution has never been effectively challenged by an alternative analysis of social power and interest in capitalist society. This is, of course, not to deny that many people have questioned the revolutionary potential of the working class and offered other revolutionary agents in its place: students, women, practitioners of various alternative 'life-styles', and popular alliances of one kind or another; more recently, the 'new social movements'. The point is simply that none of these alternatives has been supported by a systematic reassessment of the social forces that constitute capitalism and its critical strategic targets. The typical mode of these alternative visions is voluntaristic utopia or counsel of despair – or, as is often the case, both at once: a vision of a transformed society without real hope for a process of transformation.

Class-conflict and the socialist project

If the socialist project is to be redefined convincingly, several large questions must be answered, having to do with its objectives, motivating principles, and agencies. The Marxist conception of that project – as the abolition of class, carried out by means of class-struggle and the self-emancipation of the working class – provided a systematic and coherent account, in which socialist objectives were grounded in a theory of historical movement and social process. There was, in this account, an organic unity of historical processes and political objectives, not in the sense that socialism was viewed as the ineluctable end of a predictable historical evolution, but rather in the sense that the objectives of socialism were seen as real historical possibilities, growing out of existing social forces, interests, and struggles. If the social relations of production and class-struggle were the basic principles of historical movement to date, socialism was now on the historical agenda because there existed, for the first time in history, not only the forces of production to make human emancipation possible, but, more particularly, a class which contained the real possibility of a classless society: a class without property or exploitative powers of its own to protect, which could not fully serve its own class-interests without abolishing class altogether; an exploited class whose specific interest required the abolition of class-exploitation; a class whose own specific conditions gave it a collective force and capacity for collective action which made that project practicable. Through the medium of this specific class-interest and this specific capacity, the universal emancipation of humanity from class-exploitation – an objective which, in other times and places, could never be more than an abstract-utopian dream – could be translated into a concrete and immediate political programme.

No revision of the socialist project can have the same force without a similarly coherent and organic conception of ends, means, social processes, and historical possibilities. A socialist project based on the autonomy of politics is no substitute. It is not an answer, but begging the question. In the end, it simply means that anything – or, just as plausibly, nothing – is possible.

The questions can be posed this way: if not the abolition of class, then what other objective? If not class-interest, what other motive force? If not class-identity and cohesion, what other collective identity or principle of unity? And underlying these programmatic questions, more fundamental historical ones: if not class-relations, what other structure of domination lies at the heart of social and political power? More basic still: if not the relations of production and exploitation, what other social relations are at the foundation of human social organisation and historical process? If not the material conditions for sustaining existence itself, what is the 'bottom-line'?

If the objective of socialism *is* the abolition of class, for whom is this likely to be a real objective, grounded in their own life-situation, and not simply an abstract good? If not those who are directly subject to capitalist exploitation, who is likely to have an 'interest' in the abolition of capitalist exploitation? Who is likely to have the social capacity to achieve it, if not those who are strategically placed at the heart of capitalist production and exploitation? Who is likely to have the potential to constitute a collective agent in the struggle for socialism? [...]

Class-conflicts have historically structured political forces without necessarily producing political organisations which directly correspond to class-formations. It should hardly need to be said that workers have an interest in not being exploited; that this interest is in conflict with the interests of those who exploit them; that many historic struggles have been fought over this conflict of interest; and that these struggles have shaped the political 'sphere'. The absence of explicit class-'discourses' does not betoken the absence of class-realities and their effects in shaping the life-conditions and consciousness of the people who come within their 'field of force'.[11] If these class-situations and oppositions have not been directly mirrored in the political domain, it can hardly be concluded that people have no class-interests, or even that they have chosen not to express these interests politically. It is especially dangerous to generalise about the relation, or lack of it, between 'economics' and 'politics' or about the conditions of socialist struggle – as the NTS [advocates of New 'True' Socialism] tend to do – from the mechanisms by which electoral parties are formed, or from patterns of voting-behaviour.

---

11. This phrase is borrowed from Thompson 1978.

But perhaps most important of all, it is ludicrous to proceed, explicitly or implicitly, from the 'autonomy' (relative or otherwise) of political affiliations to very far-reaching conclusions which seem to suggest, among other things: that the relation between capital and labour is no longer (if it ever was) the fundamental relation upon which the structure of capitalism is built; that the working class, which stands in a direct relation to capitalist exploitation, has no more interest in the abolition of that exploitation than does anyone else, or that such interests as it has (purely 'economic') can be adequately served without being translated into political terms; that, because people partake of collective identities other than class, class-conditions are no more important in determining their life-situations than any other social fact; that class is not available as a principle of unity and a motivation for collective action, or, at least, that any other collective identity will do just as well; that the working class is no more likely – indeed perhaps less likely – than any other social collectivity to adopt the socialist project as its own, and to do so effectively; and that an effective struggle for socialism – that is, a struggle for the abolition of class – can be mounted by appealing to any number of collective motivations other than class-interests and by mobilising political movements which correspond to no class-forces. In short, we should demand a good deal more historical evidence and far more convincing arguments to persuade us that socialism can be achieved without the construction of a political force which does 'correspond' to particular class-interests and without a confrontation between political forces which does 'correspond' to the class-opposition between capital and labour.

The proposition that there is no simple or necessary correspondence between 'economic' or 'social' conditions and politics, in the particular senses in which it is obviously true, still leaves unchallenged the principle that the road to socialism is the self-emancipation of the working class by means of class-struggle. The critical questions remain: who has a specific interest in socialism? If no one in particular, why not everyone? If everyone, why not capitalists too, and why need there be *any* conflict and struggle? If 'interest' is not the relevant principle, what is? And with or without interest, what about *capacity*? What kinds of people are strategically placed and collectively defined in such a way as to make possible and likely their constitution as a collective agent in the struggle for socialism? If no one in particular, why not everyone? But, if some people and not others, on what principle of historical selection? If the analysis of history as class-struggle, and the underlying materialist principles which accord centrality to relations of production, are wrong, or if they do not entitle us to conclude that class-struggle is the most likely path to socialism, what alternative principle of historical explanation should we adopt, or what different connections should we draw between our emancipatory project and our understanding of history?

Socialism and democracy

[...]There ought to be no dispute concerning the identification of socialism with the extension of democratic control to the very foundations of social organisation. This principle in itself is not, however, what distinguishes the NTS from other conceptions of socialism. Its distinctive characteristic is the abstraction and autonomisation of democracy, an insistence on the 'indeterminacy' of bourgeois democracy and its lack of any particular class-character, and, above all, the conviction that the (relative?) autonomy of bourgeois democracy makes it in principle expandable into socialist democracy. Socialism is thus merely the completion of capitalism, and the progression from one to the other can be conceived as a seamless continuum.

All this further implies that, if the class-opposition between capital and labour remains critical in the 'economic' sphere, this is not necessarily the relevant opposition at the political level. Indeed, if it were, we could no longer conceive of the transition from capitalism to socialism as an unbroken passage, since the process would be interrupted at the point where antagonistic class-interests intervene. Instead of class, the central categories at the political level are politically constituted entities, often called 'power-blocs', or even 'official-dom', on the one hand, and the 'people' on the other. Both these categories – but especially the latter – are, in principle, capable of infinite expansion, by ideological and political means. The task of socialist strategy is to constitute the 'people' out of the available forces, more-or-less irrespective of class, depending upon the prevailing circumstances and varying susceptibilities to democratic discourse on the part of existing social groups, and thereafter to lead the 'people' against the 'power-bloc' or 'officialdom' in order to extend democracy beyond the formal-political limits of bourgeois democracy. [...]

It is, undoubtedly, important to insist that democracy belongs to the essence of socialism, and that a major task of the socialist movement is to recapture the terrain of democratic struggle, which has too often been ceded to 'liberal' or 'bourgeois' politics. The NTS, however, with its abstraction and autonomisation of democracy, does little to advance the issue. The expansion of democracy, which is here treated as a means, a strategy, for the construction of socialism, is not a means or a strategy at all, but rather the very goal that must be attained. If the democratic struggle is meant not only to improve the application of bourgeois-democratic political forms, but also, as Bob Jessop suggests, to encompass the 'fundamental social relations' that underlie them; if, in particular, 'the realization of democracy requires the reorganization of the relations of production to eliminate class-based inequalities in political freedom'[12] – then we are really back where we started.

The reformulation of the socialist project proposed by Alan Hunt, Barry Hindess, Jessop, et al. simply conceptualises out of existence the very problems that need to be solved.[13] It is merely a theoretical conjuring trick, a play on words, that makes the strategy of extending bourgeois democracy look like a method for achieving the transition to socialism and makes the transformation of a 'popular-democratic' movement into a socialist movement seem relatively unproblematic. It depends, in the first instance, on conflating the various meanings and aspects of 'democracy', so that the question of socialist democracy becomes merely a quantitative one, a matter of *extension, expansion*. We lose sight of the chasm between the forms of democracy that are compatible with capitalism and those that represent a fundamental challenge to it. We no longer see the gap in the continuum of 'democratisation': a gap which corresponds precisely to the opposition of class-interests. In other words, we are induced to forget that the struggle between capitalism and socialism can be conceived precisely as a struggle over different forms of democracy, and that the dividing line between the two forms can be located at exactly the point where fundamental class-interests diverge.

Colin Mercer, in the same collection of essays, catalogues the 'multiple definitions' of democracy in order to demonstrate that Marxists have been wrong 'to assign democracy to a necessary class-belonging'. This, he argues, is 'complicit with the liberal state's own conception of it', that is, the claim by capitalism to be the sole possessor of democracy.[14] Mercer seeks to challenge this claim by outlining the various connotations of 'democracy', many of which have no association with capitalism and are quite distinct from bourgeois democracy. His conclusion is that the concept of democracy suggests:

> a complexity which denies the possibility of collapsing the word and the reality of democracy into anyone of its possible meanings – its representative form, its popular form or its class form. It must in effect embrace all of these. There is no pure 'bourgeois' democracy which can be posed as simply opposite to 'proletarian' democracy or replaced by it in a revolutionary *fiat*. The articulation of these meanings of democracy is central to the development of a concept of transition in Marxist theory and practice which would reject the simple dichotomy of 'formal' and 'direct' democracy and its associated strategic models.[15]

---

12. Jessop 1980, p. 63.
13. See Hunt (ed.) 1980.
14. Mercer 1980, p. 109.
15. Mercer 1980, p. 110.

The flaws in this argument are obvious. The very diversity of meanings in the concept of democracy highlights the differences between bourgeois democracy and other forms; and it is precisely the conflation of these meanings that has supported the capitalist claim to exclusive ownership of democracy, encouraging us to identify democracy as such with its bourgeois-parliamentary forms. Yes, of course, it must be the objective of socialism to achieve democracy in all its multiplicity – including an extension of those bourgeois-democratic forms which serve as a protection against arbitrary power and not simply as a cover for capitalist domination. But, in a sense, it is this very objective that brings socialism into fundamental conflict with capitalism. It is precisely the multiplicity of facets contained in the socialist meaning of democracy that makes it impossible to conceive of the transition from capitalism to socialism as nothing more than an extension and completion of the democratic forms nurtured by capitalism. The extension of bourgeois democracy may be important in itself; but there is a qualitative difference between democracy conceived in formal-juridical terms, and democracy conceived, for example, as entailing the self-organisation of freely-associated producers. The fact that some institutions of the former may not be in principle antagonistic to the latter does not mean that all social interests compatible with the one are also compatible with the other. It may be that some class-interests that are compatible with, and even served by, bourgeois-democratic forms are irrevocably antagonistic to democracy in the sphere of production-relations. A careless insistence on the non-correspondence of politics and 'economics' and the 'indeterminacy' of democracy may obscure the fact that, while liberal democracy can be compatible with capitalism precisely because it leaves production-relations intact, socialist democracy by definition entails the transformation of production-relations.

In fact, the non-correspondence principle in a sense mirrors the basic presupposition of capitalist political ideology, the sharp separation between political and economic or social spheres, the very separation that makes possible the development of liberal-democratic forms while leaving capitalist production-relations intact. It is this divide that confines 'democracy' to a formal political-juridical sphere and firmly excludes it from the substance of social relations. The hegemony of capitalist ideology depends upon retaining a distinction between the principles of citizenship and the rules that apply in non-political domains.

Of course, an attack on capitalist hegemony must take the form of challenging this ideological division and expanding the meaning of democracy, but the problem is hardly just a linguistic one. The divide between the spheres in which capitalism can permit democracy to operate (and even here, it can do so only up to a point) and those in which it cannot, corresponds to the insurmountable divisions between antagonistic class-interests. Here, if not before, there must be a break in the continuum from one form of democracy to the other; here, if not before, in other words, class-determinations will become decisive – and no amount of verbal conjuring will spirit the problem away.

The idea that bourgeois democracy is 'indeterminate', and in principle classless, has been the fundamental premise of social-democratic programmes, just as it is the presupposition of the NTS. Before we look at some of the inadequacies of this axiom, it needs to be stressed that its importance has been vastly exaggerated. Even if we accept that the political and juridical forms of liberal democracy are not class-specific and need not serve the interests of capital, what does this actually tell us about the transition from capitalism to socialism? Does not the character of the transition depend less on the class-associations of bourgeois democracy than on the class-specificity of socialism? Are not the NTS asking us, in effect, to accept not only that liberal democracy is 'indeterminate', but that socialist democracy is equally so, in the sense that it represents no fundamental challenge to any class-interest and that all classes have an equal interest in attaining it? It is, of course, true that the force of socialism lies in its uniquely legitimate claim to 'indeterminacy' or, more precisely, universality – as representing the interests of all humanity against those of particular classes; but because the fulfilment of that claim presupposes the abolition of all classes and class-exploitation, the socialist project must, in the first instance, represent some class-interests and oppose others. So the whole NTS project, like the more traditional programmes of social democracy, to the extent that it proceeds from the 'indeterminacy' of bourgeois democracy to a view of socialism as merely an extension of bourgeois-democratic forms, rests on a logical fault. Neither the classlessness of these forms nor the formal compatibility of liberal-democratic institutions with socialism would tell us very much about the conditions of the struggle for socialism or the barriers that stand in its way.

The confusion of issues at the heart of the NTS project is illustrated by the following typical observation: '[…] once it is accepted that there is no Chinese Wall between "bourgeois" and "proletarian" democracy the Leninist idea of "smashing" the "bourgeois state" becomes unacceptable. There is bound to be a conflict between different types of institution, but not necessarily an irreconcilable contradiction.'[16] What, then, does it mean to say that there is no 'Chinese Wall'? At best, it means that the institutional forms of parliamentary democracy are not in themselves antithetical to socialism, that they need not

---

16. Hodgson 1984, p. 55.

be destroyed as a pre-condition to socialism, that they are not in themselves useless to socialists in their struggle to transform society, and perhaps even that they may still have their uses after the destruction of capitalism. With certain qualifications, these are not unreasonable propositions; at least, they may serve as a useful corrective to uncritical applications of Leninist principles which treat liberal-democratic forms as if they 'correspond' to capitalism so completely and exclusively that they can be dismissed – and must even be destroyed – as the enemies of socialism. These are points to which we shall return. There is, however, more to the 'indeterminacy'-argument than this. The absence of a 'Chinese Wall' between different forms of democracy means that democracy 'can grow, first within capitalism, and then beyond it', and apparently also that a focus on democracy in the struggle to transform society can transcend divisions between socialists and non-socialists. In other words, the transition from liberal democracy to socialist democracy can take place by means of more-or-less non-antagonistic increments, as one set of democratic institutions is imperceptibly transformed into another by extension, by supplementing inadequacies and filling in gaps.

What all this means is that, by some neat conceptual conjuring, the transition from capitalism to socialism has been transformed into a relatively non-antagonistic process of institutional reform. But does the transformation of society and the relations of production become less problematic and antagonistic simply because we call it an extension of democracy, rather than a transition from capitalism to socialism? When, for example, Hodgson maintains that, although 'it is possible that future developments will lead to the erosion or end of the limited democracy that survives within capitalism', the incompatibility of capitalism and democracy 'is not predetermined or inevitable',[17] how far does he want to go? Is *any* amount of democracy compatible with capitalism? If not, and if there is a point at which the expansion of democracy by definition means the end of capitalism, because it means the end of capitalist domination and exploitation, will that point pass unnoticed simply because we call it another incremental change in the process of extending democracy, instead of a revolutionary change in the relations of production?

It is not, in the end, the institutional forms of parliamentary democracy that are in question. A case could be made[...]that at least some of these forms may serve a useful purpose even under socialism. The critical point, however, is that liberal democracy entails a separation of political rights and powers from economic and social ones, as well as a limited and formalistic conception of political democracy itself. This separation belongs to the essence of

---

17. Hodgson 1984, p. 123.

liberal democracy; it is not just a flaw in the system. Parliamentary democracy is not simply a form of representation: it is a particular delineation of spheres of power, a specific definition and isolation of the spheres in which democratic principles may be allowed to prevail. It is, in fact, a *denial*, as we have seen, of democracy in the sense of popular power. And this delimitation is the very foundation of private property and its power in capitalist society. In other forms of property and exploitation, the exploitative force of property depends upon a unity of political and economic power, so that political rights must remain exclusive. In capitalism, where exploitative power does not rest directly on the exclusive possession of political force, but on absolute private property and the exclusion of producers from it, it is possible (though not necessary) to extend political rights more-or-less universally – but then, the power of property depends upon a rigid separation between political and economic spheres. This is a structural characteristic of capitalism; and it means that any effort to reunite these separate spheres, at the point where it challenges capitalist power and property, will entail all the antagonisms and struggles which attend the decisive battle between exploiting and exploited classes. No socialist strategy can be taken seriously that ignores or obscures the class-barriers beyond which the extension of democracy becomes a challenge to capitalism.

There is also another danger in this insistence on the 'indeterminacy' of democracy, as […] in [Ernesto] Laclau and [Chantal] Mouffe's conception of the 'democratic revolution'.[18] No doubt, at least some of the contributors to the Hunt volume would emphatically dissociate themselves from the extreme formulations of Laclau and Mouffe, but there is a certain logic in the detachment of democracy from social determinations that impels us towards those extremes. Stripped of its association with specific social interests, 'democracy' in the NTS becomes an abstract ideal. If as a political objective it reflects the motivations of any actually-existing social being, and is not simply an abstract good with no power to sustain collective social action, it seems that we must postulate some autonomous drive for 'democratisation' residing in the depths of human nature. We are given little guidance as to who in particular might want or need democracy, whether some kinds of people might want or need more – or different aspects – than others, how a social force capable of bringing it about might come into being – or, indeed, why there should be any difficulty or conflict about it at all. If, on the other hand, the democratic drive is not universal, or not immediately so, and yet at the same time is not constituted by material conditions and class-relations, but is constructed by ideology and

---

18. Laclau and Mouffe 1985.

politics more-or-less 'autonomously', then are we not again thrown back upon the old utopian elitism which Marx himself denounced? Must we not look to some privileged producers of 'discourse' to implant the democratic impulse from without, giving a collective identity to an otherwise shapeless mass, creating the 'people' and then imparting to them a socialist or democratic spirit which they cannot bring forth out of their own resources?

The state in classless societies

There is another side to the relation between liberal democracy and capitalism. If liberal democracy was born out of capitalist relations of production, should it also die with them? If liberal-democratic institutions have acted to *civilise* as well as to support capitalism, is the need for such institutions dependent on the persistence of capitalist relations of production, or might a socialist society be faced with problems that demand similar solutions? In other words, has liberalism produced a legacy that can and ought to be adopted by socialism? Here again, the NTS, with its insistence on the seamless continuity between liberal democracy and socialism, obscures the issue. While it may be true to say that socialism could not have existed without liberalism, our understanding of either is not advanced by regarding one as a mere extension of the other and ignoring the fundamental ways in which they are diametrically opposed. Liberalism and socialism can be conflated in this way only by means of an empty formalism that voids them of their social content.

Let us consider what social needs are served by liberal principles and institutions, and whether similar social needs will persist in a socialist society. From this point of view, it can be argued that if liberalism is about anything worth preserving, it is about certain ways of dealing with political authority: the rule of law, civil liberties, checks on arbitrary power. This function of liberalism must be conceded even if the status of 'bourgeois liberties' is at best ambiguous in a class-divided society where they may not only obscure class-oppositions with a false equality, but actively serve as instruments of class-power and hegemony. It is not, here, a question of how *democratic* 'bourgeois democracy' may or may not be. In fact, one ought perhaps to begin by again separating the 'liberal' from the 'democratic'. This coupling tends to obscure the difference between 'democracy' as *popular power*, and 'democracy' as a formal, procedural principle. It may be that the most important lesson of liberalism has little to do with democracy, but is concerned with controlling state-power – and here, the earlier *anti*-democratic forms of liberalism may have as much to say as does liberal democracy.

To say that liberalism has a lesson for socialism in this respect is, of course, to make a highly contentious assumption, namely that the state will persist as a problem in a classless society and that the most democratic society may continue to be faced with a *political* problem analogous to that of undemocratic societies. Much of socialist doctrine is based on the assumption that, if the state will not actually wither away in a classless society, state-power will at least no longer constitute a *problem*. Social democrats and NTS who have unbounded faith in the efficacy of bourgeois-democratic forms seem not to regard the state as a problem, even in capitalist society. Indeed, they treat it as an instrument of salvation. More interesting questions are raised by socialists who are convinced that the state-apparatus of bourgeois democracy must be 'smashed' and replaced by something radically different. As Ralph Miliband has argued, those who speak of the 'smashing' of the bourgeois state have not squarely faced the fact that they will – indeed, must – replace the smashed state with yet another, perhaps temporarily even strengthened, state; that the smashing of the bourgeois state and its replacement by a revolutionary state do *not* in themselves mean the 'dictatorship of the proletariat', if that concept still carries its original democratic implications; that there is always a tension between the necessity of 'direction' and 'democracy', between state-power and popular power, which has been consistently evaded.[19] So serious is the problem, suggests Miliband, that democracy can be preserved only by a system of 'dual power', in which state-power is *complemented* by widespread democratic organisations of various kinds throughout civil society.

It must be added, however, that the problem is not likely to be confined to some awkward 'transitional' phase during which a strong state will undertake to fulfil the promise of the revolution by transforming society. If, for example, as Marx suggests, the central organisational problem of *all* societies is the allocation of social labour, then there is a sense in which the *political* question will be particularly important *after* the complete overthrow of capitalism. Capitalism is, after all, a system in which that central social problem is not dealt with 'politically': a system uniquely characterised by the absence of an 'authoritative allocation' of social labour. It is a system with what Marx calls an 'anarchic' social division of labour not dictated by political authority, tradition, or communal deliberation, but by the mechanisms of commodity-exchange. One might say that it is capitalism, then, which in this very particular sense involves the 'administration of things and not people' – or perhaps the administration of people by things; while the new society will be faced

---

19. Miliband 1977, pp. 180–90.

with a new and substantial organisational problem which very much involves the administration of people.

Marxist theory has not done much to clarify the issues at stake, let alone resolve the problem of the state under socialism. Marx and Engels had little to say on the subject of the state in future society, and what they did say is often ambiguous. In particular, the debate has been plagued by a vagueness and inconsistency in the use of the term 'state'. We are told that the *state* will 'wither away' in classless society. If (as is usually, but not always the case) the state is defined as a system of class-domination, it is a mere tautology to say that the state will 'wither away' once classes are abolished. The definition of the state as synonymous with class-domination resolves nothing. It simply evades the issue. On the other hand, if the 'state' refers to *any* form of public power, it is not at all clear that the state will disappear with class – nor is it clear that Marx or Engels thought it would.

Whatever Marx and Engels may have thought about the future of the state, the real question is not whether a public power will be needed in a classless society, but whether that public power will constitute a problem. In other words, are there certain problems inherent in public power itself whether or not it is *class*-power? I take it for granted that it is hopelessly naive to believe in an advanced-socialist society administered completely by simple forms of direct and spontaneous democracy. It is difficult to avoid the conviction that even classless society will require some form of *representation*, and hence *authority* and even *subordination* of some people to others. That premise granted, it must be added that, whether or not one uses the term 'state' to describe political and administrative power in a classless society, it seems unduly optimistic to believe that there can ever be a case in which power exercised by some people on behalf of others does not constitute a problem. Socialist-political theory must, therefore, face the dangers posed by representation, authority, and subordination, and the fact that their very existence makes possible the misappropriation of power.

These problems cannot be dismissed by the mere assertion that representation, authority, and subordination will present no danger in the absence of class. Among other things, it is necessary to consider the possibility (hinted at by Marx himself, for example in his discussions of the Asiatic mode of production and other precapitalist formations) that public power may be, and historically often has been, itself the *source* of differentiation between appropriators and direct producers. There is good reason to believe that public power, instituted to undertake socially necessary functions – warfare, distribution, direction of communal labour, the construction of vital public works – has often been the original basis of the claim to and capacity for surplus-appropriation. In other words, the state – in the broad sense – has not emerged from class-divisions, but has, on the contrary, *produced* class-divisions and hence also produced the state in the narrow sense. It does not seem wise to assume that no constant and institutionalised protection will be needed in the future to prevent the similar transmutation of 'political' authority into 'economic' power, public power into something like class-domination.

However much Marx or Engels may have tended towards political utopianism, the view that public power in classless society will still be a problem requiring conscious and institutionalised control is entirely consistent with the fundamental Marxist view of the world and the meaning of the socialist revolution. Marx's belief in the complete transformation of society once class-domination disappears does not imply that all problems associated with class-domination will automatically and forever dissolve of themselves. On the contrary, the essence of the transformation itself is that socio-historical forces will, for the first time, be consciously controlled and directed, instead of left to chance. This is what Marx means when he speaks of man's history before the revolution as 'pre-history' and thereafter as 'human history'. The planned direction of social forces certainly does not refer simply to 'economic' planning in the narrow sense – the planning of production-quotas, and so on. The 'economic' is itself a *social relation*, and the social relations of production themselves must be 'planned'. Furthermore, if 'economic' power, the power to extract surplus-labour, consists in a relationship of domination and coercion, then it is also *political* power; and the planning of the social relations of production must include 'political' planning at every level of society, institutional measures to prevent the re-emergence of domination and exploitative relations.

Even in a classless society there will probably have to be organisations whose conscious and explicit object is not simply to complement, but to *check* power and prevent its misappropriation. There will have to be ongoing institutions – not simply emergency-measures such as the power of recall – to act to this specific end, and equally important, to maintain a *consciousness* of the dangers. Assuming that the political form of socialism will be a *representative* system, with some kind of administrative apparatus, there will still be tension between state-power and popular power. Representation is itself a problem; and to the extent that the political problem cannot be practically resolved by replacing representation with direct democracy, by further democratising the system of political organisation, the problem must still be faced on another plane. In other words, the very existence of a state – however democratically representative – necessarily places a special task on the agenda: not simply democratic organisation throughout civil society, but – and this may not be the same thing – what Marx calls the *subordination* of the state to society.[20]

The debate on the future of the state ought not to be reduced to a matter of textual interpretation; but discussions of the question are bound to return to the sketchy comments made by Marx and Engels on the subject. Since it is probably easier to demonstrate that they were optimistic about the disappearance of politics than to prove that they saw the state as a continuing problem, a few remarks in support of the latter interpretation should be added here. Particularly interesting is what they have to say – or at least imply – about the legacy of bourgeois liberalism and its possible application to post-revolutionary society.

It must be said, first, that both Marx and Engels may have clouded the issue by asserting that in a classless society the *state* will disappear, or that the 'public power will lose its political character'.[21] This is not the same as saying that there will *be* no public power, or even that the public power will cease to be a problem. Engels, who most often and explicitly repeated the assertion that the state 'in the proper sense of the word' would disappear, is also the man who, in attacking the anarchists, stressed the continuing need for *authority* and *subordination* and mocked the anarchists for believing that, by changing the name of the public authority, they had changed the thing itself. Even if, as Engels writes, 'public functions will lose their political character and be transformed into the simple administrative functions of watching over the true interests of society',[22] the problem is not self-evidently resolved. Is it not possible that – even in Engels's own view – institutionalised measures will be required precisely to *ensure* that the public power, vested with authority over others and subordinating others to it, will maintain its purely 'administrative' character and continue to act in the true interests of society? In a class-society, such a humane and 'unpolitical' public power would be impossible; but, if it becomes *possible* only in a classless society, it does not become inevitable.

Liberalism vs. democracy

[...]We should not[...]be too absorbed by the formula 'liberal democracy', so that our attention is focused on the opposition 'liberal democracy' versus 'socialist democracy', as if the major issue were the difference between two aspects of democracy. It may be useful to resituate the discussion by

---

20. Marx 1974, p. 354.
21. Marx and Engels 1973, p. 87.
22. Engels 1962, p. 639.

contrasting liberalism ('democratic', or 'pre-democratic') to democracy, to define democracy as *distinct* from – though not in opposition to – liberalism. If we concentrate our attention on the differences between the problems to which 'liberalism' and 'democracy' are respectively addressed, we can recognise the value of liberalism and its lessons for socialism without allowing liberalism to circumscribe our definition of democracy.

Liberalism has to do essentially with 'restricting the freedom of the state' – through the rule of law, civil liberties, and so on. It is concerned to limit the scope and the arbitrariness of political power; but it has no interest in the *disalienation* of power. Indeed, it is a fundamental liberal ideal, even in its most 'democratic' forms, that power *must* be alienated, not simply as a necessary evil, but as a positive good – for example, in order to permit fundamentally individualistic human beings to occupy themselves with private concerns. This is why, for liberalism, *representation* is a *solution*, not a *problem*.

In contrast to liberalism, *democracy* has to do precisely with the disalienation of power. To the extent that some form of alienated power or representation continues to be a necessary expedient – as, in any complex society, it undoubtedly must – from the point of view of democratic values such representative institutions must be regarded not only as a solution, but also as a problem. It is in confronting this problem that socialism has something to learn from liberalism – not about the disalienation of power, but about the control of alienated power.

Even democratic power will undoubtedly present dangers about which liberalism – with its principles of civil liberties, the rule of law, and protection for a sphere of privacy – may yet have lessons to teach; but the *limitation* of power is not the same thing as its disalienation. Democracy, unlike liberalism even in its most idealised form, furthermore implies overcoming the opposition of 'economic' and 'political' and eliminating the superimposition of the 'state' upon 'civil society'. 'Popular sovereignty' would thus not be confined to an abstract political 'sphere', but would instead entail a disalienation of power at every level of human activity, an attack on the whole structure of domination that begins in the sphere of production and continues upwards to the state. From this point of view, just as the coupling of 'liberal' and 'democracy' may be misleading, the joining of 'socialist' and 'democracy' should be redundant.

This also means that there can be no simple, non-antagonistic extension of liberal democracy into socialist democracy. Even if the term 'democracy' is allowed to stand for both these cases, it must at least be acknowledged that there have throughout history existed radically different forms of democracy, and that the institutional differences that distinguish, say, the Athenian from the modern American or British form, reflect their very different social bases. It is historical nonsense to deny that there is any correspondence between the institutional forms of these various democracies and the varying social foundations on which they rest. The configuration of social relations and power that will distinguish socialism from capitalism will necessarily be reflected in different institutional forms. The very heart of socialism will be a mode of democratic organisation that has never existed before – direct self-government by freely-associated producers in commonly-owned workplaces producing the means of material life. The very existence of such democratic institutions, by definition, means an end to capitalist relations and the forms of democracy compatible with them.

Nor is it simply a matter of tacking 'economic' democracy on to an already-existing 'political' democracy. It is not just that democracy at the level of production will require new forms of supporting institutions at other 'levels'. More immediately important is the fact that the political sphere in even the most 'liberal-democratic' capitalist society is itself constructed to maintain – bureaucratically and coercively whenever necessary – the barriers to democracy at the 'level' of production-relations. To treat the transition to socialism as just an incremental improvement on liberal democracy, as if all that is required is to 'transport' its democratic principles from the polity to the economy, is to forget not only that there is no such thing as a socially indeterminate democratic principle, but also that one of the essential functions of the liberal-democratic state is vigilantly to police, and coercively to enforce, the confinement of 'democracy' to a limited domain.

'Universal human goods'

The place of 'primary human needs' or 'universal goods' in the socialist project is a critical and painfully difficult question. The socialist movement, if it is to have any credibility as an emancipatory project, must broaden its conception of human liberation and the quality of life. But even broadening socialist objectives explicitly and emphatically to include all the human goals which must be part of a truly emancipatory vision would not, by itself, resolve the question of the socialist constituency or the nature of the socialist struggle, its forms of organisation and its specific targets. In particular, it would not imply that we can abandon the conception of the socialist project as a class-struggle whose object is the abolition of class. If we accept a vision of socialism that includes such 'human' goals as peace, security, democracy, a caring society, and a careful economy, and if at the same time we also acknowledge that the class-system of capitalism and the capitalist drive for accumulation are now the principal barriers to the achievement of these objectives, then what conclusions should we draw about the specific nature of the struggle and the social forces that are likely to carry it forward?

Two rather different conclusions are possible. One might say that, once people can be made to see that it is capitalism and its class-system that, above all, stand in the way of their non-material, human goals, the abolition of class can become everyone's project, as much as it is the specific objective of the working class. In other words, one might conclude that, even if the abolition of class is the direct and specific object of working-class 'material' or 'economic' interests, it is equally in the interests of other social groups in other respects, and that the specificity of working-class material interests does not entitle that class to a privileged role in the struggle to abolish class-exploitation. Alternatively, one might say that, if the abolition of class is the core of the socialist project, even if its ultimate object is to achieve larger human goals, socialism is not likely to become the collective project of other social groups in the way that it can be for the working class: people who are the direct objects of class-exploitation; whose collective identity springs directly from this class-system; whose organisation and strategic location are defined by it; and whose collective actions, even when they are particularist and limited in scope, are necessarily directed at the relevant target. If the latter seems more plausible, the socialist movement can still draw on other constituencies and can still connect with other social movements, but it must still be conceived and organised as an instrument of class-struggle whose first strategic concern must be to serve the class-interests, and forge the class-unity, of the working class.

Here, we encounter the difficulties that afflict the NTS project, with its tendency to shift the focus away from class-bound material interests to universal 'human' goals. Of course, these 'human' goals must be the ultimate objective of the emancipatory struggle, and, of course, there is an important sense in which even the abolition of class – let alone the satisfaction of working-class interests – must be regarded as an interim-objective, perhaps a means rather than an end. But what the NTS in effect proposes is that these ultimate 'human' goals can now be the immediate objectives (however long it may take to achieve them) of a political movement. This means not only that these concerns constitute the common interests around which an effective collective agent can be organised, but also that this collective agent can be directed against the very foundations of the capitalist system. To maintain this is to say one of two things: (1) that the material and social conditions for the achievement of these objectives now exist (in a way that has never been true before), in the sense that the existence of classes is no obstacle – either because the relations of production and exploitation are not, and perhaps never have been, critical in determining historical processes, or because these obstacles have already been removed. In such a case, it only remains to put the necessary instrumentalities in place to achieve those 'human' objectives; or (2) the threat to these human interests – peace, security, the environment, the quality of life – is so much greater than ever before that an interest in their protection overrides, in unprecedented ways and degrees, all other social interests and all other historical determinants, and is sufficient to create a force capable of transforming the social and material conditions of the prevailing order.

It is tempting to think that the most ardent exponents of an 'autonomous' socialist politics must believe in the first of these two propositions, since they appear to be convinced that only 'discourse' is required to achieve the desired objectives. This is not, however, a position that needs to be taken seriously, since a massive rewriting of history would be required to demonstrate the marginality of production-relations and class in determining historical processes; or, at least, a thorough reanalysis of capitalism to demonstrate that, alone among historic modes of production, this one subordinates production-relations and class to other historical determinants (or, perhaps, to show that classes no longer exist in advanced-capitalist societies in any significant sense?).

There is a somewhat weaker form of this argument, which actually has gained a certain currency: that 'welfare-state capitalism' has so completely altered the nature of the capitalist system that the old issues which made up the substance of class-politics have now been resolved. Given the many new class-issues created by the 'welfare-state' itself, the many new burdens that have been imposed on the working class, not to mention the dismantling of the welfare-state now underway in some advanced capitalist countries, and the continuing – indeed growing – salience of class-issues in the politics of advanced capitalist countries, however much the nature of class-forces and the 'parameters of class-politics' may have been altered by welfare-capitalism, this argument is almost as hard to take seriously as the stronger version. 'First of all', as Göran Therborn has recently reminded us,

> it should never be forgotten that welfare state capitalism is still capitalism. Not only do the classical questions of capitalist politics remain, but the current economic crisis poses a threat to the achievements of welfare-state capitalism – full employment, social security, greater equality between men and women – and thereby makes of them central political issues. It would be a fundamental error to suggest that the fully developed welfare state has, even in appearance, removed the basic objects of working-class militancy, such as wages, working conditions, employment and social security.[23]

---

23. Therborn 1984, pp. 29–30.

And to the extent that the (temporary?) resolution of some of these issues has apparently made inroads upon the political terrain of the left and cap-tured parts of its traditional constituencies, new class-issues, as well as new – and newly militant – class-forces, have also emerged. There is, therefore, no convincing evidence to suggest that the conditions of modern capitalism have pre-empted the ground of class-politics or rendered class unnecessary or unavailable as a political force.

The second argument – that the extent of the threat to basic human interests is now great enough to override other social determinations – has some force at a time when the dangers of nuclear annihilation and ecological disaster threaten not only the fulfilment of humanitarian goals, but the existence of humanity itself, and when these threats have generated large popular move-ments even among people resistant to mobilisation by other, less apocalyp-tic concerns. The moral force of these movements is unquestionable; but in a sense, the very qualities that give them their particular strength make them resistant to transformation into agents of a fundamental social change, the transition from capitalism to socialism. These movements do not reflect, and are not intended to create, a new collective identity, a new social agency, motivated by a new anti-capitalist interest which dissolves differences of class-interest. They are not constituted on the basis of the connections that exist between the capitalist order and the threats to peace and survival. On the contrary, their unity and popular appeal depend upon *abstracting* the issues of peace or ecology from the prevailing social order and the conflicting social interests that comprise it. The general interests that human-beings share sim-ply because they are human must be seen, not as requiring the transforma-tion of the existing social order and class-relations, but rather as something *detached* from the various particular interests in which human-beings partake by virtue of belonging to that social order and its system of classes. In other words, such movements have tended to rely on the extent to which they can *avoid* specifically implicating the capitalist order and its class-system.

Here, indeed, are political programmes designed to be more-or-less 'autonomous' from social conditions and material interests; but it is precisely their autonomy that makes them resistant to development as programmes for socialist change. In fact, the inadequacy of the NTS formula is perhaps nowhere more vividly evident than here. One need only try to imagine the actual modalities by which such a 'popular' movement might be transformed into a socialist force. How exactly should we envisage the process whereby a movement, mobilised precisely on the basis of its abstraction from the pre-vailing conditions of class and class-interest and a deliberate detachment of its aims from a fundamental challenge to the existing structure of social relations and domination, might be transformed into a stable collective force directed against those class-conditions and that structure of domination? Unless, of course, the movement itself becomes the terrain of class-struggle. Indeed, the very fact that such movements must rely so heavily upon bracketing off their objectives from material interests and class-conflict tells us a great deal about the importance of material interests and class-conflict in shaping political forces; for the moment these issues are allowed to surface, the very identity and unity of these popular movements is shattered. In other words, these movements can go one of two ways: they can retain their 'popular' identity and unity by forgoing the capacity to act as a strong oppositional force; or they can become more substantially effective, even in achieving their own specific ends, by harnessing their popular power to the politics of class.

These strictures apply to any notion of a socialist movement which 'begins from primary human needs', universal humanitarian goals transcending material interests and class – if by that is meant, not a movement for human emancipation and the achievement of universal humanitarian goals through the medium of class-struggle and the abolition of class, but a movement that attempts to *bypass* class-interests and class-struggle in the hope of creating a transformative collective agent simply by means of an 'autonomous' universalistic 'discourse'. What, after all, would it mean to organise a political movement around 'primary human needs' in this sense?

Again, the problem can be illustrated by asking ourselves why, in a socialist movement so conceived, capitalists themselves might not be as much a part of the collective revolutionary agent as anyone else. Since they are 'people', with the same *human* interests as everyone else, what is to prevent socialist discourse from including them? If, however, we concede that capitalism is contrary to human interests, and that, therefore, capitalists cannot be among the natural constituents of socialism, then we are also conceding that capitalist production-relations are the relevant target of the socialist struggle, the structure of power which must be attacked in order to achieve human goals, and also that people – or at least some people (only capitalists, and possibly the 'traditional' working class?) – put their class-interests before their 'human' interests. And if this is so, under what specific circumstances could we organise a political movement around a commitment to 'primary human needs'? Do we really want to say, for example, that while some people – indeed, whole classes, and particularly the principal antagonistic classes of capitalism – are bound by their material conditions to put class-interests before human goals, there is a vast middle-ground of social groups not bound in this way, and that it is they who will conduct the struggle for socialism? If so – and above all – *how*? From what strategic vantage-point, and with what collective power, will this 'autonomous' mass launch its attack upon the points of concentration of capitalist power? Indeed, by what means will it retain its identity and unity?

None of this is to say that people are incapable of being motivated by altruism, compassion, or a selfless concern for the 'general interest', or that these motivations have no role to play in the socialist project. But a transformative struggle cannot be organised by these principles, least of all in a society structured by class, with the irreducible antagonisms of interest and the configuration of power this entails.

Neither can we usefully conceive of socialism as simply a 'rational' goal which any creature of reason would adopt, once having attained the requisite level of 'intellectual sophistication'. Of course, the anti-intellectualism of certain socialist tendencies is stupid and dangerous, and, of course, an effective socialist movement requires education. But there is nothing in education or 'rationality' as such that conduces to socialism or democracy. History offers ample evidence that there is no incompatibility between 'intellectual sophistication' and a commitment to exploitative and oppressive social relations. What *is* fundamentally and irreducibly incompatible with such social relations is the interests of the exploited class; and it is to this social principle that 'intellectual sophistication' must be harnessed, if 'reason' is to be a force for socialism.

Nevertheless, if the pursuit of working-class interests is still the indispensible vehicle of socialism, still the only form in which 'universal human goods' can constitute a practicable political programme, there remains a need to link those interests explicitly with those universal objectives. The democratic impulse of socialism, its commitment to human emancipation and the quality of life, must always be kept clearly in sight if the class-struggle is to stay on course as a struggle for socialism. There is, then, an important sense in which the language of 'universal human goods' is the language of translation from working-class consciousness to socialist consciousness. And it may also be the language of appeal which most effectively spells out the better quality of life offered by socialism to those so-called 'intermediate groups' who may be torn between their exploitation by capital and the benefits they derive from their service to it. The mistake of the new 'true' socialism lies not in the belief that there must be ideological mediations between the material interests of the working class and the ultimate objectives of socialism, but, rather, in the conviction that the need for such mediation means that there is no organic or 'privileged' connection between working-class interests and social objectives.

Either we maintain that, because all human-beings *qua* human-beings have an interest in socialism – or in freedom from exploitation, in democratic control, peace, security, and a decent quality of life – they are all equally candidates for socialist commitment through persuasion; or else we have to admit that, even if, at bottom and in the long run, all human-beings have such an interest, there are more immediate structures of interest and power standing massively in the way of its realisation. If the latter is so, then socialism must still be conceived, in the first instance, not simply as an abstract-moral good, but as a concrete political objective that mobilises the social forces most immediately directed against the capitalist structure of interest and power. Socialism takes the form of such a concrete project, with identifiable targets and agencies – yet one which is, at the same time, capable of 'connecting' with the 'general interest' – only insofar as it is embodied in the interests and struggles of the working class.

The self-emancipation of the working class

What, then, is specific to the Marxist conception of the collective agent, the revolutionary working class? The first premise, of course, is that production is essential to human existence and the organisation of social life. (It cannot be emphasised enough that the NTS rejection of Marxism begins here, with an effective denial of this elementary fact and everything that follows from it.) On the assumption that political movements must be grounded in social relations and interests, the critical question for Marxism is, what social relations and interests are commensurate with, and provide the surest grounding for, a political project that has as its object the transformation of production-relations and the abolition of class? Marxism's answer is that there is such a thing as a working class, people who by virtue of their situation in the relations of production and exploitation share certain fundamental interests, and that these class-interests coincide with the essential objective of socialism, the abolition of class and, more specifically, the classless administration of production by the direct producers themselves.

   This is not to say that the condition of the working class directly determines that its members will have socialism as their immediate class-objective. It does, however, mean that they can uniquely advance the cause of socialism (though not completely achieve it) even *without* conceiving socialism as their class-objective, by pursuing their material class-interests, because these interests are, by nature, essentially opposed to capitalist class-exploitation and to a class-dominated organisation of production. Since the material interests of the working class cannot be satisfied within the existing framework of social relations, and since a pursuit of these interests will inevitably encounter the opposing interests of capital, the process of struggle will tend to expose its own limitations, spill over into the political arena, and carry the battle closer to the centres of capitalist power. Furthermore, since the working class itself *creates* capital, and since the organisation of production and appropriation places the collective labourer at the heart of the whole capitalist structure, the working class has a unique capacity to destroy capital. The conditions of production, and of working-class struggle, are also such as to encourage the organisation of workers into a collective force potentially suited to carrying out this project. This does not mean that the working class is immediately available as a political organisation ready-made to prosecute the struggle for socialism. It simply means that the organisational and political efforts of socialists will most fruitfully be devoted to unifying the working class and serving its interests, while the boundaries of class-struggle are pushed forwards. To say – as the NTS repeatedly do – that *classes* are never political agents, while undoubtedly true in its limited way, is therefore quite beside the point.

There is one unique characteristic of socialism which adds an even greater force to the Marxist argument that the revolution must come by the self-emancipation of the working class: although the struggle between exploiting and exploited classes has been a major force in every transformation of production-relations, no other social revolution has ever placed the exploited class of the old social order in command of the new one. No transformation of production-relations has had as its principal object the interests of the exploited class, however much those interests may have moved the revolution forwards. Even more specifically, socialism alone presupposes both a continuity between the direct producers of the old order and the new, and a social organisation of production administered by those direct producers themselves. The Marxist project is based on the premise that the collective labourer of advanced-industrial capitalism will be the direct producer of the socialist order, and that socialist democracy will be constituted by the self-organisation of freely-associated producers. This places the collective labourer in capitalism at the centre of the socialist project as no exploited class has ever been in any other social revolution. Thus, unless the class-interests of the working class themselves direct them into political struggle and to the transformation of the mode of production, the socialist project must remain an empty and utopian aspiration. This does not mean that socialism is inevitable, only that it will come about in this way or not at all.

The socialist movement

[…]If a political party or movement is not only an electoral machine but also an instrument of mobilisation, struggle, and ideological change in the service of socialist transformation, then it cannot be based on ephemeral social identities and the superficial bonds of expediency. For its principles of cohesion, it must look to more fundamental and enduring social bonds; and for its motive force, it must appeal to interests much closer to the material foundations of social existence, interests that are commensurate with the objectives of socialism. If, in other words, a political party or movement is to engage in the struggle for power, electoral or otherwise, while acting as an instrument of mass-mobilisation and ideological transformation, if it is to pursue immediate objectives which at the same time advance the struggle for socialism, then that party or movement can only be – above all – a *class*-party, guided by and organised around the interests of the working class.

This does not mean that there is no place for coalitions and alliances with other social movements. The nexus of politics and working-class interests can – and, indeed, should – be extended to social issues beyond the immediate material interests of class, to the politics of peace, gender, environment, and culture; and, as we have seen, it is in any case a mistake to treat these issues as if they take us 'beyond class-politics'. But the vital interests of the collective labourer must remain the guiding thread for any political movement which has as its goal the construction of socialism. This may mean that, in some cases, alliances and coalitions will be explicitly limited and temporary, clearly directed at the attainment of limited specific objectives. Sometimes, alliances will take the form of support by the working-class movement for the causes of others, without organisational unity. Sometimes, as in the miners' strike [in Great Britain in 1984–5], the struggles of workers will engage other loyalties and interests and be strengthened by them, as the miners were strengthened by community-ties and the solidarity of women. But, just as in the miners' strike, these other loyalties and interests were mobilised as a strong oppositional force by their articulation with the class-interests of the workers, so other social movements can be forged into forces for socialism by their intersection with the interests of the working class.

There is no question that the socialist movement will have to find new forms of working-class organisation and new ways of incorporating the emancipatory aspirations expressed by the 'new social movements'. The experience of the miners' strike has, again, pointed the way, revealing the possibilities of new solidarities, new forms of organisation, and new points of contact between workers' struggles and other social movements. But the first principle of socialist organisation must remain the essential correspondence between working-class interests and socialist politics. Unless class-politics becomes the unifying force that binds together all emancipatory struggles, the 'new social movements' will remain on the margins of the existing social order: at best able to generate periodic and momentary displays of popular support, but destined to leave the capitalist order intact, together with all its defences against human emancipation and the realisation of 'universal human goods'.

While the power of the state is being used to fight the class-war on behalf of capital, it cannot be the job of a socialist movement to encourage the divorce

of politics from class, as the NTS project requires. On the contrary, the principal task is to encourage and to build upon the political impulses which grow
out of working-class interests and struggles. That task is clearly not an easy
one. Concerted action by widely scattered and disparate working-class formations, even when joined by common class-interests, is not something that
can happen spontaneously. A united working class, in this sense, is certainly
not 'given' directly in the relations of production. But this is very far from
saying that the building-blocks of socialist politics are not to be found in the
struggles, large and small, against capital which have constituted working-
class history, or that a better foundation for socialism exists somewhere else.
There are many obstacles to class-organisation; but to treat these obstacles as
if they were absolute determinants, irrevocably overriding the common interests of class, is to accept the very mystifications that sustain the hegemony of
capitalism.

There are many lessons to be learned from the thousands of working-class
struggles that have taken place in Britain and elsewhere. Above all, they have
shown that, while the task is long and difficult, the material of socialism is
there in the interests, solidarities, and strategic capacities of the working class.
In their victories, and even in their defeats, these struggles have shown us
what might be accomplished if the labour-movement had a political instrument ready to do its job, the tremendous goals that might be achieved if all the
isolated and particular struggles for emancipation and 'universal goods' were
unified not simply by the phantoms of 'discourse' or by the superficial bonds
of electoral expediency, but by the politics of *class*.

Democracy as an economic mechanism

[…][It] seems to me that the main long-term theoretical task for the left is
to think about alternative mechanisms for regulating social production. The
old choice between the market and centralised planning is barren. Both, in
their various ways, have been driven by the imperatives of accumulation – in
one case imposed by the demands of competition and profit-maximisation
internal to the system, in the other by the requirements of accelerated industrial development. Neither has involved the reappropriation of the means
of production by the producers; neither has been motivated by the interests of the workers whose surplus-labour is appropriated, nor indeed by
the interests of the people as a whole; and in neither case has production
been susceptible to democratic accountability. Nor does the social market
or even 'market-socialism' provide an alternative, since, with or without a
human face, market-imperatives remain the driving mechanism. In today's

world-economy, as the social market begins to look more utopian, less feasible, even a contradiction in terms, it may now be more rather than less
realistic to think about radical alternatives.

I have suggested throughout this book that the capitalist market is a *political*
as well as an economic space: a terrain not simply of freedom and choice, but
of domination and coercion. I now want to suggest that *democracy* needs to be
reconceived not simply as a political category, but as an economic one. What I
mean is not simply 'economic democracy' as a greater equality of distribution.
I have in mind democracy as an economic regulator, the *driving mechanism* of
the economy.

Here, Marx's free association of direct producers (which does not, even in
Marx's terms, include only manual workers or people directly involved in
material production)[24] is a good place to start. It stands to reason that the like-
liest place to begin the search for a new economic mechanism is at the very
base of the economy, in the organisation of labour itself. But the issue is not
simply the internal organisation of enterprises; and even the reappropriation
of the means of production by the producers, while a necessary condition,
would not be sufficient, as long as possession remains market-dependent and
subject to the old imperatives. The freedom of the free association implies not
only democratic organisation, but emancipation from 'economic' coercions of
this kind.

Establishing a democratic organisation of direct producers, as distinct
from the present hierarchical structure of the capitalist enterprise, is, in some
respects, the easy part. Up to a point, even capitalist firms can accommodate
alternative organisations – such as the 'team-concept'. There is, to be sure,
nothing especially democratic about the team-concept as it actually operates
in capitalist enterprises; but even with the most democratically organised
'teams', such enterprises would be governed not by the self-determined objectives of those who work in them, but by imperatives imposed upon them from
without – not even by the needs and desires of the majority of citizens, but by
the interests of employers and the coercions imposed by the capitalist market
itself: the imperatives of competition, productivity, and profit-maximisation.

24. A good starting point for understanding Marx's concept of the producing
class is his concept of the 'collective labourer', which, in capitalist societies, includes
a wide variety of workers, both blue- and white-collar, situated at various points in
the process of creating and realising the surplus-value appropriated by capital. (For a
discussion of this point, see Meiksins 1986.) This is the class whose self-emancipation
would constitute socialism; but, of course, with the abolition of capitalist exploitation,
the nature of the 'producers' would no longer be defined by their contribution to the
production of capital.

And, of course, the workers would remain vulnerable to dismissal and plant-closures, the market's ultimate discipline. At any rate, these new modes of organisation are conceived not as new forms of democracy, making the organisation more accountable to its workers, or to the community at large, but on the contrary, as means of making the workers more responsive to the economic needs of the organisation. These organisations do not satisfy the most basic criteria of democracy, since the 'people' – neither the workers nor the citizen-body as a whole – are not in any sense sovereign, nor is the primary purpose of the organisation to enhance the quality of life enjoyed by its members, or even to pursue goals which they have set for themselves.

Even outright takeover by workers would not by itself circumvent the alienation of power to the market. Anyone who has listened in on the debates surrounding the [1994] buy-out of United Airlines in the USA will understand the problem. The most powerful argument the workers were able to muster in defence of their bid was that they would be no less responsive than their capitalist employers had been to market-imperatives – including, it must be supposed, the disciplines of closure and dismissal without which the market cannot function as a regulator.

New, more democratic ways of organising the workplace and workers' takeovers are admirable objectives in themselves and potentially the basis of something more; but, even if all enterprises were taken over in this way, there would remain the problem of detaching them from market-imperatives. Certain instruments and institutions now associated with 'the market' would undoubtedly be useful in a truly democratic society, but the moving force of the economy would have to emanate not from the market, but from within the self-active association of producers. And if the motivating force of the economy were to be found within the democratic enterprise, in the interests and objectives of the self-active workers themselves, modalities would have to be found for harnessing those interests and objectives to the management of the economy as a whole and to the well-being of the larger community; and that means, in the first instance, working out the modalities of interaction among enterprises.

I do not pretend to know the answers; but, as always, the questions need to be clarified first. And, on that score, we have barely made a start, to judge by the state of current debates. For the moment, I simply want to emphasise one point: what we are looking for is not only new forms of ownership, but also a new driving mechanism, a new rationality, a new economic logic; and if, as I think is the case, the most promising place to start is in the democratic organisation of production, which presupposes the reappropriation of the means of production by the producers, then it also needs to be emphasised

that the benefits of replacing the rationality of the market as a driving mechanism would accrue not to workers alone, but to everyone who is subject to the
consequences of market-imperatives, from their effects on the terms and conditions of work and leisure – indeed, the very organisation of time itself – to
their larger implications for the quality of social life, culture, the environment,
and 'extra-economic' goods in general.

Bibliography of Works by Ellen Meiksins Wood, 1970–2012

1970

'Canada and the American Science of Politics', with Neal Wood, in *Close the 49th Parallel etc: The Americaniza-tion of Canada*, edited by Ian Lums-den, pp. 179–95. Toronto: University of Toronto Press.

1972

Mind and Politics: An Approach to the Meaning of Liberal and Socialist Indi-vidualism, Berkeley and Los Angeles: University of California Press.

1978

'C.B. Macpherson, Liberalism, and the Task of Socialist Political Theory', in *The Socialist Register 1978*, edited by Ralph Miliband and John Saville, pp. 215–40. London: Merlin.

Class Ideology and Ancient Political The-ory: Socrates, Plato, and Aristotle in Social Context, with Neal Wood. New York: Oxford University Press.

1979

'For Sale! Strategies for Winning the Class Struggle!', *Canadian Dimension*, 14, 1: 13–16.

1981

'Liberal Democracy and Capitalist Hegemony: A Reply to Leo Pan-itch on the Task of Socialist Political Theory', in *The Socialist Register 1981*, edited by Ralph Miliband and John Saville, pp. 169–89. London: Merlin.

'Marxism and Ancient Greece', *History Workshop Journal*, 11: 3–22.

'The Separation of the Economic and the Political in Capitalism', *New Left Review*, I, 127: 66–95.

1982

'The Politics of Theory and the Concept of Class: E.P. Thompson and His Critics', *Studies in Political Economy*, 9: 45–75.

1983

'Agricultural Slavery in Classical Athens', *American Journal of Ancient History*, 8: 1–47.

'Marxism without Class Struggle?', in *The Socialist Register 1983*, edited by Ralph Miliband and John Saville, pp. 239–71. London: Merlin.

'The State and Popular Sovereignty in French Political Thought: A Geneal-ogy of Rousseau's "General Will"', *History of Political Thought*, 4: 281–315.

1984

'Marxism and the Course of History', *New Left Review*, I, 147: 95–107.

Review of *Medieval Slavery and Libera-tion*, by Pierre Dockès, *Social History*, 9: 101–3.

1985

'Beyond Class? A Reply to Chantal Mouffe', with Peter Meiksins, *Studies in Political Economy*, 17: 141–65.

'The State and Popular Sovereignty in French Political Thought: A Geneal-ogy of Rousseau's "General Will"', in *History from Below: Studies in Popular Protest and Popular Ideology in Honour of George Rudé*, edited by Frederick Krantz, pp. 117–39. Montréal: Concordia University.

1986
The Retreat from Class: A New 'True' Socialism, London: Verso.
'Socrates and Democracy: A Reply to Gregory Vlastos', with Neal Wood. *Political Theory*, 14: 55–82.

1987
'A Reply to "Looking for Alternatives to Reformism"', *International Socialism*, 35: 129–38.
'Why Class Struggle Is Central', *Against the Current*, 10: 7–9.

1988
'Capitalism and Human Emancipation', *New Left Review*, I, 167: 3–20.
Peasant-Citizen and Slave: The Foundations of Athenian Democracy. London: Verso.

1989
'Oligarchic "Democracy"', *Monthly Review*, 41, 3: 42–51.
'Power and Oppression', *New Statesman and Society*, 2, 70: 30.
'Rational Choice Marxism: Is the Game Worth the Candle?', *New Left Review*, I, 177: 41–88.

1990
'Explaining Everything or Nothing?', *New Left Review*, I, 184: 116–28.
'Falling Through the Cracks: E.P. Thompson and the Debate on Base and Superstructure', in *E.P. Thompson: Critical Perspectives*, edited by Harvey J. Kaye and Keith McClelland, pp. 125–52. Philadelphia: Temple University Press.
'The Uses and Abuses of "Civil Society"', in *The Socialist Register 1990*, edited by Ralph Miliband, Leo Panitch, and John Saville, pp. 60–84. London: Merlin.

1991
The Pristine Culture of Capitalism: A Historical Essay on Old Regimes and Modern States, London: Verso.

Review of *Bread and Circuses: Historical Sociology and Political Pluralism*, by Paul Veyne. *History of the Human Sciences*, 4: 469–71.

1992
'Custom against Capitalism', *New Left Review*, I, 195: 21–8.
'Locke against Democracy: Consent, Representation, and Suffrage in the *Two Treatises*', *History of Political Thought*, 13: 657–89.

1994
'Democracy: An Idea of Ambiguous Ancestry', in *Athenian Political Thought and the Reconstruction of American Democracy*, edited by J. Peter Euben, John R. Wallach, and Josiah Ober, pp. 59–80. Ithaca: Cornell University Press.
'E.P. Thompson: Historian and Socialist', *Monthly Review*, 45, 8: 8–14.
'Edward Palmer Thompson: In Memoriam', *Studies in Political Economy*, 43: 26–31.
'From Opportunity to Imperative: The History of the Market', *Monthly Review*, 46, 3: 14–40.
'History of the Market: From Opportunity to Imperative', *Mainstream*, 32, 41: 11–21.
'Radicalism, Capitalism, and Historical Contexts: Not Only a Reply to Richard Ashcraft on John Locke', *History of Political Thought*, 15: 323–72.
'Ralph Miliband, 1924–1994: The Common Sense of Socialism', *Radical Philosophy*, 68: 62–3.
'A Tale of Two Democracies', *History Today*, 44, 5: 50–55.

1995
'A Chronology of the New Left and Its Successors, or: Who's Old-Fashioned Now?', in *The Socialist Register 1995*, edited by Leo Panitch (with special coeditors Ellen Meiksins Wood and John Saville), pp. 22–49. London: Merlin.
Democracy against Capitalism: Renewing Historical Materialism, Cambridge: Cambridge University Press.

'An Inheritance Reaffirmed: Marx', in *Class*, edited by Patrick Joyce, pp. 64–8. Oxford: Oxford University Press.

'Rational Choice Marxism: Is the Game Worth the Candle?', in *Rational Choice Marxism*, edited by Terrell Carver and Paul Thomas, pp. 79–135. University Park: Pennsylvania State University Press.

'What Is the "Postmodern" Agenda? An Introduction', *Monthly Review*, 47, 3: 1–12.

1996

'Capitalism, Merchants, and Bourgeois Revolution: Reflections on the Brenner Debate and Its Sequel', *International Review of Social History*, 41: 209–32.

'Democracy and Capitalism: Friends or Foes? [Interview with Ellen Meiksins Wood]', *New Socialist*, 1, 1: 14–16.

'Demos versus "We, the People": Freedom and Democracy Ancient and Modern', in *Dēmokratia: A Conversation on Democracies, Ancient and Modern*, edited by Josiah Ober and Charles Hedrick, pp. 121–37. Princeton: Princeton University Press.

'Intellectuals and Universalism', *Imprints*, 1, 1: 65–71.

'Marxism and Postmodernism: A Reply to Roger Burbach', with John Bellamy Foster, *Monthly Review*, 47, 10: 41–6.

'Modernity, Postmodernity, or Capitalism?', *Monthly Review*, 48, 3: 21–39.

1997

'Back to Marx', *Monthly Review*, 49, 2: 1–9.

In Defense of History: Marxism and the Postmodern Agenda, edited with John Bellamy Foster, New York: Monthly Review Press.

'Labor, the State, and Class Struggle', *Monthly Review*, 49, 3: 1–17.

'Locke against Democracy: Consent, Representation, and Suffrage in the *Two Treatises*', in *Locke*, Vol. 2, edited by John Dunn and Ian Harris, pp. 570–602. Cheltenham: Edward Elgar.

'Modernity, Postmodernity, or Capitalism?', *Review of International Political Economy*, 4: 539–60.

'The Non-History of Capitalism', *Historical Materialism*, 1: 5–21.

'A Note on Du Boff and Herman', *Monthly Review*, 49, 6: 39–43.

'A Reply to A. Sivanandan', *Monthly Review*, 48, 9: 21–32.

A Trumpet of Sedition: Political Theory and the Rise of Capitalism, 1509–1688, with Neal Wood. London: Pluto; New York: New York University Press.

'What Is the "Postmodern" Agenda?', in *In Defense of History: Marxism and the Postmodern Agenda*, edited by Ellen Meiksins Wood and John Bellamy Foster, pp. 1–16. New York: Monthly Review Press.

1998

'The Agrarian Origins of Capitalism', *Monthly Review*, 50, 3: 14–31.

Capitalism and the Information Age: The Political Economy of the Global Communication Revolution, edited with Robert W. McChesney and John Bellamy Foster. New York: Monthly Review Press.

'Capitalist Change and Generational Shifts', *Monthly Review*, 50, 5: 1–10.

'Class Compacts, the Welfare State, and Epochal Shifts: A Reply to Frances Fox Piven and Richard A. Cloward', *Monthly Review*, 49, 8: 24–43.

'The *Communist Manifesto* after 150 Years', *Monthly Review*, 50, 1: 14–35.

'The Communist Manifesto 150 Years Later', in *The Communist Manifesto / Karl Marx and Friedrich Engels, Principles of Communism / Friedrich Engels, The Communist Manifesto 150 Years Later / Ellen Meiksins Wood*, pp. 87–112. New York: Monthly Review Press.

'Introduction to the New Edition', in *The Retreat from Class: A New 'True' Socialism*, pp. xi–xv. London: Verso.

'Labor, Class, and State in Global Capitalism', in *Rising from the Ashes? Labor in the Age of 'Global' Capitalism*, edited by Ellen Meiksins Wood,

Peter Meiksins, and Michael Yates, pp. 3–16. New York: Monthly Review Press.

'Modernity, Postmodernity, or Capitalism?', in *Capitalism and the Information Age: The Political Economy of the Global Communication Revolution*, edited by Robert W. McChesney, Ellen Meiksins Wood, and John Bellamy Foster, pp. 27–49. New York: Monthly Review Press.

Rising from the Ashes? Labor in the Age of 'Global' Capitalism, edited with Peter Meiksins and Michael Yates. New York: Monthly Review Press.

1999

'Horizontal Relations: A Note on Brenner's Heresy', *Historical Materialism*, 4: 171–9.

'An Interview with Ellen Meiksins Wood', interview by Christopher Phelps. *Monthly Review*, 51, 1: 74–92.

'Kosovo and the New Imperialism', *Monthly Review*, 51, 2: 1–8.

The Origin of Capitalism, New York: Monthly Review Press.

'The Politics of Capitalism', *Monthly Review*, 51, 4: 12–26.

'Unhappy Families: Global Capitalism in a World of Nation-States', *Monthly Review*, 51, 3: 1–12.

2000

'The Agrarian Origins of Capitalism', in *Hungry for Profit: The Agribusiness Threat to Farmers, Food, and the Environment*, edited by Fred Magdoff, John Bellamy Foster, and Frederick H. Buttel, pp. 23–41. New York: Monthly Review Press.

'Capitalism or Enlightenment?', *History of Political Thought*, 21: 405–26.

'Kosovo and the New Imperialism', in *Masters of the Universe? NATO's Balkan Crusade*, edited by Tariq Ali, pp. 190–200. London: Verso.

2001

'Contradiction: Only in Capitalism?', in *The Socialist Register 2002*, edited by Leo Panitch and Colin Leys, pp. 275–93. London: Merlin.

'Eurocentric Anti-Eurocentrism', *Against the Current*, 92: 29–35.

'War without Boundaries', *Canadian Dimension*, 35, 6: 16–17.

2002

'Class, Race, and Capitalism', *Political Power and Social Theory*, 15: 275–84.

'Explaining 11 September', *Studies in Political Economy*, 67: 25–31.

'Global Capital, National States', in *Historical Materialism and Globalization*, edited by Mark Rupert and Hazel Smith, pp. 17–39. London: Routledge.

'Infinite War', *Historical Materialism*, 10, 1: 7–27.

'Landlords and Peasants, Masters and Slaves: Class Relations in Greek and Roman Antiquity', *Historical Materialism*, 10, 3: 17–69.

The Origin of Capitalism: A Longer View, London: Verso.

'The Question of Market Dependence', *Journal of Agrarian Change*, 2: 50–87.

2003

'Capitalist Empire and the Nation State', *Against the Current*, 106: 21–6.

'Christopher Hill and the Recovery of History', *Against the Current*, 104: 43–5.

Empire of Capital, London: Verso.

'Globalisation and the State: Where Is the Power of Capital?', in *Anti-Capitalism: A Marxist Introduction*, edited by Alfredo Saad-Filho, pp. 127–41. London: Pluto.

'A Manifesto for Global Capital?', in *Debating Empire*, edited by Gopal Balakrishnan, pp. 61–82. London: Verso.

2006

'Democracy as Ideology of Empire', in *The New Imperialists: Ideologies of Empire*, edited by Colin Mooers, pp. 9–23. Oxford: Oneworld.

'Logics of Power: A Conversation with David Harvey', *Historical Materialism*, 14, 4: 9–34.

2007
'A Reply to Critics', *Historical Materialism*, 15, 3: 143–70.

2008
Citizens to Lords: A Social History of Western Political Thought from Antiquity to the Middle Ages, London: Verso.
'Historical Materialism in "Forms Which Precede Capitalist Production"', in *Karl Marx's Grundrisse: Foundations of the Critique of Political Economy 150 Years Later*, edited by Marcello Musto, pp. 79–92. London: Routledge.
'Kapitalismusentstehung' (Origin of Capitalism), *Historisch-kritisches Wörterbuch des Marxismus*. Vol. 7, Part 1, edited by Wolfgang Fritz Haug, Frigga Haug, and Peter Jehle, cols. 273–92. Hamburg: Argument.
'Why It Matters' [Review of *Hobbes and Republican Liberty*, by Quentin Skinner], *London Review of Books*, 30, 18: 3, 5–6.

2009
'Getting What's Coming to Us: Capitalism and Social Rights', *Against the Current*, 140: 28–32.
'Peasants and the Market Imperative: The Origins of Capitalism', in *Peasants and Globalization: Political Economy, Rural Transformation, and the Agrarian Question*, edited by A. Haroon Akram-Lodhi and Cristóbal Kay, pp. 37–56. London: Routledge.
'Redéfinir la démocratie', *Contretemps*, new series, 4: 59–62.

2010
'Britain vs. France: How Many *Sonderwegs*?', in *Rechtsstaat statt Revolution, Verrechtlichung statt Demokratie?*, Vol. 1, *Die historischen Voraussetzungen*, edited by Detlef Georgia Schulze, Sabine Berghahn, and Frieder Otto Wolf, pp. 83–97. Münster: Westfälisches Dampfboot.
'Happy Campers' [Review of *Why Not Socialism?*, by G.A. Cohen], *London Review of Books*, 32, 2: 26–7.
'Les origines agraires du capitalisme', *Sciences Humaines*, special issue no. 11 (La grande histoire du capitalisme): 18–19.

2011
'Ellen Meiksins Wood: Empire in the Age of Capital [Interview]', in *Capital and Its Discontents: Conversations with Radical Thinkers in a Time of Tumult*, edited by Sasha Lilley, pp. 27–42. Oakland: PM Press.
'Foreword', in *The American Road to Capitalism: Studies in Class-Structure, Economic Development, and Political Conflict, 1620–1877*, by Charles Post. Leiden: Brill. 'Le marxisme politique et ses débats [Interview by Frédérick-Guillaume Dufour and Jonathan Martineau]', *Actuel Marx*, 50: 98–118.

2012
'Capitalism', in *The Elgar Companion to Marxist Economics*, edited by Ben Fine and Alfredo Saad-Filho. Cheltenham: Edward Elgar.
'Democracy', in *The Marx Revival: Essays on the Critique of Contemporary Society*, edited by Marcello Musto. Houndmills: Palgrave Macmillan.
Liberty and Property: A Social History of Western Political Thought from Renaissance to Enlightenment, London: Verso.
'Universal Capitalism', in *Marx for Today*, edited by Marcello Musto, New York: Routledge.

References

Albo, Greg 1996, 'The World Economy, Market Imperatives, and Alternatives', *Monthly Review*, 48, 7: 6–22.

Anderson, Benedict 1983, *Imagined Communities: Reflections on the Origin and Spread of Nationalism*, London: Verso.

Anderson, Perry 1964, 'Origins of the Present Crisis', *New Left Review*, I, 23: 26–53.

—— 1966, Socialism and Pseudo-Empiricism', *New Left Review*, I, 35: 2–42.

—— 1968, 'Components of the National Culture', *New Left Review*, I, 50: 3–57.

—— 1974, *Passages from Antiquity to Feudalism*, London: NLB.

—— 1976–7, 'The Antinomies of Antonio Gramsci', *New Left Review*, I, 100: 5–78.

—— 1980, *Arguments within English Marxism*, London: NLB.

—— 1987, 'The Figures of Descent', *New Left Review*, I, 161: 20–77.

—— 2002, 'Confronting Defeat', *London Review of Books*, 24, 20: 10–17.

Andrewes, Antony 1977, 'Cleisthenes' Reform Bill', *Classical Quarterly*, 27: 241–8.

Andreyev, V.N. 1974, 'Some Aspects of Agrarian Conditions in Attica in the Fifth to Third Centuries BC', *Eirene*, 12, 5–46.

Arato, Andrew 1981, 'Civil Society against the State: Poland 1980–81', *Telos*, 47: 23–47.

—— 1981–2, 'Empire vs. Civil Society: Poland 1981–82', *Telos*, 50: 19–48.

Aston, Trevor H. and Charles H.E. Philpin (eds.) 1985, *The Brenner Debate: Agrarian Class Structure and Economic Development in Pre-Industrial Europe*, Cambridge: Cambridge University Press.

Audring, Gert 1974, 'Grenzen der Konzentration von Grundeigentum in Attika während des 4. Jh. v. u. Z.', *Klio*, 56: 445–56.

Badian, Ernst 1968, *Roman Imperialism in the Late Republic*, Second Edition, Oxford: Blackwell.

Beringer, Walter 1985, 'Freedom, Family, and Citizenship in Early Greece', in *The Craft of the Ancient Historian: Essays in Honor of Chester G. Starr*, edited by John W. Eadie and Josiah Ober, Lanham: University Press of America.

Bisson, Thomas N. 1994, 'The "Feudal Revolution"', *Past and Present*, 142: 6–42.

Blackburn, Robin 1988, *The Overthrow of Colonial Slavery, 1776–1848*, London: Verso.

—— 1997, *The Making of New World Slavery: From the Baroque to the Modern, 1492–1800*, London: Verso.

Blackledge, Paul 2002–3, 'Political Marxism: Towards an Immanent Critique', *Studies in Marxism*, 9: 5–25.

—— 2008, 'Political Marxism', in *Critical Companion to Contemporary Marxism*, eds. Jacques Bidet and Stathis Kouvelakis, Leiden: Brill.

Blaut, James M. 1993, *The Colonizer's Model of the World: Geographical Diffusionism and Eurocentric History*, New York: Guilford Press.

Bloch, Marc 1970 [1931], *French Rural History: An Essay on Its Basic Characteristics*, Berkeley: University of California Press.

Bodemann, Y. Michal and Willfried Spohn 1989, 'The New "True" Socialism and the Old "Correct" Marxism', *Critical Sociology*, 16: 105–20.

Bodin, Jean 1955 [1576], *Six Books of the Commonwealth*, Oxford: Blackwell.

Braudel, Fernand 1986, *The Identity of France*, Vol. 2, *People and Production*, trans. Sian Reynolds, New York: Harper & Row.

Brenner, Robert 1977, 'The Origins of Capitalist Development: A Critique of Neo-Smithian Marxism', *New Left Review*, I, 104: 25–92.

—— 1985a, 'Agrarian Class Structure and Economic Development in Pre-Industrial Europe', in Aston and Philpin (eds.) 1985.

—— 1985b, 'The Agrarian Roots of European Capitalism', in Aston and Philpin (eds.) 1985.

—— 1986,'The Social Basis of Economic Development', in *Analytical Marxism*, edited by John Roemer, Cambridge: Cambridge University Press.

—— 1989, 'Bourgeois Revolution and Transition to Capitalism', in *The First Modern Society: Essays in English History in Honour of Lawrence Stone*, ed. A.L. Beier et al., Cambridge: Cambridge University Press.

—— 1993, *Merchants and Revolution: Commercial Change, Political Conflict, and London's Overseas Traders, 1550–1653*, Princeton: Princeton University Press.

—— 2001, 'The Low Countries in the Transition to Capitalism', *Journal of Agrarian Change*, 1: 169–241.

—— 2006a, *The Economics of Global Turbulence: The Advanced Capitalist Economies from Long Boom to Long Downturn, 1945–2005*, London: Verso.

—— 2006b, 'What Is, and What Is Not, Imperialism', *Historical Materialism*, 14, 4: 79–105.

Burckhardt, Jacob 1929, *Griechische Kulturgeschichte*, ed. Rudolf Marx, Leipzig: A. Kröner.

Burford, Alison 1972, *Craftsmen in Greek and Roman Society*, London: Thames and Hudson.

Burns, James H. (ed.) 1988, *The Cambridge History of Medieval Political Thought, c. 350–c. 1450*, Cambridge: Cambridge University Press.

Callinicos, Alex 1990,'The Limits of "Political Marxism"', *New Left Review*, I, 184: 110–15.

Chun, Lin 1993, *The British New Left*, Edinburgh: Edinburgh University Press.

Cohen, Jean L. 1982, *Class and Civil Society: The Limits of Marxian Critical Theory*, Amherst: University of Massachusetts Press.

Coleman, Janet 1988, 'Property and Poverty', in Burns (ed.) 1988.

—— 2000, *A History of Political Thought: From the Middle Ages to the Renaissance*, Oxford: Blackwell.

Colletti, Lucio 1972, 'Bernstein and the Marxism of the Second International', in *From Rousseau to Lenin: Studies in Ideology and Society*, London: NLB.

Condorcet, Antoine-Nicolas de 1955 [1794], *Sketch for a Historical Picture of the Progress of the Human Mind*, trans. June Barraclough, London: Weidenfeld and Nicolson.

Davis, Mike 1986, *Prisoners of the American Dream: Politics and Economy in the History of the U.S. Working Class*, London: Verso.

Derathé, Robert 1970, *Jean-Jacques Rousseau et la science politique de son temps*, Paris: J. Vrin.

De Ste. Croix, Geoffrey E.M. 1981, *The Class Struggle in the Ancient Greek World: From the Archaic Age to the Arab Conquests*, Ithaca: Cornell University Press.

De Vries, Jan and Ad van der Woude 1997, *The First Modern Economy: Success, Failure, and Perseverance of the Dutch Economy, 1500–1815*, Cambridge: Cambridge University Press.

Dockès, Pierre 1982, *Medieval Slavery and Liberation*, trans. Arthur Goldhammer, London: Methuen.

Duby, Georges 1968 [1962], *Rural Economy and Country Life in the Medieval West*, trans. Cynthia Postan, Columbia, SC.: University of South Carolina Press.

Eagleton, Terry 2011, *Why Marx Was Right*, New Haven: Yale University Press.

Ehrenberg, Victor 1962, *The People of Aristophanes: A Sociology of Old Attic Comedy*, Second Edition, New York: Schocken Books.

—— 1969, *The Greek State*, Second Edition, London: Methuen.

—— 1973, *From Solon to Socrates: Greek History and Civilization during the Sixth and Fifth Centuries B.C.*, Second Edition, London: Methuen.

Elliott, Gregory 1994, 'Missing Ingredients', *Radical Philosophy*, 68: 45–8.

Engels, Friedrich 1962 [1872], 'On Authority', in *Marx-Engels Selected Works*, Vol. 1, Moscow: Foreign Languages Publishing House.

Ferguson, Adam 1978 [1767], *An Essay on the History of Civil Society*, ed. Duncan Forbes, Edinburgh: Edinburgh University Press.

Finley, Moses I. 1965, *The World of Odysseus*, New York: Viking Press.

—— 1973, *The Ancient Economy*, Berkeley: University of California Press.

—— 1980, *Ancient Slavery and Modern Ideology*, London: Chatto and Windus.

—— 1981, *Economy and Society in Ancient Greece*, London: Chatto and Windus.

Frank, André Gunder 1998, *ReOrient: Global Economy in the Asian Age*, Berkeley: University of California Press.

Franklin, Julian 1969, introduction to *Constitutionalism and Resistance in the Sixteenth Century: Three Treatises by Hotman, Beza, and Mornay*, ed. and trans. Julian Franklin, New York: Pegasus.

Fried, Morton H. 1967, *The Evolution of Political Society: An Essay in Political Anthropology*, New York: Random House.

Garnsey, Peter and Richard Saller 1987, *The Roman Empire: Economy, Society, and Culture*, London: Duckworth.

Geras, Norman 1990, 'Seven Types of Obloquy: Travesties of Marxism', in *Socialist Register 1990*, ed. Ralph Miliband and Leo Panitch, London: Merlin Press.

Gindin, Sam 1997, 'Notes on Labor at the End of the Century: Starting Over?', *Monthly Review*, 49, 3: 140–57.

Gowan, Peter 2002, 'The American Campaign for Global Sovereignty', in *Socialist Register 2003*, ed. Leo Panitch and Colin Leys, London: Merlin Press.

Gray, John 1995, *Liberalism*, Second Edition, Minneapolis: University of Minnesota Press.

Hale, John 1993, *The Civilization of Europe in the Renaissance*, New York: Atheneum.

Harrison, Alick R.W. 1968, *The Law of Athens: The Family and Property*, Oxford: Clarendon Press.

Harvey, David 1990, *The Condition of Postmodernity: An Enquiry into the Origins of Cultural Change*, Oxford: Blackwell.

—— 2003, *The New Imperialism*, Oxford: Oxford University Press.

Heller, Agnes 1988, 'On Formal Democracy', in Keane (ed.) 1988.

Hendel, Charles W. 1934, *Jean-Jacques Rousseau: Moralist*, Indianapolis: Bobbs-Merrill.

Henwood, Doug 1999, 'Booming, Borrowing, and Consuming: The U.S. Economy in 1999', *Monthly Review*, 51, 3: 120–33.

Hexter, Jack H. 2003, 'History', in *The Blackwell Dictionary of Modern Social Thought*, Second Edition, ed. William Outhwaite, Oxford: Blackwell.

Hilton, Rodney 1973, *Bond Men Made Free: Medieval Peasant Movements and the English Rising of 1381*, London: Temple Smith.

—— 1978, 'A Crisis of Feudalism', *Past and Present*, 80: 3–19.

Hobsbawm, Eric J. 1987, *The Age of Empire, 1875–1914*, London: Weidenfeld and Nicolson.

—— 1990, *Echoes of the Marseillaise: Two Centuries Look Back on the French Revolution*, London: Verso.

Hodgson, Geoff 1984, *The Democratic Economy: A New Look at Planning, Markets, and Power*, Harmondsworth: Penguin.

Hopkins, Keith 1978, *Conquerors and Slaves*, Cambridge: Cambridge University Press.

Hotman, François 1969 [1573], *Francogallia*, in Franklin (ed.) 1969.

Hume, David 1773, *History of England*, Vol. 3, London.

Hunt, Alan (ed.) 1980, *Marxism and Democracy*, London: Lawrence and Wishart.

James, Cyril Lionel Robert 1989 [1938], *The Black Jacobins: Toussaint L'Ouverture and the San Domingo Revolution*, New York: Vintage Books.

Jameson, Fredric 1996, 'Five Theses on Actually Existing Marxism', *Monthly Review*, 47, 11: 1–10.

Jameson, Michael H. 1977–8, 'Agriculture and Slavery in Classical Athens', *Classical Journal*, 73: 122–45.

Jessop, Bob 1980, 'The Political Indeterminacy of Democracy', in Hunt (ed.) 1980.

Jones, Arnold H.M. 1969 [1957], *Athenian Democracy*, Oxford: Blackwell.

Kaye, Harvey J. 1984, *The British Marxist Historians: An Introductory Analysis*, Cambridge: Polity.

Keane, John 1988a, *Democracy and Civil Society: On the Predicaments of European Socialism, the Prospects for Democracy, and the Problem of Controlling Social and Political Power*, London: Verso.

—— 1988b, 'Introduction' in Keane (ed.) 1988.

—— (ed.) 1988, *Civil Society and the State: New European Perspectives*, London: Verso.

Keohane, Nannerl O. 1980, *Philosophy and the State in France: The Renaissance to the Enlightenment*, Princeton: Princeton University Press.

Kramnick, Isaac (ed.) 1987, *The Federalist Papers*, Harmondsworth: Penguin.

Krauthammer, Charles 2001, 'How fast things change', *Washington Post*, 30 November.

Laclau, Ernesto and Chantal Mouffe 1985, *Hegemony and Socialist Strategy: Towards a Radical Democratic Politics*, London: Verso.

Lash, Scott and John Urry 1987, *The End of Organized Capitalism*, Cambridge: Polity Press.

Le Roy Ladurie, Emmanuel 1980, *Carnival in Romans*, New York: Braziller.

Luxemburg, Rosa 1963 [1913], *The Accumulation of Capital*, London: Routledge.

Magdoff, Harry 1998, 'A Letter to a Contributor: The Same Old State', *Monthly Review*, 49, 8: 1–10.

Manicas, Peter 1988, 'The Foreclosure of Democracy in America', *History of Political Thought*, 9: 137–60.

Marx, Karl 1971 [1894], *Capital*, Vol III, Moscow: Progress Publishers.

—— 1973 [1939], *Grundrisse: Foundations of the Critique of Political Economy*, trans. Martin Nicolaus, Harmondsworth: Penguin.

—— 1974 [1875], *Critique of the Gotha Programme*, in *The First International and After*, edited by David Fernbach, Harmondsworth: Penguin.

—— 1978 [1879], 'Circular Letter to Bebel, Liebknecht, Bracke, and Others, 17–18 September 1879', in *The Marx-Engels Reader*, Second Edition, edited by Robert C. Tucker, New York: Norton.

—— 1981 [1894], *Capital*, Vol. III, edited by Ernest Mandel, New York: Vintage Books.

Marx, Karl and Frederick Engels 1947 [1932], *The German Ideology: Parts I and II*, edited by R. Pascal, New York: International Publishers.

—— 1973 [1848], *The Manifesto of the Communist Party*, in *The Revolutions of 1848*, edited by David Fernbach, Harmondsworth: Penguin.

McNally, David 1988, *Political Economy and the Rise of Capitalism: A Reinterpretation*, Berkeley: University of California Press.

—— 1989, 'Locke, Levellers and Liberty: Property and Democracy in the Thought of the First Whigs', *History of Political Thought*, 10: 17–40.

—— 1999, 'Turbulence in the World Economy', *Monthly Review*, 51, 2: 38–52.

Meiksins, Peter 1986, 'Beyond the Boundary Question', *New Left Review*, I, 157: 101–20.

Mercer, Colin 1980, 'Revolutions, Reforms or Reformulations? Marxist Discourse on Democracy', in Hunt (ed.) 1980.

Miliband, Ralph 1977, *Marxism and Politics*, Oxford: Oxford University Press.

Mitford, William 1814, *The History of Greece*, London: T. Cadell and W. Davies.

Murray, Oswyn 1980, *Early Greece*, Glasgow: W. Collins.

Nairn, Tom 1964a, 'The British Political Elite', *New Left Review*, I, 23: 19–25.

—— 1964b, The English Working Class', *New Left Review*, I, 24: 43–57.

—— 1964c, 'The Nature of the Labour Party', *New Left Review*, I, 27: 38–65 and *New Left Review*, I, 28: 33–62.

—— 1970, 'The Fateful Meridian', *New Left Review*, I, 60: 3–35.

—— 1977, 'The Twilight of the British State', *New Left Review*, I, 101–2: 3–61.

—— 1988, *The Enchanted Glass: Britain and Its Monarchy*, London: Radius.

Nederman, Cary J. 1983, 'State and Political Theory in France and England, 1250–1350: Marsiglio of Padua, William of Ockham, and the Emergence of National Traditions of Discourse in the Late Middle Ages', Ph.D. diss., York University.

Osborne, Robin 1985, *Demos: The Discovery of Classical Attika*, Cambridge: Cambridge University Press.

—— 1987, *Classical Landscape with Figures: The Ancient Greek City and Its Countryside*, London: G. Philip.

Patriquin, Larry 2007, *Agrarian Capitalism and Poor Relief in England, 1500–1860: Rethinking the Origins of the Welfare State*, Houndmills: Palgrave Macmillan.

Phelps, Christopher 1999, 'An Interview with Ellen Meiksins Wood', *Monthly Review*, 51, 1: 74–92.

Pirenne, Henri 1956 [1939], *Mohammed and Charlemagne*, London: G. Allen and Unwin.

—— 1969 [1925], *Medieval Cities: The Origins and the Revival of Trade*, Princeton: Princeton University Press.

Piven, Frances Fox and Richard A. Cloward 1998a, *The Breaking of the American Social Compact*, New York: New Press.

—— 1998b, 'Eras of Power', *Monthly Review*, 49, 8: 11–23.

Pocock, John G.A. 1985, *Virtue, Commerce, and History*, Cambridge: Cambridge University Press.

Polanyi, Karl 1957 [1944], *The Great Transformation: The Political and Economic Origins of Our Time*, Boston: Beacon Press.

Reynolds, Susan 1994, *Fiefs and Vassals: The Medieval Evidence Reinterpreted*, Oxford: Oxford University Press.

Riley, Patrick 1979, 'The General Will before Rousseau', *Political Theory*, 6: 485–516.

Rousseau, Jean-Jacques 1964a, *Oeuvres complètes*, Vol. 3, ed. Bernard Gagnebin and Marcel Raymond, Paris: Gallimard.

—— 1964b [1755], 'Discours sur l'économie politique', in Rousseau 1964a.

—— 1964c [1762], *Contrat social*, in Rousseau 1964a.

—— 1965–98 [1758], 'Letter to Theodore Tronchin, 26 November 1758', in *Correspondance complète de Jean Jacques Rousseau*, Vol. 5, ed. R.A. Leigh, Geneva: Institut et musée Voltaire.

—— 1967 [1758], *Lettre à M. d'Alembert sur son article Genève*, Paris: Garnier-Flammarion.

Rupert, Mark and Hazel Smith (eds.) 2002, *Historical Materialism and Globalization*, London: Routledge.

Sahlins, Marshall 1974, *Stone Age Economics*, London: Tavistock Publications.

Saxonhouse, Arlene 1981, 'Review of *Ancient Slavery and Modern Ideology*, by Moses I. Finley', *Political Theory*, 9: 577–9.

Shanin, Teodor 1971, 'Peasantry as a Political Factor', in *Peasants and Peasant Societies: Selected Readings*, edited by Teodor Shanin, Harmondsworth: Penguin.

Skinner, Quentin 1978, *The Foundations of Modern Political Thought*, Vol. 1, *The Renaissance*, Cambridge: Cambridge University Press.

Smith, Sir Thomas 1982 [1583], *De Republica Anglorum*, ed. Mary Dewar, Cambridge: Cambridge University Press.

Starr, Chester G. 1982, *The Roman Empire, 27 B.C. to A.D. 476: A Study in Survival*, New York: Oxford University Press.

Sweezy, Paul et al. 1976, *The Transition from Feudalism to Capitalism*, introduction by Rodney Hilton, London: Verso.

Syme, Ronald 1960 [1939], *The Roman Revolution*, London: Oxford University Press.

Therborn, Göran 1984, 'The Prospects of Labour and the Transformation of Advanced Capitalism', *New Left Review*, I, 145: 5–38.

Thompson, Edward Palmer 1968 [1963], *The Making of the English Working Class*, Harmondsworth: Penguin.

—— 1975, *Whigs and Hunters: The Origin of the Black Act*, London: Allen Lane.

—— 1978, 'Eighteenth-Century English Society: Class Struggle without Class?', *Social History*, 3: 133–65.

—— 1993, *Customs in Common*, New York: New Press.

Van Caenegem, Raoul 1988, 'Government, Law and Society', in Burns (ed.) 1988.

Weber, Max 1968 [1922], *Economy and Society*, edited by Guenther Roth and Claus Wittich, New York: Bedminster Press.

Whitehead, David 1986, *The Demes of Attica: 508/7–ca. 250 BC*, Princeton: Princeton University Press.

Wickham, Chris 1994, *Land and Power: Studies in Italian and European Social History, 400–1200*, London: British School at Rome.

—— 2005, *Framing the Early Middle Ages: Europe and the Mediterranean, 400–800*, Oxford: Oxford University Press.

Williams, Eric 1961 [1944], *Capitalism and Slavery*, New York: Russell & Russell.

Williams, Raymond 1979, *Politics and Letters: Interviews with New Left Review*, London, NLB.

Wirszubski, Chaim 1950, *Libertas as a Political Idea at Rome during the Late Republic and Early Principate*, Cambridge: Cambridge University Press.

Wolf, Eric R. 1966, *Peasants*, Englewood Cliffs: Prentice-Hall.

—— 1971, 'On Peasant Rebellions', in Shanin (ed.) 1971.

Wood, Ellen Meiksins 1981a, 'The Separation of the Economic and the Political in Capitalism', *New Left Review*, I, 127: 66–95.

—— 1981b, 'Marxism and Ancient Greece', *History Workshop Journal*, 11: 3–22.

—— 1983a, 'The State and Popular Sovereignty in French Political Thought: A Genealogy of Rousseau's "General Will"', *History of Political Thought*, 4, 281–315.

—— 1983b, 'Agricultural Slavery in Classical Athens', *American Journal of Ancient History*, 8: 1–47.

—— 1984, 'Marxism and the Course of History', *New Left Review*, I, 147: 95–107.

—— 1986, *The Retreat from Class: A New 'True' Socialism*, London: Verso.

—— 1988, *Peasant-Citizen and Slave: The Foundations of Athenian Democracy*, London: Verso.

—— 1989, 'Rational Choice Marxism: Is the Game Worth the Candle?', *New Left Review*, I, 177: 41–88.

—— 1990, 'Explaining Everything or Nothing?', *New Left Review*, I, 184: 116–28.

—— 1991, *The Pristine Culture of Capitalism: A Historical Essay on Old Regimes and Modern States*, London: Verso.

—— 1992a, 'Custom against Capitalism', *New Left Review*, I, 195, 21–8.

—— 1992b, 'Locke against Democracy: Consent, Representation, and Suffrage in the *Two Treatises*', *History of Political Thought*, 13: 657–89.

—— 1994a, 'Radicalism, Capitalism, and Historical Contexts: Not Only a Reply to Richard Ashcraft on John Locke', *History of Political Thought*, 15: 323–72.

—— 1994b, 'E.P. Thompson: Historian and Socialist', *Monthly Review*, 45, 8: 8–14.

—— 1994c, 'Edward Palmer Thompson: In Memoriam', *Studies in Political Economy*, 43: 26–31.

—— 1994d, 'From Opportunity to Imperative: The History of the Market', *Monthly Review*, 46, 3: 14–40.

—— 1995a, *Democracy against Capitalism: Renewing Historical Materialism*, Cambridge: Cambridge University Press.

—— 1995b, 'What Is the "Postmodern" Agenda? An Introduction', *Monthly Review*, 47, 3: 1–12.

—— 1996, 'Capitalism, Merchants, and Bourgeois Revolution: Reflections on the Brenner Debate and Its Sequel', *International Review of Social History*, 41: 209–32.

—— 1997, 'Modernity, Postmodernity, or Capitalism?', *Review of International Political Economy*, 4: 539–60.

—— 1999a, 'Horizontal Relations: A Note on Brenner's Heresy', *Historical Materialism*, 4, 1: 171–9.

—— 1999b, 'The Politics of Capitalism', *Monthly Review*, 51, 4: 12–26.

—— 2000, 'Capitalism or Enlightenment?', *History of Political Thought* 21: 405–26.

—— 2001a, 'Contradiction: Only in Capitalism?', in *The Socialist Register 2002*, edited by Leo Panitch and Colin Leys, London: Merlin Press.

—— 2001b, 'Eurocentric Anti-Eurocentrism', *Against the Current*, 92: 29–35.

—— 2002a, *The Origin of Capitalism: A Longer View*, London: Verso.

—— 2002b, 'The Question of Market Dependence', *Journal of Agrarian Change*, 2: 50–87.

—— 2002c, 'Landlords and Peasants, Masters and Slaves: Class Relations in Greek and Roman Antiquity', *Historical Materialism*, 10, 3: 17–69.

—— 2008a, *Citizens to Lords: A Social History of Western Political Thought from Antiquity to the Middle Ages*, London: Verso.

—— 2008b, 'Historical Materialism in "Forms Which Precede Capitalist Production"', in *Karl Marx's Grundrisse: Foundations of the Critique of Political Economy 150 Years Later*, edited by Marcello Musto, London: Routledge.

—— 2009, 'Getting What's Coming to Us: Capitalism and Social Rights', *Against the Current*, 140: 28–32.

—— 2010, 'Britain vs. France: How Many Sonderwegs?', in *Rechtsstaat statt Revolution, Verrechtlichung statt Demokratie?*, Vol. 1, *Die historischen Voraussetzungen*, ed. Detlef Georgia Schulze et al., Münster: Westfälisches Dampfboot.

—— 2012, *Liberty and Property: A Social History of Western Political Thought from Renaissance to Enlightenment*, London: Verso.

Wood, Ellen Meiksins and Neal Wood 1978, *Class Ideology and Ancient Political Theory: Socrates, Plato, and Aristotle in Social Context*, New York: Oxford University Press.

—— 1986, 'Socrates and Democracy: A Reply to Gregory Vlastos', *Political Theory*, 14: 55–82.

—— 1997, *A Trumpet of Sedition: Political Theory and the Rise of Capitalism, 1509–1688*, London: Pluto Press.

Wood, Gordon S. 1972 [1969], *The Creation of the American Republic, 1776–1787*, New York: Norton.

Wood, Neal 1978, 'The Social History of Political Theory', *Political Theory*, 6: 345–67.

—— 1984, *John Locke and Agrarian Capitalism*, Berkeley: University of California Press.

—— 1988, *Cicero's Social and Political Thought*, Berkeley: University of California Press.

Index

Bloch, Mark, 124n33
Bodin, Jean, 133, 164–5
boule. *See* council (Athens)
bourgeois democracy, 286–92
bourgeois paradigm, 32–6
bourgeois revolution, 132, 227, 240
bourgeoisie
    capitalism and, 31, 32–6, 42, 44
    French, 33, 34–5, 223
Braudel, Fernand, 54n22
Brenner, Robert, 31n10, 50–1, 93n3, 275, 276–7
British Empire, 251, 256–7. *See also* England; Great Britain
Burckhardt, Jacob, 88
burghers, 44–6
Burke, Edmund, 178–9
Bush, George W., 265

Caesar, Julius, 112
Callicles, 150
Cambridge school, the, 142–3
Canada, 253
Cape Colony, 253
capital, 47–8, 189, 192. *See also* capitalism
    labour and, 37, 268–74, 278–81, 304–5
    relations among capitals, 275–6
    as a social relation of production, 4
capitalism. *See also* agrarian capitalism; industrial capitalism
    assumed to have always existed, 36, 226
    bourgeoisie and, 31, 32–6, 42
    and cities, 44–6
    citizenship and, 189–92
    civil society and, 211
    class-struggle and, 27–30
    coercion and, 20, 27, 40, 56, 71, 215
    crises of, 239
    critique of, 17, 210, 231
    democracy and, 189–92, 202–10, 288–9, 292–6
    effect on political rights, 184–5, 197, 204–5
    Enlightenment and, 38, 232–6
    'extra-economic' goods and, 45, 46, 47, 49–50, 56
    formal equality and, 197–8
    as imperative not opportunity, 36, 39–40, 227
    imperialism and, 254–60, 262–6
    labour and, 37, 268–74, 278–81, 304–5
    left intellectuals and, 241–3
    Locke's theories and, 176–7
    modern expressions of, 241–3

modernity and history of, 221–8
    origin of, 30–2, 37–40, 58, 226–7
    postmodernity and history of, 224–6
    privatisation of political power and, 20–1, 22, 26–7
    'proto-capitalism', 37
    separation of 'political' and 'economic' in, 18–21, 26–7, 191, 209–10, 244–5
    slavery and, 77–9, 251
    specificity of, 42–3
    technological progress and, 38–9, 41, 224, 225
    and 'universal human goods', 298–304
    universalisation of, 246–8, 254–5
    welfare-state, 300–1
Charlemagne, 124–5
Chartism, 193
China, early imperial, 23, 62–6, 114
Christianity, 68
Chun, Lin, 242
Cicero, Marcus Tullius, 112, 148, 198
cities, 41, 44–6, 126–7. *See also* city-states; towns; urbanisation
citizenship. *See also* peasant-citizens
    in Athens, 64, 67, 97, 100–2, 107–8, 147, 204
    class and, 105
    electoral franchise and, 197–8
    equality and, 183–4, 192–3
    freedom and, 162
    French, 223
    limited under capitalism, 189–92
    modern democracy and, 185–8, 205
    peasants and, 82–8
    Roman, 64, 67–8, 114–15, 116–17, 119
city-states, 64
    in ancient Greece, 64
    in medieval Italy, 45, 69–72
civil liberties, 186, 220
civil society
    capitalism and, 211
    conceptual problems of, 213–17
    democracy and, 217–20
    freedom and, 213
    idea of, 210–13
    state and, 197, 201, 204, 212–17, 219–20
Civil War, English, 35, 129, 178
class. *See also* aristocracy; 'banausic classes'; bourgeoisie; class-relations; class-struggle; landlords; lordship; oligarchy; peasant-citizens; peasants; ruling class; serfs/serfdom; slavery; working class
    -'compacts', 267–70
    -control, 27

Montchrétien, Antoine de, 164
Montesquieu, Charles-Louis de
    Secondat, baron de, 166, 168
Mouffe, Chantal, 291
multiple states, system of, 250, 256,
    258–60, 265
Mycenaeans, the, 92, 94–5, 97, 98

Nairn, Tom, 180, 181, 239
'Nairn-Anderson' theses, 181–2
Napoleon Bonaparte, 133, 134, 179, 180
nation-states
    globalisation and, 244–6
    and universalisation of capitalism,
        246–8
nationalism, 128, 231
natural rights
    concept of, 178–9
    Locke's use of concept, 173
needs, human. *See* 'universal human
    goods'
neoliberalism, 17, 267, 270, 276–8
Netherlands, 52–3, 56–8. *See also*
    Amsterdam
Neville, Henry, 187
New Deal, 269–70
New Left, the, 230–2, 238–43
'new social movements', 26, 283, 307
New 'True' Socialism, 281n10, 284,
    286–7, 289–90, 291, 299, 301, 304
nomos, 116
Norman Conquest, 49, 128–9, 135

office-holding, 94–5
oikos, the, 95, 96, 116, 154
oligarchy, 127–8, 194, 195
Osborne, Robin, 86n20, 107, 156

papacy, the, 127
Parliament, English. *See also* 'Crown
    in Parliament'; elections; franchise,
    electoral
    enclosures and, 178
    the franchise and, 187
    representation by, 186–7
    sovereignty and, 138
Pasion, 102
patricians, 115, 126–7
patronage, 115
Paul, Saint, 68
peasant-citizens, 73, 76–7, 82–8, 91, 147,
    156–7
peasants. *See also* agriculture; feudalism;
    land; peasant-citizens

Athenian, 92–4, 109, 190
autonomy, 190
Chinese, 63
citizenship and, 73
economic role of, 9–10, 37, 45, 55–6
'extra-economic' domination of, 45,
    47–8, 190–1
freedom of, 25, 47, 69, 73, 125–6,
    156–63, 190
French, 54, 137
in Italian city-states, 69–72
land-possession of, 37, 58–9, 63
lordship and, 125–6
medieval *vs.* Athenian, 191
and rise of feudalism, 76–7, 80–81,
    121–2
Roman, 64–5, 92–4
slavery and, 24, 26n9, 74–7, 81–2
Peloponnesian War, 111
people, sovereignty of, 189–90, 309
Pericles, 104, 116, 198
periodisation, 224–6, 238–41
Petition of Right, 193
Petty, William, 177
Physiocrats, 34–5
Pinochet, Augusto, General, 203
Pirenne, Henri, 41
Piven, Frances Fox, 267, 268, 271–2
Plato, 141–2, 218n32
    'argument from the arts', 151–2
    class-inequality and, 103–4, 152–6
    contempt for labour, 104–5, 153–4
    against democracy, 150–1, 154, 162
    on land-tenure, 155
    rulers and producers, 80
    technē and, 151
plebeians, 115
pluralism, 214
Pocock, J.G.A., 1n3, 142n2
Polanyi, Karl, 18
polis, the, 90, 154. *See also* Athens,
    ancient
    class and, 101–6
    development of, 94–7
    freedom and, 100–1, 156–63, 204
    oikos and, 116
    village and state in, 106–9
'political', the
    and separation from the 'economic',
        18–21, 26–7, 191, 209–10, 226–7,
        244–6, 262–5, 285–6
political economy
    critique of, 43, 163–7, 169–70
    origins of, 177

Protagoras, 104
'Protestant ethic', 44

rationalisation, 221–2, 230, 236
Reagan, Ronald, 267
redistributive kingdoms, 63–4, 94, 103, 122, 123n33, 166
Ree, Jonathan, 242
Renaissance, Italian, 128
representation, 186–7, 194–8, 295–6, 297
republicanism, 127–8, 187–8, 189, 194–5
resistance
  individual right to, 169
  justified by Locke, 169n39
  theories of, 229
revolution
  idea of, 178–82
  production modes and, 29
  socialist, 295
Reynolds, Susan, 121n32
rights. *See also* natural rights
  concept of, 178–9
  human, 201, 205
  political, 184, 199
Roman Empire
  class and state in, 62–6, 111–12
  decline of, 24, 68–9, 76–7, 120–31
  importance of land in, 65–6, 112–13
  rise of, 111–12
  slavery in, 26n9, 65, 76–7
Roman law, 66, 68, 114–20, 122–3, 129–30, 147
Rome, ancient, 65. *See also* Roman Empire; Roman law
  administration in, 113–4, 118, 121, 124
  citizenship in, 64, 67–8, 114–15, 116–17, 119
  class and state in, 62–6, 92–4, 109–14
  compared with Athens, 63–4, 67–8, 73, 109–10, 117–18
  concept of the state in, 63–4, 109–14, 118–19
  democracy in, 218n32
  dominium, 117–18
  freedom in, 161n27
  imperialism in, 62, 65
  inequality in, 116–7
  oligarchy in, 112–13
  peasantry in, 64–5
  property in, 66–9, 112–13, 114–20
  the Republic, 109–12
  Senatus Populusque Romanus, 118–9, 198
  slavery in, 64, 73

tributary system, 123n33
Rousseau, Jean-Jacques, 136
  idea of 'general will', 163–5, 170–2
  on 'intermediate bodies', 167–9
  on popular sovereignty, 164–7
rule of law, 97, 98, 161, 166, 204, 209n20, 217, 218n32, 292, 297
rulers and ruled, 93, 110, 147, 163–5
ruling class, 149
  English compared with French, 136–40
  public powers of, 22, 25, 129, 219, 294–6
  Roman, 111
  taxation and, 67, 83, 84–5, 123n33, 137, 138, 190

Saville, John, 238
Scandinavia, 268
self-propriety, 172–3
self-sufficiency, 54, 91, 96, 106, 157, 171
serfs/serfdom, 69, 77, 190
Shaftesbury, first Earl of, 177
Shanin, Teodor, 106
Sidney, Algernon, 187
Skinner, Quentin, 1n3, 142n2
'slave-mode of production', 77–82, 88
slavery
  agricultural, 82–8
  in ancient societies, 100
  in Athens, 72–3, 79–82, 84–91, 101–2, 108, 157
  and capitalism, 77–9, 251
  democracy and, 88–91
  Locke and, 236n11
  Marxist view of, 256
  in medieval Italy, 70
  peasant-dependence and, 126
  peasantry and, 24, 26n9, 74–7, 81–2
  in Rome, 26n9, 64, 65, 73, 76–7
Smith, Adam, 34, 44, 134
Smith, Sir Thomas, 186–7, 189n5
social contract, theory of, 170–1. *See also* consent
social democracy, 271–3
  and class-'compacts', 267–70
social provisions, 248–50
socialism. *See also* working-class movements
  as the abolition of class, 283, 292–6
  capitalism and, 182, 272–4, 280–1
  democracy and, 30, 286–92
  the socialist movement, 305–7
  the state under, 292–6